Guide to the Building Regulations

Huw M A Evans

WITHDRAWN from collection

RIBA Publishing

Moulton College

T56098

Guide to the Building Regulations

© RIBA Enterprises Ltd., 2014

First published by RIBA Publishing, 15 Bonhill Street, London EC2P 2EA

ISBN 978 1 85946 506 6

Stock code 80587

The right of Huw M A Evans to be identified as the Author of this Work has been asserted in accordance with the Copyright, Design and Patents Act 1988.

All rights reserved. No part of this publication may be reproduced, stored in a retrieval system, or transmitted, in any form or by any means, electronic, mechanical, photocopying, recording or otherwise, without prior permission of the copyright owner.

© Crown copyright material is reproduced with the permission of the Controller of HMSO and the Queen's Printer for Scotland.

All diagrams in this book are © Crown copyright unless stated otherwise.
Tables are © Crown copyright or © Huw M A Evans, where stated.

Permission to reproduce extracts from British Standards is granted by the British Standards Institution (BSI).
No other use of this material is permitted. British Standards can be obtained in PDF or hard copy formats from the BSI online shop:
http://shop.bsigroup.com or by contacting BSI Customer Services for hard copies only: Tel: +44 (0)20 8996 9001;
Email: cservices@bsigroup.com

British Library Cataloguing in Publications Data
A catalogue record for this book is available from the British Library.

Publisher: Steven Cross
Commissioning Editor: Lucy Harbor
Project Editor: Melanie Thompson
Designed by Liaison Design
Typeset by Academic + Technical Typesetting
Printed and bound by Polestar Wheatons

While every effort has been made to check the accuracy and quality of the information given in this publication, neither the Author nor the Publisher accept any responsibility for the subsequent use of this information, for any errors or omissions that it may contain, or for any misunderstandings arising from it.

RIBA Publishing is part of RIBA Enterprises Ltd.
www.ribaenterprises.com

Preface and acknowledgements

One of the oldest pieces of legislation to address the safety of buildings is the Code of Hammurabi, which dates from approximately 1750 BC. Law 229 states:

If a builder build a house for some one, and does not construct it properly, and the house which he built fall in and kill its owner, then that builder shall be put to death.

A further four laws set out the penalties for unstable buildings which kill people other than the owner, or damage property.

As first sight that seems straightforward enough, but on a second reading, I am left wondering what exactly 'construct it properly' means and how the builder of a collapsed house could demonstrate he had indeed done that. What, in eighteenth century BC Mesopotamia, would be considered to be 'constructed properly'?

Similar questions haunt us today: what exactly is 'suitable installation' for the provision of heated wholesome water, an 'adequate system' of drainage, or 'reasonable provision' for conservation of fuel and power? After all, one person's 'reasonable provision' might be another's 'unreasonable imposition'. The answers to those and other, comparable questions are contained in the Approved Documents to the Building Regulations, the tertiary guidance documents and numerous national and international standards and guides. There is a lot to grasp.

But most people in the construction industry do not want to spend their time poring over the Regulations and the supporting documents: they want to design and construct buildings. They need to know enough to ensure their buildings will comply with the Regulations, but little more than that: what counts as 'constructed properly'? In writing this guide I have attempted to answer that question. I have not set out to write a line-by-line, clause-by-clause examination of the Regulations; rather a straightforward, functional guide to what the Regulations require, and what compliance methods are available.

This second edition incorporates the 2013 changes to the Building Regulations and associated guidance documents. The changes include:

- revisions to the Regulations to transpose the recast Energy Performance of Buildings Directive (see **L.1.6** and **L.3.1.7**);
- the adoption of the Eurocodes in Parts A and C (e.g. **A.2.1.1** and **C.5.3.1**);
- minor changes to the treatment of internal linings in Part B (see **B.4.1**);
- a rationalisation of the overlapping requirements of Parts K, M and N, which resulted in the expansion of Part K and the elimination of Part N (summarised in **K.1**);
- a tightening of carbon dioxide emissions targets for new buildings in Part L (see **L.1.1**);
- a modest relaxation of the requirements for notification of electrical work in Part P (see **P.1.1**).

Moulton College
Class No. 343.07869 EVA
Acc. No. T56098
Learning Resource Centre

R
T
C

One other change which was not part of the consultation package, and does not directly affect the Building Regulations in England was the transfer of powers to make Building Regulations in Wales to Welsh ministers (see **I.6** for details), bringing further fragmentation of the regulatory framework of construction within the UK.

Initially, the change had little impact, coming as it did in the lull of the triennial revision cycle, but on 9 January 2013 the two sets of regulations began to diverge. Few of the 2013 revisions affect Wales, which, at the time of writing (January 2014), still has Building Regulations as they stood in England at the end of 2011 (although there is a new Approved Document to Regulation 7 to address the Construction Products Regulation – see **I.4** for the comparable changes in England). Looking ahead, there is likely to be a steady divergence between Building Regulations in England and those in Wales.

In arranging the structure of the book I have, at the top level, shadowed the Regulations, so for example, the Requirements for Part H are discussed in chapter H. However, within each chapter the arrangement of sub-sections and information does not necessarily follow that of the related Approved Document. I have not hesitated to re-order information where logical presentation demands it. As a general principle, common provisions which apply to more than one Requirement are addressed first, with those which address individual Requirements following.

Beyond that, the structure of each chapter is driven by the corresponding Requirements – so J (combustion appliances and fuel storage systems) reflects the prescriptive nature of the guidance (the flue goes here, just so), while L (conservation of fuel and power) reflects the more performance-based guidance of those Approved Documents (get the emissions *down*, don't mind how you do it).

To make it easy to find related information, cross references to other sections in this book are given in bold – for example, **H.4.3.2**. References in the text to other documents, such as standards, are usually only by number, with the full details given in the margin, as close to the citation as possible. Inevitably, some of the documents referred to in the Approved Documents have been updated, withdrawn or superseded since the Approved Documents were published, but for the purposes of compliance with Building Regulations it is still the referenced editions of those documents which contain the means of demonstrating compliance (**I.1.2**). Where a referenced document has changed, I have listed both the original document and, wherever possible, the new edition or document.

There are two points where new or updated standards are a substantial issue: Part B, where BS 9999 has replaced most of BS 5588 (**B.1.2**); and Part M, where the 2001 edition of BS 8300 has been replaced by the 2009 edition (amended 2010, see **M.1.4**), but Approved Document M still refers to the earlier edition. There is only one rule for situations where it is unclear whether guidance in a new edition still meets the Regulation – get the agreement of the Building Control Body as soon as possible.

The text of this guide follows the Building Regulations as revised up to 6 April 2014, when the bulk of the revisions to Part L come into force. To help readers identify revised requirements, sections which have undergone significant changes have a marginal notes – labelled 2013 changes – which outline the differences introduced since 2010.

Revision is a different process from writing a book from scratch, as part of the existing work has to be unpicked and restitched to incorporate new patterns and remove redundant features. There are many people who have helped me address those challenges: David Fuller had the arduous task of reviewing the changes against the amended approved documents, while James Hutchinson had the unenviable job of keeping me to timetable. I would also like to thank Steven Cross, Lucy Harbor and the team at RIBA Publications who have carried those changes into print, all the while dealing with the government's increasingly flexible timetable of revisions.

I should also like to thank John Potter for my introduction to the intricacies of the Building Regulations; the many hours we have spent drafting – and re-drafting – technical documents have shown me it is possible to convey complex concepts in lucid English. My greatest debt, though, is to my wife and children who have supported and encouraged me through the process of revision (even though two of the latter have left home rather than find out more about the Building Regulations): thank you.

Huw M A Evans
January 2014

About the author

Huw M A Evans has worked as a technical author and trainer in the construction industry since 1996 and holds a Postgraduate Diploma in Technical Authorship from Sheffield Hallam University. From 1996–2006 he worked at JPA Technical Literature in Newcastle-upon-Tyne, developing technical documentation both in the UK and Europe, and providing technical support for thermal calculation software.

He has been a freelance consultant (www.writelines.biz) since 2006, authoring technical documents, and writing and delivering training courses for designers, energy assessor and construction product manufacturers. He has particular interests in building physics and energy efficiency, and how they are addressed by building regulations.

Contents

An introduction to the Building Regulations

I.1 The legal framework of the Building Regulations

The Building Regulations in England are intended to:

- secure the health, safety, welfare and convenience of people in and around buildings, and people who might be affected by those buildings;
- conserve fuel and power;
- prevent waste, undue consumption, misuse or contamination of water.

I.1.1 Building Act 1984

The Building Act 1984 gives the Secretary of State powers to make regulations regarding the design and construction of buildings, and the provision of services, fittings and equipment. Those regulations may impose continuing requirements – particularly with regard to the inspection and maintenance of services and fittings.

The Regulations may specify that the use of certain methods of construction or types of material will be deemed to comply with certain requirements of the Regulations (so introducing 'deemed to satisfy' solutions).

Under the powers conferred by the Building Act, the Secretary of State has issued and amended the Building Regulations 2010 (hereafter simply the Building Regulations, or the Regulations) and the Building (Approved Inspectors etc.) Regulations 2010 (hereafter the Approved Inspectors Regulations).

The Building Regulations and the Approved Inspectors Regulations consist mainly of procedural requirements. The substantive requirements of the Regulations are largely set out in Schedule 1 of the Building Regulations, divided into Parts A–P. Parts A to D, F to K and P (except for paragraphs G2, H2 and J6) of Schedule 1 do not require anything to be done, except to ensure the health and safety of people in and around buildings and of people who may be affected by them. Parts E and M require measures for the convenience of building users, while L requires measures for the conservation of energy.

Part III (sections 59–83) of the Building Act contain other provisions affecting buildings (such as those governing dangerous and defective premises) which are commonly administered by local authorities.

I.1.2 Approved Documents

Under the Building Act, the Secretary of State can issue and/or approve documents which give practical guidance for compliance with the requirements of the Regulations. Guidance is necessary because, in many cases, the substantive requirements of Schedule 1 are expressed in terms of 'reasonable provision'; but what is reasonable to one person may be not be reasonable to another.

The Approved Documents set out what is considered to be 'reasonable provision' and describe constructions and arrangements which, if adopted, would be deemed to satisfy the Regulations. There is no obligation to adopt the solutions in the Approved Documents, but additional measures might be required in order to demonstrate that a different solution satisfies the Regulations.

2013 changes
On 31 December 2011 the powers to make building regulations in Wales were devolved to Welsh Ministers (see **I.6**).

Further guidance
Building Act 1984.
www.opsi.gov.uk/acts/acts1984/pdf/ukpga_19840055_en.pdf

The Building Regulations 2010.
http://www.legislation.gov.uk/uksi/2010/2214/made/data.pdf

The Building (Approved Inspectors etc.) Regulations 2010.
http://www.legislation.gov.uk/uksi/2010/2215/made/data.pdf

The Building Regulations &c. (Amendment) Regulations 2012.
http://www.legislation.gov.uk/uksi/2012/3119/contents/made

The Building Regulations &c. (Amendment) (No.2) Regulations 2013
http://www.legislation.gov.uk/uksi/2013/1959/contents/made

2013 changes
Since coming into force in October 2010 the Building Regulations have been amended on nine different occasions. The most substantial amendments were introduced by SI 2012/3119 The Building Regulations &c. (Amendment) Regulations 2012, and SI 2013/1959 The Building Regulations &c. (Amendment) (No.2) Regulations 2013. Full details of the amendments can be viewed at http://www.legislation.gov.uk/changes/affected/uksi/2010/2214

If, in the course of civil or criminal proceedings, it is alleged that a person has contravened the Regulations then not following an Approved Document may tend to establish liability, whereas complying with an Approved Document may tend to negative liability.

The Approved Documents make frequent reference to British Standards and European Standards. The relevant version of a standard is the one listed at the end of the Approved Document. However, where a standard has been updated since the publication of the Approved Document the new version may be used as a source of guidance, provided it continues to address the relevant requirements of the Regulations.

I.1.3 Other legislation affecting building work

The Building Act is not the only legislation which imposes requirements regarding buildings and building work. Most of the other statutes that affect particular aspects of building work are addressed in the relevant chapter of this book (for example, The Water Supply (Water Fittings) Regulations 1999 are covered in chapter G). However, some Acts have broader implications:

I.1.3.1 Health and Safety at Work etc. Act 1974 (HSWA), and the Workplace (Health, Safety and Welfare) Regulations 1992

Compliance with the Building Regulations can be used to demonstrate compliance with some of the requirements of the HSWA. The Act can also indirectly impose the requirements of the Building Regulations where they would not otherwise apply. Common areas of residential premises such as stairwells and corridors may constitute a workplace for service staff such as caretakers and cleaners. The most straightforward way of providing a safe workplace may be to comply with functional requirements of the Building Regulations in such common areas, even though those standards may not be required by the Regulations themselves.

I.1.3.2 Party Wall etc. Act 1996

The Act applies to work on an existing shared wall, building on the boundary with a neighbouring property and excavating near a boundary.

I.1.3.3 Local Acts

The Building Act 1984 rationalised many of the controls over buildings, but there remain a number of local Acts of Parliament which are enforced by local authorities. The local authorities are obliged (by section 90 of the Building Act) to keep a copy of any local provisions available for inspection. In London, the London Building Acts operate in a similar way.

2013 changes
The provisions in Local Acts for the fire protection of large storage buildings, car parks and tall buildings were repealed on 9 January 2013. Provisions relating to fire and rescue service access remain in place. See **B.1.3**.

I.2 Building work

I.2.1 The definition of building work

The Regulations apply when building work takes place. Building work is defined as:

- the erection or extension of a building;
- the provision or extension of a controlled fitting or service in, or in connection with, a building (**I.2.4**);

- the material alteration of a building, or a controlled fitting or service (**I.2.2**);
- work required as the result of a material change of use (**I.2.3**);
- the insertion of insulating material into the cavity wall of a building;
- work involving the underpinning of a building;
- work required by Regulation 23 – requirements relating to thermal elements (**I.2.5**);
- work required by Regulation 22 – requirements relating to a change of energy status (**I.2.6**);
- work required by Regulation 28 – consequential improvements to energy performance (**I.2.7**).

Any building work must be carried out so as to comply with the applicable requirements of Schedule 1 of the Building Regulations and must not result in a failure to comply with other requirements. Work relating only to thermal elements, change of energy status or consequential improvements to energy performance need only comply with the applicable requirements of Part L, provided the work does not constitute a material alteration.

After the completion of building work the following *must* comply with the applicable requirements of Schedule 1:

- any building which is extended, or to which a material alteration is made; or
- any building in which, or in connection with which, a controlled service or fitting is provided, extended or materially altered; or
- any controlled service or fitting.

Any building or controlled service or fitting which did not comply with an applicable requirement before the work was carried out should be no more unsatisfactory once the work is finished.

I.2.2 Material alterations

For the purposes of the Building Regulations, an alteration to a building is regarded as material (that is, of significance) if it would result in:

- a building, controlled fitting or service which previously complied with a relevant requirement no longer complying; or
- a building or controlled fitting or service which previously did not comply with a relevant requirement, being more unsatisfactory than before.

The relevant requirements in Schedule 1 are:

- Part A (Structure)
- B1 (Means of warning and escape)
- B3 (Internal fire spread – structure)
- B4 (External fire spread)
- B5 (Access and facilities for the fire service)
- Part M (Access to and use of buildings).

I.2.3 Material change of use

Some changes of use are regarded as being material (significant) for the purposes of the Building Regulations. Where a material change of use takes place, the building must comply with certain of the requirements of Schedule 1. Table I.1 lists the categories of material change of use together with the parts of Schedule 1 which apply. Some requirements apply to all material changes of use; others apply only to some changes of use.

Table I.1 Requirements for material changes of use		
Change of use	**Common requirements**	**Specific requirements**
(a) The building is used as a dwelling, where previously it was not.	B1 (means of warning and escape) B2 (internal fire spread – linings)	C1(2) (resistance to contaminants) C2 (resistance to moisture) E1 to E3 (resistance to the passage of sound)
(b) The building contains a flat, where previously it did not.	B3 (internal fire spread – structure)	C1(2) (resistance to contaminants) E1 to E3 (resistance to the passage of sound)
(c) The building is used as an hotel or a boarding house, where previously it was not.	B4(2) (external fire spread – roofs) B5 (access and facilities for the fire service)	A1 to A3 (structure) C1(2) (resistance to contaminants) E1 to E3 (resistance to the passage of sound) M1 (access and use)[1]
(d) The building is used as an institution, where previously it was not.	C2(c) (interstitial and surface condensation)	A1 to A3 (structure) C1(2) (resistance to contaminants) M1 (access and use)
(e) The building is used as a public building, where previously it was not.	F1 (ventilation) G1 (cold water supply)	A1 to A3 (structure) M1 (access and use)
(e) The building is used as a public building, where previously it was not and consists of or contains a school.	G3(1) to (3) (hot water supply and systems)	A1 to A3 (structure) M1 (access and use) E4 (acoustic conditions in schools)
(f) The building is not a building described in Classes I to VI in Schedule 2, where previously it was.	G4 (sanitary conveniences and washing facilities)	A1 to A3 (structure)
(f) The building is not a building described in Classes I to VI in Schedule 2, where previously it was and provides new residential accommodation.	G5 (bathrooms)	A1 to A3 (structure) C1(2) (resistance to contaminants)
(g) The building, which contains at least one dwelling, contains a greater or lesser number of dwellings than it did previously.	G6 (kitchens and food preparation areas)	C1(2) (resistance to contaminants) E1 to E3 (resistance to the passage of sound)
(h) The building contains a room for residential purposes, where previously it did not.	H1 (foul water drainage) H6 (solid waste storage)	C1(2) (resistance to contaminants) E1 to E3 (resistance to the passage of sound)
(i) The building, which contains at least one room for residential purposes, contains a greater or lesser number of such rooms than it did previously.	J1 to J4 (combustion appliances)	C1(2) (resistance to contaminants) E1 to E3 (resistance to the passage of sound)
(j) The building is used as a shop, where previously it was not.	L1 (conservation of fuel and power) P1 (electrical safety)	M1 (access and use)
Any of the above where the building is more than 15m high.		B4(1) (external fire spread – walls)[2]

[1] Where only part of the building is subject to material change of use, the requirement applies to that part of the building, and sanitary conveniences provided in or in connection with it; and the whole building should comply with Approved Document M1(a), to extent that reasonable provision should be made to provide either suitable independent access to that part, or suitable access through the building to that part.

[2] Applies to the whole building, even if material change of use only applies to part of the building.

I.2.4 Controlled fittings and services

A controlled fitting or service is a fitting or service to which Parts G, H, J, L or P impose a requirement, such as windows, doors and space heating systems.

I.2.5 Thermal elements

A thermal element is a wall, floor or roof (but not a window, roof window, rooflight or door) which separates a thermally conditioned part of the building ('the conditioned space') from the external environment (including the ground).

Walls and floors will also be thermal elements if they separate the conditioned space from another part of the building which is:

- unconditioned;
- an extension in Class VII of Schedule 2;
- conditioned to a different temperature, provided the building is not a dwelling and the two parts of the building are used for different purposes.

The 'thermal element' includes all parts of the element between the surface bounding the conditioned space and the external environment or other part of the building. Renovated thermal elements, or replacement thermal elements must comply with L1(a)(i) of Schedule 1 (**L.4.6.2**).

I.2.6 Change of energy status

A change of energy status occurs when building work makes a building subject to the requirements of Part L of Schedule 1 where previously it was not – for example, installing a space heating system to a previously unconditioned building would constitute a change of energy status. (The change of energy status may apply to all or part of a building.) Further building work may be required in order to make the building compliant with Part L.

I.2.7 Consequential improvements

Building work to buildings with a total useful floor area in excess of 1000m² will require improvement to the energy efficiency of the whole building if the work consists of, or includes:

- an extension;
- the initial provision of any fixed building services;
- an increase to the installed capacity of any fixed building services.

Such consequential improvements need only be carried out in so far as they are technically, functionally and economically feasible (**L.4.7**).

I.3 Exemptions from the Building Regulations

Building work must comply with all the requirements of the Building Regulations unless:

- the building belongs to an exempt body or the work is being carried out on behalf of such a body;

- the building is one of the exempt categories listed in Schedule 2 of the Regulations;
- it is minor work for which notification is not required.

I.3.1 Buildings belonging to exempt bodies

Buildings belonging to the following bodies are exempt from the Building Regulations:

- statutory undertakers, such as water and sewage authorities (but not private water companies);
- the UK Atomic Energy Authority;
- the Civil Aviation Authority;
- a person/organisation holding a licence for air traffic services.

Although, houses or buildings used as offices or showrooms (which do not form part of a railway station or aerodrome) must still comply with the Regulations.

Work carried out under Crown immunity, such as that to Crown buildings (such as government offices and courts of law), or carried out by or on behalf of the Crown, is not subject to the procedural requirements of the Building Regulations, but must still comply with their substantive requirements. Health service buildings no longer have Crown immunity and work must comply with all the requirements of the Regulations.

However, buildings of statutory undertakers, crown buildings and building work carried out by the crown authorities are not exempt from the regulations regarding energy efficiency. They must comply with Regulations 11(3), 21, 23(1)(a), 25(a), 25A, 25B, 26, 29 (but not 29(4)(e), 29(9A), 29(10), 29(11) and 29(12)), 29A and 35(2), unless exempt under Regulation 21(I.3.2).

The Mayor's Office for Policing and Crime is also exempt from the procedural requirements of the Regulations, but must still comply with their substantive requirements, and the requirements for Energy Performance Certificates in Regulation 29.

I.3.2 Exempt buildings

A building in one of the seven classes of Schedule 2 of the Regulations will be exempt from the Building Regulations, provided that, when the work is completed, the building is still in one of those categories (Regulation 9).

The classes are:

I – Buildings controlled by other legislation;

II – Buildings not frequented by people;

III – Greenhouses and agricultural buildings;

IV – Temporary buildings;

V – Ancillary buildings;

VI – Small detached buildings;

VII – Extensions.

However, an exempt building may still be subject to the following conditions of Parts G, L and P of Schedule 1.

The requirements for hot and cold water supplies in Parts G1, G3(2) and G3(3) apply to:

- a greenhouse which receives a hot or cold water supply from a source shared with, or located inside, a dwelling;
- a small detached building falling within Class VI of Schedule 2 or an extension falling within Class VII of Schedule 2 which receives a hot or cold water supply shared with or located inside any building that is subject to the Regulations.

The energy efficiency requirements of the Regulations (Part L) apply to the erection or extension of any building (except an extension in Class VII of Schedule 2) and any associated work. In this context, a building is defined as: a roofed construction having walls, which uses energy to condition the indoor climate.

The only buildings exempt from the energy efficiency requirements are:

- historic buildings (scheduled ancient monuments, listed buildings and buildings in Conservation Areas) which would have their appearance or character unacceptably altered by compliance with the energy efficiency requirements;
- buildings used primarily, or solely, as places of worship;
- temporary buildings with a planned time of use of two years or less;
- industrial sites, workshops and non-residential agricultural buildings with low energy demand;
- stand-alone buildings, other than dwellings, with a total useful floor area of less than 50m^2.

Note that the addition of a conservatory or porch which falls in Class VII of Schedule 2 will only be exempt if:

- the existing walls, windows or doors are retained, or replaced if removed; and
- the heating system of the building is not extended into the conservatory or porch.

The requirements for electrical safety in Part P apply to the following, if it receives its electricity from a source shared with, or located inside, a dwelling:

- a greenhouse used for domestic purposes;
- a small detached building falling within Class VI in Schedule 2;
- an extension of a building falling within Class VII in Schedule 2.

I.3.3 Minor work exempt from notification

Under Regulation 12(6), minor work of a type listed in Schedule 4 (reproduced in Table I.2) is exempt from the requirement for notification by either building notice or full plans. However, the work must still comply with the substantive requirements of the Regulations.

I.3.4 Historic buildings

Although historic buildings are not of themselves exempt from the Building Regulations, it is recognised that any building work should conserve their special character. Consequently it may be neither appropriate nor feasible for a historic building to reach the performance standards expected for other buildings.

Historic buildings include:

- listed buildings;
- buildings situated in a Conservation Area;
- buildings of local architectural and historical interest and which are referred to as a material consideration in a local authority's development plan;
- buildings within national parks, areas of outstanding natural beauty and world heritage sites;
- vernacular buildings of traditional form and construction.

Particular issues warranting sympathetic treatment include:

- restoring the historic character of a building previously subject to inappropriate alteration (such as replacement windows, doors and rooflights);
- rebuilding a former building (for example, following a fire or filling a gap site in a terrace);
- making provisions to enable the fabric of a historic building to 'breathe' in order to control moisture and prevent decay.

The advice of the local planning authority's conservation officer should be taken into account when determining appropriate performance standards.

Further guidance
BS 7913:1998. Guide to the principles of the conservation of historic buildings.

National Planning Policy Framework. CLG. March 2012. [Section 12 addresses the historic environment.]

Historic environment planning practice guide, CLG. 2010. Although originally offering guidance on meeting PPS 5 the guide remains valid for the NPPF.

Table I.2 Minor works exempt from notification	
Work	**Limitations**
On an existing fixed building service, which is not a fixed internal or external lighting system: • replacing any part which is not a combustion appliance; • adding an output device; or • adding a control device.	Testing and adjustment of the work is not possible or would not affect the use by the fixed building service of no more fuel and power than is reasonable in the circumstances.
Providing a self-contained fixed building service, which is not a fixed internal or external lighting system	• The service is not a combustion appliance. • Any electrical work associated with its provision is exempt from the requirement to give a building notice or to deposit full plans. • Testing and adjustment is not possible or would not affect its energy efficiency. • In the case of a mechanical ventilation appliance, the appliance is not installed in a room containing an open-flued combustion appliance whose combustion products are discharged through a natural draught flue.
Replacing an external door	The door together with its frame has not more than 50% of its internal face area glazed.
Providing fixed internal lighting in existing buildings other than dwellings	No more than 100m² of the floor area of the building is to be served by the lighting.

continued

Table I.2 continued	
Work	**Limitations**
Replacing: • a sanitary convenience; • a washbasin; • a fixed bath; • a fixed shower bath; • a rainwater gutter; • a rainwater downpipe.	The work does not include any work to underground drainage, and includes no work to the hot or cold water system or above ground drainage, which may prejudice the health or safety of any person on completion of the work. A sanitary convenience must use no more water than the one it replaces.
In relation to an existing cold water supply: (i) replacing any part; (ii) adding an output device; or (iii) adding a control device.	–
Providing a hot water storage system that has a storage vessel with a capacity not exceeding 15 litres	Any electrical work associated with its provision is exempt from the requirement to give a building notice or to deposit full plans.
Installation of thermal insulation in a roof space or loft space	The work consists solely of the installation of such insulation, and the work is not carried out in order to comply with any requirement of the Regulations.
Installation of thermal insulation to a suspended timber floor	The work consists solely of the installation of such insulation, and the work is not carried out in order to comply with any requirement of the Regulations.

I.4 Materials and workmanship

Regulation 7 requires building work to be carried out in a workmanlike manner, with adequate and proper materials which are:

- appropriate for the circumstances of use;
- adequately mixed or prepared;
- applied, used or fixed so as to perform adequately their intended functions.

For this Regulation, 'materials' includes products, components, fittings, naturally occurring materials, items of equipment and backfilling for excavations.

I.4.1 Establishing suitability of materials

The suitability of a material for a specific purpose may be assessed in several ways:

- It is CE marked under the Construction Products Regulation (305/2011/EU-CPR). Construction products covered by a harmonised European product standard must be CE marked, while products not covered by a harmonised standard can be CE marked through a European Technical Assessment (ETA). Building control bodies should assume the information in the CE marking and associated declaration of performance is accurate (unless there are indications to the contrary) and not prohibit or impede the use of the product.
- It is CE marked under other EU directives or legislation, such as the Gas Appliances Directive.
- It is manufactured and assessed against a British standard.

2013 changes
Although Regulation 7 has not changed, the guidance in the Approved Document to Regulation 7 has been revised to take account of the Construction Products Regulation (305/2011/EU-CPR) which requires mandatory CE marking of construction products from 1 July 2013. **I.4** has been revised accordingly.

- It is assessed against a national technical specification from another country, or against an international technical specification.
- It is certified by an independent certification scheme as complying with the requirements of a recognised document appropriate to the material's purpose. The certification body should be accredited by a national accreditation body belonging to the European co-operation for Accreditation (EA), such as the United Kingdom Accreditation Service (UKAS).
- Tests and calculations show the material is fit for purpose. The use of nationally accredited testing laboratories ensures the reliability of test results.
- Past experience shows the material to be capable of performing the intended function.

Under Regulation 46 the local authority has the power to take samples of materials used in building work in order to establish compliance with Regulations. The right does not apply where an initial notice has been given, nor where the local authority has accepted an Approved Inspector's final certificate. Approved Inspectors may also take samples to ensure that materials are suitable.

The Secretary of State can approve a particular type of building matter as complying with particular requirements of the Regulations.

I.4.2 Short-lived materials

Some materials may, without special care, deteriorate rapidly in comparison with the expected service life of the building. Such a short-lived material may meet the requirements of the Regulations provided:

- it is readily accessible for inspection, maintenance and replacement; and
- should it fail, the health and safety consequences are not serious.

A short-lived material which does not meet those conditions is unlikely to meet the requirements of the Regulations. Under Section 19 of the Building Act local authorities can place conditions on the use of a prescribed material with a short life. However, because no materials have been prescribed, at the time of writing, that section has no effect.

I.4.3 Materials susceptible to changes in properties

The properties and performance of some materials can change over time. Such materials may be used in building work provided their residual properties (that is their properties after the change, including structural properties):

- can be estimated at the time of construction; and,
- will be adequate throughout the expected life of the building.

I.4.4 Workmanship

The adequacy of workmanship may be established by:

- CE marking: workmanship may be specified in the harmonised product standard or ETA.
- Standards: British Standards and other technical specifications give methods for carrying out work.

- Independent certification schemes: some schemes specify how workmanship will deliver the declared performance, while schemes that register installers of materials offer a means of ensuring work is carried out by knowledgeable contractors.
- Management systems: the work is covered by a quality management system which complies with BS EN ISO 9000.
- Past experience: experience of a building in use may be used to demonstrate the method of workmanship can meet its intended function.
- Tests: building control bodies have powers to make tests of building work in order to establish whether it complies with Regulation 7.

I.5 Control of building work

There are two main systems for ensuring building work complies with the Building Regulations:

- Local Authority Building Control, which has no power to refuse to oversee building work within its geographic area;
- Approved Inspectors, who can oversee building work at any location in England and Wales.

A person proposing to carry out building work may elect to use the local authority or an Approved Inspector to supervise the work. Public bodies are allowed to supervise their own building work (**I.5.3**).

I.5.1 Local Authority Building Control

I.5.1.1 Giving a building notice or deposit of plans

A person intending to carry out building work supervised by Local Authority Building Control must, before work begins:

- give the local authority a building notice (**I.5.1.2**); or
- deposit full plans with the local authority (**I.5.1.3**).

Full plans must be deposited where the proposed building work:

- affects a building to which the Regulatory Reform (Fire Safety) Order 2005 applies or will apply;
- includes the erection of a building fronting onto a private street;
- is within 3m of the centre line of a drain, sewer or disposal main as described in Part H4 (**H.5**).

However, there is no need to give a notice or to deposit plans if the building work consists entirely of work which may be self-certified by a competent person (**I.5.4**).

Emergency repairs may begin without a building notice, provided a notice is given to the local authority as soon as reasonably practical.

Where the work comes under the supervision of the local authority following the cessation of an initial notice from an Approved Inspector (**I.5.2.1**) the person carrying out the work should provide plans to show the work would comply with the Regulations.

Further guidance
BS 8000. Workmanship on building sites.
[The series of standards combines guidance from other BSI codes and standards.]

13

I.5.1.2 Building notice

The content of the building notice should comply with Table I.3. The local authority can make a written request for any additional plans it needs to ensure that compliance. Neither the building notice nor any accompanying or requested plans are treated as being deposited under Section 16 of the Building Act.

If the work is not begun, or if the change of use or energy status are not made within three years the building notice lapses.

I.5.1.3 Full plans

The required contents of a 'full plans' submission is given in Table I.3. The local authority has five weeks in which to consider the plans. That period may be extended to two months, with the consent of the person depositing the plans. The local authority must pass the plans unless they:

- are defective (for example being incomplete);
- show the proposed work would contravene the Regulations;
- do not include satisfactory provision for water supply;
- do not show compliance with any local Acts.

The local authority may then reject the plans or, with the written consent of the person depositing them, pass them subject to modifications. A rejection notice must specify the defects or contraventions.

The local authority has a duty to consult:

- the fire authority, where the work involves the erection, extension or change of use of a building to which the Regulatory Reform (Fire Safety) Order 2005 applies or will apply (a 'relevant use');
- the sewerage undertaker, where work is going to take place within 3m of the centre line of drain, sewer or disposal main (as described in Part H4 (**H.5**)).

The local authority cannot pass the plans until the sewerage undertaker has responded, which it must do within fifteen days.

Where it is not possible to deposit full plans at the outset, the local authority can pass plans subject to either or both of the following conditions:

- specified modifications must be made to the deposited plans;
- further plans must be deposited, enabling the plans to be passed in stages.

If the work does not begin within three years of the deposit of plans the local authority can, by giving a notice, declare that the deposit of plans is no longer in effect.

I.5.1.4 Notifications

Under a building notice the local authority must be informed that work will begin, with at least two clear working days' notice of commencement. Under full plans, work may not begin until the local authority has granted notice of approval; the local authority must then be notified of commencement, with at least two working days' notice.

Table I.3 Requirements for a building notice or full plans submission

Type of information	Building notice	Full plans
Identification	The name and address of the person intending to carry out the work. The submission must be signed by that person or on their behalf.	
Statement	A statement that the notice is given for the purpose of Regulation 12(2)(a).	A statement that the plans are deposited for the purpose of Regulation 12(2)(b).
Description	Description of the proposed building work, renovation or replacement of a thermal element, change to the building's energy status or material change of use.	
	Particulars of the location of the building and its use or intended use.	
Information required for the erection or extension of a building	A plan to a scale of not less than 1:1250 showing: • the size and position of the building, or the building as extended, and its relationship to adjoining boundaries; • the boundaries of the curtilage of the building, or the building as extended, and the size, position and use of every other building or proposed building within that curtilage; • the width and position of any street on or within the boundaries of the curtilage of the building or the building as extended.	
	A statement specifying the number of storeys (each basement level being counted as one storey), in the building.	
	The provision to be made for the drainage of the building or extension.	
	The steps to be taken to comply with any local enactment which applies.	
Information required when H4 of schedule 1 applies	Not applicable	Details of the precautions to be taken in building over a drain, sewer or disposal main.
Fire	Not applicable	A statement as to whether the Regulatory Reform (Fire Safety) Order 2005 applies, or will apply after the completion of the work.
Additional information	Not applicable	Any other plans required to show the work would comply with the Regulations.
Number of copies of the submission	One	Two, of which the local authority may retain one. Where Part B of Schedule 1 (fire safety) imposes a requirement, an additional two copies of any such plans as demonstrate compliance with that requirement, both of which may be retained by the local authority (that requirement does not apply to a dwellinghouse or flat).

When a local authority receives a notice of intention to commence building work it may issue a notice which lists the stages of work at which the person carrying out the work must notify the authority. For each notification stage the authority may specify:

- a period before or after the work during which notification must be made; and,

- a period during which the work concerned may not be covered up.

The local authority may specify a notification stage only if it intends to carry out an inspection at that stage, based on an assessment of the risk of the Regulations being breached if there were to be no inspection. Where notification is not given the local authority can require work to be opened up or pulled down in order to ascertain whether work complies with the Regulations.

When building work is complete, the person carrying it out must notify the local authority within five days. When a building subject to the Regulatory Reform (Fire Safety) Order 2005 is to be occupied before completion the local authority must be given at least five days notice.

The local authority can require reasonable tests to be carried out to ensure that building work complies with the Regulations. It may also carry out tests itself. Tests may examine soil, sub-soil, materials of construction, and services, fittings or equipment provided in connection with the building.

2013 changes
The prescriptive list of work stages in the 2010 Regulations has been replaced with an inspection procedure which is intended to reduce unnecessary inspections and focus upon non-compliance.

I.5.1.5 Relaxation of requirements

The local authority has the power to dispense with or relax any requirement of the Building Regulations, except:

- 23(1)(a) – Major renovation of thermal elements;

- 25A – Consideration of high-efficiency alternative systems for new buildings;

- 25B – Nearly zero-energy requirements for new buildings;

- 26 – Target carbon dioxide emission rates;

- 29 – Energy Performance Certificates (apart from regulations 29(4)(e), 29(9A), 29(10), 29(11) and 29(12));

- 29A – Recommendation reports associated with Energy performance certificates.

2013 changes
The list of regulations which may not be dispensed with or relaxed has been revised. It contains those regulations which are required for transposition of the recast Energy Performance of Buildings Directive into UK law.

Where a relaxation would be likely to affect public health and safety the details of the application must be published in a local newspaper. If it is likely to affect a neighbouring property then the owner of that property must be notified. The fire authority must be consulted on matters affecting structural fire safety or means of escape.

If the local authority refuses an application to relax a requirement the applicant has a right of appeal (**I.5.5**).

I.5.1.6 Completion Certificates

A local authority must give a completion certificate within eight weeks of receiving notification of completion of building work, provided it is satisfied the building complies with provisions of Schedule 1 to the Regulations, and Regulations 25A, 26, 29, 36 and 38 (those Regulations address: high efficiency alternative systems, target CO_2 emission rates, energy performance certificates, water efficiency and fire safety information).

Where a building subject to the Regulatory Reform (Fire Safety) Order 2005 is to be occupied before completion, the local authority must give a completion certificate for those parts of the building which are to be occupied, provided it is satisfied those parts comply at that time with Part B of schedule 1 and Regulation 38 (fire safety information. The certificate must be provided within four weeks of notification of occupation (**I.5.1.4**).

In both cases the certificate is evidence, but not conclusive evidence that the relevant requirements have been complied with. Any certificate must contain a statement to that effect.

I.5.1.7 Contraventions and unauthorised building work

If, during the course of the building work, or within a year of completion, the local authority considers the work contravenes any requirement of the Building Regulations it may issue a notice requiring the work to be taken down or altered within 28 days. The person carrying out the work may obtain an independent expert's report (doing so extends the notice period to 70 days), and the local authority may withdraw the notice in the light of the report. If the local authority does not withdraw the notice there is a right of appeal to a magistrate's court.

If building work is carried out without a building notice or without full plans being deposited, or following rejection of plans, or in a way which contravenes any requirements which the local authority imposed when passing the plans, the local authority may require the owner to:

- pull down or remove the work; or
- pull down or remove the work, or if the owner so elects, to make such alterations as would be necessary to make it comply.

Should the owner not co-operate, the local authority has powers to pull down or remove work, or make alterations and recover expenses from the owner. The owner may also be liable to legal sanctions.

Where building work is carried out without notifying the local authority the building owner may apply for a regularisation certificate. The application should include plans showing the unauthorised work and any building work needed to ensure compliance with the requirements of the Regulations in force at the time the work was carried out. The local authority may then require the owner to lay open the work or make tests, in order to determine what work is necessary to ensure compliance. Once the necessary work has been satisfactorily completed the local authority can issue a regularisation certificate.

The local authority has a right of entry to premises at reasonable hours in order to ascertain whether there has been contravention of the Building Regulations, subject to giving 24 hours' notice.

2013 changes
Local authorities must now provide completion certificates for all work carried out under a building notice or deposit of full plans. There is no longer any need to request a completion certificate. A separate certificate is required when a building subject to the Regulatory Reform (Fire Safety) Order 2005 is occupied before completion.

I.5.2 Approved Inspectors

Approved Inspectors are private sector companies or individuals authorised under the Building Act 1984 to provide a Building Control service. The Construction Industry Council (CIC) is currently the designated body which maintains the register of Approved Inspectors. Inspectors must have suitable insurance cover in place and must ensure the designated body is in possession of a declaration of insurance before undertaking any work.

Where it is proposed to use an Approved Inspector, the inspector must be competent for that type of work and be independent of the designer, builder or owner, with no professional interest in the work being supervised, unless it is a minor work consisting of:

- material alteration or extension of a one- or two-storey house, provided it has no more than three storeys on completion of the work;
- the provision, extension or material alteration of a controlled service or fitting in any building;
- underpinning work to any building.

Further guidance
Construction Industry Council
http://cic.org.uk/services/approved-inspectors.php

I.5.2.1 Initial notice

The person intending to carry out the work, together with the Approved Inspector, must give an initial notice to the local authority, together with evidence that an approved scheme of insurance applies to the work. The initial notice should conform to Form 1 of Schedule 1 of the Approved Inspectors Regulations. The local authority has five days in which to consider the initial notice, and may reject it only on grounds prescribed in Schedule 2 of those Regulations.

If the local authority accepts, or is deemed to have accepted, the initial notice then the Approved Inspector is responsible for supervising the work and ensuring it complies with the substantive requirements of the Building Regulations.

The local authority can cancel an initial notice if it appears that work has not begun within three years of the acceptance date.

I.5.2.2 Plans certificate

An Approved Inspector may be asked to certify the plans as complying with the Building Regulations and issue a plans certificate, with a copy provided to the local authority. The plans certificate may be issued at the same time as the initial notice, or later. The plans certificate provides a measure of protection for the person carrying out the work, in the event of the initial notice being cancelled or ceasing to be in force.

The local authority can rescind its acceptance of a plans certificate if it appears no work has taken place within three years.

I.5.2.3 Consultation with other bodies

Where work involves the erection, extension or change of use of a building to which the Regulatory Reform (Fire Safety) Order 2005 applies or will apply (a 'relevant use') the Approved Inspector must consult the fire authority:

- before, or as soon as practically after, giving an initial notice – supplying plans to show the work described will comply with Part B;
- before giving a plans certificate – supplying a copy of plans for which the plans certificate will be given;
- before giving a final certificate.

The fire authority must be allowed fifteen days to respond before the plans certificate or final certificate may be issued.

Where work is going to take place within 3m of the centre line of a drain, sewer or disposal main (as described in Part H4 (**H.5**), the Approved Inspector must consult with the sewerage undertaker when issuing an initial notice or amendment notice.

I.5.2.4 Variations

Where it is proposed to vary work which is the subject of an initial notice, the Approved Inspector and the person carrying out the work should give an amendment notice to the local authority. The local authority may reject the amendment notice within five days, but only on prescribed grounds.

If, for any reason, the Approved Inspector ceases to supervise the work, they must cancel the initial notice. A new Approved Inspector may issue an initial notice together with the person carrying out the work, provided it is accompanied by an undertaking from the original Approved Inspector to withdraw the original initial notice once the new one is accepted.

I.5.2.5 Final certificate

When the work is complete the Approved Inspector must give the local authority a final certificate. The certificate is evidence, but not conclusive evidence, that the work complies with the requirements specified in the certificate. The local authority can reject the certificate only on grounds given in Schedule 4 of the Approved Inspectors Regulations, and within ten days of submission. If the final certificate is rejected then the initial notice ceases to be in force four weeks from the date of rejection.

If the building is occupied following completion of the work without a final certificate being issued, the initial notice ceases to have an effect, but there is a period of grace:

- eight weeks for erection, extension, material alteration, material change of use;
- four weeks for erection, extension or material alteration for a building to which the Regulatory Reform (Fire Safety) Order 2005 applies (a 'relevant use').

Once the initial notice ceases to have effect the Approved Inspector cannot issue a final certificate and the local authority's power to enforce the Building Regulations can revive, although the local authority can extend the period of grace, especially if it is confident a final certificate will be provided soon.

I.5.2.6 Contraventions of the Building Regulations

Approved Inspectors have no power to enforce the Building Regulations but can issue written notices if they believe work carried out under their supervision contravenes the Regulations. The person carrying out the work has three months in which to remedy the alleged contravention, otherwise the Approved Inspector must cancel the initial notice. The cancellation notice must be given in the prescribed form (Form 6 in Schedule 1 of the Approved Inspectors Regulations) with a copy supplied to the local authority. The cancellation of the initial notice brings the work back under the supervision of the local authority, which may then exercise its powers of enforcement.

I.5.3 Public bodies

Public bodies may supervise their own building work following procedures similar to those followed by Approved Inspectors. Before work begins the public body must give the local authority a 'public body notice' (which acts much as an Approved Inspector's initial notice). The local authority can accept or reject a public body notice and impose requirements, as with deposition of plans. The public body can issue a public body's plans certificate and, when the work is complete, a public body's final notice.

I.5.4 Competent person self-certification schemes

Self-certification schemes enable individuals and enterprises to certify building work they have carried out as compliant with the applicable requirements of the Building Regulations. A competent person carrying out work within the scope of their scheme membership need not notify the local authority or an Approved Inspector in advance of the work. Instead, on completion of the work a certificate of compliance is issued (usually by the scheme operator) to the building occupier with a notice or copy certificate supplied to the local authority or Approved Inspector. Where work is wholly or partly paid for by a green deal plan the certificate and notice must include a statement identifying which part was paid for by that plan.

A self-certification certificate is evidence, but not conclusive evidence, that the work complies with the requirements specified: any certificate must include a statement to that effect. Local authorities are authorised to accept such certificates as evidence of compliance, but they retain their powers of inspection.

2013 changes
The requirements for self-certification certificates and notices have been extended to take account of the green deal (as defined in the Energy Act 2011). Local authorities are now obliged to store 'in a retrievable form' copies of self-certification notices and certificates.

Further guidance
www.communities.gov.uk
[Search for 'competent persons schemes'.]

I.5.5 Determinations and appeals

The Building Act provides two means of resolution for disputes as to whether proposed building work complies with the Building Regulations:

- Determinations – Where the local authority or Approved Inspector does not consider that the proposed work would comply with the Regulations the person carrying out the work may apply to the Secretary of State for a determination to establish that it does in fact comply. A determination may not be obtained for work carried out under a building notice.

- Appeals – Where the local authority has refused to relax or dispense with a requirement (**I.5.1.5**) the person carrying out the work may appeal against the refusal to the Secretary of State. An appeal may be made on work subject to full plans or a building notice; the work may be proposed, in progress or completed. An appeal must be made within one month of the local authority's refusal.

Further guidance
Guide to determinations and appeals. CLG. 2007.

I.6 Building Regulations in Wales

On 31 December 2011 the powers to make buildings regulations in Wales were transferred from the Secretary of State to Welsh ministers. Consequently, amendments made to the Building Regulations from 2012 onwards do not apply to Wales. The only exception in the transfer was 'excepted energy buildings' (a category which includes power stations, power lines and gas pipelines and storage facilities) which remain under the Secretary of State.

The transfer of power will result in building regulations in England and Wales diverging, most particularly in the area of energy efficiency and carbon dioxide emissions.

Further guidance
The Welsh Ministers (Transfer of Functions) (No. 2) Order 2009 (Statutory Instrument 2009/3019).

A. Structure

A.1 General considerations

A.1.1 Scope

Part A is intended to ensure the stability of buildings.

Part A: Structure
Requirements
Loading
A1 (1) The building shall be constructed so that the combined dead, imposed and wind loads are sustained and transmitted by it to the ground – (a) safely; and (b) without causing such deflection or deformation of any part of the building, or such movement of the ground, as will impair the stability of any part of another building. (2) In assessing whether a building complies with sub-paragraph (1) regard shall be had to the imposed and wind loads to which it is likely to be subjected in the ordinary course of its use for the purpose for which it is intended.
Ground movement
A2 The building shall be constructed so that ground movement caused by – (a) swelling, shrinkage or freezing of the sub-soil; or (b) land-slip or subsidence (other than subsidence arising from shrinkage), in so far as the risk can be reasonably foreseen will not impair the stability of any part of the building.
Disproportionate collapse
A3 The building shall be constructed so that in the event of an accident the building will not suffer collapse to an extent disproportionate to the cause.

2013 changes
There have only been minor changes to the requirements of Part A, although the introduction of the Eurocodes has resulted in the majority of the references being revised (see **A.2.1.1**). Notable changes include:

- A.2.1.1 Approved Document A now refers to the Eurocodes instead of the withdrawn British Standards.
- A.2.2.3 The method for calculating maximum permitted building height has been revised.
- A.2.2.3 The specifications for cavity wall ties have been revised following the withdrawal of BS 1243.
- A.2.2.5 The minimum depth to the underside of strip foundations has been increased for some shrinkable clay soils.
- A.3.1 The maximum area of a storey at risk of collapse has been increased to 100m^2.
- A.3.3 Analysis for seismic design should be considered for some buildings.

A.1.2 Existing buildings

Where a building is subject to a material change of use a structural appraisal should be undertaken to ensure that it will meet the requirements of Part A.

The re-roofing of a building will constitute a material alteration if the construction is unable to withstand the proposed increased loading, and strengthening work or replacement of roof members is required (**A.2.4**).

Further guidance
BRE Digest 366: *Structural appraisal of existing buildings, including for a material change of use.* 2012.

Appraisal of existing structures. The Institution of Structural Engineers. 2010.

A.1.3 Definitions

Buttressing wall A wall which provides lateral support from the base to the top of a wall perpendicular to it.

Cavity width The horizontal distance between the two leaves of a cavity wall.

Compartment wall A wall to a fire-resisting compartment (**B.5.2**).

Dead load The load due to the weight of all walls, permanent partitions, floors, roofs and finishes including services.

Imposed load The load produced by the use of the building, including snow loads, but not wind loads.

Pier A thickened section of a wall which provides lateral support.

Separating wall A wall or part of a wall common to adjoining buildings, and constructed to meet Requirement B3(2).

Spacing The centre to centre distance between two adjacent timber members, measured in the plane of floor, ceiling or roof structure.

Span The distance measured along the centre line of a member between the centres of any two adjacent bearings or supports.

Supported wall A wall that receives lateral support by buttressing walls, piers or chimneys acting in conjunction with floor(s) or roof.

Wind load The load due to the effect of wind pressure or suction.

A.2 Loading and ground movement (Requirements A1 and A2)

The requirements for loading and ground movement may be met by:
- following the recommendations in the documents listed in **A.2.1**; or
- by adopting the detailed guidance in sections **A.2.2** to **A.2.4**.

The design should take account of the hazards to which the building is likely to be subject. Loading should be assessed in accordance with current Codes of Practice (**A.2.1**) and should account for dynamic, concentrated and peak load effects likely to occur during ordinary use of the building for its intended purpose.

Grandstands and structures in places of public assembly may need to sustain synchronous or rhythmic movement of numbers of people without impairing the structure or alarming those using it. Safety factors should be appropriate for the overall design.

Stability also depends on:
- the use of materials with suitable properties;
- detailed design and assembly of the structure;
- standards of workmanship.

Further guidance
Dynamic performance requirements for permanent grandstands subject to crowd action – Recommendations for management, design and assessment. The Institution of Structural Engineers. 2008.

A.2.1 All building types

A.2.1.1 Reference standards

The building should be designed to the appropriate standards listed in Table A.1.

2013 changes
The majority of the British Standards for structural design referenced in the 2004 edition of Approved Document A were replaced in 2010 by the Eurocodes. A list of the Eurocodes and the corresponding withdrawn design standards is given in Annex A of a CLG circular dated 30 July 2013, which is available here: https://www.gov.uk/building-regulations-divisional-circular-letters.

Table A.1 Reference standards

Requirement	Standards
Basis of structural design and loading	BS EN 1990:2002+A1:2005 Eurocode – Basis of structural design; with UK National Annex to BS EN 1990:2002+A1:2005
	BS EN 1991-1-1:2002 Eurocode 1: Actions on structures – Part 1.1: General actions – Densities, self weight, imposed loads for buildings; with UK National Annex to BS EN 1991-1-1:2002
	BSI PD 6688-1-1:2011 Published Document – Recommendations for the design of structures to BS EN 1991-1-1
	BS EN 1991-1-3:2003 Eurocode 1: Actions on structures – Part 1.3: General actions – Snow loads; with UK National Annex to BS EN 1991-1-3:2003
	BS EN 1991-1-4:2005+A1:2010 Eurocode 1: Actions on structures – Part 1.4: General actions – Wind actions; with UK National Annex to BS EN 1991-1-4:2005+A1:2010
	BSI PD 6688-1-4:2009 Published Document – Background information to the National Annex to BS EN 1991-1-4 and additional guidance
	BS EN 1991-1-5:2003 Eurocode 1: Actions on structures – Part 1.5: General actions – Thermal actions; with UK National Annex to BS EN 1991-1-5:2003
	BS EN 1991-1-6:2005 Eurocode 1: Actions on structures – Part 1.6: General actions – Actions during execution; with UK National Annex to BS EN 1996-1-6:2005
	BS EN 1991-1-7:2006 Eurocode 1: Actions on structures – Part 1.7: General actions – Accidental actions; with UK National Annex to BS EN 1991-1-7:2006
	BSI PD 6688-1-7:2009 Published Document – Recommendations for the design of structures to BS EN 1991-1-7
	BS EN 1991-3:2006 Eurocode 1: Actions on structures – Part 3: Actions induced by cranes and machines; with UK National Annex to BS EN 1991-3:2006
Structural work of reinforced, pre-stressed or plain concrete	BS EN 1992-1-1:2004 Eurocode 2: Design of concrete structures – Part 1.1: General rules and rules for buildings; with UK National Annex to BS EN 1992-1-1:2004
	BSI PD 6687-1:2010 Published Document – Background paper to the UK National Annexes to BS EN 1992-1 and BS EN 1992-3
	BS EN 13670:2009 Execution of concrete structures
Structural work of steel	BS EN 1993-1-1:2005 Eurocode 3: Design of steel structures – Part 1.1: General rules and rules for buildings; with UK National Annex to BS EN 1993-1-1:2005
	BS EN 1993-1-3:2006 Eurocode 3: Design of steel structures – Part 1.3: General rules – Supplementary rules for cold-formed members and sheeting; with UK National Annex to BS EN 1993-1-3:2006
	BS EN 1993-1-4:2006 Eurocode 3: Design of steel structures – Part 1.4: General rules – Supplementary rules for stainless steels; with UK National Annex to BS EN 1993-1-4:2006
	BS EN 1993-1-5:2006 Eurocode 3: Design of steel structures – Part 1.5: Plated structural elements; with UK National Annex to BS EN 1993-1-5:2006
	BS EN 1993-1-6:2007 Eurocode 3: Design of steel structures – Part 1.6: Strength and stability of shell structures

continued

Table A.1 continued

Requirement	Standards
	BS EN 1993-1-7:2007 Eurocode 3: Design of steel structures – Part 1.7: Plated structures subject to out of plane loading
	BS EN 1993-1-8:2005 Eurocode 3: Design of steel structures – Part 1.8: Design of joints; with UK National Annex to BS EN 1993-1-8:2005
	BS EN 1993-1-9:2005 Eurocode 3: Design of steel structures – Part 1.9: Fatigue; with UK National Annex to BS EN 1993-1-9:2005
	BSI PD 6695-1-9:2008 Published Document – Recommendations for the design of structures to BS EN 1993-1-9
	BS EN 1993-1-10:2005 Eurocode 3: Design of steel structures – Part 1.10: Material toughness and through-thickness properties; with UK National Annex to BS EN 1993-1-10:2005
	BSI PD 6695-1-10:2009 Published Document – Recommendations for the design of structures to BS EN 1993-1-10
	BS EN 1993-1-11:2006 Eurocode 3: Design of steel structures – Part 1.11: Design of structures with tension components; with UK National Annex to BS EN 1993-1-11:2006
	BS EN 1993-1-12:2007 Eurocode 3: Design of steel structures – Part 1.12: Additional rules for the extension of EN 1993 up to steel grades S 700; with UK National Annex to BS EN 1993-1-12:2007
	BS EN 1993-5:2007 Eurocode 3: Design of steel structures – Part 5: Piling; with UK National Annex to BS EN 1993-5:2007+A1:2012
	BS EN 1993-6:2007 Eurocode 3: Design of steel structures – Part 6: Crane supporting structures; with UK National Annex to BS EN 1993-6:2007
	BS EN 1090-2:2008+A1:2011 Execution of steel structures and aluminium structures – Part 2. Technical requirements for the execution of steel structures
	BRE Digest 437 Industrial platform floors: mezzanine and raised storage
Structural work of composite steel and concrete	BS EN 1994-1-1:2004 Eurocode 4: Design of composite steel and concrete structures – Part 1.1: General rules and rules for buildings; with UK National Annex to BS EN 1994-1-1:2004
Structural work of timber	BS EN 1995-1-1:2004+A1:2008 Eurocode 5: Design of timber structures – Part 1.1: General – Common rules and rules for buildings; with UK National Annex to BS EN 1995-1-1:2004+A1:2008
	BSI PD 6693-1:2012 Published Document – Recommendations for the design of timber structures to Eurocode 5: Design of timber structures Part 1: General – Common rules and rules for buildings
	BS 8103-3:2009 Structural design of low-rise buildings – Part 3: Code of practice for timber floors and roofs for housing
Structural work of masonry	BS EN 1996-1-1:2005+A1:2012 Eurocode 6: Design of masonry structures – Part 1.1: General rules for reinforced and unreinforced masonry structures; with UK National Annex to BS EN 1996-1-1:2005+A1:2012
	BS EN 1996-2:2006 Eurocode 6: Design of masonry structures – Part 2: Design considerations, selection of materials and execution of masonry; with UK National Annex to BS EN 1996-2:2006
	BSI PD 6697:2010 Published Document – Recommendations for the design of masonry structures to BS EN 1991-1-1 and BS EN 1996-2
	BS EN 1996-3:2006 Eurocode 6: Design of masonry structures – Part 3: Simplified calculation methods for unreinforced masonry structures; with UK National Annex to BS EN 1996-3:2006
	BS 8103-1:2011 Structural design of low-rise buildings – Part 1: Code of Practice for stability, site investigation, foundations, precast concrete floors and ground floor slabs for housing
	BS 8103-2:2005 Structural design of low-rise buildings – Part 2: Code of practice for masonry walls for housing

continued

Table A.1 continued	
Requirement	**Standards**
Geotechnical work and foundations	BS EN 1997-1:2004 Eurocode 7: Geotechnical design – Part 1: General rules; with UK National Annex to BS EN 1997-1:2004
	BS EN 1997-2:2007 Eurocode 7: Geotechnical design – Part 2: Ground investigation and testing; with UK National Annex to BS EN 1997-2:2007
Seismic aspects	BS EN 1998-1:2004+A1:2013 Eurocode 8: Design of structures for earthquake resistance – Part 1. General rules, seismic actions and rules for buildings; with UK National Annex to BS EN 1998-1:2004
	BS EN 1998-5:2004 Eurocode 8: Design of structures for earthquake resistance – Part 5. Foundations, retaining structures and geotechnical aspects; with UK National Annex to BS EN 1998-5:2004
	BSI PD 6698:2009 Published Document – Recommendations for the design of structures for earthquake resistance to BS EN 1998
Structural work of aluminium	BS EN 1999-1-1:2007+A1:2009 Eurocode 9: Design of aluminium structures – Part 1.1: General structural rules; with UK National Annex to BS EN 1999-1-1:2007+A1:2009
	BS EN 1999-1-3:2007+A1:2011 Eurocode 9: Design of aluminium structures – Part 1.3: Structures susceptible to fatigue; with UK National Annex to BS EN 1999-1-3:2007+A1:2011
	BSI PD 6702-1:2009 Published Document – Structural use of aluminium – Part 1. Recommendations for the design of aluminium structures to BS EN 1999
	BS EN 1999-1-4:2007+A1:2011 Eurocode 9: Design of aluminium structures – Part 1.4: Cold-formed structural sheeting; with UK National Annex to BS EN 1999-1-4:2007
	BS EN 1999-1-5:2007 Eurocode 9: Design of aluminium structures – Part 1.5: Shell structures; with UK National Annex to BS EN 1999-1-5:2007
	BS EN 1090-3:2008 Execution of steel structures and aluminium structures – Part 3. Technical requirements for aluminium structures
	BSI PD 6705-3:2009 Published Document – Structural use of steel and aluminium – Part 3. Recommendations for the execution of aluminium structures to BS EN 1090-3

A.2.1.2 Ground movement

Unstable ground – resulting from landslides, mining or unstable strata – can have a devastating effect on a building and its surroundings. The design of the building and its foundations should take account of such conditions where they are known or recorded.

Further guidance
Planning Policy Guidance 14 (PPG 14) *Development on unstable land*. CLG. 1990. [Replaced by the National Planning Policy Framework (CLG. 2012), which makes one reference to unstable land in paragraph 109.]

A.2.2 Residential buildings and other small buildings of traditional construction

The guidance in Approved Document A for the design and construction of residential buildings of traditional construction, and other small buildings covers:

- basic requirements for stability (**A.2.2.1**);
- sizing and treatment of timber members in floors and roofs (**A.2.2.2**);
- thickness of masonry walls (**A.2.2.3**);
- proportions for masonry chimneys (**A.2.2.4**);
- foundations of plain concrete (**A.2.2.5**).

Guidance in **A.2.2.1** should be observed when following **A.2.2.2** and **A.2.2.3**.

A.2.2.1 Basic requirements for stability

To ensure that a low-rise residential building is stable under likely imposed and wind loading conditions:

- the overall size and proportioning of the building should comply with the guidance for that form of construction;
- the internal and external walls should form a robust three-dimensional box structure, no larger than the maximum cell size;
- the internal and external walls should be adequately connected by masonry bonding or mechanical connections;
- the roof and any intermediate floors should provide local support to the walls and transfer wind forces to buttressing elements.

Traditional cut timber roofs (with purlins, rafters and ceiling joists) generally have sufficient built-in resistance to instability and wind forces. However, diagonal rafter bracing (equivalent to that recommended for trussed rafter roofs in BS EN 1995-1-1:2004 with its UK National Annex, BSI PD 6693-1:2012 and BS 8103-3:2009) should be considered for non-hipped or single-hipped roofs of greater than 40° pitch on detached houses.

A.2.2.2 Timber members for floors and roofs

Guidance on sizing members in floors and roofs is given in span tables published by TRADA and in BS EN 1995-1-1:2004, PD 6693-1:2012 and BS 8103-3:2009.

To prevent infestations by house longhorn beetle (*Hylotrupes bajulus L*) in the areas listed in Table A.2, all softwood timber used in roof construction and within roof spaces should be treated with preservative.

Table A.2 Areas at risk from house longhorn beetle
Geographical area
In the Borough of Bracknell Forest the parishes of Sandhurst and Crowthorne
The Borough of Elmbridge
In the District of Hart, the parishes of Hawley and Yateley
The District of Runnymede
The Borough of Spelthorne
The Borough of Surrey Heath
In the Borough of Rushmoor the area in the former district of Farnborough
The Borough of Woking

Further guidance
Eurocode 5 span tables: for solid timber members in floors, ceilings and roofs for dwellings. TRADA. 2009. [The previous edition, compatible with BS 5268, is still available.]

BS EN 1995-1-1:2004+A1:2008. Design of timber structures. General. Common rules and rules for buildings. With UK National Annex.

PD 6693-1:2012 Recommendations for the design of timber structures to Eurocode 5: Design of timber structures Part 1: General – Common rules and rules for buildings.

BS 8103-3:2009. Structural design of low-rise buildings. Code of practice for timber floors and roofs for housing.

Industrial wood preservation specification and practice. The Wood Protection Association. 2011.

A.2.2.3 Masonry walls

The guidance on wall thickness and construction in this section applies to residential buildings of not more than three storeys and small non-residential buildings and annexes, and is valid only when both the building and the wall itself meet the conditions set out below.

Where this section does not give guidance, the walls should comply with the recommendations of BS EN 1996-2:2006 (with UK National Annex) and PD 6697:2010.

The guidance is based on the worst combination of circumstances, so it is permitted to make minor departures, on the basis of judgement and experience, or where calculation shows the wall will perform satisfactorily.

Wall thickness determination

The thickness of a wall should not be less than:

- the general minimum values given in Table A.3; and
- the specific minimum values for the type of construction given in Table A.4.

Table A.3 Minimum thickness of certain external walls, compartment walls and separating walls

Height of wall (m)	Length of wall (m)	Minimum thickness of wall
≤3.5	≤12	190mm for whole of its height
>3.5 and ≤9	≤9	190mm for whole of its height
	≤9 and ≤12	290mm from the base of the height of one storey, and 190mm for the rest of its height
>9 and ≤12	≤9	290mm from the base of the height of one storey, and 190mm for the rest of its height
	>9 and ≤12	290mm from the base for the height of two storeys, and 190mm for the rest of its height

Table A.4 Minimum thicknesses for particular wall types

Wall type	Minimum wall thickness
Solid external walls, compartment walls and separating walls of coursed brickwork or blockwork	At least as thick as 1/16 of storey height (subject to minimum thicknesses in **Table A.3**)
Solid external walls, compartment walls and separating walls in uncoursed stone, flints, clunches, bricks or other burnt or vitrified material	1.33 times the thickness required of a similar wall with coursed brickwork or blockwork (subject to minimum thicknesses in **Table A.3**)
Cavity walls in coursed brickwork or blockwork	Leaves at least 90mm thick and cavities at least 50mm wide. For external walls, compartment walls and separating walls in cavity construction, the combined thickness of 2 leaves + 10mm should be at least as thick as 1/16 of storey height (subject to minimum thicknesses in **Table A.3**). Wall ties as **Table A.12** at 900mm horizontal spacing and 450mm vertical spacing or at least 2.5 ties/m²; and ties within 225mm of vertical edges of all openings, movement joints and roof verges at no more than 300mm vertical spacing
Walls providing vertical support to other walls	Irrespective of material used in construction, should not be less thick than any part of wall to which it gives vertical support (subject to minimum thicknesses in **Table A.3**)
Internal loadbearing walls in brickwork or blockwork (except compartment walls or separating walls)	Thickness = ((Thickness from **Table A.3**)/2) – 5mm but a wall in the lowest storey of a three-storey building carrying load from both upper storeys must be a minimum of 140mm thick
Parapet walls	Minimum width and maximum height as **Figure A.3**
Single leaves of external walls of small, single-storey non-residential buildings and of annexes	90mm (notwithstanding **A.2.2.3**)

Note: Where walls are constructed of bricks or blocks having modular dimensions, wall thicknesses which derive from a dimension of brick or block may be reduced by an amount not exceeding the deviation from the work size permitted by a British Standard relating to equivalent-sized bricks or blocks made of the same material.

Table A.5 Wall types and building proportions

Building type	Limiting proportions of building	Wall types
Residential building up to three storeys (**Figure A.1**)	Maximum height, H, from lowest finished ground level adjoining building to highest point of roof or wall not greater than 15m.[1]	External walls Internal loadbearing walls Compartment walls Separating walls
	Height of building, H, should not exceed twice the least width, W1.	
	For a wing where the projection, P, exceeds twice the least width, W2, the height of wing, H2, should not exceed W2.	
Small single-storey non-residential buildings (**Figure A.2**)	Height H should not exceed 3m, and the greatest width of the building, W, should not exceed 9m.[1]	External walls Internal loadbearing walls
Annexes	Height H should not exceed 3m.[1]	

[1] Subject to limits of wind loading: **A.2.2.3** Building heights.

Conditions relating to the building

Size and proportion of building:

The building should not exceed the proportions shown in Figures A.1 and A.2 and Table A.5. The wall must extend to full storey height unless it is a parapet wall, in which case it should not exceed the heights shown in Figure A.3.

Figure A.1 Size and proportion of residential buildings of not more than three storeys

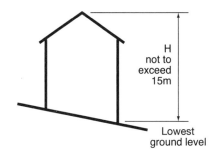
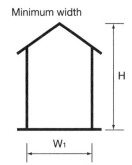
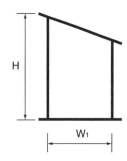

H not to exceed 15m

Lowest ground level

Minimum width

W_1 to be not less than 0.5 H

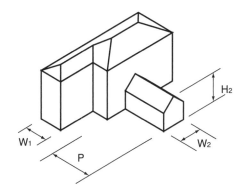

If P is more than 2W_2 then W_2 to be not less than 0.5 H_2

Figure A.2 Size and proportion of non-residential buildings and annexes

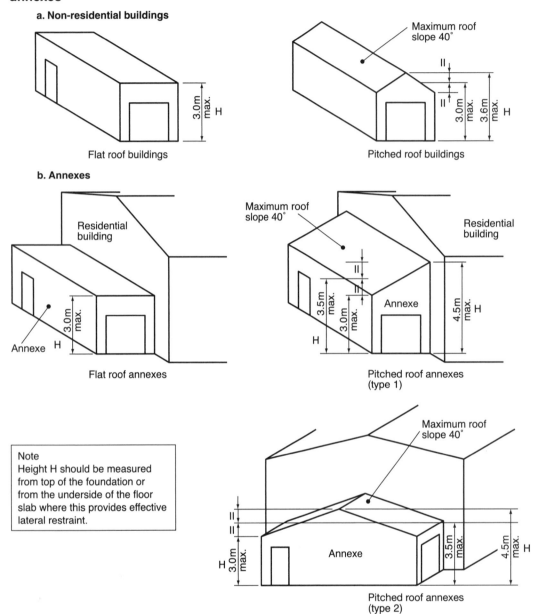

a. Non-residential buildings

Flat roof buildings

Pitched roof buildings

b. Annexes

Flat roof annexes

Pitched roof annexes (type 1)

Pitched roof annexes (type 2)

Note
Height H should be measured from top of the foundation or from the underside of the floor slab where this provides effective lateral restraint.

Floor areas:
No floor enclosed by structural walls on all sides may exceed 70m² and no floor without a structural wall on one side may exceed 36m².

Imposed loads:
Imposed loads should not exceed those in Table A.6.

Building heights:
The permissible height of the building is limited by the site exposure and wind speed; it may be determined by the following method, based on BS EN 1991-1-4:2005 (with UK National Annex):

1. Determine the site wind speed, V, from Figure A.4.
2. Determine the site's orographic zone from Figure A.5.
3. Determine the Factor O for that zone using Table A.7 (or use Figure A.6 and A.7 – interpolation between curves may be used).
4. Determine Factor A for the site altitude using Table A.8.
5. Calculate Factor S, where $S = V \times O \times A$.
6. Use Factor S to determine the maximum allowable height of the building from Table A.9.

Note: Heights should be measured in accordance with Figure A.8.

2013 changes
The maximum permissible height is now determined using the method in BS EN 1991-1-4:2005, instead of BS 6399-2. The topographic zone factor, T, has been replaced by the orographic zone factor, O. Figures A.4 and A.5, and Tables A.7, A.8 and A.9 have been revised, and there are additional Figures A.6 and A.7 which offer a graphical method for determining Factor O.

Figure A.3 Parapet walls: height

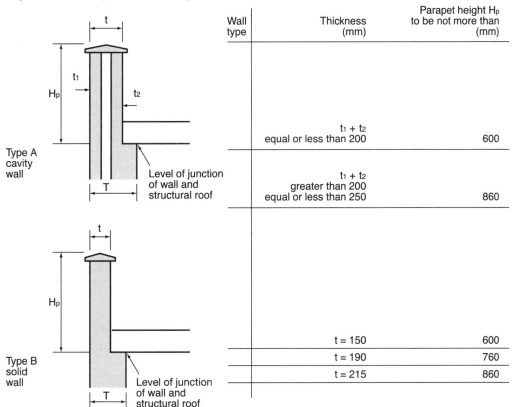

Wall type	Thickness (mm)	Parapet height H_p to be not more than (mm)
	$t_1 + t_2$ equal or less than 200	600
	$t_1 + t_2$ greater than 200 equal or less than 250	860
	$t = 150$	600
	$t = 190$	760
	$t = 215$	860

Type A cavity wall — Level of junction of wall and structural roof

Type B solid wall — Level of junction of wall and structural roof

Note: t should be less than or equal to T

Table A.6 Maximum imposed loads	
Element	**Loading**
Roof	Distributed loads • 1.00kN/m² for spans not exceeding 12m • 1.5kN/m² not exceeding 6m
Floor	Distributed load • 2.00kN/m²
Ceilings	Distributed load • 0.25kN/m² (together with concentrated load 0.9kN)

Figure A.4 Map of wind speeds (V) in m/s

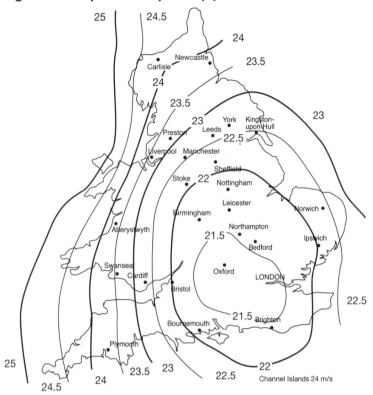

Figure A.5 Orographic zones for Factor O

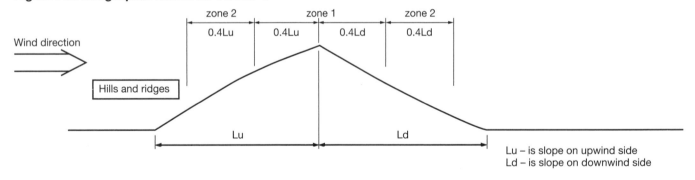

Wind direction

Hills and ridges

zone 2 — 0.4Lu | zone 1 — 0.4Lu | 0.4Ld | zone 2 — 0.4Ld

Lu

Ld

Lu – is slope on upwind side
Ld – is slope on downwind side

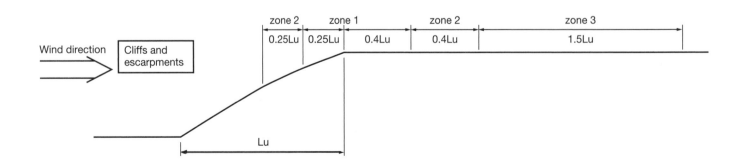

Wind direction

Cliffs and escarpments

zone 2 — 0.25Lu | 0.25Lu | zone 1 — 0.4Lu | zone 2 — 0.4Lu | zone 3 — 1.5Lu

Lu

Figure A.6 Alternative graphical method for determining orography Factor O for hills and ridges

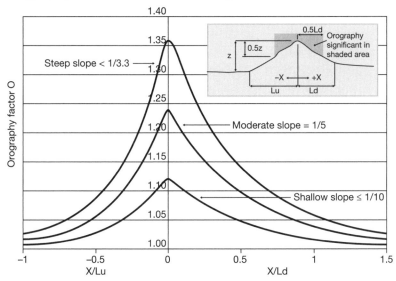

Figure A.7 Alternative graphical method for determining orography Factor O for cliffs and escarpments

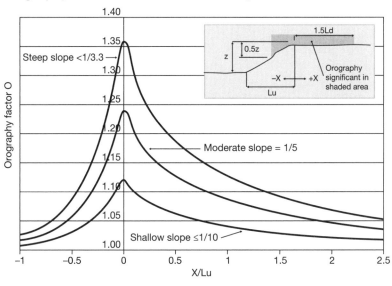

Table A.7 Factor O			
Topographic category and average slope of whole hillside, ridge, cliff or escarpment	Factor O		
	Zone 1	Zone 2	Zone 3
Category 1: Nominally flat terrain, average slope <1/20	1.0	1.0	1.0
Category 2: Shallow terrain, average slope <1/10	1.12	1.07	1.05
Category 3: Moderately steep terrain, average slope <1/5	1.24	1.13	1.10
Category 4: Steep terrain, average slope >1/5	1.36	1.20	1.15

Note: Outside these zones Factor O = 1.0.

Table A.8 Wind speed, Factor A

Site altitude (m)	Factor A
0	1.00
50	1.05
100	1.10
150	1.15
200	1.20
300	1.30
400	1.40
500	1.50

For elevated sites where orography is significant a more accurate assessment of Factor A can be obtained by using the altitude at the base of the topographic feature instead of the altitude at the site, see Figure A.5 or, alternatively, Figures A.6 and A.7.

Interpolation may be used.

Table A.9 Maximum allowable building height (m)

Factor S	Distance to the coast[1]					
	Country sites			Town sites[2]		
	<2km	2–20km	>20km	<2km	2–20km	>20km
≤25	15	15	15	15	15	15
26	11.5	13.5	15	15	15	15
27	8	11	14.5	15	15	15
28	5.5	8	11	15	15	15
29	4	6.5	8.5	12.5	15	15
30	3	5	6.5	10	12.5	15
31	–	4	5.5	8.5	11	13.5
32	–	3.5	4.5	7	9.5	11.5
33	–	3	3.5	6	8	10
34	–	–	3	5.5	7	8.5
35	–	–	–	4.5	6.5	7.5
36	–	–	–	4	5.5	6.5
37	–	–	–	3.5	5	6
38	–	–	–	3	4.5	5.5
39	–	–	–	–	4	5
40	–	–	–	–	3.5	4.5
41	–	–	–	–	3	4
42	–	–	–	–	–	3.5
43	–	–	–	–	–	3.5
44	–	–	–	–	–	3

[1] Where a site is closer than 1km to an inland area of water which extends more than 1km in the wind direction, the distance to the coast should be taken as <2km.

[2] Sites in town less than 300m from the edge of the town should be assumed to be in Country terrain.

Interpolation may be used.

Figure A.8 Measuring storey and wall heights

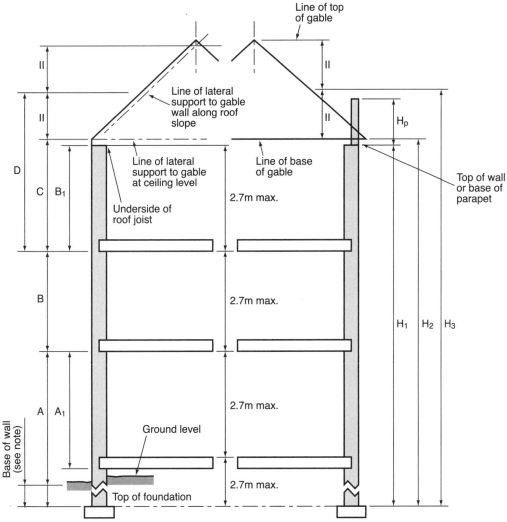

Key

(a) Measuring storey heights

A_1 is the ground storey height if the ground floor provides effective lateral support to the wall, i.e. is adequately tied to the wall or is a suspended floor bearing on the wall.

A is the ground storey height if the ground floor does not provide effective lateral support to the wall.

Note: If the wall is supported adequately and permanently on both sides by suitable compact material, the base of the wall for the purposes of the storey height may be taken as the lower level of this support. (Not greater than 3.7m ground storey height.)

B is the intermediate storey height.

B_1 is the top storey height for walls which do not include a gable.

C is the top storey height where lateral support is given to the gable both at ceiling level and along the roof slope.

D is the top storey height for the external walls which include a gable where lateral support is given to the gable only along the roof slope.

(b) Measuring wall heights

H_1 is the height of an external wall that does not include a gable.

H_2 is the height of an internal or separating wall which is built up to the underside of the roof.

H_3 is the height of an external wall which includes a gable.

H_p is the height of a parapet (see Figure A.3). If H_p is more than 1.2m add H_p to H_1.

Conditions relating to the wall

Materials:

Walls should be built of masonry units conforming to Table A.10, properly bonded with mortar. The masonry units should have compressive strengths shown in Table A.11, as appropriate for the three conditions (A, B and C) shown in Figure A.9.

Table A.10 Standards for masonry units	
Masonry units	**Standards**
Clay bricks or blocks	BS EN 771-1:2003 Specification for masonry units. Clay masonry units.
Calcium silicate bricks	BS EN 771-2:2003 Specification for masonry units. Calcium silicate units.

Concrete bricks or blocks	BS EN 771 Specification for masonry units
	    -3:2003 Aggregate concrete masonry units (dense and lightweight aggregates).
	    -4:2003 Autoclaved aerated concrete masonry units.

Manufactured stone	BS EN 771-5:2003 Specification for masonry units. Manufactured stone masonry units.
Square dressed natural stone	The appropriate requirements are described in BS EN 771-6:2005 Specification for masonry units. Natural stone masonry units.

Table A.11 Declared compressive strength of masonry units (N/mm^2)							
Condition (as Figure A.7)	Unit type	Clay masonry unit to BS EN 771-1		Calcium silicate masonry units to BS EN 771-2		Aggregate concrete masonry units to BS EN 771-3	Autoclaved aerated concrete masonry units to BS EN 771-4	Manufactured stone masonry units to BS EN 771-5
		Group 1[1]	Group 2	Group 1[1]	Group 2			
		Declared compressive strength of masonry units (N/mm^2)						
Condition A	Brick	6.0	9.0	6.0	9.0	6.0	–	Any unit
	Block	5.0	8.0	5.0	8.0	2.9[2]	2.9	Any unit
Condition B	Brick	9.0	13.0	9.0	13.0	9.0	–	Any unit
	Block	7.5	11.0	7.5	11.0	7.3[2]	7.3	Any unit
Condition C	Brick	18.0	25.0	18.0	25.0	18.0	–	Any unit
	Block	15.0	21.0	15.0	21.0	7.3[2]	7.3	Any unit

[1] Group 1 units have not more than 25% formed voids (frogged bricks: 20%). Group 2 units have formed voids greater than 25% but not more than 55%.

[2] Dry strengths to BS EN 772-1. Otherwise, table shows mean compressive strengths, except for blocks to BS EN 771-1 and -2, which are normalised compressive strengths.

Figure A.9 Compressive strength zones for masonry units

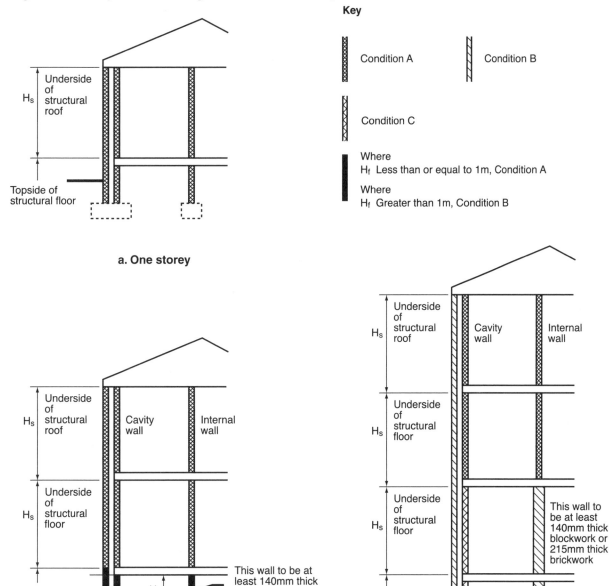

Key

Condition A

Condition B

Condition C

Where
H_f Less than or equal to 1m, Condition A

Where
H_f Greater than 1m, Condition B

a. One storey

b. Two storeys

c. Three storeys

Notes

1 If H_s is not greater than 2.7m, the compressive strength of bricks or blocks should be used in walls as indicated by the key.

2 If H_s is greater than 2.7m, the compressive strength of bricks or blocks used in the wall should be at least Condition B, or as indicated by the key, whichever is the greater.

3 If the external wall is solid construction, the masonry units should have a compressive strength of at least that shown for the internal leaf of a cavity wall in the same position.

4 The guidance given in the diagram for walls of two- and three-storey buildings should only be used to determine the compressive strength of the masonry units where the roof construction is of timber.

A. Structure

Mortor should be:

- Mortar designation (iii) to BS EN 1996-1-1:2005 with UK National Annex;
- Strength Class M4 to BS EN 998-2;
- 1:1:5 to 6 CEM I, lime and fine aggregate measured by volume of dry materials; or
- of equivalent or greater strength and durability.

Wall ties should comply with BS EN 845-1 and be material references 1 or 3 in BS EN 845 Table A1 Austenitic Stainless Steel and sized as Table A.12.

Table A.12 Cavity wall ties

Nominal cavity width (mm)[1]	Tie length (mm)[2]	BS EN 845-1 wall tie
50–75	200	Type 1, 2, 3 or 4 to PD 6697:2010 and selected on the basis of the design loading and design cavity width.
76–100	225	
101–125	250	
126–150	275	
151–175	300	
176–300	[2]	

[1] For face insulated blocks the cavity width should be measured from the face of the masonry.
[2] The embedment depth of the tie should not be less than 50mm in both leaves. For cavities wider than 175mm calculate the length as the nominal cavity width plus 125mm and select the nearest stock length. For ties requiring embedment depths greater than 50mm, increase the calculated tie length accordingly.

Loading on walls:
The span of any floor supported by a wall should not exceed 6m, measured from the centre line of the bearing.

Vertical loading on walls should be distributed. This may be assumed for concrete floor slabs, precast concrete floors and timber floors designed in accordance with **A.2.2.2** provided the bearing length for lintels is:

- 150mm for a clear span greater than 1200mm; or
- 100mm for a clear span of 1200mm or less.

Walls should not be subject to lateral load, other than wind load, and the load resulting from differences in levels between one side of the wall and the other. In the case of the latter, the difference should not exceed four times the wall thickness (Figure A.10). The combined dead and imposed load should not exceed 70kN/m at the base of the wall (Figure A.10).

2013 changes
With the withdrawal of BS 1243 wall ties are now specified solely to BS EN 845-1. Table A.12 has been revised accordingly.

Further guidance
BS 845-1:2003+A1:2008. Specification for ancillary components of masonry. Ties, tension straps, hangers and brackets.

Figure A.10 Differences in ground level

a. Situations where differences in level may occur

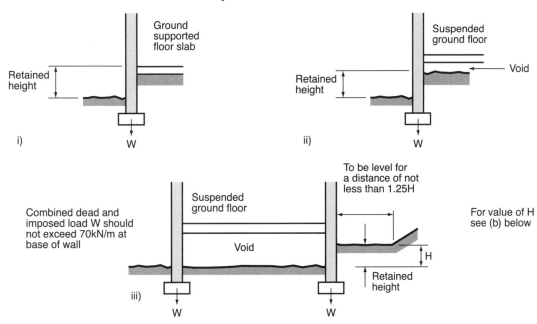

b. Maximum differences in permitted level

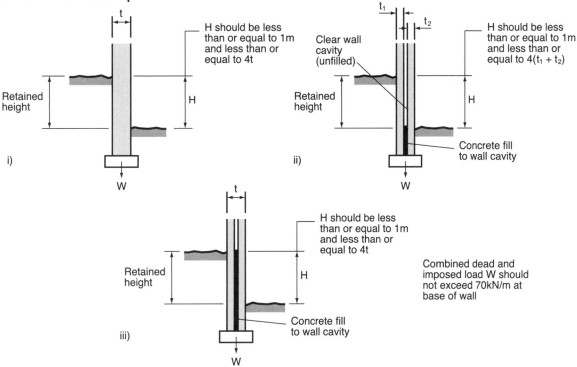

Notes

1   In (b), floor slabs have been omitted for clarity and may be on either side of the walls shown.

2   Cavity walls should be tied in accordance with Table A.12.

3   These recommendations apply only to circumstances where there is a full storey height of masonry above the upper retained level.

End restraint:

The ends of every wall should be bonded or otherwise securely tied throughout their full height to a buttressing wall, pier or chimney. Long walls may have intermediate buttressing walls, piers or chimneys, dividing the wall into distinct lengths within each storey. Each distinct length should then be treated as a supported wall. The lateral supports should provide restraint to the full height of supported wall, but may be staggered at each storey.

A buttressing wall which is not itself supported should have a thickness, T2, which is not less than:

- half the thickness required for an external or separating wall of similar height and length, less 5mm; or
- 75mm if the wall forms part of a dwelling and does not exceed 6m in total height and 10m in length; or
- 90mm in other cases.

The length of the buttressing wall should be at least 1/6 (one-sixth) of the overall height of the supported wall. It should be bonded or securely tied to the supported wall, and at the other end to a buttressing wall, pier or chimney. Openings in a buttressing wall should not exceed those shown in Figure A.11.

Figure A.11 Openings in a buttressing wall

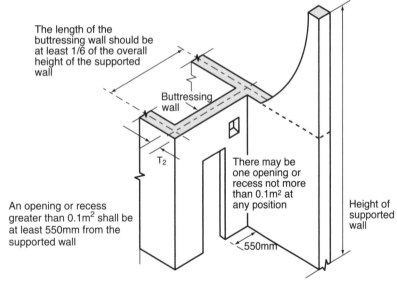

The length of the buttressing wall should be at least 1/6 of the overall height of the supported wall

Buttressing wall

T_2

There may be one opening or recess not more than 0.1m² at any position

An opening or recess greater than 0.1m² shall be at least 550mm from the supported wall

Height of supported wall

550mm

The opening height should not be more than 0.9 times the floor to ceiling height and the depth of the lintel including any masonry over the opening should be not less than 150mm

Notes:

1   The buttressing wall should be bonded or securely tied to the supported wall and at the other end to a buttressing wall, pier or chimney.

2   Openings or recesses in the buttressing wall should be as shown – the position and shape of the openings should not impair the lateral support to be given by the buttressing wall.

3   Refer to Figure A.8 for the rules for measuring the height of the supported wall.

Restraint may also be provided by piers and chimneys:

- A pier should have at least 3 times the thickness of the supported wall, with a minimum width of 190mm.

- A chimney should have a plan area – excluding openings for chimneys and flues – not less than that required for a pier in the same wall, and the overall thickness should be not less than twice the required thickness of supported wall.

Openings, recesses and chases:
The number, size and position of openings and recesses should not impair the stability of the wall, or the lateral restraint afforded by a buttressing wall. Construction over openings and recesses should be adequately supported. The dimensional limits for openings and recesses are given in Figure A.12 and Table A.13.

2013 changes
In Figure A.12, note 8 the limiting value for the compressive strength of bricks or blocks has been increased from 7.0 to 7.3N/mm².

Figure A.12 Sizes of openings and recesses

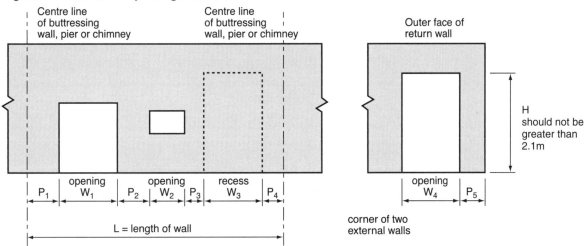

Notes:
Requirements (refer to Table A.13 for values of Factor X).

1 $W_1 + W_2 + W_3$ should not exceed $\dfrac{2L}{3}$

2 W_1, W_2 or W_3 should not exceed 3m

3 P_1 should be greater than or equal to $\dfrac{W_1}{X}$

4 P_2 should be greater than or equal to $\dfrac{W_1 + W_2}{X}$

5 P_3 should be greater than or equal to $\dfrac{W_2 + W_3}{X}$

6 P_4 should be greater than or equal to $\dfrac{W_3}{X}$

7 P_5 should be greater than or equal to $\dfrac{W_4}{X}$ but should not be less than 665mm.

8 Take the value of the Factor X from Table A.13 or it can be given the value 6, provided the compressive strength of the bricks or blocks (in the case of a cavity wall – in the loaded leaf) is not less than 7.3N/mm².

There should be no openings in walls below the ground floor, except for services and ventilation, which should not exceed 0.1m² at 2m minimum centres.

Chases should not be positioned so as to impair the stability of the wall – particularly with hollow blocks – and should be no deeper than:

- vertical chases: 1/3 (one-third) wall or leaf thickness;
- horizontal chases: 1/6 (one-sixth) wall or leaf thickness.

Overhangs and projections should not impair the stability of the wall.

Table A.13 Value of factor 'X' for sizing openings and recesses

Nature of roof span	Maximum roof span (m)	Minimum thickness of wall inner (mm)	Span of floor is parallel to wall	Span of timber floor into wall (m)		Span of concrete floor into wall (m)	
				max 4.5m	max 8.0m	max 4.5m	max 6.0m
				Value of X			
Roof spans parallel to wall	Not applicable	100	6	6	6	6	6
		90	6	6	6	6	5
Timber roof spans into wall	9	100	6	6	5	4	3
		90	6	4	4	3	3

Lateral support by roofs and floors:

Walls should be secured to adjoining floors and roofs in order to transfer lateral forces to buttressing walls, piers or chimneys and so restrict their horizontal movement. Lateral restraint should be provided as Table A.14.

Table A.14 Lateral support for walls

Wall type	Wall length	Lateral support required
Solid or cavity: external, compartment, separating	Any length	Roof lateral support by every roof forming a junction with the supported wall
	>3m	Floor lateral support by every floor forming a junction with the supported wall
Internal loadbearing wall, but not a compartment or separating wall	Any length	Roof or floor lateral support at the top of each storey

Walls should be strapped to floors above ground level, at intervals not exceeding 2m, and as shown in Figure A.11, tension straps should conform to BS EN 845-1, have a declared tensile strength not less than 8kN, and be of material reference 14 or 16.1 or 16.2 (galvanised steel), or other more resistant material including material references 1 or 3 (austenitic stainless steel).

Strapping is not required:

- in the longitudinal direction of joists in houses of not more than two storeys, provided that joists are at not more than 1.2m centres with at least 90mm bearing on the supported walls, or 75mm bearing on the timber wall plate at each end;
- in the longitudinal direction of joists in houses of not more than two storeys, provided that joists are carried on a supported wall by joist hangers conforming to BS EN 845-1, of the restraint type described in PD 6697:2010 and shown in Figure A.13(c) and are incorporated at not more than 2m centres;
- when a concrete floor has at least 90mm bearing on the supported wall (Figure A.13(d));
- where floors are at or about the same level on each side of a supported wall, and contact between the floors and wall is either continuous, or at intervals not exceeding 2m. Intermittent contact should be in line or nearly in line on plan (Figure A.13(e)).

Figure A.13 Lateral support by floors

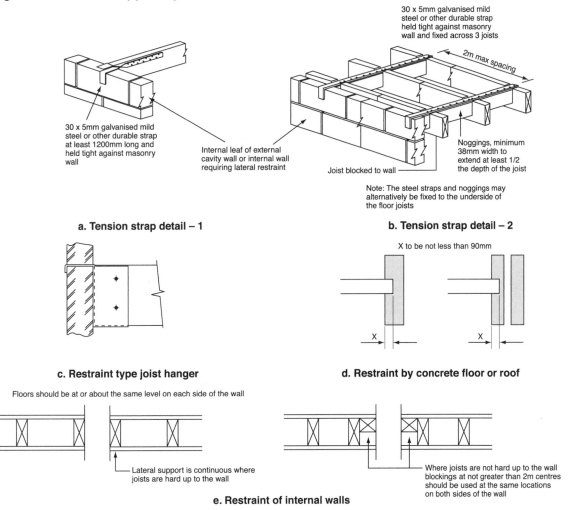

30 x 5mm galvanised mild steel or other durable strap held tight against masonry wall and fixed across 3 joists

2m max spacing

30 x 5mm galvanised mild steel or other durable strap at least 1200mm long and held tight against masonry wall

Internal leaf of external cavity wall or internal wall requiring lateral restraint

Joist blocked to wall

Noggings, minimum 38mm width to extend at least 1/2 the depth of the joist

Note: The steel straps and noggings may alternatively be fixed to the underside of the floor joists

a. Tension strap detail – 1

b. Tension strap detail – 2

X to be not less than 90mm

X

X

c. Restraint type joist hanger

d. Restraint by concrete floor or roof

Floors should be at or about the same level on each side of the wall

Lateral support is continuous where joists are hard up to the wall

Where joists are not hard up to the wall blockings at not greater than 2m centres should be used at the same locations on both sides of the wall

e. Restraint of internal walls

Gable walls should be strapped to roofs as shown in Figure A.14 (a) and (b) by tension straps as described above.

Vertical strapping at least 1m in length should be provided at eaves level at intervals not exceeding 2m, as Figure A.14 (c) and (d). It may be omitted if the roof:

- has a pitch of 15° or more; and
- is tiled or slated; and
- is of a type known by local experience to be resistant to wind gusts; and
- has main timber members spanning onto the supporting wall at not more than 1.2m centres.

Figure A.14 Lateral support at roof level

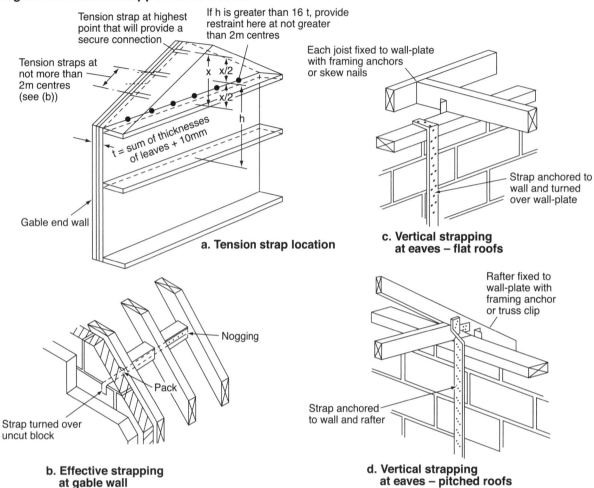

Tension strap at highest point that will provide a secure connection

If h is greater than 16 t, provide restraint here at not greater than 2m centres

Tension straps at not more than 2m centres (see (b))

Each joist fixed to wall-plate with framing anchors or skew nails

x   x/2

x/2

h

t = sum of thicknesses of leaves + 10mm

Gable end wall

Strap anchored to wall and turned over wall-plate

a. Tension strap location

c. Vertical strapping at eaves – flat roofs

Nogging

Pack

Rafter fixed to wall-plate with framing anchor or truss clip

Strap turned over uncut block

Strap anchored to wall and rafter

b. Effective strapping at gable wall

d. Vertical strapping at eaves – pitched roofs

Interruption of lateral support

Where the opening in a floor or roof – such as for a stairway – adjoins a supported wall and interrupts the continuity of lateral support then:

- the opening, measured parallel to the supported wall, should not exceed 3m;

- where mild steel anchors are used, they should be spaced closer than 2m on each side of the opening to provide the same number of anchors as if there were no opening;

- where a connection is provided by a means other than an anchor, this should be provided throughout the length of each portion of the wall, situated on each side of the opening; and

- there should be no other interruption of lateral support.

Small single-storey non-residential buildings and annexes

General – size and proportion:

The following guidance only applies if:

- the floor area of the building or annexe is not more than 36m²;

- the walls are solidly constructed of brickwork or blockwork, using materials as set out above (see **A.2.2.3** Conditions relating to the wall);

- where the floor area exceeds 10m^2 the walls have a mass not less than 130kg/m^2 (there are no mass limitations for smaller floor areas);
- access to the roof is for maintenance and repair only;
- the only lateral loads are wind loads;
- the maximum length or width of the building does not exceed 9m;
- the height does not exceed the lower value derived from Figure A.2;
- the roof is braced at rafter level, horizontally at eaves level and at base of any gable by roof decking, rigid sarking or diagonal timber bracing, to BS EN 1995-1-1:2004 with UK National Annex and PD 6693-1:2012 or BS 8013-3:2009;
- the walls are tied to the roof structure vertically and horizontally as set out above (see **A.2.2.3** Conditions relating to the wall), and with horizontal lateral restraint at roof level as described below;
- the roof structure of an annexe is secured to the structure of the main building at both rafter and eaves level.

Size and location of openings:
One or two major openings, not more than 2.1m in height, are permitted in one wall of the building or annexe only. The width of a single opening, or the combined width of two openings should not exceed 5m. The only other openings permitted in a building or annexe are those for windows and a single leaf door. The size and location of these openings should be as Figure A.15.

Wall thickness and piers:
The minimum thickness of walls is 90mm. Walls which do not contain a major opening, but exceed 2.5m in length or height, should be bonded or tied to piers for their full height at not more than 3m centres as shown in Figure A.16(a).

Walls which contain one or two major openings should, in addition, have piers as shown in Figure A.16(b) and A.16(c). Ties used to connect piers and walls should be flat, 20mm × 3mm in cross-section, be stainless steel (material 1 or 3 to BS EN 845-1) and should be placed in pairs at 300mm vertical centres.

Horizontal lateral restraint at roof level:
Walls should be tied horizontally to the roof structure at no more than 2m centres:

- at eaves level;
- at the base of gables;
- along roof slopes.

Straps should be fixed as set out above (see **A.2.2.3** Conditions relating to the building). Where straps cannot pass through a wall they should be adequately secured to the masonry using suitable fixings. Isolated columns should also be tied to the roof structure.

Figure A.15 Size and location of openings

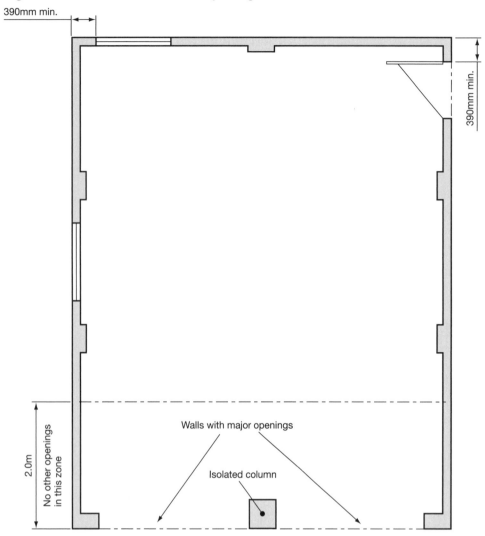

Notes:

1 Major openings should be restricted to one wall only. Their aggregate width should not exceed 5.0m and their height should not be greater than 2.1m.

2 There should be no other openings within 2.0m of a wall containing a major opening.

3 The aggregate size of openings in a wall not containing a major opening should not exceed 2.4m².

4 There should not be more than one opening between piers.

5 Unless there is a corner pier the distance from a window or a door to a corner should not be less than 390mm.

Figure A.16 Wall thickness

a. Wall without a major opening

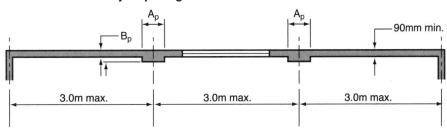

b. Wall with a single major opening

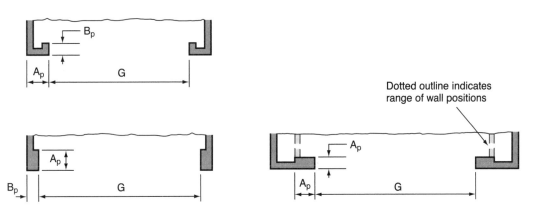

Orientation of piers with opening width G not greater than 2.5m

Orientation of piers with opening width G greater than 2.5m

Dotted outline indicates range of wall positions

c. Wall with two major openings

Dotted outline indicates range of wall positions

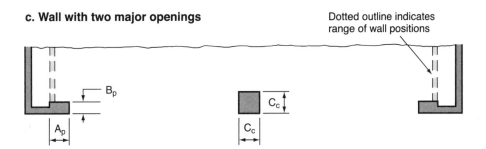

Notes

1   In all cases the minimum pier size ($A_p \times B_p$) should be 390mm × 190mm or 327mm × 215mm depending on the size of the masonry units.

2   Isolated column (Case c) to be 325mm × 325mm minimum ($C_c \times C_c$).

A.2.2.4 Masonry chimneys

A chimney which is not restrained or tied may be up to 4.5 times as high as it is wide, provided the density of masonry is greater than 1500kg/m³ (Figure A.17).

Figure A.17 Proportions for masonry chimneys

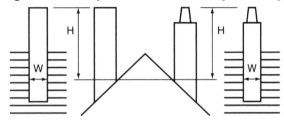

H: measured from highest point of intersection between chimney and roof to top of chimney pot or flue terminal.
W: least horizontal dimension of chimney at line of intersection.

A.2.2.5 Foundations of plain concrete

The area to be loaded should not contain:

- non-engineered fill;
- widely varying ground conditions;
- weaker or more compressible ground below the foundations that could impair the stability of the structure.

In normal soils, concrete for foundations should consist of Portland cement to BS EN 197-1 and -2, and fine and coarse aggregates to BS EN 12620, either:

- in a mix of 1 part Portland cement to not more than 4 parts fine aggregate and 8 parts coarse aggregate; or
- to grade ST2 or GEN I concrete to BS 8500-2.

In aggressive soils the concrete mix should comply with BS 8500-1 and BRE Special Digest 1.

Basic dimensions:
Foundations should be located centrally under the wall; the minimum dimensions of strip foundations should be taken from Table A.15. The minimum thickness of foundations, T, should be the greater of 150mm or P, where:

P = (foundation width – wall width)/2.

To avoid frost action, the underside of strip foundations should be at least 0.45m below ground level, except where they bear directly onto rock. A greater depth may be required where long periods of frost are expected. For clays which shrink on drying (shrinkable clays with plasticity index ≥10%) the underside of strip foundations should be at least 0.75m below ground level on low shrinkage clay soils, 0.90m on medium shrinkage clay soils, and 1.0m on high shrinkage clay soils. The influence of vegetation and trees may require a greater depth, as may the need to transfer the loading to satisfactory ground.

Further guidance
BRE Digest 427 *Low-rise buildings on fill*. 1997. [Describes non-engineered fill.]

2013 changes
The 0.75m minimum depth for shrinkable clay soils has been replaced by three minimum depths, for low, medium and high shrinkage clay soils.

Table A.15 Minimum width of strip footings

Type of ground (including engineered fill)	Condition of ground	Field test applicable	Total load of loadbearing walling not more than (kN/linear metre)					
			20	30	40	50	60	70
			Minimum width of strip foundations (m)					
I Rock	Not inferior to sandstone, limestone or firm chalk	Requires at least a pneumatic or other mechanically operated pick for excavation	In each case equal to the minimum width of the wall					
II Gravel or sand	Medium dense	Requires pick to excavate. Wooden peg 50mm square in cross-section hard to drive beyond 150mm	250	300	400	500	600	650
III Clay Sandy clay	Stiff Stiff	Can be indented slightly by thumb	250	300	400	500	600	650
IV Clay Sandy clay	Firm Firm	Thumb makes impression easily	300	350	450	600	750	850
V Sand Silty sand Clayey sand	Loose Loose Loose	Can be excavated with a spade. Wooden peg 50mm in cross-section can be easily driven	400	600	Foundations on soil types V and VI fall outside the provisions of this table if the total load exceeds 30kN/m.			
VI Silt Clay Sandy clay Clay or silt	Soft Soft Soft Soft	Finger pushed in up to 10mm	450	650				
VII Silt Clay Sandy clay Clay or silt	Very soft Very soft Very soft Very soft	Finger easily pushed in up to 25mm	Take specialist advice					

Foundations for piers, buttresses and chimneys should project as Figure A.18, with the projection, X, never being less than P, where there is no local thickening of the normal wall width.

Steps in foundations (Figure A.19) should not be higher than the thickness of the foundation, T, with the minimum overlap in strip foundations being the greatest of:

- twice the height of the step;
- the thickness of the foundation;
- 300mm.

Trench fill foundations should overlap by the greatest of 1 m, or twice the height of the step.

Figure A.18 Piers and chimneys

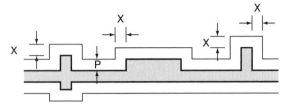

Projection X should not be less than P

Figure A.19 Elevation of stepped foundations

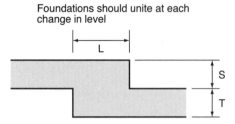

Foundations should unite at each change in level

Minimum overlap L = twice height of step, or
thickness of foundation
or 300mm, whichever is greater

S should not be greater than T

(For trench fill foundations,
minimum overlap L = twice height of step, or 1m,
whichever is greater)

A.2.3 Wall cladding

In order to prevent wall cladding detaching from the building and becoming a hazard, the support and fixing system must:

- sustain the dead, imposed and wind loads and transfer them to the supporting structure;
- be securely fixed to and supported by the building structure;
- provide both vertical support and horizontal restraint to the cladding;
- allow for differential movement between the cladding and the building structure;
- have durable, corrosion-resistant components, which are suitable for the local environment; and
- the design life of fixings should not be less than that of cladding.

Wind loads should be calculated from BS EN 1991-1-4:2005 with UK National Annex, taking account of local effects such as wind funnelling between buildings. Loading calculations should allow for fixtures which are supported by cladding (such as handrails), and allow for increased lateral loading where cladding acts as pedestrian guarding or as a vehicle barrier (see **K.3** and **K.4**).

Fixings should be of proven performance and suitable for the application which should be designated as:

- Non-redundant – The failure of a single fixing could result in the cladding becoming detached; or
- Redundant – The failure or excessive movement of one fixing would result in the load being sharing by adjacent fixings.

The strength of fixings should be derived from tests in materials representative of the actual substrate, taking account of inherent weaknesses, such cracks in concrete due to shrinkage or flexure, or voids in masonry construction. Anchors are available with European Technical Approval (ETA) to ETAG 001 Parts 1–6. The ETA should cover cracked or non-cracked concrete, as appropriate. Guidance documents on fixing selection are listed in Approved Document A clauses 3.9–3.11.

Further guidance
Guide to safety at sports grounds. TSO. 1997.
(Fifth edition. DCMS 2008.)

BS EN 1991-1. Eurocode 1. Actions on structures. General actions.
-1:2002. Densities, self-weight, imposed loads for buildings; with UK National Annex.
-4:2005+A1:2010. Wind actions; with UK National Annex.

Further guidance
Use of anchors with European Technical Approvals. UK Guidance – Distinction between cracked and non-cracked concrete. British Board of Agrément.
www.fixingscfa.co.uk/downloads/ETAG1-SUP.pdf

A.2.4 Roof coverings

All materials used to cover roofs must be capable of safely withstanding the concentrated imposed loads specified in BS EN 1991-1-1:2002 with its UK National Annex. The only exceptions are:

- residential buildings: glass windows in roofs at pitches of not less than 15°;
- all buildings: transparent and translucent coverings on roofs only accessible for normal maintenance and repair, provided they are non-fragile or protected against collapse.

Where an existing roof is subject to an increase in loading of more than 15% – for example as a result of re-covering, or the addition of insulation – the structural integrity of the roof structure and supporting structure should be checked (bearing in mind the covering to be replaced may not be the original covering). A roof unable to accept the increased loading would have to be strengthened. Increased stress in a structural member does not, of itself, mean the roof would no longer be compliant, provided an adequate margin of safety is maintained.

Where work will significantly decrease the roof loading an adequate factor of safety must be maintained against uplift under wind loading.

2013 changes
There have been two minor changes, in addition to the updated references to the Eurocodes:

- The requirements for roof covering materials to withstand imposed loads have been clarified.
- When assessing increased loading on a roof as a result of a change of covering, it should be borne in mind that the covering to be replaced may not be the original 'as-built' covering.

Further guidance
BS EN 1991-1-1:2002. Eurocode 1. Actions on structures. General actions. Densities, self-weight, imposed loads for buildings; with UK National Annex.

A.3 Disproportionate collapse (Requirement A3)

An accident must not result in the collapse of a building which is disproportionate to its cause. The measures required to prevent such a collapse depend upon the Consequence Class of building as defined in Table A.16.

- Consequence Class 1 – no additional measures provided the building complies with Requirements A1 and A2 in normal use.
- Consequence Class 2a – in addition to the Consequence Class 1 measures, provide effective horizontal ties or anchorage of suspended floors to walls, as described in **A.3.2**.
- Consequence Class 2b – either:
  - in addition to the Consequence Class 1 measures, provide effective horizontal ties as described in **A.3.2** together with effective vertical ties in all supporting columns and walls; or
  - ensure key elements meet performance standards in **A.3.1**.
- Consequence Class 3 – undertake a systematic risk assessment, examining all hazards reasonably likely to occur during the life of the building then design the building in accordance with **A.3.2**.

For other buildings outside the scope of Table A.16 or for which consequences of collapse require special consideration, follow the recommendations in the documents listed [overleaf].

Further guidance
[For the assessment of Consequence Class 3 buildings:] Annexes A and B to BS EN1991-1-7:2006. Eurocode 1: Actions on structures. General actions – Accidental actions; with UK National Annex to BS EN 1991-1-7:2006.

BS EN 1990:2002+A1:2005 Eurocode – Basis of structural design; with UK National Annex to BS EN 1990:2002+A1:2005.

[For buildings which are outside the scope of Table A.16:] *Guidance on robustness and provision against accidental actions.* DTLR. 1989.[Available via www.planningportal. gov.uk]

Calibration of proposed revised guidance on meeting compliance with the requirements of Building Regulation Part A3. Revision of Allott and Lomax proposals. Project Report No. 205966.
[Available via www.planningportal.gov.uk]

Practical guide to structural robustness and disproportionate collapse in buildings. The Institution of Structural Engineers. October 2010.

Table A.16 Building consequence classes

Consequence Class	Building type and occupancy
1	Houses not exceeding 4 storeys Agricultural buildings Buildings into which people rarely go, provided no part of the building is closer than a distance of 1.5 × building height to another building, or an area where people do go
2a lower risk group	Five-storey single occupancy houses Hotels not exceeding 4 storeys Flats and other residential buildings not exceeding 4 storeys Offices not exceeding 4 storeys Industrial buildings not exceeding 3 storeys Retailing premises not exceeding 3 storeys of less than 2000m² floor area in each storey Single-storey educational buildings All buildings not exceeding 2 storeys to which members of the public are admitted and which contain floor areas not exceeding 2000m² at each storey
2b upper risk group	Hotels, blocks of flats, apartments and other residential buildings greater than 4 storeys but not exceeding 15 storeys Educational buildings greater than 1 storey but not exceeding 15 storeys Retailing premises greater than 3 storeys but not exceeding 15 storeys Hospitals not exceeding 3 storeys Offices greater than 4 storeys but not exceeding 15 storeys All buildings to which members of the public are admitted which contain floor areas exceeding 2000m² but less than 5000m² at each storey Car parking not exceeding 6 storeys
3	All buildings defined above as Consequence Class 2a and 2b that exceed the limits on area and/or number of storeys Grandstands accommodating more than 5000 spectators Buildings containing hazardous substances and/or processes

Notes:

For buildings intended for more than one type of use, take the most onerous consequence class.

In determining the number of storeys in a building, basement storeys may be excluded provided they fulfil the requirements of Consequence Class 2b buildings.

BS EN 1991-1-7:2006 with its UK National Annex also provides compatible guidance to Table A.16.

A.3.1 Key elements

A key element is: a supporting column; a beam supporting one or more columns; or any nominal length of loadbearing wall (in each storey of the building) whose notional removal would result in:

- the building being unstable; or

- the risk of collapse of an area of floor in any storey greater than the smaller of 15% or 100m²; or

- a collapse which would extend over more than the immediately adjacent storeys.

2013 changes
The maximum area of a storey which may be at risk of collapse has been increased to 100m².

When testing key elements with accidental damage loads all normal wind and imposed loads are assumed to act simultaneously in an accidental damage loading combination: previously only 1/3 of such loads were considered to be acting simultaneously.

The nominal length of the loadbearing wall is taken as:

- reinforced concrete wall – the distance between lateral supports, up to a maximum of 2.25H;

- external masonry wall, timber or steel stud wall – length between vertical lateral supports;

- internal masonry wall, timber or steel stud wall – a length not exceeding 2.25H

(where H is height in metres).

Key elements should be capable of sustaining an accidental design load of $34kN/m^2$ applied to the element (and any attached components such as cladding) horizontally or vertically, in one direction at a time. The accidental load should be assumed to act simultaneously with wind and imposed loading in accidental actions loading combination.

Further guidance
Annex A of BS EN 1991-1-7:2006 with its UK National Annex. See **A.2.1.1**. [Guidance on key elements.]

BS EN 1990:2002+A1:2005 with its UK National Annex. See **A.2.1.1** [Guidance on accidental design loading and accidental actions loading combination.].

A.3.2 Integrity

The standards listed (see *Further guidance*) give methods for checking structural integrity and design guidance for horizontal and vertical ties.

Further guidance
BS EN 1990:2002+A1:2005.
BS EN 1991-1-7:2006.
PD 6688-1-7: 2009
BS EN 1992-1-1:2004.
PD 6687-1:2010.
BS EN 1993-1-1:2005.
BS EN 1994-1-1:2004.
BS EN 1995-1-1:2004+A1:2008.
PD 6693-1:2012.
BS EN 1996-1-1:2005+A1.2012.
PD 6697:2010.
BS EN 1999-1-1:2007+A1:2009.

See **A.2.1.1**.

A.3.3 Seismic design

While seismic design is not an explicit requirement for buildings in Consequence Class 3, the risk assessment should consider whether seismic design is necessary. It is not usually required for buildings in Consequence Classes 1 and 2.

2013 changes
This is the first time seismic design has been addressed in Approved Document A.

B. ■ Fire safety

B.1 General considerations

B.1.1 Scope

Part B is intended to protect life in the event of a fire by enabling building occupants to escape, reducing the risk to firefighters and preventing fire spreading to other buildings.

2013 changes
There are three minor changes to the guidance to Part B, addressing the standard for smoke alarms (**B.3.2.2**) and the provisions for spread of flame over internal linings (**B.4.1**). In addition, the fire protection provisions of local acts have been repealed (**B.1.3**).

Part B: Fire safety	
Requirement	**Limits on application**
Means of warning and escape	
B1 The building shall be designed and constructed so that there are appropriate provisions for the early warning of fire, and appropriate means of escape in case of fire from the building to a place of safety outside the building capable of being safely and effectively used at all material times.	Requirement B1 does not apply to any prison provided under section 33 of the Prison Act 1952 (power to provide prisons etc.).
Internal fire spread (linings)	
B2 (1) To inhibit the spread of fire within the building, the internal linings shall – (a) adequately resist the spread of flame over their surfaces; and (b) have, if ignited, either a rate of heat release or a rate of fire growth, which is reasonable in the circumstances. (2) In this paragraph 'internal linings' means the materials or products used in lining any partition, wall, ceiling or other internal structure.	
Internal fire spread (structure)	
B3 (1) The building shall be designed and constructed so that, in the event of fire, its stability will be maintained for a reasonable period. (2) A wall common to two or more buildings shall be designed and constructed so that it adequately resists the spread of fire between those buildings. For the purposes of this sub-paragraph a house in a terrace and a semi-detached house are each to be treated as a separate building. (3) Where reasonably necessary to inhibit the spread of fire within the building, measures shall be taken, to an extent appropriate to the size and intended use of the building, comprising either or both of the following – (a) sub-division of the building with fire-resisting construction; (b) installation of suitable automatic fire suppression systems. (4) The building shall be designed and constructed so that the unseen spread of fire and smoke within concealed spaces in its structure and fabric is inhibited.	Requirement B3(3) does not apply to material alterations to any prison provided under section 33 of the Prison Act 1952.

External fire spread	
B4 (1) The external walls of the building shall adequately resist the spread of fire over the walls and from one building to another, having regard to the height, use and position of the building. (2) The roof of the building shall adequately resist the spread of fire over the roof and from one building to another, having regard to the use and position of the building.	
Access and facilities for the fire service	
B5 (1) The building shall be designed and constructed so as to provide reasonable facilities to assist firefighters in the protection of life. (2) Reasonable provision shall be made within the site of the building to enable fire appliances to gain access to the building.	

Approved Document B is divided into two volumes:

- volume 1 covers dwellinghouses;

- volume 2 covers all other buildings, including flats.

This chapter treats both volumes together.

The guidance in Approved Document B does not exclude alternative approaches to compliance. When an alternative approach is adopted it should be followed as a whole, although in some circumstances it may be necessary to supplement one set of provisions by another, particularly where the use of a building (for example the sale of fuel) requires additional precautions.

In situations beyond the scope of Approved Document B provisions should follow the principles of fire safety engineering, which provide a disciplined framework for assessing fire safety measures in buildings, particularly large complex buildings with multiple uses. Fire safety engineering may also be used for resolving design problems in buildings which would otherwise follow the Approved Document.

Although Part B does not cover building management, any design which relies on an unrealistic or unsustainable management system will not be acceptable.

Fire safety provisions must take account of the needs of all persons who may access and work in a building. Only rarely will it be appropriate to presume some groups will be excluded from a building because of its use. Some specific groups may require additional provision.

Further guidance
BS 7974. 2001. Application of fire safety engineering principles to the design of buildings.

B.1.2 Standards

Approved Document B makes reference to BS 5588 which – with the exception of part one – has been withdrawn and replaced by BS 9999:2008. Nonetheless, the references to BS 5588 remain part of the approved guidance. Designers electing to follow BS 9999 must satisfy themselves and the Building Control Body that the guidance adequately addresses the requirements of Part B.

B.1.3 Other legislation

- **The Regulatory Reform (Fire Safety) Order 2005** – The order applies to non-domestic premises, including common parts of blocks of flats and houses in multiple occupation (defined by the Housing Act 2004 as self-contained dwellings for no more than six residents which are generally licensed by the local authority). A person carrying out building work which affects the fire safety of a building covered by the order must provide the owner or occupier with information about the safe operation of the building to enable them to meet their statutory duties to implement appropriate fire protection measures.
Small buildings will require only basic information on the location and nature of fire protection measures, while large buildings will require a record of the fire safety strategy, together with procedures for the operation and maintenance of fire protection measures.
Although the order applies only to buildings in use, it may be useful for designers to carry out a preliminary fire risk assessment as part of the design process and to include it in the Building Regulations submission; this will assist the Fire and Rescue Authority to determine the additional provision which may be required once the building is occupied.

- **Construction (Design and Management) Regulations 2007** – The CDM Regulations 2007 (and the Regulatory Reform (Fire Safety) Order 2005 address fire safety during the construction process. Responsibility for enforcement rests with the Health and Safety Executive for construction sites and unoccupied buildings, and the Fire and Rescue Authority for occupied buildings.

- **Environmental Protection** – The Environment Agency has issued Pollution Prevention Guidelines 18 (PPG 18), which contains guidance on minimising the environmental effect of water run-off from fire-fighting, including requirements for containment of contaminated water.

B.1.4 Purpose Groups

The uses of buildings and their associated fire hazards are addressed in Approved Document B by a number of 'Purpose Groups', each of which represents a broad category of use (Table B.1).

Where part of a building or compartment has a use ancillary to its main use – for example a staff canteen in a large shop – that part may either be considered as falling within the main Purpose Group, or be treated as a Purpose Group in its own right. An ancillary use should be considered as a separate Purpose Group where:

- the ancillary use is a flat; or
- the ancillary use employs more than 20% of the floor area of a building compartment of more than 280m²; or
- storage makes up 1/3 (one-third) of the floor area of a Purpose Group 4 building or compartment of more than 280m² floor area.

Other non-ancillary uses, such as an independent flat over a shop, should be treated as belonging to separate Purpose Groups. Large buildings may include many Purpose Groups, some of which may increase the risks to other Purpose Groups and so require additional precautions.

Further guidance
Building Regulations and Fire Safety Procedural Guidance. Department for Communities and Local Government. 2007. [Guidance on the interaction between the Building Regulations and the Fire Safety Order, and the Building Control Body and the Fire Safety Enforcing Authority.]

Housing health and safety rating system operating guidance. Office of the Deputy Prime Minister. 2006. [Guidance for houses in multiple occupation.]

Construction Information Sheet 51: Construction fire safety. HSE. 1997.

HSF 168 Fire Safety in Construction Work. HSE. 1997. [replaced by HSF 168 Fire safety in construction. HSE. 2010.]

Pollution Prevention Guidelines 18 (PPG 18) *Managing fire water and major spillages.* Environment Agency. 2000.

2013 changes
Many Local Acts (**I.1.3.3**) contained provisions for fire precautions which were more onerous than the requirements of Part B. In order to remove unnecessary regulatory burdens the provisions in Local Acts for the fire protection of large storage buildings, car parks and tall buildings were repealed on 9 January 2013. Provisions relating to fire and rescue service access remain in place. Details of the affected Local Acts can be found in Statutory Instrument 2012/3124 at www.legislation.gov.uk.

Table B.1 Purpose Groups

Title	Group	Intended use of building or building compartment
Residential (dwellings)	1(a)	Flat, including live/work unit (**B.3.6.6**).
	1(b)	Dwellinghouse where at least one habitable storey has a floor level more than 4.5m above ground level.[1]
	1(c)	Dwellinghouse where no habitable storey has a floor level more than 4.5m above ground level,[1] detached garages/carports up to 40m².
Residential (institutional/other)	2(a)	Hospital, home, school or similar, used as living accommodation and/or for treatment.
	2(b)	Hotel, boarding house, residential college, hall of residence, hostel.
Office	3	Offices or premises for administration, clerical work, handling money, communications or audio-visual media work.
Shop and commercial	4	Shops or premises for retail trade or business involving sale of goods or services to the public, including those for hire or repair of goods.
Assembly and recreation	5	Places of assembly, entertainment or recreation, such as conference centres, and leisure centres, cinemas, theatres, buildings for worship, libraries, railway stations and airports.
Industrial	6	Factories and other premises for: manufacturing, repair, adapting or processing any article; generating power; slaughtering livestock.
Storage and other non-residential	7(a)	Place of storage or deposit of goods or materials (other than as 7(b)), and any other building not in Groups 1–6.
	7(b)	Car parks for cars, motorcycles and passenger or light goods vehicles up to 2500kg gross weight.

[1] Includes offices up to 50m² used by the occupants in a profession or business.

B.1.5 Special building types

Health care premises The fire safety strategy will depend on the level of dependency of the patients and the design and operation of the building. Total evacuation of the premises is unlikely to be appropriate for high-dependency patients. As a result, many assumptions of Approved Document B will not apply. New buildings should comply with HTM 05-02; work to existing buildings should follow the Department of Health Firecode guidance documents.

Unsupervised group homes an existing one- or two-storey house converted for use as an unsupervised group home for up to six mental health service users should be treated as Purpose Group 1c if means of escape are provided in accordance with HTM 88. A new building should be treated as Purpose Group 2(b).

Assembly buildings Fixed seating will limit people's ability to escape in the event of a fire. The guidance in sections 3 and 5 of BS 5588-6:1991 should be followed. Premises to which the Safety of Sports Grounds Act 1975 applies should comply with 'Guide to safety at sports grounds'.

Schools Designed to Building Bulletin 100 (BB100) will typically satisfy the requirements of Part B.

Buildings containing atria A building containing an atrium which passes through compartment floors may need special fire safety measures.

Sheltered housing complexes May require additional fire protection measures according to the nature of the occupancy.

Further guidance
Firecode. Department of Health [Health Technical Memoranda dealing with fire precautions. Includes: HTM 05-02 *Guidance in support of functional provisions for health care premises*. Available at: https://www.gov.uk/government/uploads/system/uploads/attachment_data/file/142863/HTM_05-02.pdf

HTM 88. Guide to fire precautions in NHS housing in the community for mentally handicapped (or mentally ill) people. [Updated by: HTM 88 update: Fire precautions in housing providing NHS-supported living in the community. NHS Estates. 2001.]

BS 5588. Fire precautions in the design, construction and use of buildings.
-6:1991. Code of practice for places of assembly.
-7:1997. Code of practice for the incorporation of atria in buildings. [Withdrawn 2009. Replaced by BS 9999:2008. Code of practice for fire safety in the design, management and use of buildings. Annex D covers theatres, cinemas and similar venues. Annexes B and C cover atria.]

Guide to safety at sports grounds. TSO. 1997. (Fifth edition. DCMS 2008.)

Building Bulletin (BB) 100. *Designing and managing against the risk of fire in schools*. DfES [replaced by Building Bulletin 100. *Design for fire safety in schools*. DfE. 2007.]

Buildings of architectural or historical interest To preserve the special character of such a building, safety features should be adopted on the basis of a risk assessment.

B.1.6 Material alterations

Requirements B1, B3, B4 and B5 are defined as 'relevant requirements' (**I.2.2**). Building work which results in the building being less satisfactory with regard to those requirements than it was before constitutes a 'material alteration'. At the completion of the work the building must either comply with the relevant requirements or, where it did not previously comply, must be no more unsatisfactory than it was before.

B.1.7 Protection of property

Part B is concerned solely with the preservation of life. Designing the building to protect property is likely to require additional measures to limit damage to the building and contents, and minimise business interruption. Stakeholders, including insurers, will be interested in fire protection measures and may require higher standards of provision.

Further guidance
Fire Protection Association Design Guide.
www.thefpa.co.uk
[Now, *The LPC design guide for the fire protection of buildings 2000. A code of practice for the protection of business.* This document is currently being revised.]

B.1.8 Sprinklers

Sprinkler systems can reduce risk to life and significantly reduce fire damage. Sprinkler systems specifically recommended in the Approved Document should be provided throughout the building or separated part. However, it may be acceptable for a sprinkler system which is compensating for a specific risk to be installed in only part of a building.

Design and installation should follow BS 9251:2005 and DD 252 for dwellings and residential buildings, and BS 5306-2:1990 or BS EN 12845:2004 for non-residential buildings (and dwellings and residential buildings outside scope of BS 9251). The design should follow the requirements for the relevant hazard classification together with the additional requirements for a life safety system. Non-residential systems should have two single water supplies, or two stored water supplies in appropriate tanks. These water supplies should not be used in connection with other services or fixed firefighting systems.

Further guidance
BS 9251:2005. Sprinkler systems for residential and domestic occupancies. Code of practice.

DD 252:2002. Components for residential sprinkler systems. Specification and test methods for residential sprinklers. [Withdrawn, replaced by BS 9252:2011 Components for residential sprinkler systems. Specification and test methods for residential sprinklers.]

BS 5306-2:1990. Fire extinguishing installations and equipment on premises. Specification for sprinkler systems. [Current, but obsolete. Superseded by BS EN 12945:2004.]

BS EN 12845:2004. Fixed firefighting systems. Automatic sprinkler systems. Design, installation and maintenance. [Amended: A2:2009.]

B.2 Performance of materials, products, structures

The likely behaviour of a material, product, structure or system when exposed to fire is established by fire tests, which address different aspects of performance. As tests do not directly assess hazard, the results must be used in conjunction with other criteria to ensure appropriate overall performance.

As part of the process of harmonising standards for construction products across the European Union, national fire performance tests and classifications are being replaced with European test and classification systems. National standards will

2013 changes
The Construction Products Directive (89/106/EEC) has been replaced by the Construction Products Regulation (305/2011). The majority of its provisions came into effect on 1 July 2013. CE marking is now mandatory for all products covered by a harmonised European standard, and is likely to extend the use of European fire test standards.

eventually be withdrawn, but there is a transitional period during which national and European classes co-exist.

The fire performance of products may be measured against national UK standards or European standards. However, as the two systems are not strictly compatible a classification under one system must not be equated to a classification under the other. Products covered by harmonised standards must be CE marked (**I.1.4**).

B.2.1 Fire resistance of construction elements

The fire resistance of a building element can be assessed against three criteria:

- Resistance to collapse – the ability of the element to maintain its **loadbearing** capacity (denoted R in European classifications).

- Resistance to fire penetration – the ability of the element to maintain its **integrity** (denoted E in European classifications).

- Resistance to the transfer of excessive heat – the ability of an element to provide **insulation** from high temperatures (denoted I in European classifications).

The standard of fire resistance required of an element takes account of the severity of fires in buildings of a particular Purpose Group and the consequences of the failure of that element. The main factors to be considered are:

- the fire load (amount of combustible material/unit of floor area), which is common to each Purpose Group;

- the height of the top floor above ground level, which affects the ease of evacuation and firefighting, and the consequences of large-scale collapse;

- the occupancy type, which affects ease of evacuation;

- the presence of basements, which can increase the intensity of a fire and complicate firefighting;

- whether a building is single storey.

The general standards of fire resistance are given in Table B.2, with specific standards for Purpose Groups in Table B.3. Table A3 of Approved Document B volume 2 defines the performance standards required in order for suspended ceilings to contribute to the fire resistance of floors.

Performance is determined by reference to:

- BS 476-20–24. 1987 (national tests); or

- BS EN 13501-2 and -4 (European tests).

B.2.2 External fire exposure of roofs

The resistance of roofs to external fire exposure is classified by:

- BS 476-3:2004 (national tests). Classification is by a two letter code (XX), each running from A to D, with AA being the best. The first letter represents the time to penetration and the second letter the spread of flame.

- BS EN 13501-5:2005 (European tests). Roofs are classified from $B_{ROOF}(t4)$ (the highest performance) to $F_{ROOF}(t4)$. The suffix t4 indicates the classification is based on test 4 referred to in BS EN 13501-1.

Further guidance
BS 476. Fire tests on building materials.
-20:1987. Method for determination of the fire resistance of elements of construction (general principles).
-21:1987. Methods for determination of the fire resistance of loadbearing elements of construction.
-22:1987. Methods for determination of the fire resistance of non-loadbearing elements of construction.
-23:1987. Methods for determination of the contributions of components of the fire resistance of a structure.
-24:1987. Method for determination of the fire resistance of ventilation ducts.

BS EN 13501. Fire classification of construction products and building elements.
-2:2007. Classification using data from fire resistance tests, excluding ventilation services. [Amended: A1:2009.]
-4:2007. Classification using data from fire resistance tests on components of smoke control systems. [Amended: A1:2009.]

Table B.2 Specific provisions of test for fire resistance of elements of structure, etc.

Part of building	Minimum provision to the relevant part of BS 476 (minutes)			Minimum provision to European Standards (minutes)	Method of exposure
	Loadbearing[1]	Integrity	Insulation		
1. Structural frame, beam or column	See **Table B.3**	Not applicable	Not applicable	R see **Table B.3**	Exposed faces
2. Loadbearing wall (excluding any below)	See **Table B.3**	Not applicable	Not applicable	R see **Table B.3**	Each side separately
3. Floors[2] a. Between a shop and a flat above	Greatest of 60 or **Table B.3**	Greatest of 60 or **Table B.3**	Greatest of 60 or **Table B.3**	Greatest of REI 60 or **Table B.3**	From underside
b. Upper storey of two-storey dwellinghouse (but not over garage or basement)	30	15	15	R 30 and REI 15	
c. Any other floor – including compartment floors	See **Table B.3**	See **Table B.3**	See **Table B.3**	REI see **Table B.3**	
4. Roofs a. Any part forming an escape route	30	30	30	REI 30	From underside
b. Any roof that performs as a floor	See **Table B.3**	See **Table B.3**	See **Table B.3**	REI see **Table B.3**	
5. External walls a. Any part less than 1000mm from any point on relevant boundary	See **Table B.3**	See **Table B.3**	See **Table B.3**	REI see **Table B.3**	Each side separately
b. Any part 1000mm or more from the relevant boundary	See **Table B.3**	See **Table B.3**	15	RE see **Table B.3** REI 15	From inside building
c. Any part adjacent to an external escape route	30	30	No provision[3]	RE 30	From inside building
6. Compartment walls separating: a. A flat from another part of the building b. Other occupancies	Least of 60 or **Table B.3**	Least of 60 or **Table B.3**	Least of 60 or **Table B.3**	Least of REI 60 or **Table B.3**	Each side separately
7. Other compartment walls	See **Table B.3**	See **Table B.3**	See **Table B.3**	REI see **Table B.3**	Each side separately
8. Protected shafts (excluding firefighting shafts) a. Any glazing between the shaft and protected lobby/corridor	Not applicable	30	No provision (but see AD Bv2 Table B.7)	E 30	Each side separately
b. Any other part between the shaft and protected lobby/corridor	30	30	30	REI 30	
c. Any other part	See **Table B.3**	See **Table B.3**	See **Table B.3**	REI see **Table B.3**	
9. Enclosure (but not part of compartment wall or protected shaft) to a: a. Protected stairway	30	30	30[4]	REI 30[4]	Each side separately
b. Lift shaft	30	30	30	REI 30	

Table B.2 continued

Part of building	Minimum provision to the relevant part of BS 476 (minutes)			Minimum provision to European Standards (minutes)	Method of exposure
	Loadbearing[1]	Integrity	Insulation		
10. Firefighting shafts a. Construction separating the shaft from the rest of the building	120	120	120	REI 120	From side remote to shaft
	60	60	60	REI 60	From shaft side
b. Construction separating firefighting stair, firefighting lift shaft and firefighting lobby	60	60	60	REI 60	Each side separately
11. Enclosure (which is not 6, 7 or 8) to a a. Protected lobby	30	30	30	REI 30	Each side separately
b. Protected corridor	30	30	30	REI 30	
12. Sub-division of a corridor	30	30	30	REI 30	Each side separately
13. Fire resisting construction: a. Enclosing places of special fire hazard	30	30	30	REI 30	Each side separately
b. Between store rooms and sales areas in shops	30	30	30	REI 30	
c. Fire-resisting sub-division for means of escape from flats	30	30	30	REI 30	
d. Enclosing bedrooms and ancillary accommodation in care homes	30	30	30	REI 30	
14. Enclosure in a flat to a protected entrance hall or protected landing	30	30	30	REI 30	Each side separately
15. Cavity barrier	Not applicable	30	15	E 30 and EI 15	Each side separately
16. Ceiling (**Figure B.23**)	Not applicable	30	30	EI 30	From underside
17. Duct passing through cavity barrier (**B.5.3.3**)	Not applicable	30	No provision	E 30	From outside
18. Casing around drainage system (**Figure B.25**)	Not applicable	30	No provision	E 30	From outside
19. Flue walls (**B.5.4.3**)	Not applicable	Half the period in **Table B.3** for the compartment wall/floor	Half the period in **Table B.3** for the compartment wall/floor	EI half the period in **Table B.3** for the compartment wall/floor	From outside
20. Fire doors	See AD Bv2 Table B.11				
21. Wall separating attached or integral garage from a dwellinghouse	30	30	30	REI 30	From garage side
21. Fire resisting construction in dwellinghouse not described elsewhere	30	30	30	REI 30	

[1] Loadbearing elements only.

[2] A suspended ceiling will only contribute to the extent described in Approved Document B, volume 3, Table A3.

[3] Unless needed as part of a wall in 5a or 5b.

[4] See **Table B.7** for permitted extent of uninsulated glazed elements.

Table B.3 Minimum periods of fire resistance by Purpose Group

Purpose Group	Minimum period of fire resistance (minutes)					
	Basement storey including floor over		Ground or upper storey			
	Depth (m) of lowest basement		Height (m) of top floor above ground, in a building or separated part of a building			
	More than 10	Not more than 10	Not more than 5	Not more than 18	Not more than 30	More than 30
1. Residential a. Block of flats						
– not sprinklered	90	60	30[1]	60[2]	90[2]	Not permitted
– sprinklered	90	60	30[1]	60[2]	90[2]	120[2]
b. & c. Dwellinghouses	N/A	30[1]	30[1]	60[3]	N/A	N/A
2. Residential a. Institutional	90	60	30[1]	60	90	Not permitted
b. Other	90	60	30[1]	60[1]	60	120[4]
3. Office – not sprinklered	90	60	30[1]	60	90	Not permitted
– sprinklered	60	60	30[1]	30[1]	60	120[4]
4. Shop and commercial – not sprinklered	90	60	60	60	90	Not permitted
– sprinklered	60	60	30[1]	60	60	120[4]
5. Assembly and recreation – not sprinklered	90	60	60	60	90	Not permitted
– sprinklered	60	60	30[1]	60	60	120[4]
6. Industrial – not sprinklered	120	90	60	90	120	Not permitted
– sprinklered	90	60	30[1]	60	90	120[4]
7. Storage a. any building or part not described elsewhere:						
– not sprinklered	120	90	60	90	120	Not permitted
– sprinklered	90	60	30[1]	60	90	120[4]
b. car park for light vehicles i open sided car park	Not applicable	Not applicable	15[1] [5]	15[1] [5]	15[1] [5]	60
ii any other car park	90	60	30[1]	60	90	120[4]

Note: Sprinklered indicates the building is fitted throughout with an automatic sprinkler system in accordance with **B.1.8**.

[1] 60 minutes for compartment walls separating buildings.

[2] 30 minutes for floor within a flat with more than one storey which does not contribute to the support of the building.

[3] 30 minutes for three-storey dwellinghouse, but 60 for compartment walls separating buildings.

[4] 90 minutes for elements not forming part of structural frame.

[5] 30 minutes for elements protecting the means of escape.

Some roof coverings, such as natural slates and concrete tiles, can be considered to meet the requirements for external fire performance without the need for testing (Commission Decision 2000/553/EC). Approved Document B volume 2 Table A5 sets out notional classifications for generic roof coverings.

B.2.3 Reaction to fire

The reaction to fire classification is a European classification that assesses the extent to which a material fuels a fire. It is related to, but not the same as, the national classification of 'surface spread of flame'. Either classification may currently be used.

The classification is set out in BS EN 13501-1:2007, and combines the results from four other tests:

- Non-combustibility test (BS EN ISO 1182:2002);
- Determination of gross calorific values (BS EN ISO 1716:2002);
- Exposure to single burning item (BS EN 13823:2002);
- Ignitability with direct impingement of flame (BS EN ISO 11925-2:2002).

The classification runs from A1 (best) to F (worst), with Classes A2–E being further sub-divided according to the emission of smoke (s1–s3) and burning particles and droplets (d0–d2). Classes which include 's3, d2' have no limit on the production of smoke or flaming droplets/particles.

B.2.3.1 Non-combustible materials

Materials are considered non-combustible if they:
- meet the performance standards in BS 476-4:1970 or BS 476-11:1982; or
- achieve Class A1 to BS EN 13501-1:2007 when tested to BS EN ISO 1182:2002 and BS EN ISO 1716:2002; or
- are defined in Approved Document B volume 2 Table A6.

B.2.3.2 Materials of limited combustibility

Materials are considered as having limited combustibility if they:
- comply with the method in BS 476-11:1982 (national classes); or
- achieve Class A2-s3, d2 to BS EN 13501-1:2007 (European classes), when tested to BS EN ISO 1182:2002 and BS EN ISO 1716:2002; or
- are defined in Approved Document B volume 2 Table A7.

Approved Document B volume 2 Table A7 includes composite products such as plasterboard. Where these materials form exposed linings they should also meet the appropriate spread of flame rating.

B.2.3.3 Surface spread of flame

The speed at which flame spreads over internal linings (walls and ceilings) can be classified to national standards using the surface spread of flame rating (the national equivalent of the European reaction to fire classification).

Surface spread of flame is tested to BS 476-7:1971, 1987, or 1997. Materials or products are classified from 1 to 4, with 4 being the lowest. The classification

Further guidance
BS 476. Fire tests on building materials and structures.
-3:2004. Classification and method of test for external fire exposure to roofs.

BS EN 13501. Fire classification of construction products and building elements.
-1:2007. Classification using test data from reaction to fire tests. [Amended: A1:2009.]
-5:2005. Classification using data from external fire exposure to roofs tests. [Amended: A1:2009.]

Further guidance
BS EN 13501-1:2007 [See **B.2.2**.]

BS EN ISO 1182:2002. Reaction to fire tests for building products. Non-combustibility test. [Withdrawn, replaced by BS EN ISO 1182:2010.]

BS EN ISO 1716:2002. Reaction to fire tests for building products. Determination of the heat of combustion. [Withdrawn, replaced by BS EN ISO 1716:2010. Reaction to fire tests for products. Determination of the gross heat of combustion (calorific value).]

BS EN ISO 13823:2002. Reaction to fire tests for building products. Building products excluding floorings exposed to thermal attack by a single burning item. [Withdrawn, replaced by BS EN 13823:2010.]

BS EN ISO 11925-2:2002. Reaction for fire tests. Ignitability of building products subjected to direct impingement of flame. Single-flame source test. [Withdrawn, replaced by BS EN ISO 11925-2:2010. Reaction to fire tests. Ignitability of products subjected to direct impingement of flame. Single-flame source test.]

Further guidance
BS 476. Fire tests on building materials and structures.
-4:1970. Non-combustibility test for materials.
-11:1982. Method for assessing the heat emission from building materials.

BS EN 13501-1:2007 [See **B.2.2**.]

BS EN ISO 1182:2002 [See **B.2.3**.]

BS EN ISO 1716:2002 [See **B.2.3**.]

Further guidance
[See **B.2.3.1**.]

system includes 'fire propagation' indices (BS 476-6:1981 or 1989) which assess whether materials are likely to ignite rapidly, have a high release of heat and/or contribute to flashover. Index (I) refers to the overall test index, while (i1) refers to the first three minutes of test.

Class 0 – the highest class – is not established by a test in any British Standard, but is defined in Approved Document B as including:

- materials, or the surfaces of composites, which are composed throughout of materials of limited combustibility; and

- Class 1 materials with a fire propagation index (I) of not more than 12 and a sub-index (i1) of not more than 6.

Approved Document B volume 2 Table A8 gives typical performance ratings for commonly used materials.

Further guidance
BS 476. Fire tests on building materials and structures.
-6:1989. Methods of test for fire propagation for products. Amended: A1:2009.
-7.1997. Method of test to determine the classification of the surface spread of flame of products.

B.2.3.4 Thermoplastic materials

Thermoplastic materials are defined as synthetic polymers with a softening point below 200°C (tested to BS EN ISO 306:2004 method A120). Thermoplastic materials cannot be assumed to protect a substrate when used as a lining, so both products must have an appropriate surface classification. Where a thermoplastic is bonded to a substrate then only the substrate need comply.

Further guidance
BS 476-4. and -5. [See **B.2.3.3**.]

BS EN ISO 306:2004. Plastics. Thermoplastic materials. Determination of Vicat softening temperature (VST).

Under requirements B2 and B4 thermoplastic materials should either be classified to BS 476-6 and 7, or be classified as TP(a) rigid, TP(a) flexible or TP(b) (Table B.4).

Table B.4 Classification of thermoplastic materials	
Class	**Definition**
TP(a) rigid	• Rigid, solid PVC sheet. • Solid, polycarbonate sheet at least 3mm thick. • Multi-skinned rigid sheet of uPVC or polycarbonate which achieves Class 1 to BS 476-7:1971, 1976 or 1997. • Any other rigid thermoplastic, tested to BS 2782-0:2004 method 508A, on which the test flame extinguishes before the first test mark and the flaming or afterglow does not exceed 5 seconds.
TP(a) flexible	• Flexible product not more than 1mm thick which meets Type C of BS 5867-2:1980.
TP(b)	• Rigid solid polycarbonate sheets less than 3mm thick, or multi-skin polycarbonates which do not meet Class TP(a) rigid by test. • Other products which, when specimens 1.5–3mm thick are tested to BS 2782-0:2004 method 508A, have a rate of burn not exceeding 50mm/minute.

B.2.4 Fire doors

B.2.4.1 Fire resistance

The fire resistance of fire doors may be established by testing to:

- British Standards – BS 476-22, with integrity expressed in minutes, for example, FD30. An 'S' suffix indicates restricted smoke leakage at ambient temperatures.

- European Standards – BS EN 13501-2:2007, with integrity (E) measured in minutes. The additional 'Sa' classification indicates restricted smoke leakage at ambient temperatures.

- BS EN 1634-1:2008 – results are acceptable until harmonised product standards are introduced.

Results from different test methods are not equivalent. Typically, testing to European Standards will give a lower result than testing to national standards.

Doors should be tested to both sides (lift doors need only be tested from the landing side), and results should adequately represent the performance of the completed assembly, because relatively small differences in detail may affect the rating. Hinges should be made from materials with a melting point of at least 800°C, unless testing of the whole door assembly has shown them to be satisfactory.

The required performance standards are given in Approved Document B volume 2 Table B1. Fire doors should not form more than 25% of a compartment wall unless they provide the integrity and insulation required for that wall. (The figure may be greater if a clear space is maintained on both sides of the doorway.)

B.2.4.2 Closing

In dwellinghouses, only fire doors to attached or integral garages need be fitted with self-closers. In all other buildings, all fire doors should be fitted with self-closing devices (the only exceptions being fire doors to cupboards and service ducts which are normally kept locked shut, and fire doors within flats).

Where self-closing devices would hinder normal use of the building (including access for people with disabilities, **M.2.5**) the fire doors may be held open by:

- an automatic release mechanism actuated by an automatic fire detection or alarm system;
- a door closer delay device;
- a fusible link – this is only acceptable on an escape route if two fire doors are fitted across the same opening and the other door is easily openable by hand and has a fire resistance of at least 30 minutes.

Rolling shutters across an escape route should be released only by a heat sensor (e.g. a fusible link or electric heat detector) in the immediate vicinity. Smoke detectors and alarm systems should only initiate closure of such a shutter where its partial descent forms a boundary for a smoke reservoir. Rolling shutters should be capable of being opened and closed manually for firefighting purposes.

B.2.4.3 Marking

Fire doors should be marked with signs to BS 5499-5:2002 indicating:

- 'Fire door keep shut';
- 'Fire door keep locked shut';
- 'Automatic fire door keep clear – doors held open by automatic release mechanism or swing free device'.

Signs should be provided to both sides of fire doors, except those to cupboards and service ducts. Signs are not required for:

- doors in dwellinghouses;
- doors to and within flats;

Further guidance
BS 476-22.1987. [See **B.2.1.**]

BS EN 13501-2:2007. [See **B.2.1.**]

BS EN 1634-1:2008. Fire resistance tests for door, shutter and, openable window assemblies and elements of building hardware. Fire resistance tests doors, shutters and openable windows.

- bedroom doors in premises in Purpose Group 2b, Residential (Other);
- lift entrance/landing doors.

B.2.5 Insulating core panels

Composite panels typically consist of an inner core of insulation sandwiched between and bonded to steel facings. The core may be mineral fibre or a polymeric material such as polyisocyanurate or polystyrene. When used to form an internal lining or structure, the panels often rely for their support on a jointed construction augmented by lightweight fixings.

Composite panels can present specific problems during a fire:

- polymeric materials degrade, often producing large quantities of smoke;
- facings can delaminate from the core, resulting in collapse of the system;
- fire spread behind and within the panels may be difficult to detect;
- rapid fire spread, leading to flashover.

Where composite panels are specified, designers should identify potential fire risks then adopt one or more of the following measures:

- remove the risk;
- separate the risk from the panels by an appropriate distance;
- provide a fire suppression system for the risk, or for the enclosure;
- provide fire-resisting panels;
- specify appropriate materials/fixing and jointing systems.

Wherever possible, core panel materials should be matched to the application, with mineral core panels specified in areas of high fire risk, as fire breaks in combustible panels and for general fire protection. Construction details should prevent core materials being exposed to fire, while the panel envelope and support systems should be designed to retain structural stability should the facings de-bond.

B.3 Means of warning and escape (Requirement B1)

A building should have:

- system(s) to give the occupants early warning of a fire; and
- routes by which the occupants can escape from a fire.

The escape routes should be sufficient to enable all the building occupants to escape; they should, where necessary, be protected from the effects of fire, be adequately lit and be suitably signed. The ingress of smoke to an escape route should be limited, or there should be facilities to remove smoke.

B.3.1 Principles for escape

The occupants of any part of a building should be able to escape safely without external assistance. They should be able to turn their backs on a fire, wherever it

Further guidance
BS 5499-5:2002: Graphical symbols and signs. Safety signs, including fire safety signs. Signs with specific safety meanings. [Withdrawn, replaced by BS EN ISO 7010:2012. Graphical symbols. Safety colours and safety signs. Registered safety signs.]

Further guidance
Design, construction, specification and fire management of insulated envelopes for temperature controlled environments. International Association of Cold Storage Contractors (European Division). 1999. [Replaced by 2008 edition.]

breaks out, and to travel either to a place of safety or to a protected escape route. The ultimate place of safety is the open air, away from the building, although in large complex buildings with suitable protection measures, it may be possible to reach a place of reasonable safety within the building.

Wherever possible, escape routes should be direct; otherwise occupants should be able to reach a protected stairway or corridor rapidly. Unprotected portions of escape routes should be limited to avoid exposure to fire and smoke, while the length of the protected route should also be limited, because even fire-resistant structures will not give indefinite protection. Wheelchair users will require refuges on escape routes and the use of evacuation lifts or manual assistance down, or up, stairs. The means of escape for institutional buildings may be designed on the basis of staff-assisted evacuation.

Lifts, portable and throw-out ladders, fold-down ladders, chutes and the like, are not acceptable means of escape. Escalators should not be included when assessing escape capacity, although mechanised walkways can be included in static mode. Potential conflicts between requirements for escape and building security should be identified and addressed early in the design process.

B.3.2 Fire detection and alarm systems

Fire detection and alarm systems are intended to give early warning of fire to enable building occupants to escape. The system should be matched to the:

- occupancy – for example, residential accommodation where people will be sleeping is likely to require a better detection system than an office where people will be alert and able to raise the alarm;
- evacuation strategy – simultaneous evacuation requires all alarm sounders to be triggered at once, whereas phased evacuation may require a staged alarm system.

In small buildings where all the occupants are near each other, a basic mechanical or electrical sounder may be sufficient, but most other buildings will require an electrical system with manual call points by exit doors and sounders audible throughout the building.

B.3.2.1 Fire alarms

Fire alarms should comply with BS 5839-6 for dwellings and BS 5839-1:2002 for other buildings (Table B.5). Call points should comply with BS 5839-2:1983, or be Type A. direct operation, to BS EN 54-11:2001. Type B call points, which require a separate action following breaking/displacement of a frangible element, may be used only with approval of the BCB.

B.3.2.2 Smoke alarms

Smoke alarms should conform to BS EN 14604:2005 and heat alarms to BS 5446-2:2003. Both alarm types should be mains operated and have a stand-by power supply. Smoke detectors should be matched to the likely hazard and location:

- Ionisation chamber smoke detectors are sensitive to small particles of smoke produced by flaming fires, but are slightly less sensitive to smouldering fires.

Further guidance
BS 5839. Fire detection and alarm systems for buildings.
-1:2002. Code of practice for system design, installation, commissioning and maintenance. [Withdrawn, replaced by -1:2013. Code of practice for design, installation, commissioning and maintenance of systems in non-domestic premises.]
-2:1983. Specification for manual call points. [Withdrawn, replaced by BS EN 54-11:2001.]
-6:2004. Code of practice for the design, installation and maintenance of fire detection and fire alarm systems in dwellings.

BS EN 54-11:2001. Fire detection and alarm systems. Manual call points.

2013 changes
The standard for smoke alarms is now BS EN 14604:2005 instead of BS 5446-1:2000.

Table B.5 Categories of fire alarm system

Category		Description
M		Manual systems with no automatic detectors
L		Automatic systems for protection of life
	L1	Systems installed throughout all parts of the building.
	L2	Systems installed in only defined parts of the building.
	L3	Systems designed to warn early enough to enable escape before fire, smoke or toxic gases block escape routes.
	L4	Systems within circulation areas which form part of escape routes.
	L5	Systems designed to satisfy a specific fire objective (other than L1–4).
LD		Automatic system for protection of life in dwellings
	LD1	System installed throughout dwelling with detectors in all circulation areas that form escape routes and in all rooms/areas where a fire might start.
	LD2	System with detectors in all circulation areas that form escape routes and in all rooms/areas that present high fire risk to occupants.
	LD3	System with detectors in all circulation areas that form escape routes.
P		Automatic systems for protection of property
	P1	Installed throughout building to offer earliest possible warning of fire.
	P2	Installed in part of building, for areas of high hazard or risk.
PD		Automatic systems for protection of property in dwellings
	PD1	Installed throughout the dwelling with detectors in all rooms and areas where a fire might start (other than toilets, bathrooms and shower rooms).
	PD2	Detectors installed only in rooms or areas where risk to property warrants their provision.

- Optical (photo-electric) smoke detectors are more effective at detecting larger particles of smoke from slow-burning fires and are more appropriate for use near kitchens..

B.3.2.3 Dwellinghouses and flats

Dwellinghouses and flats should have fire alarms to the standard in Table B.6.

Table B.6 Fire alarms in new dwellinghouses and flats: to BS 5839-6:2004

Type	Fire alarm category
Dwellinghouses	Grade D, Category LD2
Large dwellinghouse – 2 storeys, at least one >200m²	Grade B, Category LD3
Large dwellinghouse – 3 storeys, at least one >200m²	Grade A, Category LD2, with detectors sited as Category L2
Flats	Grade D, Category LD3

Further guidance

BS EN 14604:2005. Smoke alarm devices.

BS 5446-2:2003. Fire detection and fire alarm devices for dwellings. Specification for heat alarms.

There should be at least one smoke alarm on every storey of a dwellinghouse or flat, positioned in circulation spaces between sleeping accommodation and places where fires are most likely to start (such as kitchens and living rooms), with an alarm within 7.5m of the door to every habitable room. Where there is no door between a kitchen area and a circulation space or stair then there should be an additional heat detector or alarm in the kitchen. Multiple alarms should be linked so that detection of smoke by one unit triggers the alarm in all units.

Ceiling-mounted units should be at least 300mm from walls and light fittings. Sensors on smoke alarms should be 25–600mm below the ceiling and those for smoke detectors 25–150mm below. Wall-mounted units should be above the level of doorways. All units should be accessible for testing and cleaning; consequently they should not be installed over stairs. Units should not be sited where air currents may keep smoke away from them, such as very cold or very hot places. To prevent false alarms, units should not be sited above heaters or in areas where steam and fumes are produced.

Alarms and detectors should be powered from the mains supply, either on a separate circuit or on a single, regularly used lighting circuit. Fire-resistant cabling is only required on large dwellings. BS 5839-1 and -6 contain further guidance on power supplies.

At commissioning, an installation and commissioning certificate should be provided and occupants should be given information to enable them to use and maintain the systems.

Special cases

Supervised sheltered housing should have a central monitoring point so the warden/supervisor is made aware when a fire has been detected and in which dwelling.

Communal areas should comply with **B.3.2.4**. Student accommodation designed as self-contained flats for up to six students should be alarmed in the same way as flats.

Material alterations

New habitable rooms above ground floor level, and new ground floor rooms without a final exit, should have a fire detection system, and smoke alarms should be provided in circulation spaces.

Further guidance
BS 5839-1:2002, and -6:2004. [See **B.3.2.1**.]

B.3.2.4 Other buildings

Fire alarms should comply with BS 5839-1 Table A.1 and should be properly designed and maintained. An installation and commissioning certificate should be provided.

In premises where many members of the public are present – for example large shops – an initial general alarm may be undesirable. Discrete sounders and paging systems may be used initially to enable trained staff to carry out pre-planned emergency procedures. Where people are unfamiliar with the fire warning arrangements a voice alarm system (to BS 5839-8:1998) may be desirable.

Where it is likely that one or more people with impaired hearing may be relatively isolated (e.g. hotel rooms and sanitary accommodation) both visual and audible signals should be provided. In buildings with a more controlled population (e.g. schools and offices) a vibrating paging system may be more appropriate.

Residential and institutional occupancies require automated detectors and alarms. These are not required elsewhere except:

- as part of an agreed departure from Approved Document B;
- to trigger automatic door releases and other protection systems;
- where fire in unoccupied parts of premises could prejudice escape from occupied parts.

Interfaces between fire detection and alarm systems and other systems, such as those for smoke control or door release, must be very reliable.

B.3.3 General provisions for escape

B.3.3.1 Calculation of capacity

The number and size of escape routes is largely determined by the number of people each part of a building is intended to accommodate. The occupant capacity of a room, storey or building is:

- the maximum number of persons it is designed to hold; or
- the number calculated by dividing the area of the room or storey(s) by a floor space factor, such as those in Approved Document B volume 2 Table C1 (areas should exclude stair enclosures, lifts and sanitary accommodation).

B.3.3.2 Protection of escape routes

Generally, 30 minutes' fire resistance is sufficient for the protection of means of escape. Requirements for limiting internal fire spread (**B.5.2.1**) or provision for the Fire and Rescue Service (**B.7.3**) may impose more stringent standards. Fire-resisting elements should provide the performance specified in Tables B.2 and B.3.

B.3.3.3 Doors and glazed elements

Doors on escape routes should open at least 90° with a swing clear of a change of floor level, other than a clearly marked step or threshold. The door swing should not reduce the effective width of an escape route across a landing, and doors opening to corridors or stairways should be recessed so as not to reduce the effective width. Where practicable, doors should be hung to open in the direction of escape. They should always open in the direction of escape where more than 60 people are expected to use the door for escape, or where there is a very high fire risk.

Doors required to be fire-resisting should meet the criteria in **B.2.4** and Approved Document B volume 2 Table B1. Any glazing should meet the provisions set out below. Doors which swing both ways and those sub-dividing corridors require vision panels. Revolving doors, automatic doors and turnstiles must provide the required escape width and either:

- fail safely to outward opening from any position of opening; or
- have a failsafe system which opens the doors on mains failure; or
- fail safely to open in the event of power failure.

Alternatively, an adjacent non-automatic swing door of the required width should be provided.

Fastenings

Doors should be readily openable, either not fitted with locks or fastenings, or else fitted with one keyless fastening with readily apparent operation. Doors which have to be secured against entry should be secured with a lock or fastening which can be operated from the escape side without a key, code or swipe card. In places of assembly, shops or commercial buildings, doors on escape routes for more than 60 people should either not have a lock or fastening or else be fitted with panic fastenings to BS EN 1125:1997.

Closers and hold-open devices should comply with **B.2.4**. Electrically powered locks should return to unlocked on:

- operation of the fire alarm;
- loss of power or system error;
- activation of a manual door release (Type A to BS EN 54-11:2001) (note that a door used both ways needs a unit on both sides).

Glazed elements

Glazing, including that in doors, which satisfies the standards for integrity and insulation may be used without limitation. If it provides integrity only then its use is limited by Table B.7, and possibly by requirements for protected shafts (**B.5.2.3**).

B.3.3.4 Stairs

Construction

The flights and landings of an escape stair should be constructed of materials of limited combustibility where:

- it is the only stair to a building or part of a building (unless the building is Purpose Group 1a or 3 and has only two or three storeys);
- it is within a basement storey (except a private stair in a flat);
- it serves a storey with a floor more than 18m above the ground;
- it is an external stair (except one that connects ground or paving with a floor or flat roof less than 6m above);
- it is a firefighting stair.

All those stairs, except firefighting stairs, may have combustible materials to horizontal surfaces.

Special stairs

Helical and spiral stairs to BS 5395-2:1984 may form part of an escape route, but if they will serve members of the public must be to type E. Fixed ladders are only acceptable where a conventional stair is not feasible, and then not for public access.

Further guidance
BS EN 1125:1997. Building hardware. Panic exit devices operated by a horizontal bar, for use on escape routes. Requirements and test methods. [Superseded by 2008 edition.]

BS EN 54-11:2001. [See **B.3.2.1**.]

Table B.7 Limitations on the use of glazed elements on escape routes

Position of glazed element	Maximum total glazed area in parts of building with access to:			
	A single stairway		More than one stairway	
	Walls	Door leaf	Walls	Door leaf
Flats				
1. Within the enclosures of a protected entrance hall or protected landing or within fire-resisting separation shown in **Figure B.13**	Fixed fanlights only	Unlimited above 1100mm from floor	Fixed fanlights only	Unlimited above 1100mm from floor
General				
2. Between residential/sleeping accommodation and a common escape route (corridor, lobby or stair)	Nil	Nil	Nil	Nil
3. Between a protected stairway and: – the accommodation – corridor which is not a protected corridor (other than item 2)	Nil	25% of door area	Unlimited above 1100mm[1]	50% of door area
4. Between – a protected stairway and a protected lobby or protected corridor – accommodation and a protected lobby (other than item 2)	Unlimited above 1100mm	Unlimited above 100mm[2]	Unlimited above 100mm	Unlimited above 100mm
5. Between the accommodation and a protected corridor forming a dead end (other than item 2)	Unlimited above 1100mm	Unlimited above 100mm	Unlimited above 1100mm	Unlimited above 100mm
6. Between accommodation and any other corridor or sub-dividing corridor	N/A	N/A	Unlimited above 100mm	Unlimited above 100mm
7. Adjacent to external escape route as **B.3.4.5**	Unlimited above 1100mm	Unlimited above 1100mm	Unlimited above 1100mm	Unlimited above 1100mm
8. Adjacent to external escape stair or roof escape	Unlimited	Unlimited	Unlimited	Unlimited

[1] Measured vertically from landing floor or pitch line.

[2] 100mm limit to reduce risk of fire spread from floor covering.

Note: Fire-resisting glass to be marked with manufacturer and product name.

External walls of protected stairways

Fire within the building at internal corners and projections which are close to the external wall of a protected stairway could compromise safe use of the stair. To prevent that, an external wall within 1800mm of any unprotected area of the stair enclosure must be fire-resistant (Figure B.1).

External escape stairs

External escape stairs must meet the following requirements:

- Access doors onto the stair must be fire-resisting and self-closing (except for a single access door at the head of a downward-going stair).
- Stairs over 6m high should be protected from the weather.
- The external wall must be of fire-resisting construction (Figure B.2), within:
  - 1800mm horizontally;
  - 9m vertically below;
  - 1100mm vertically above the top level of stair (providing it does not lead from a basement);
  - 1800mm of the escape route from the foot of the stair to a place of safety.

Glazing in that fire-resisting construction should be fire-resisting (integrity) and fixed shut.

Further guidance

BS 5395-2:1984. Stairs, ladders and walkways. Code of practice for the design of helical and spiral stairs.

Figure B.1 External protection to protected stairways

CONFIGURATIONS OF STAIRS
AND EXTERNAL WALL

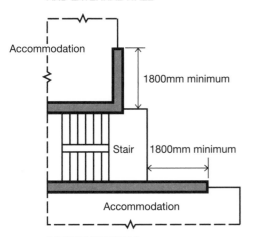

CONFIGURATION A

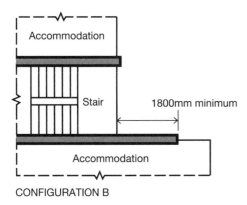

CONFIGURATION B

Key

Fire-resisting construction
— Non fire-resisting construction

B.3.3.5 General

Escape routes should have clear headroom of at least 2m, except in doorways, with flooring – including that of stairs and ramps – chosen to minimise slipperiness when wet. Ramps should comply with Part M (**M.2.2**) and be no steeper than 35°. For areas of fixed seating, see **K.2.2.2** and BS 5588-6:1991.

Final exits

Final exits should enable people to move rapidly away from the building to the street, passageway, or other open space. They should be at least as wide as the escape route they serve and should be clear of any risk of fire or smoke from a basement or from openings to a plant room.

2013 changes
Although Approved Document B volume 2 still refers to Part M for ramps, the guidance is now in Part K (**K.2.3**).

Figure B.2 External escape stairs

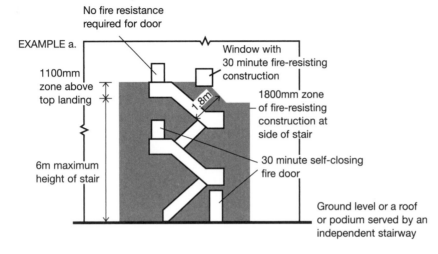

EXAMPLE a.

No fire resistance required for door

1100mm zone above top landing

6m maximum height of stair

1.8m

Window with 30 minute fire-resisting construction

1800mm zone of fire-resisting construction at side of stair

30 minute self-closing fire door

Ground level or a roof or podium served by an independent stairway

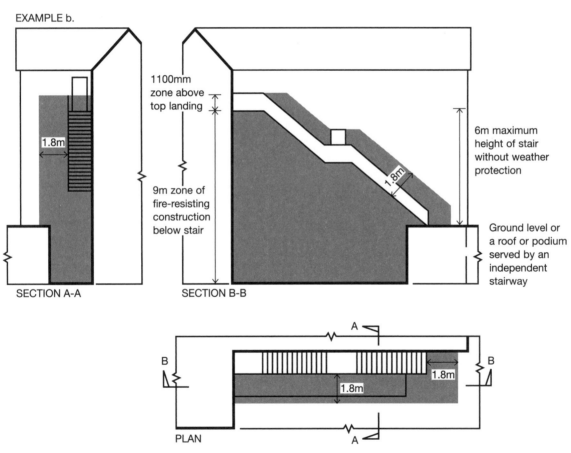

EXAMPLE b.

1.8m

SECTION A-A

1100mm zone above top landing

9m zone of fire-resisting construction below stair

SECTION B-B

6m maximum height of stair without weather protection

1.8m

Ground level or a roof or podium served by an independent stairway

PLAN

1.8m

1.8m

A

B

Final exits should be readily apparent to users, especially where the exit opens off a continuing stair. There should be no obstacle to wheelchair users and other people with disabilities; the exit should have a level threshold if there are no steps.

Escape routes over roofs

Escape routes may go over flat roofs, where:

- the roof is part of the same building from which escape is being made; and
- the route leads to a storey exit or an external escape route; and
- the roof within 3m of the escape route, together with its supporting structure, is fire-resisting; and
- the route is adequately defined and guarded by walls and/or barriers to Part K (**K.3**).

Lighting

All escape routes should have adequate artificial lighting. Routes and areas listed in Table B.8 should also have escape lighting (to BS 5266-1:2005) which illuminates if the main supply fails. Lighting to escape stairs should be on a different circuit to the rest of the route.

Exit signs

Every escape route, other than routes in ordinary use, should have clear emergency exit signs that comply with the Health and Safety (Safety Signs and Signals) Regulations 1996 (for example, signs with symbols/pictograms to BS 5499-1:2002).

Table B.8 Escape lighting	
Purpose Group of the building or part of the building	**Areas requiring escape lighting**
1. Residential	All common escape routes[1], except in two-storey flats
2. Office, industrial, storage and other non-residential	a. Underground or windowless accommodation b. Stairways in a central core or serving storey(s) more than 18m above ground level c. Internal corridors more than 30m long d. Open-plan areas of more than 60m²
3. Shop and commercial and car parks	a. Underground or windowless accommodation b. Stairways in a central core or serving storey(s) more than 18m above ground level c. Internal corridors more than 30m long d. Open-plan areas of more than 60m² e. All escape routes to which the public are admitted[1] (except in shops of three or fewer storeys with no sales floor more than 280m², provided that the shop is not a restaurant or bar)
4. Assembly and recreation	All escape routes[1], and accommodation except for: a. accommodation open on one side to view sport or entertainment during normal daylight hours
5. Any Purpose Group	a. All toilet accommodation with a floor area over 8m² b. Electricity and generator rooms c. Switch room/battery room for emergency lighting system d. Emergency control room

[1] Including external escape routes.

Protected power circuits

Circuits which must function in the event of a fire should be protected power circuits, with the possibility of damage limited by the use of robust cables, careful selection of routes and, possibly, physical protection to the cables. Cable supports should be non-combustible and as robust as the cable.

A protected circuit for operating equipment in the event of fire should achieve category PH30 to BS EN 50200:2006 (including Appendix E), should be routed to avoid fire risk and should be separate from circuits for any other purpose. Where systems must operate for an extended period, cables should be selected on the basis of BS 5839-1, BS 5266-1 and BS 7346-6.

B.3.3.6 Lifts

Generally, lifts should not be used in the event of fire because there is a danger of people being trapped within them. However, with appropriate provision, a lift may form part of an evacuation plan (see BS 5588-8:1999). Firefighting lifts (**B.7.3**) may be used for the evacuation of disabled people, but the evacuation plan should include a contingency for the arrival of the Fire and Rescue Service.

Without proper protection, lifts may compromise escape routes. Therefore a lift well should either:

- be within the enclosure of a protected stairway; or
- where it would prejudice escape routes, be enclosed with fire-resisting construction for its whole height.

A lift well connecting different compartments should form a protected shaft (**B.5.2.3**). A lift without a conventional well, such as one rising in a mall or atrium, may be at risk if it runs through a smoke reservoir. Measures will be required to protect the lift's occupants and preserve the integrity of the reservoir.

A lift which is not within the enclosure of a protected stair should open to a protected lobby/corridor, where it serves:

- a basement;
- an enclosed car park;
- a storey containing high fire risk areas;
- a corridor serving sleeping accommodation.

A lift shaft should not serve a basement if:

- it is within the enclosure of a stair which terminates at ground level; or
- if there is only one escape stair, and smoke from the basement could prejudice escape from other storeys.

Lift machine rooms should, wherever possible, be sited over the lift well. Where a lift is in the protected enclosure of a building's only stairway, the machine room should be sited outside the stairway if it cannot be sited over the lift well.

Further guidance

BS 5588. Fire precautions in the design, construction and use of buildings.
-6:1991. Code of practice for places of assembly. [Withdrawn 2009. Replaced by BS 9999:2008. Code of practice for fire safety in the design, management and use of buildings. Annex D covers theatres, cinemas and similar venues.]

BS 5266-1:2005. Emergency lighting. Code of practice for the emergency lighting of premises.

BS 5499-1:2002. Graphical symbols and signs. Safety signs, including fire safety signs. Specification for geometric shapes, colours and layout. [Withdrawn, replaced by BS ISO 3864-1:2011. Graphical symbols. Safety colours and safety signs. Design principles for safety signs and safety markings.]

Safety signs and signals. Health and safety (safety signs and signals) regulations 1996. Guidance on the Regulations. HSE. 1996. [Superseded by the 2009 edition.]

BS EN 50200:2006. Methods of test for resistance to fire of unprotected small cables for use in emergency circuits.

BS 5839-1:2002. [See **B.3.2.1**.]

BS 7346-6:2005. Components for smoke and heat control systems. Specifications for cable systems. [Withdrawn, superseded by BS 8519:2010. Selection and installation of fire-resistant power and control cable systems for life safety and fire-fighting applications. Code of practice.]

Further guidance

BS 5588-8:1999. Fire precautions in the design, construction and use of buildings. Code of practice for means of escape for disabled people. [Withdrawn, replaced by BS 9999:2008. Code of practice for fire safety in the design, management and use of buildings. Paragraph 46 covers the Evacuation of disabled people.]

B.3.3.7 Mechanical ventilation systems

Ductwork for mechanical ventilation systems should not transfer fire and smoke through the building:

- Ventilation ducts to protected escape routes should not serve other areas and each protected stair should have a separate ventilation system.
- Ductwork serving more than one part of a sub-divided escape route requires a fire damper at the sub-division, operated by a smoke detector or fire detection system.
- Systems which recirculate air should have smoke detectors which either shut down or switch wholly to extraction with no recirculation.
- Non-domestic kitchens, car parks and plant rooms should have separate, independent extraction systems with no recirculation.
- Ventilation and air-conditioning systems should be compatible with a pressure differential system when operating under fire conditions (BS 5720:1979 and BS 5839-1:2002).
- Any duct which passes through the enclosure of a protected escape route should be fire-resisting, or have a fire-resisting enclosure (**B.5.4**).
- Exhaust points should be sited away from final exits, openings or combustible materials.

Further guidance

BS 5720:1979. Code of practice for mechanical ventilation and air-conditioning in buildings. [Withdrawn.]

BS 5839. Fire detection and fire alarm systems for buildings.
-1:2002. Code of practice for system design, installation, commissioning and maintenance. [See **B.3.2.1**.]

BS 5588-6:1991. Fire precautions in the design, construction and use of buildings. Code of practice for places of assembly. [Withdrawn; replaced by BS 9999:2008. Code of practice for fire safety in the design, management and use of buildings. Annex D covers theatres, cinemas and similar venues.]

B.3.3.8 Refuse chutes and storage

Chutes, storage chambers and hoppers for refuse should be sited and constructed to BS 5906. Chutes and refuse storage rooms should:

- be separated by fire-resisting construction from other parts of the building;
- not be within protected stairways or lobbies.

Rooms containing chutes, or which are used for refuse storage, should be approached either from the open air, or from a protected lobby with (minimum) 0.2m² of permanent ventilation. The access to storage chambers should not be next to escape routes, final exits or windows of flats.

Further guidance

BS 5906:1980. Code of practice for storage and on-site treatment of solid waste from buildings.
[Replaced by BS 5906:2005. Waste management in buildings. Code of practice.]

B.3.3.9 Shop store rooms

Fully enclosed, walk-in store rooms in shops which, by their location, would prejudice means of escape, should:

- be separated from retail areas by fire-resisting construction; or
- be fitted with an automatic fire detection system; or
- be fitted with sprinklers.

B.3.4 Horizontal escape (excluding dwellinghouses and flats)

Horizontal escape routes should enable people to get from any point on a storey to a storey exit, which will take them either out of the building or to a vertical escape route. The guidance is intended for smaller, simpler buildings. For more complex buildings see **B.1.5**. Special provisions apply to smaller buildings (**B.3.4.6**) and some institutional buildings (**B.3.4.7**).

Table B.9 Limitations on travel distance

Purpose Group	Use of premises/part of premises	Maximum travel distance[1] where travel possible in:	
		One direction only (m)	More than one direction (m)
2(a)	Institutional	9	18
2(b)	Other residential:		
	a. in bedrooms[2]	9	18
	b. in bedroom corridors	9	35
	c. elsewhere	18	35
3	Office	18	45
4	Shop and commercial[3]	18	45
5	Assembly and recreation:		
	a. buildings primarily for disabled people	9	18
	b. areas with seating in rows	15	32
	c. elsewhere	18	45
6	Industrial:		
	Normal hazard	25	45
	Higher hazard	12	25
7	Storage and other non-residential:		
	Normal hazard	25	45
	Higher hazard	12	25
2–7	Place of special fire hazard[4]	9	18
2–7	Plant room or rooftop plant:		
	a. distance within the room	9	35
	b. escape route not in open air (overall distance)	18	45
	c. escape route in open air (overall distance)	60	100

[1] Where internal layout not known, use direct distances, with 2/3 of the travel distances shown.

[2] Maximum part of travel distance permitted in room.

[3] See BS 5588:10 for shopping malls, with reduced travel distances for units with only one exit in shopping complexes.

[4] Defined in Approved Document B volume 2 Appendix E: Distances apply within the room/area. Normal distances for Purpose Group apply for the remainder of the route.

B.3.4.1 Levels of provision

The number of routes and exits is determined by:

- the number of occupants in a room, tier or storey; derived either from the figure specified as the basis of the design or from the calculation method in **B.3.3.1**; and
- the permitted travel distance from any point to the nearest storey exit (Table B.9);
- the minimum number of escape routes and exits required (Table B.10).

Table B.10 Minimum number of escape routes and exits

Number of persons	Minimum number of escape routes/exits
≤60	1
61–600	2
>600	3

Multi-storey buildings may need more than one stair, in which case every part of every storey will need access to more than one stair. Mixed-use buildings require separate means of escape for storeys or parts used for residential or assembly and recreation purposes.

Access control measures must not affect fire safety provisions. For example, it might be reasonable for some escape routes to be secured outside normal business hours, but there should still be sufficient provision for anyone left in the building to evacuate safely (**B.3.3.3**).

B.3.4.2 Design of escape routes

A single escape route is acceptable for:

- a storey within the one-direction travel distance of Table B.9 and an occupant capacity of no more than 60;
- those parts of a floor where the storey exit is within the one-direction distance of Table B.9 and the occupant capacity is no more than:
  - 60 for place of assembly or bar;
  - 30 for institutional use (PG 2a).

In all other cases, alternative routes are required from all parts of the building. The lack of an alternative at the start of a route – for example where there is only one exit from a room to a corridor (Figure B.3) – will be acceptable provided both the one-direction travel distance and the overall travel distance do not exceed the limits in Table B.9. Alternative routes are only useful if they are unlikely to be disabled simultaneously, so will only count if they are:

- 45° apart; or
- less than 45° apart, but separated by fire-resisting construction (Figure B.4).

An inner room which has its sole escape route through an access room, is at risk if fire starts in the access room. Such an arrangement is acceptable only where all the conditions in Table B.11 are met.

Figure B.3 Travel distance in dead-end condition

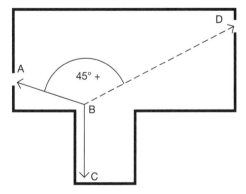

Angle ABD should be at least 45°. CBA or CBD (whichever is less) should be no more than the maximum distance of travel given for alternative routes and CB should be no more than the maximum distance for travel where there are no alternative routes.

Figure B.4 Alternative escape routes

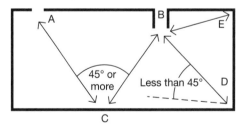

Alternative routes are available from C because angle ACB is 45° or more and therefore CA or CB (whichever is the less) should be no more than the maximum distance for travel given for alternative routes.

Alternative routes are not available from D because angle ADB is less than 45° (therefore see Figure B.3). There is also no alternative route from E.

Table B.11 Provisions for inner rooms

Requirement	Conditions
Occupant capacity of inner room	≤30 for Purpose Group 2a, Institutional ≤60 for all other occupancies
Use of inner room	Not a bedroom
Use of access room	Not a place of special fire hazard
Access to inner room	Directly from access room
Escape route from inner room	Travel distance from any point in inner room to exit of access room not to exceed **Table B.9** Passes through only one access room
Occupancy	Inner room and access room in the control of the same occupier
Fire detection measures	One of: • the walls or partitions of the inner room stop 500mm short of the ceiling; • the door or walls of the inner room have a suitably located 0.1m^2 vision panel to allow its occupants to see if a fire has started; • the access room has an automatic fire detection and alarm system to warn occupants of the inner room.

Where a building has more than one exit into a central core the exits should be remote from each other and should not be approached from a shared lift hall or lobby, or an undivided corridor (Figure B.5). Ancillary areas for the consumption of food or drink should have at least two escape routes (unless an inner room). Those routes should lead directly to a storey exit without entering a kitchen or other high fire hazard area.

The means of escape from an occupancy should not pass through a different occupancy in the same storey (whether a separate ownership or different tenancies). Where the means of escape includes a common corridor or circulation space an automatic fire detection and alarm system should be fitted throughout the storey.

Escape routes should not pass within 4.5m of openings between floors (such as those for escalators) unless the direction of travel is away from the opening, or there is an alternative route which passes more than 4.5m away (Figure B.6). It should not be necessary to pass through one stairway to reach another, although it is acceptable to pass through one stairway's protected lobby to reach another.

Self-closing fire doors to protected stairways on primary circulation routes may be rendered ineffectual by the building occupants wedging them open or removing closers to prevent them from being an impediment to normal traffic. Consequently such doors must be fitted with an automatic release mechanism (**B.2.4**).

B.3.4.3 Sizing escape routes

The width of an escape route is determined by how many people will use it. The minimum width should comply with Table B.12 and also with Part M (**M.5.3**). The width of the escape route may affect the width of the stairs, which must be as wide as any storey exit which opens onto them. Where there are two or more exits, each must be sized on assumption that the fire has blocked one of the other exits, with remaining exits being wide enough for all occupants to leave quickly. The largest exit should be discounted first.

Figure B.5 Exits in a central core

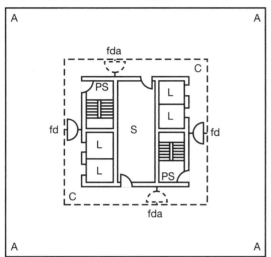

Note: The doors at both ends of the area marked 'S' should be self-closing fire doors unless the area is sub-divided such that any fire in that area will not be able to prejudice both sections of corridor at the same time. If that area is a lift lobby, doors should be provided as shown in Figure 8 in BS 5588: Part 11: 1997.

Key

L	Life
S	Services, toilets, etc.
fd	Self-closing FD20S fire doors
fda	Possible alternative position for fire door
C	Corridor off which accommodation opens
PS	Protected stairway
A	Accommodation (e.g. office space)

Figure B.6 Openings between floors

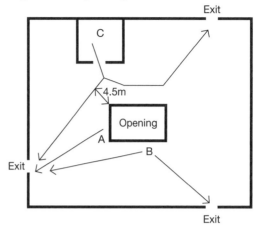

From A and B at least one direction of travel is away from the opening. From C where the initial direction of travel is towards the opening, one of the escape routes is not less than 4.5m from the opening.

Table B.12 Width of escape routes and exits	
Number of persons	**Minimum width (mm)**
≤60	750
61–110	850
111–220	1050
>220	5mm per person

The total number of people who can use the exits is found by adding together the maximum number of people for each exit width. For example, 3 exits, 850mm wide allow 3 × 110 = 330 people (and not the 510 people who could pass through a single exit 2550mm wide).

Any final ground floor storey exit which shares a final exit with a stair to a ground floor lobby should be wide enough to accommodate the maximum combined flow rate. The width of such an exit, W, can be calculated from:

$$W = ((N/2.5) + 60S)/80$$

where:
N is the number of people served by the ground floor storey exit; and
S is the stair width in metres.

Where N is greater than 60, the distance from both the stair and storey exit to the final exit should be more than 2m. Otherwise:

W = width of stair + width of storey exit.

B.3.4.4 Corridors

Corridors which form part of the means of escape should be protected (generally having 30 minutes' fire resistance) where they:

- serve bedrooms;
- are dead-end corridors (excluding recesses and extensions less than 2m deep);
- are common to two or more occupancies.

Other corridors that form part of the means of escape but which are not protected should offer some defence against the spread of smoke in the early stage of a fire. Partitions should therefore be carried up to the soffit of the structural floor or suspended ceiling, and openings from rooms should be fitted with doors, although not necessarily fire doors.

To prevent smoke spreading in corridors and making two, alternative, escape routes impassable, any corridor which connects two or more storey exits and is more than 12m long should be divided approximately midway between the exits by self-closing fire doors, which may be set in fire-resisting screens. In buildings other than dwellinghouses and flats (Purpose Groups 2–7) smoke transmission in any cavities above the enclosures should be limited by:

- fitting cavity barriers to and across the corridor at the line of the enclosure; or
- sub-dividing the storey with fire-resisting construction and cavity barriers at the line of sub-division; or
- enclosing the lower side of the cavity with a fire-resisting ceiling which extends throughout the building compartment or separated part.

Doors which might provide a smoke path through the sub-division should be self-closing but need not be fire-resisting. (See **B.5.3** for further guidance on cavity barriers and safeguarding from smoke.)

Dead-end portions of corridors more than 4.5m long should be protected from smoke by self-closing fire doors (with screens), sited so as to separate the dead end from any part of a corridor which:

- provides two directions of escape (Figure B.7a); or
- continues past one storey exit to another (Figure B.7b).

Open-plan areas present no resistance to the spread of smoke, but do enable early awareness of a fire.

B.3.4.5 External escape

External escape stairs should comply with **B.3.3.4** and **B.3.5.3**. Where an external escape route other than a stair runs beside an external wall then any part of that wall within 1800mm of the route should be fire-resisting, up to 1100mm above the paving level of the route.

Figure B.7 Dead-end corridors

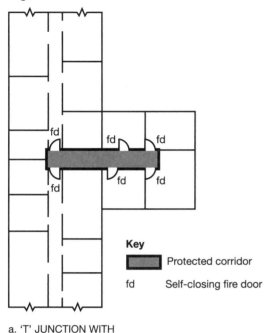

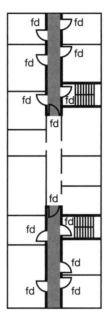

Key

▬	Protected corridor
fd	Self-closing fire door

a. 'T' JUNCTION WITH
MAIN CORRIDOR

b. CONTINUATION
PAST STAIRWAY

A flat roof may serve as one of multiple escape routes, provided it does not serve an institutional building or part of the building intended for use by members of the public (**B.3.3.5**).

B.3.4.6 Smaller buildings

Small premises are generally occupied by a limited number of people; the size of the premises – when undivided – enables occupants to escape quickly in the event of a fire. It is therefore possible to reduce the number of exits and stairs, although other provisions remain in place.

A building qualifies as a 'small premises' if:

- it is a single occupancy, comprising no more than basement, ground and first floor, with no floor greater than 280m²; and
- any kitchen or other open cooking arrangement is at the extremity of a dead end remote from the exit(s); and
- planned seating or assessed standing accommodation for a bar or restaurant does not exceed 30 people per storey (100 people for a ground storey with an independent final exit); and
- the premises are not used for the storage and/or sale of highly flammable liquids or materials; and
- the floor areas are undivided (except for kitchens, ancillary offices and stores) with exits visible from all parts; and
- store rooms are enclosed with fire-resisting construction; and
- partitions separating kitchens or offices from open areas have clear glazed areas to give occupants early visual warning of fire, or the outer room has an automatic fire detection and alarm system.

Table B.13 Travel distances in small premises with protected stair

Storey	Maximum travel distance (m)	Maximum direct distance (if internal layout not known) (m)
Ground storey – single exit	27	18
Basement or first storey – single stair	18	12
Storey with more than one exit/stair	45	30

The maximum travel distances for the escape routes with a protected stair should comply with column 2 of Table B.13. If the internal layout is not settled at time of deposition of plans then the maximum direct distance should comply with column 3 of Table B.13. For open stairs, travel distance is measured to the foot of the stairs in a basement and head of the stairs on the first floor. Multiple exits should be sited to give effective alternate directions of travel.

Further guidance
Small units in covered shopping complexes are treated in BS 5588-10:1991.

B.3.4.7 Residential care homes

The fire safety strategy for a residential care home will be affected by the level of dependency of the residents, staffing levels, and the design and furnishing of the building. In care homes for the elderly it is presumed that some residents will require assistance, and that a progressive horizontal evacuation (PHE) will be required. Other care homes will require a judgement as to whether PHE or simultaneous evacuation is most appropriate. That decision should be recorded and communicated to building management so that appropriate procedures are adopted. The guidance in Approved Document B is intended for care homes which are not covered by a Firecode document (**B.1.5**).

PHE depends on moving residents from an area under direct threat of fire to the relative safety of a protected area from which they can – if necessary – be subsequently evacuated, but at less pressure of time. The building is therefore divided into protected areas by compartment walls and floors, with each storey for care of residents divided into at least three protected areas.

Each protected area must have at least two exits to adjoining, but separate, protected areas. The travel distances within protected areas to exits should not exceed Table B.9, and the travel distance to the storey exit or final exit should not exceed 64m. Fire in one protected area should not prevent residents in another protected area reaching the final exit, and escape routes should not pass through ancillary accommodation. Protected areas should have sufficient floor area to accept their own residents and those from the largest adjacent protected area.

There should be no more than 10 resident beds in any one protected area. Each bedroom should contain only one single or double bed, and should be enclosed with fire-resisting construction with fire-resisting doors. Every corridor serving bedrooms should be protected and ancillary accommodation – such as store rooms and plant rooms – should be enclosed by fire-resisting construction.

The fire detection and alarm system should be type L1 to BS 5839-1:2002. Door closers for fire doors should be to BS EN 1155:1997. Bedroom doors should have free swing devices, and doors to circulation spaces should have hold-open devices.

If sprinklers are fitted (**B.1.8**) the requirements are less onerous:

- fire doors to bedrooms need not have self-closers;
- each protected area can have more than 10 beds;
- bedrooms may have more than one bed.

B.3.5 Vertical escape (excluding dwellinghouses and flats)

Protected escape stairs should enable the building's occupants to reach a protected escape route or final exit independently. Some people, notably wheelchair users, will not be able to use stairways without assistance. Their evacuation will require refuges on escape routes, assistance up and/or down stairs, or the use of lifts.

B.3.5.1 Number of stairs

The number of escape stairs is determined by:

- constraints on the design of horizontal escape routes (**B.3.4**);
- whether occupancies in a mixed occupancy building require independent stairs;
- whether a single stair is acceptable;
- the provision of adequate width for escape, taking account of other stairs being blocked by fire and smoke.

A single stair will be sufficient in a single-use building, as follows:

- From a basement allowed to have a single escape route (**B.3.4.2**).
- A building with no floor level more than 11m above ground level, and where every storey is allowed a single escape route.
- Small premises (**B.3.4.6**).
- An office building with ground floor and five storeys above, provided:
  - the travel distance for each storey does not exceeds the one-direction distance in Table B.9; and
  - every storey at height greater than 11m has an alternative means of escape.
- A factory where the one-direction travel distance from every point on every storey complies with Table B.9 and is either:
  - a low fire risk building consisting of a ground storey and two storeys above; or
  - a normal fire risk building consisting of a ground storey and one other.
- A process plant building with occupant capacity less than 10.

In mixed-use buildings one use may have a serious effect on another (for example, fire in a shop could compromise escape from a hotel). Designers must consider whether common routes will be sufficient or if completely separate means of escape should be provided.

Access provisions for firefighters may require some escape stairs to be used as firefighting stairs (**B.7.3**).

Further guidance
BS 5839-1:2002. [See **B.3.2.1**.]

BS EN 1155:1997. Building hardware. Electrically powered hold-open devices for swing doors. Requirements and test methods.

Table B.14 Minimum widths of escape stairs		
Situation of stair	**Maximum number of people served**	**Minimum stair width (mm)**
Institutional building (unless only used by staff)	150	1000
Assembly building, serving assembly area (unless area less than 100m²)	220	1100
In any other building and serving an occupancy of more than 50	Over 220	Simultaneous evacuation: **Table B.15** Phased evacuation: **Table B.16**
Any other stair	50	800

B.3.5.2 Width of stairs

As a minimum, stairs should:

- be at least as wide as exits which open onto them;
- meet or exceed the minimum widths in Table B.14; and
- not reduce in width on the way towards the final exit.

Stairs taller than 30m should not be wider than 1400mm without having a central handrail. Where such a handrail is provided, the escape capacity of each side of the stair should be evaluated separately. Stairs wider than 1800mm will also require central handrails (**K.2.1.3**).

The width of a stair is based on the occupant capacity of the building (**B.3.3.1**) and whether simultaneous or phased evacuation is intended. The calculations should discount each stair in turn to allow for the possibility of a stair being rendered unusable by fire and/or smoke. Discounting applies to buildings with sprinklers, but is not necessary for stairs with a smoke control system or with a protected lobby on each floor (although the storey exit will still need to be discounted; **B.3.4.3**).

Simultaneous evacuation

Simultaneous evacuation must be used for all stairs serving:

- basements;
- buildings with open spatial planning;
- other residential or assembly and recreation buildings.

The escape stairs must have the capacity to evacuate all floors at the same time. The minimum width for a stair, W, can either be determined from Table B.15 or, for stairs 1100mm or wider, by the formula:

$$W = (P + 15n - 15)/(150 + 50n)$$

where:
P = population served, which should be divided among the available stairs; and
n = number of storeys served.

Separate calculations should be made for basements and for upper storeys.

2013 changes

The 2013 changes to Approved Document K have created a new anomaly. Approved Document Bv2, at paragraph 4.16, requires stairs wider than 1800mm to have a central handrail, but refers to guidance in Approved Document K, which in the 1998 edition used the same limiting dimension. Approved Document K 2013, at paragraph 1.15c, now requires stairs wider than 2000mm to be divided. The case for following the more recent guidance in AD K 2013 is strong, but the 1800mm figure is still in AD Bv2.

Table B.15 Stair capacity for simultaneous evacuation

No. of floors served	Maximum number of persons served by a stair of width:								
	1000mm	1100mm	1200mm	1300mm	1400mm	1500mm	1600mm	1700mm	1800mm
1	150	220	240	260	280	300	320	340	360
2	190	260	285	310	335	360	385	410	435
3	230	300	330	360	390	420	450	480	510
4	270	340	375	410	445	480	515	550	585
5	310	380	420	460	500	540	580	620	660
6	350	420	465	510	555	600	645	690	735
7	390	460	510	560	610	660	710	760	810
8	430	500	555	610	665	720	775	830	885
9	470	540	600	660	720	780	840	900	960
10	510	580	645	710	775	840	905	970	1035

Note:
The capacity of stairs serving more than 10 storeys may be obtained by using linear extrapolation.

Phased evacuation

In phased evacuation, people with reduced mobility are evacuated first, together with those on the storey most at risk from fire. Any subsequent evacuation is done two floors at a time. It requires the provision and maintenance of supporting facilities such as fire alarms, but allows for stairs to be narrower. Phased evacuation is suitable for buildings which do not require simultaneous evacuation, and where:

- stairways are approached through a protected lobby or protected corridor at each storey except the top storey;
- lifts are approached through protected lobbies;
- every floor is a compartment floor;
- floors more than 30m above ground level have sprinkler systems;
- the fire warning system is at least category L3;
- there is an internal speech communication system for conversation between a control point at the Fire and Rescue Service access level and the fire warden on every storey.

The recommendations on phased evacuation in BS 5839-1 should be followed. Any voice alarm should comply with BS 5839-8:1998.

The minimum width for a stair, W, can be determined from Table B.16 or calculated from the formula:

$$W = [(P \times 10) - 100]\text{mm}$$

where:
P represents the number of people in the most heavily occupied storey.

Table B.16 Minimum stair widths for phased evacuation	
Maximum number of people in any storey	Stair width (mm)
100	1000
120	1100
130	1200
140	1300
150	1400
160	1500
170	1600
180	1700
190	1800

For buildings over 30m in height evacuation may be impeded by firefighters entering the building; that possibility can be addressed by appropriate evacuation procedures, but in buildings over 45m other measures may be necessary – for example discounting a stair.

Further guidance
BS 5839-1 and -8:1998. [See **B.3.2.1**.]

B.3.5.3 Protection of escape stairs

Internal escape stairs should be protected stairs within a fire-resisting enclosure. There may be more onerous requirements if the stairs are within a protected shaft which penetrates compartment floors, or a firefighting shaft. Unprotected stairs may form part of an internal route to a storey exit or to a final exit, provided the travel distances are short and number of people will be limited.

In small premises other than a bar or restaurant, a stair may be open if:

- it does not connect more than two storeys and delivers into the ground storey not more than 3m from final exit, and the storey is also served by protected stairway; or

- it is a single stair in small premises, where no storey has a floor area greater than 90m², and, where there are three storeys, the stair serving the top or bottom storey is enclosed at the ground storey with fire-resisting construction, and discharges to final exit independent of ground storey (Figure B.8).

Access lobbies and corridors

Escape stairs should have protected lobbies or corridors at all levels, except the top storey and at all basement levels, where:

- the stair is the only one serving the building (or part of the building) with more than one storey above or below ground storey (excluding small premises);

- the stair serves a storey more than 18m above ground;

- the building is designed for phased evacuation;

- the stair is a firefighting stair;

- a stair is not being discounted in calculating stair widths;

- a place of special fire hazard adjoins the stair – a 0.4m² vent or mechanical smoke control will also be required.

Figure B.8 Single stairs in small premises

a. FIRST STOREY

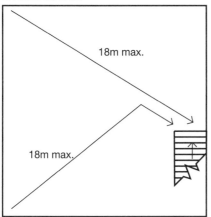

a. FIRST STOREY

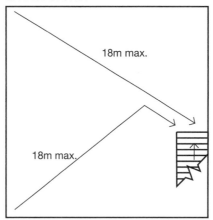

b. GROUND STOREY

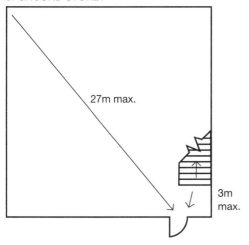

b. GROUND STOREY

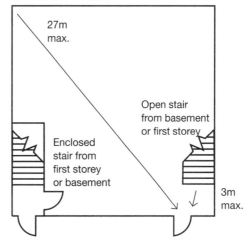

c. BASEMENT

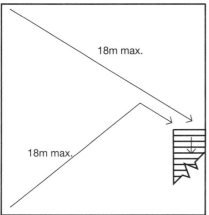

c. BASEMENT

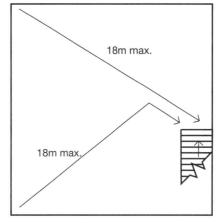

Note 1: Maximum floor area in any one storey 90m².
Note 2: The premises may not be used as a restaurant or bar.
Note 3: Only acceptable in two-storey premises (a+b or b+c).
Note 4: Travel distances are set out in Table B.13.

Note 1: Maximum floor area in any one storey 90m².
Note 2: Enclosed stair at ground storey level may be from
either the basement or the first storey.
Note 3: The premises may not be used as a restaurant or bar.
Note 4: Travel distances are set out in Table B.13.

For the first three situations a smoke control system may provide a suitable alternative.

Protected stairways should discharge to the final exit either directly or through a protected exit with the same standard of fire protection (**B.3.3.2**). Adjacent protected stairways and their exit passageways should be separated by an imperforate enclosure. External sides of the enclosure may also have to be fire-resisting where they are close to other, unprotected parts of the building (**B.3.3.4**).

Use of space

To keep protected stairways free of potential sources of fire they may only contain:

- sanitary accommodation – but not a cloakroom;
- a lift well – but not in a firefighting stair;
- a reception or enquiry desk/area not more than 10m², provided the stair is not the only one to the building;
- cupboards enclosed in fire-resisting construction, provided the stair is not the only one to the building.

A protected stairway may only contain gas service and installation pipes where the installation complies with the Pipelines Safety Regulations 1996 (SI 1996:825) and the Gas Safety Regulations 1998 (SI 1998:2451). For a stairway within a protected shaft the requirements of **B.5.2.3** will also apply.

Basement stairs

Because basement stairs are at a greater risk of filling with smoke and heat, any escape stair forming part of the sole escape route should not continue to the basement. Where there are multiple escape routes, one stair must terminate at ground floor level; other stairs may connect with the basement provided a protected lobby or protected corridor separates the stairs and accommodation at each basement level.

External stairs

Where there is more than one escape route, one route or part of a route may be formed by an external escape stair if:

- there is at least one internal stair from every part of each storey; and
- in an assembly and recreation building the route is not intended for use by the public; or
- in an institutional building, the route serves only office or residential staff accommodation.

The external stair should comply with **B.3.3.4** and **B.3.3.5**.

B.3.5.4 Refuges

Refuges are intended to provide relatively safe waiting areas for short periods for disabled people – particularly wheelchair users. They are not intended for leaving disabled people alone indefinitely.

There should be a refuge for each protected stairway which provides an exit from the storey, except storeys which consist only of plant rooms. There is no need to provide a refuge for each wheelchair user who may be present in the building because, during evacuation, successive wheelchair users may occupy the same refuge.

A refuge need not be within the stair enclosure, but should give suitable direct access to the stair. It may be formed by:

- an enclosure such as a compartment, protected lobby or protected stairway (Figure B.9);

- an area in the open air – such as a flat roof, balcony, podium – which is sufficiently protected or remote from risk, and has its own means of escape.

Figure B.9 Refuge formed by protected stairway

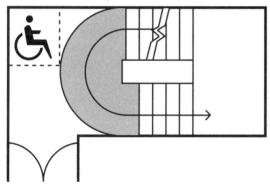

Provision where access to the wheelchair space is counter to the access flow within the stairway

 Wheelchair space

 Occupied by escape flow

Each refuge should:

- Provide a wheelchair-accessible area 900mm × 1400mm – A refuge in a protected stairway or lobby should not reduce the width of the escape route or impede the escape flow.

- Be clearly marked – In a lobby or stairway the sign should be accompanied by a blue mandatory sign worded: 'Refuge – keep clear'.

- Have an Emergency Voice Communication (EVC) system which complies with BS 5839-9:2003, with type B outstations communicating with a master station in the building control room or adjacent to the fire alarm panel. In some buildings wireless systems may be more suitable.

Further guidance
BS 5839-9:2003. Fire detection and alarm systems for buildings. Code of practice for the design, installation, commissioning and maintenance of emergency voice communication systems. [Withdrawn, replaced by 2011 edition.]

B.3.6 Escape from dwellinghouses and flats

B.3.6.1 Common provisions

Emergency egress windows or external doors

Any window for emergency egress or any external door for escape should:

- have an unobstructed openable area of 0.33m², with minimum dimensions of 450mm × 450mm (which may be measured at an angle);
- enable anyone escaping to reach a place free from danger of fire. A courtyard or inaccessible back garden should be at least as deep as the height of the dwellinghouse to be acceptable (Figure B.10).

The bottom of an escape window must be no more than 1100mm above the floor, but must comply with the minimum guarding height of 800mm (600mm for roof windows) in Part K (**K.3**). Windows should be designed to remain open without needing to be held and may be fitted with locks and stays, so long as any stay has a release catch.

Figure B.10 Exit into a controlled space

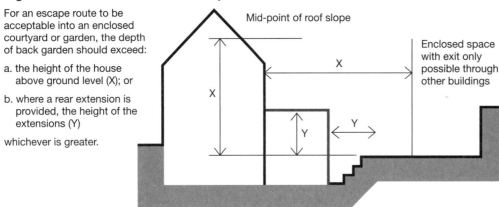

For an escape route to be acceptable into an enclosed courtyard or garden, the depth of back garden should exceed:

a. the height of the house above ground level (X); or

b. where a rear extension is provided, the height of the extensions (Y)

whichever is greater.

Mid-point of roof slope

Enclosed space with exit only possible through other buildings

Inner rooms

An inner room where the only escape route goes through another room presents a risk of trapping if fire starts in that access room. An inner room is only permitted where it is:

- a kitchen;
- a laundry or utility room;
- a dressing room;
- a bathroom, shower, or WC;
- on a floor not more than 4.5m above ground level and has an emergency egress window;
- a gallery which complies with the conditions below.

An inner-inner room (that is, an inner room accessed via an inner room) is acceptable if:

- it is one of those listed above; and
- is separated from an interlinked fire alarm by no more than one door; and none of the access rooms is a kitchen.

Galleries

Galleries should either:

- have an alternative exit; or

- an emergency egress window, provided the gallery floor is no more than 4.5m above ground; or

- meet all the following criteria:
  - the gallery should overlook 50% of the room;
  - the foot of the access stair should be within 3m of the door to the room;
  - all the gallery should be within 7.5m of the head of the access stair;
  - any cooking facilities should be enclosed in fire-resisting construction or remote from the stair.

Basements

Basement storeys which contain habitable rooms should have either:

- an external escape door or window to the basement; or

- a protected stairway leading from the basement to a final exit.

Flat roofs and balconies

Where a flat roof forms part of a means of escape:

- it should be part of the same building as that from which the escape is being made;

- the route should lead to a storey exit or external escape route;

- the part of the roof forming the escape route and within 3m of it, together with the supporting structure, should offer 30 minutes' fire resistance.

Protected stairways

Cavity barriers or fire-resistant ceilings should be provided above the enclosures to a protected stairway.

External escape stairs

External escape stairs should comply with **B.3.3.4**.

Air circulation systems

An air circulation system in an individual flat or dwellinghouse must not permit smoke or fire to spread to an internal protected stairway or entrance hall.

- Walls, doors, floors and ceilings enclosing the protected place should not contain transfer grilles.

- Ducts passing through the enclosure should be of rigid steel, with firestopped joints between the ductwork and enclosure.

- Ducts supplying the protected enclosure should not serve other areas.

- Recirculating mechanical ventilation systems that supply the protected enclosure and other areas should shut down on the detection of smoke within the system.

- Ducted warm air systems should have a thermostat which should be mounted in the living room at 1370–1830mm from the floor, with a maximum setting of 27°C.

- Ventilation ducts passing through compartment walls should comply with **B.5.4.2**.

B.3.6.2 Escape from dwellinghouses

The escape provisions for dwellinghouses are straightforward for one- and two-storey dwellings, but become more complex at greater heights as escape through emergency windows becomes more hazardous. Above 7.5m there is the further risk of stairs becoming impassable before occupants of upper storeys have escaped. The provisions for escape are set out in Table B.17 and Figures B.11 and B.12.

Table B.17 Means of escape from dwellinghouses		
Storey		**Means of escape**
Ground storey		All habitable rooms (excluding kitchens) either: • open directly onto a hall leading to a suitable exit (which may be the building entrance); or • have an emergency egress window or external door.
Upper floors		
Upper floors not more than 4.5m above ground level		All habitable rooms in the upper storey (except kitchens) either: • have an emergency egress window (which may in some circumstances serve two rooms); or • direct access to a protected stairway.
Upper floors more than 4.5m above ground level	One floor more than 4.5m above ground level: • one internal staircase	Dwellinghouse to have either: • a protected staircase (protected at all levels) which either extends to final exit or gives access to two ground level escape routes, separated by fire-resisting construction and fire doors; OR • the top storey should be separated from lower storeys by fire-resisting construction AND have an alternative exit route leading to final exit (**Figure B.12**).
	Two or more floors more than 4.5m above ground level: • one internal staircase	As above, and either: for each floor more than 7.5m above ground level, an alternative escape route with access; • either via the protected stairway to an upper storey; or • a landing within the protected stairway enclosure to an alternative escape route on same storey. AND • protected stairway should be separated by fire-resisting construction from lower storeys; OR • dwellinghouse fitted with sprinklers throughout.
	One or more floors more than 4.5m above ground level AND Dwelling has more than one internal staircase	Stairs must provide effective alternative means of escape and be physically separated. Physical separation may be achieved by fire-resisting construction or by a number of rooms.
	Passenger lifts serving floors more than 4.5m above ground level	Sited within enclosure of a protected stairway or be in a fire-resisting lift shaft.

Figure B.11 Means of escape from dwellinghouses

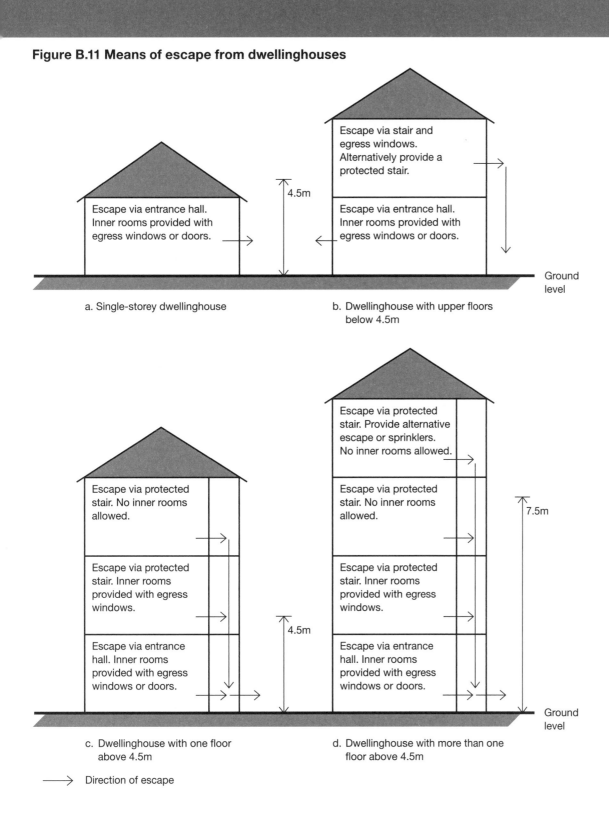

a. Single-storey dwellinghouse

b. Dwellinghouse with upper floors below 4.5m

c. Dwellinghouse with one floor above 4.5m

d. Dwellinghouse with more than one floor above 4.5m

→ Direction of escape

Figure B.12 Alternative arrangements for final exits

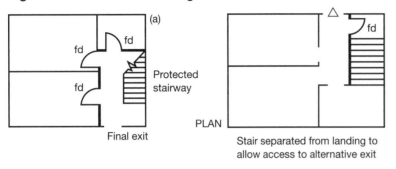

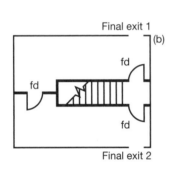

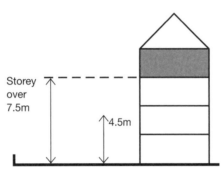

Key
fd   Fire door
━━   30 minute fire-resisting construction
∧   Alternative escape route (see AD Bv1 Appendix E)

B.3.6.3 Work to existing houses

Replacement windows

Where the original window is in a position which would require an escape window in a new dwellinghouse, and is large enough to be used for escape, then the replacement window should be sized to give at least the same escape. If the opening is larger than the requirements for escape it may be reduced in size to that minimum. There may be a need to provide cavity barriers (**B.5.3.3**).

Material alterations

Approved Document B volume 1 states, unhelpfully, that 'reasonable provision' in the event of material alterations 'would depend on the circumstances of the case' and offers some guidance on smoke alarms and loft conversions. Where new habitable rooms are formed smoke alarms should be provided as **B.3.2.3**.

Loft conversions

Where a new storey is provided by conversion the whole escape route should be considered and, where necessary, upgraded. This may require fire-resisting doors and partitions to an existing stair.

Open-plan areas will require new partitions to enclose the escape route, but an alternative solution would be to provide:

• sprinklers to the open-plan area; and

- cooking facilities separated from the open-plan area by fire-resistant construction; and
- a fire-resisting door or partition to separate the ground floor from other storeys, but placed to give the occupants of the loft access to a first floor escape window.

B.3.6.4 Escape from flats

The escape provisions for flats on a floor no more than 4.5m above ground level are relatively straightforward, but become more complex at greater heights as escape through emergency windows becomes more hazardous. The provisions presume:

- the fire is generally in a flat;
- no reliance on external rescue;
- a high degree of compartmentation and low risk of fire spread between flats, to make simultaneous evacuation of the building unlikely;
- fires in common areas are unlikely to spread, given the materials and fabric involved.

Escape is considered in two parts:

- escape from within each flat; then
- escape from each flat to the final exit.

Escape from within each flat

Table B.18 and Figures B.13–15 set out the means of escape required within flats.

Figure B.13 Flats where all habitable rooms have access to entrance hall

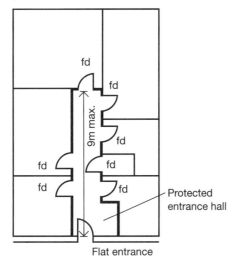

Note: Bathrooms need not have fire doors providing the bathroom is separated by fire-resisting construction from the adjacent rooms.

Key
fd   Fire door
━━   30 minute fire-resisting construction around entrance hall

Table B.18 Means of escape from flats

Floor not more than 4.5m above ground level		Means of escape
	Ground storey	• All habitable rooms open directly onto hall leading to suitable exit; or • All rooms have emergency egress window or external door.
	Upper floors	• All habitable rooms have emergency egress window;[1] or • In multi-storey flat, direct access to protected staircase leading to final exit.
Flats with one floor more than 4.5m above ground level		• All habitable rooms open directly onto a protected hall, with their doors within 9m travel of entrance door (**Figure B.13**); or • Travel distance from any point in habitable rooms to entrance door no more than 9m, and cooking facilities are remote from entrance and do not prejudice escape; or • Provide an alternative exit from the part of the flat containing bedrooms, with bedrooms separated from living accommodation by 30 minute fire-resisting construction and fire doors (**Figure B.14**).
Flats with more than one storey		
	Flats with independent ground floor entrance	As flats with floor not more than 4.5m above ground level.

	Flats with at least one floor more than 4.5m above ground level	• Provide an alternative exit from each habitable room not on entrance floor; or
		• Provide an alternative exit from each floor not on entrance floor, with protected landing entered directly from each habitable room (**Figure B.15**); or
		Where no floor is more than 7.5m above or below floor of entrance storey:
		• Provide a protected stairway plus either:
		  – smoke alarms (**B.3.2.2**) in all habitable rooms and heat alarm in any kitchen; or
		  – sprinkler system (**B.1.8**).

Alternative exits		Remote from entrance door. Lead to final exit or common stairway by: • door to access corridor, access lobby or common balcony; • internal private stair to access corridor or lobby or common balcony at another level; • door into common stair; • door onto external stair; • door onto escape route over a flat roof. And meet appropriate provisions for escape from common parts of building.

[1] In some conditions the window may serve two rooms.

Figure B.14 Flats where all habitable rooms do not have access to entrance hall

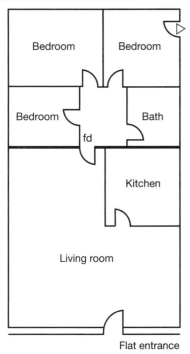

Note: The bedrooms are not classified as inner rooms because escape is possible in two directions.

Key
fd Fire door
━ 30 minute fire-resisting construction between living and bedroom accommodation
△ Alternative exit

Figure B.15 Multi-storey flat with protected entrance hall and landing

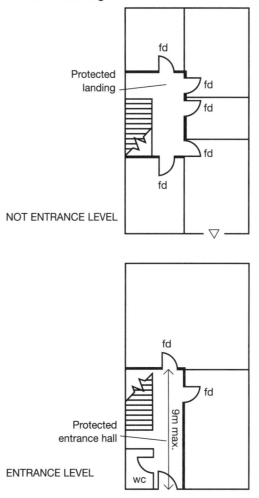

Note: This only applies where at least one storey is more than 4.5m above ground level.

Key
fd Fire door
━ 30 minute fire-resisting stair enclosure
△ Alternative exit

Escape from each flat to the final exit

Each flat should have access to alternative escape routes. Travel distances should not exceed those in Table B.19, and routes should not lead through one stairway enclosure to another, although they may pass through a protected lobby. Common corridors should be protected corridors, with compartment walls separating flats from the corridor. One of the multiple escape routes from storey or building may be over a flat roof, provided the roof complies with **B.3.3.5**.

Those requirements may be modified for flats with a balcony or deck approach, by following the recommendations of BS 5588-1:1990 clause 13, which include the provision of downstands on decks or balconies more than 2m wide in order to prevent the spread of smoke along the deck.

Table B.19 Limitations on travel distance from flat entrance doors		
	Maximum travel distance to common stair or lobby[1] (m)	Notes
Escape in one direction	7.5	4.5m in a building with small single stair building (**Figure B.18**) Not applicable if all flats have independent alternative means of escape: but access requirements for Fire Service may apply (**B.7**)
Escape in more than one direction	30	Not applicable if all flats have independent alternative means of escape: but access requirements for Fire Service may apply (**B.7**) Sheltered housing may require increased provision

[1] Lobby: no access to other flat, storage room or fire hazard.

A single escape route from the flat entrance door is acceptable if:

- each flat served by a common entrance stair is separated from the stair by a common corridor or protected lobby and travel distances in Table B.19 are observed (Figure B.16); or
- it is a flat in the dead end of a corridor which is served by two common stairs and the one-direction travel distance complies with Table B.19 (Figure B.17).

A single stair is acceptable in a small building (Figure B.18), where:

- the top floor is no more than 11m above ground level; and
- there are no more than three storeys above ground level; and
- the stair does not connect to a covered car park (except an open-sided car park); and
- the stair does not serve ancillary accommodation (unless separated by a protected lobby or corridor with either a mechanical smoke control system or at least 0.4m² permanent ventilation); and
- there is ventilation for the use of the Fire and Rescue Service, consisting of either:
  - a high-level openable vent of 1m² minimum free area at each level; or
  - a single openable vent at the head of the stair which is remotely operated at Fire and Rescue Service access level.

Ancillary accommodation such as stores should not be located in, or accessed from, a protected lobby or corridor which forms part of the sole escape route for a flat on that storey.

The requirement for alternative means of escape does not apply to flats where the top floor is less than 4.5m above ground level and which comply with Table B.18 (although requirements regarding compartment walls, protected shafts and access for the Fire and Rescue Service must still be observed).

Figure B.16 Flats served by a common stair

a. CORRIDOR ACCESS DWELLINGS

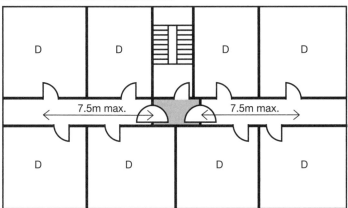

b. LOBBY ACCESS DWELLINGS

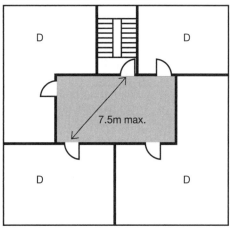

Note:
1.   The arrangements shown also apply to the top storey.
2.   See **Figure B.18** for small single stair buildings.
3.   All doors shown are fire doors.
4.   Where travel distance is measured to a stair lobby, the lobby must not provide direct access to any storage room, flat or other space containing a potential fire hazard.

Key
D   Dwelling
Shaded area indicates zone where ventilation should be provided in accordance with AD Bv2 paragraph 2.26 or 'Smoke control'
(An external wall vent or smoke shaft located anywhere in the shaded area)

Figure B.17 Flats served by more than one common stair

a. CORRIDOR ACCESS WITHOUT DEAD ENDS

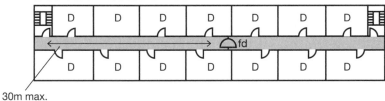

30m max.

c. 'T' JUNCTION WITH MAIN CORRIDOR

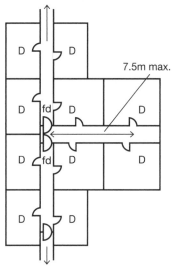

b. CORRIDOR ACCESS WITH DEAD ENDS
The central door may be omitted if maximum travel distance is not more than 15m

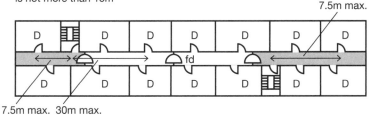

7.5m max. 30m max.

Note:
The arrangements shown also apply to the top storey.

Key
D   Dwelling
fd   Fire door
Shaded area indicates zone where ventilation should be provided in accordance with AD Bv2 paragraph 2.26 or 'Smoke control'
(An external wall vent or smoke shaft located anywhere in the shaded area)

Figure B.18 Common escape route in small single stair building

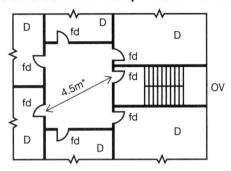

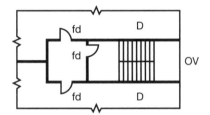

a. SMALL SINGLE STAIR BUILDING
*If smoke control is provided in the lobby, the travel distance can be increased to 7.5m maximum (see Figure B.16, example b).

b. SMALL SINGLE STAIR BUILDING WITH NO MORE THAN 2 DWELLINGS PER STOREY
The door between stair and lobby should be free from security fastenings.

If the dwellings have protected entrance halls, the lobby between the common stair and dwelling entrance is not essential.

Notes:
1. The arrangements shown also apply to the top storey.
2. If the travel distance across the lobby in Figure B.18a exceeds 4.5m, Figure B.16 applies.
3. Where, in Figure B.18b, the lobby between the common stair and the dwelling is omitted in small single stair buildings, an automatic opening vent with a geometric free area of at least 1.0m^2 is required at the top of the stair, to be operated on detection of smoke at any storey in the stair.

Key
— Fire-resisting construction
OV Openable vent at high level for fire service use (1.0m^2 minimum free area) see AD Bv2 paragraph 2.21e or see 'Escape from each flat to the final exit'
D Dwelling
fd Fire door

Smoke control

The spread of smoke to stairs from common areas must be controlled either by mechanical ventilation (BS EN 12101-6:2005) or by natural ventilation. Natural ventilation requires:

*   a vent of 1m^2 free area from the top of the stairway to outside;

*   a vent from each corridor or lobby adjoining a common stair, sited as high as practicable (and at least with the top edge as high as the top of the door to the stair).

Vents from corridors/lobbies should either:

*   be on the external wall with 1.5m^2 free area; or

*   should discharge to a vertical smoke shaft which complies with Table B.20.

These ventilation provisions do not apply to small single-stair buildings which comply with Figure B.18.

In single-stair buildings, vents on the fire floor and at the head of the stair should be actuated by smoke detectors in the common access space. In multiple-stair buildings vents may be manually actuated, but the controls should ensure that the vent at the top of the stair opens before or at the same time as the vents on the fire floor.

Table B.20 Requirements for smoke shafts

Specification	Requirements
Arrangement	Closed at base Vertical (a deviation of up to 30° permitted for no more than 4m)
Construction	Shaft of non-combustible materials Vents with fire/smoke performance equivalent to E30Sa fire door
Cross-sectional area (minimum) Minimum dimension	1.5m² 0.85m
Height	At least 2.5m above ceiling of highest storey served
Roof level opening	At least 0.5m above any surround structure within 2m
Free area of vents and opening at head of shaft	1m²
Activation	On detection of smoke in the common corridor/lobby the vents on the fire floor and at the top of the shaft should open. All other vents should remain closed

A common corridor which connects two or more storey exits should be sub-divided with self-closing fire doors, which may be set in a fire-resisting screen. Door(s) should be positioned so smoke will not affect access to more than one stairway. A dead end should be separated from the rest of the corridor with a self-closing fire door.

B.3.6.5 Common stairs

Width

Stairs of 'acceptable width for every day use' (AD B volume 2, para. 2.33) will be wide enough for escape, although if they also serve as firefighting stairs they should be at least 1100mm wide.

Protection

Common stairs should be protected stairways within fire-resisting enclosures to Tables B.2 and B.3 (see also **B.5.2.3** for limiting the spread of fire between floors). Firefighting stairs should comply with **B.7.3.1**. Adjoining stairways and/or exit passageways should be separated by an imperforate enclosure. Protected stairways should discharge to a final exit either directly or through a protected exit passageway with the same standard of fire protection. Basement stairs should follow **B.3.5.3**.

Protected stairways must be relatively free of potential sources of fire. They should contain only a lift well (**B.3.3.6**) or electricity meters. In buildings with a single stair, meters should be sited within a secure cupboard which has fire-resisting construction to the escape side. Gas services should comply with **B.3.5.3**.

Ancillary accommodation

A common stair which forms part of the only escape route from a flat should not serve places of fire risk such as covered car parks, boiler rooms or fuel stores. (Small single-stair buildings are exempt from that requirement.) A common stair which is not part of the only escape route may serve such ancillary accommodation provided it is separated by a protected lobby or corridor. Where the stair serves an enclosed car park or a place of special fire hazard then the

Further guidance
BS 5588-1:1990. Fire precautions in the design, construction and use of buildings. Code of practice for residential buildings. [Withdrawn, replaced by BS 9991:2011. Fire safety in the design, management and use of residential buildings. Code of practice.]

BS EN 12101-6:2005. Smoke and heat control systems. Specification for pressure differential systems. Kits.

lobby or corridor requires either 0.4m² permanent ventilation or a mechanical smoke control system.

External escape stairs

An external escape stair is permitted for a building with a single stair provided it serves no floor more than 6m above ground level. Where there are multiple escape stairs, one may be an external stair, provided:

- there is an internal escape stair from every storey; and
- the external stair serves no floor more than 6m above either ground level or a roof or podium served by an independent protected escape stair.

External escape stairs should comply with **B.3.3.4**.

Mixed use buildings

In mixed use buildings with no more than three storeys above the ground storey the same stairs can serve flats and other occupancies, provided they are separated from each occupancy by protected lobbies at all levels.

Otherwise, stairs can serve both flats and other occupancies, provided:

- the flat is ancillary to the main use and has an independent alternative escape route; and
- the stair is separated from other occupancies on the lower storeys by protected lobbies at those levels; and
- the fire detection and alarm system covers the flat as well as the main building; and
- security measures do not prevent escape.

There may be a need for increased fire resistance between a flat and any fuel storage area.

B.3.6.6 Live/work units

Where a flat serves as a workplace both for the occupants and for others who do not live there, additional provisions apply:

- The maximum distance from the work area to the flat entrance door or alternative means of escape (but not a window) is 18m.
- Windowless accommodation should have escape lighting which illuminates the escape route if the main supply fails (see BS 5266-1:2005).

Where the requirement for the escape distance cannot be met it is likely that the general assumptions for flats are inappropriate.

Further guidance

BS 5266-1:2005. Emergency lighting. Code of practice for the emergency lighting of premises.

B.4 Internal fire spread (linings) (Requirement B2)

Although linings are unlikely to be the first materials to be ignited in a fire, they can make a substantial difference to the rate at which the fire spreads. In circulation routes, linings may be the main means of spread. To inhibit fire spread, the linings of walls, partitions, ceilings and other internal structures must:

- resist the spread of flame over their surfaces; and
- have a low rate of heat release or fire growth if ignited.

There are no requirements for the surfaces of floors and stairs because they play little part in the early spread of a fire, although the construction of stairs and landings may be affected by **B.3.3.4** and **B.7.3**.

B.4.1 Wall and ceiling linings

The linings of walls and floors (as defined in Table B.21) should comply with the performance requirements of Table B.22. Rooflights should also comply with Table B.22, but rooflights to Class 3 may be used even where their performance is poorer than required by Table B.22, so long as they comply with Tables B.34 and B.44.

Thermoplastic materials which do not meet the performance standards required by Table B.22 can be used, subject to the provisions in Tables B.23 and B.24 and Figure B.19. Flexible membranes should comply with Appendix A of BS 7157:1989. For PTFE membrane in tension-membrane roofs and structures see BR 274.

2013 changes
Decorative wall claddings rated Class O under the national classification system tend to be rated Class C under the European classification system. As that presents a disincentive to adopt the European system the provisions have been modified to allow the use of Class C wall coverings bonded to Class A2 substrates. This has been done by adding an additional footnote to Table B.22 (based on AD B V2 table 11).

In order to allow for more energy efficient lighting layouts, whilst maintaining reasonable standards of fire safety, the limitations on the use of TPb materials have been revised. Table B.24 (based on AD B V2 Table 11) now includes an additional line for smaller panels, and is supported by a new Figure B.19b (based on AD B V2 Diagram 27A).

Further guidance
BS 7157:1989. Method of test for ignitability of fabrics used in the construction of large tented structures.

BR 274. *Fire safety of PTFE-based materials used in buildings*. BRE. 1994.

BS EN 15102:2007. Decorative wall coverings–roll and panel form products.

Table B.21 Linings of walls and ceilings	Walls	Ceilings
Includes	The wall surface The surface of glazing (except glazing in doors) Any part of a ceiling at more than 70° to horizontal	The ceiling surface The surface of glazing Any part of a wall at less than 70° to horizontal Underside of a mezzanine floor or gallery Underside of roof exposed to the room below
Excludes	Doors and their frames Window frames and frames in which glazing is fitted Architraves, cover moulds, skirting boards and similar thin members Fire surrounds, mantle shelves and fitted furniture	Trap doors and their frames Frames of windows and rooflights Architraves, cover moulds, skirting boards and similar thin members
Variations	Poorer performance than **Table B.22** is permitted, if: • no worse than Class 3/D-s3,s2;a and, • area is no more than half of floor area; and • area is no more than 20m² in residential; or • area is no more than 60m² in non-residential.	A suspended ceiling can contribute to the overall fire resistance of a ceiling or floor: it should comply with **Table B.22** and AD Bv2 Table A.3. A fire-resistant ceiling can also reduce the use of any cavity barriers which would otherwise be required (**B.5.3.1**)

Table B.22 Classification of wall and floor linings

Location	National class	European class
Small rooms of area no more than: • 4m² in residential accommodation • 30m² in non-residential accommodation	3	D-s3,d2
Domestic garages <40m²	3	D-s3,d2
Other rooms (including garages)	1	C-s3,d2
Circulation spaces within dwellings	1	C-s3.d2
Other circulation spaces inc. common areas of blocks of flats	0	B-s3,d2*

Note: s3,d2 = no limit for smoke production and/or flaming droplets/particles.

*This includes decorative wall coverings which conform to BS EN 15102:2007 and achieve at least Class C-s3,d2 and are bonded to a Class A2-s3,d2 substrate.

Table B.23 Use of thermoplastic materials

Item	Conditions for acceptability
External windows	Material classified as TP(a) rigid.
Rooflights	Lower surface classified as TP(a) rigid or TP(b). Size and layout of rooflights as **Table B.24**.
Lighting diffusers forming part of a ceiling[1][2]	The surfaces of walls and ceilings above the suspended ceiling to comply with **Table B.22**. Size and layout of rooflights as **Table B.24**.
Suspended or stretched skin ceilings	Material classified as TP(a) flexible. Each panel should be supported on all sides, and not exceed 5m².

[1] Can only be used in fire-resisting ceiling if the whole assembly has been tested for fire resistance.

[2] No restriction when the diffuser forms part of a lighting unit below the ceiling.

Table B.24 Limitations on thermoplastic rooflights and diffusers

Condition/use of space	Classification of inner/lower surface	Maximum area of each panel or rooflight (m²)	Maximum total area of panels/rooflights as % of floor area (%)	Minimum separation between panels or rooflights (m)
Rooms	TP(a) rigid	No limits	No limits	No limits
	D-s3,d2/TP(b)/Class 3	5	50	3 (see **Figure B.19a**)
		1	50	A distance equal to the largest plan dimension of the largest diffuser or rooflight (see **Figure B.19b**)
Circulation spaces	TP(a) rigid	No limits	No limits	No limits
	D-s3,d2/TP(b)/Class 3	5	15	3
Protected stairways	None permitted	N/A	N/A	N/A

Notes:

(1) Walls and ceilings exposed above luminaires to comply with Table B.32 according to the space below.

(2) Class 3/D-s3,d2 rooflights to rooms in industrial and other non-residential purpose groups may be spaced 1800mm apart, provided they are evenly spaced and do not exceed 20% of the room's floor area.

Figure B.19a Layout restrictions

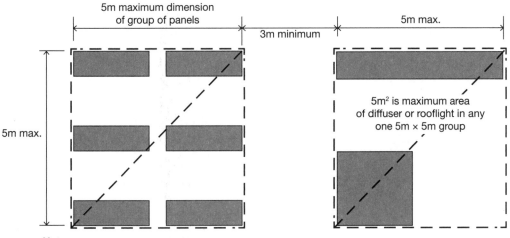

Notes:
a   No restriction on Class 3 rooflights in small rooms
b   See second note on Table B.24

Figure B.19b Layout restrictions on small rooflights and light diffusers

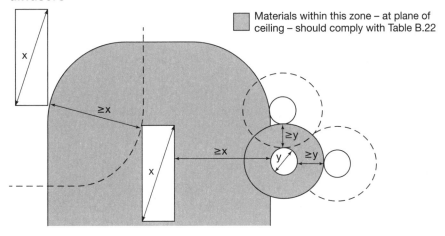

Materials within this zone – at plane of ceiling – should comply with Table B.22

B.5 Internal fire spread (structure) (Requirement B3)

The structural requirements for controlling internal fire spread are intended to ensure that buildings retain their stability in event of fire, to inhibit the spread of fire between parts of the same building and to resist the spread of fire between buildings, including between semi-detached and terraced houses.

Key provisions include:

• ensuring loadbearing elements can withstand the effects of fire for appropriate periods of time without loss of stability (**B.5.1**);

• sub-dividing the building into compartments with fire-resisting construction (**B.5.2**);

- protecting openings in fire-resisting elements (**B.5.2.2**);
- inhibiting unseen spread of fire and smoke within concealed spaces (**B.5.3**).

There are particular requirements for car parks (**B.5.5**) and shopping complexes (**B.5.6**).

B.5.1 Loadbearing elements of structure

Elements of loadbearing structure should have adequate resistance to collapse, in order to prevent premature failure and to:

- minimise the risk to those occupants who may still be inside the building while evacuation proceeds;
- reduce the risk to firefighters engaged in search and rescue operations;
- reduce the danger to people in the vicinity of the building who might be injured by debris or in the collapse of adjoining buildings.

Elements of structure should therefore have fire resistance to the standards of Tables B.2 and B.3. Elements which support or give stability to other elements must have fire resistance no less than the elements they support or stabilise. An element common to more than one building or compartment must be constructed to the highest of any applicable standards.

Elements of structure include:

- a member which forms part of the structural frame of a building, or any other column or beam;
- a loadbearing wall or part of a loadbearing wall;
- a floor;
- a gallery;
- an external wall;
- a compartment wall, including one common to two or more buildings.

The following are not considered elements of structure:

- a structure which only supports a roof – unless the roof performs as a floor for parking, or as means of escape, or provides stability for an external wall which requires fire resistance;
- the lowest floor of a building;
- a platform floor;
- galleries such as loading galleries, fly galleries and lighting bridges, or similar structures used for maintenance and repair.

B.5.1.1 Raised storage areas

A raised, free-standing storage area within a single-storey building which would normally have to comply with Table B.2 need not do so if it meets all the following conditions:

- it has one tier;
- it is used only for storage;
- it is only used by low numbers of people and there is no public access;
- it occupies no more than half of the floor area;
- it is open above and below to the space;

- it has an appropriate means of escape; and
- it is not more than 10m in either length or width (20m if lower level has automatic detection and alarm system to BS 5839-1:2002). Where sprinklers are fitted those size limits do not apply, although the safety of firefighters must still be considered.

B.5.1.2 Flats formed by conversion

Retained timber floors may be difficult to upgrade to the standards in Table B.2. Consequently, 30 minutes' fire resistance will be acceptable for elements of structure, provided the building is no more than three storeys high and has suitable means of escape. Elements in buildings of four or more storeys must meet Table B.2.

B.5.1.3 Loft conversions in dwellinghouses

Where an existing two-storey dwellinghouse is being altered by the addition of a further storey, all new and existing floors should have full 30 minutes' fire resistance (Table B.2). However, the existing first floor construction may have lower standards of integrity and insulation, where:

- there is only one new storey containing one or two habitable rooms; and
- the total floor area is less than 50m²; and
- the floor separates rooms not circulation spaces.

That concession does not apply to the floor which forms part of the enclosure to the circulation space between loft and the final exit.

Further guidance
BS 5839-1:2002. [See **B.3.2.1**.]

B.5.2 Compartmentation

Buildings may need to be sub-divided into a number of compartments separated by fire-resisting walls and floors to prevent occupants being trapped by the rapid spread of fire, and to reduce the likelihood of a fire becoming large. The number and size of such compartments is governed by:

- the use and fire load of the building – which affects the potential for fires and their severity;
- the height to the floor of the top storey – which affects the ease of evacuation and Fire and Rescue Service intervention;
- the presence of sprinkler systems to limit the rate at which a fire grows.

Buildings should be divided into compartments with compartment walls and/or floors to meet Tables B.25 and B.26.

Protected shafts are spaces such as stairways and service shafts that connect compartments and must therefore restrict fire spread between them. Any wall or floor bounding a protected shaft is considered a compartment wall or floor.

B.5.2.1 Construction of compartment walls and floors

Compartment walls and floors should form a complete barrier between the compartments and have the appropriate fire resistance to Tables B.2 and B.3. Compartment walls should run the full height of each storey and those in the top storey should be continued through the roof space. Where they are common to two or more buildings, or used to separate parts of the building which have different fire requirements, they should run the full height of the building in a vertical plane.

Table B.25 Provision of compartmentation

Condition	Requirement	Exemptions
Wall common to two or more buildings, including semi-detached and terraced houses	Constructed as compartment wall.	
Domestic garage – integral or attached	Separated from rest of house by compartment walls and/or floors. Door openings should either be 100mm above garage floor level or garage floor laid to falls away from door.	
Flats	Separated from each other by compartment floors.	A floor within an individual dwelling.
	Separated from other parts of building by compartment walls.	A wall between a flat and an external balcony or deck access.
	Walls enclosing refuse storage chambers to be compartment walls.	
Institutional buildings, including healthcare	All floors to be compartment floors.	
Other residential buildings	All floors to be compartment floors.	
Parts of building occupied for different purposes	Separated by compartment walls and/or floors.	Where one of the purposes is ancillary to the other.
Shopping complexes	Walls and floors which BS 5588-10:1991 section 5 requires to be compartment walls and floors.	
Shops, commercial, industrial or storage premises	Walls and floors which divide building into separate occupancies to be separated by compartment walls and floors, irrespective of whether in the same Purpose Group.	Two-storey buildings in shop, commercial and industrial PG may be treated as a single storey for compartmentation purposes if the upper storey is compartmented from the lower, has escape routes independent from lower and area does not exceed 20% of ground storey and 500m².
Non-residential building, a floor at more than 30m above ground level	All floors must be compartment floors.	Atrium buildings to follow appropriate guidance in BS 5588-7.
Non-residential with no floor more than 30m above ground level	Floor of the ground storey to be a compartment floor.	Buildings without basements.
	Floor of every basement storey (except lowest) to be compartment floors.	Buildings with basement floor less than 10m below ground level.
Non-residential buildings	Compartments to be limited to sizes in **Table B.26**.	
Places of special fire hazard	To be enclosed by fire-resisting construction.	

Construction

Timber members may be carried through masonry or concrete walls, but openings should be as small as practicable and fire stopped. Trussed rafters may bridge a wall, but failure of part of the truss in one compartment must not cause failure in another compartment. Services built into walls should not risk fire developing or spreading prematurely.

Table B.26 Sizing of compartments			
Purpose Group of building or part	**Height of top storey above ground level (m)**	**Floor areas of any one storey in the building or any one storey in a compartment (m²)**	
		In multi-storey buildings	In single-storey buildings
Office	No limit	No limit	No limit
Assembly and recreation, shops and commercial			
a. Shops – not sprinklered	No limit	2000	2000
Shops – sprinklered[1]	No limit	4000	No limit
b. Elsewhere – not sprinklered	No limit	2000	No limit
Elsewhere – sprinklered[1]	No limit	4000	No limit
Industrial[2] Not sprinklered	Not more than 18 More than 18	7000 2000[3]	No limit N/A
Sprinklered[1]	Not more than 18 More than 18	14,000 4000[3]	No limit N/A
	Height of top storey above ground level (m)	**Maximum compartment volume (m³)**	**Maximum floor area (m²)** / **Maximum height (m)[4]**

	Height of top storey above ground level (m)	**Maximum compartment volume (m³)**	**Maximum floor area (m²)**	**Maximum height (m)[4]**
		Multi-storey buildings	Single-storey buildings	
Storage[2] and other non-residential a. Car park for light vehicles	No limit	No limit	No limit	No limit
b. Any other building or part: Not sprinklered	Not more than 18 More than 18	20,000 4000[3]	20,000 N/A	18 N/A
Sprinklered[1]	Not more than 18 More than 18	40,000 8000[3]	No limit	No limit

[1] 'Sprinklered' means that the building is fitted throughout with an automatic sprinkler in accordance with **B.1.8**.

[2] There may be additional limitations on floor area and/or sprinkler provisions in certain industrial and storage uses under other legislation, for example in respect of storage of LPG and certain chemicals.

[3] This reduced limit applies only to storeys that are more than 8m above ground level. Below this height the higher limit applies.

[4] Compartment height is measured from finished floor level to underside of roof or ceiling.

Junctions with other walls and floors

The junctions between a compartment wall and/or floor and another compartment wall or external wall should maintain the fire resistance of the compartment, with fire stopping as **B.5.4**. Where the external wall has no fire stopping it should be restrained to reduce movement away from the floor in the event of fire.

Compartment walls should accommodate the deflection of the floor above, either by a deflection head to maintain integrity or by constructing a wall to resist the additional load from the sagging floor.

Junctions with roofs

Compartment walls should be taken to the underside of the roof covering or deck. Junctions should be fire stopped. To prevent fire spreading between

Figure B.20 Junction of compartment wall with roof

a. ANY BUILDING OR COMPARTMENT

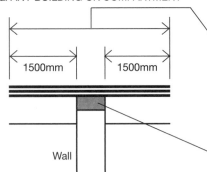

1500mm | 1500mm

Wall

Roof covering over this distance to be designated AA, AB or AC on deck of material of limited combustibility. Roof covering and deck could be composite structure, e.g. profiled steel cladding.

Double-skinned insulated roof sheeting should incorporate a band of material of limited combustibility at least 300mm wide centred over the wall.

If roof support members pass through the wall, fire protection to these members for a distance of 1500mm on either side of the wall may be needed to delay distortion at the junction (see B.5.2.1 Construction).

Resilient fire-stopping to be carried up to underside of roof covering, e.g. roof tiles.

b. RESIDENTIAL (NOT INSTITUTIONAL), OFFICE OR ASSEMBLY USE AND NOT MORE THAN 15M HIGH

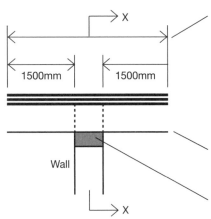

X

1500mm | 1500mm

Wall

X

Roof covering to be designated AA, AB or AC for at least this distance.

Boarding (used as a substrate), wood wool slabs or timber tiling battens may be carried over the wall provided that they are fully bedded in mortar (or other no less suitable material) where over the wall.

Thermoplastic insulation materials should not be carried over the wall.

Double-skinned insulated roof sheeting with a thermoplastic core should incorporate a band of material of limited combustibility at least 300mm wide centred over the wall.

Sarking felt may also be carried over the wall.

If roof support members pass through the wall, fire protection to these members for a distance of 1500mm on either side of the wall may be needed to delay distortion at the junction (see **B.5.2.1** Construction).

Fire-stopping to be carried up to underside of roof covering, boarding or slab.

Section X–X

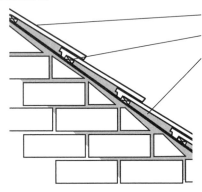

Roof covering to be designated AA, AB or AC for at least 1500mm either side of wall.

Roofing battens and sarking felt may be carried over the wall.

Fire-stopping to be carried up to underside of roof covering. Above and below sarking felt.

Notes:
1 Fire-stopping should be carried over the full thickness of the wall.
2 Fire-stopping should be extended into any eaves.
3 The compartment wall need not necessarily be constructed of masonry.

c. ANY BUILDING OR COMPARTMENT

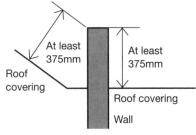

At least 375mm

At least 375mm

Roof covering

Roof covering

Wall

The wall should be extended up through the roof for a height of at least 375mm above the top surface of the adjoining roof covering.

Where there is a height difference of at least 375mm between two roofs or where the roof coverings on either side of the wall are AA, AB or AC the height of the upstand/parapet wall above the highest roof may be reduced to 200mm.

compartments across the roof surface the roof covering within 1500mm of both sides of the compartment wall must have a fire classification of AA, AB or AC (**B.2.2**) and have a substrate or deck of limited combustibility (Figure B.20). Rooflights classified to AA or B_{ROOF}(t4) are not suitable. Alternatively, the compartment wall may be carried through the roof to terminate at least 375mm above the external surface of the roof.

Where the building is less than 15m high – and is for residential (not institutional), office, or assembly and recreation Purpose Groups – some combustible materials (such as, boarding used for substrate, wood wool slabs, tiling battens) can be carried over the compartment wall, provided they are well bedded in mortar or the like for the width of the wall.

Double-skinned roof panels with a thermoplastic core need a band of limited combustibility at least 300mm wide, centred over the wall.

B.5.2.2 Openings in compartment walls

Openings in a compartment wall common to two buildings, or between different occupancies, should be limited to:

- a door which is needed to provide a means of escape, which has the same fire resistance as the wall (see AD vol 2, Table B1) and fitted as **B.2.4**;
- a pipe, which meets **B.5.4**.

Openings in other compartment walls or floors should be limited to:

- doors, with appropriate fire resistance (see AD vol 2, Table B1);
- pipes, ventilation ducts, service cables and the like (**B.5.4**);
- refuse chutes of non-combustible construction;
- atria to BS 5588-7:1997;
- protected shafts.

Further guidance
BS 5588-7:1997. [See **B.3.6.4**.]

B.5.2.3 Protected shafts

A protected shaft should form a complete barrier between the compartments it connects, and should have fire resistance to Tables B.2 and B.3. The enclosure may include an uninsulated glazed screen between the stair and an adjoining lobby or corridor, provided:

- the stair enclosure requires no more than 60 minutes' fire resistance; and
- the screen has 30 minutes' integrity; and
- the area of glazing conforms with Table B.7; and
- the lobby/corridor has 30 minutes' resistance.

A protected shaft may contain:

- stairs;
- lifts;
- escalators;
- sanitary accommodation;
- washrooms;
- chutes;

- ducts, but not a ventilating duct, other than for pressurising or ventilating the stairway;
- pipes, but not one conveying oil.

Any natural gas or LPG pipes within a protected shaft should be of screwed or welded steel construction and the shaft should be ventilated to outside air, with openings top and bottom. The storey floor must not obstruct free movement of air.

Openings

A wall to a protected shaft which is also a compartment wall may only have openings in accordance with **B.5.2.2**. Other parts of the enclosure may have openings only for:

Figure B.21 Provisions for cavity barriers

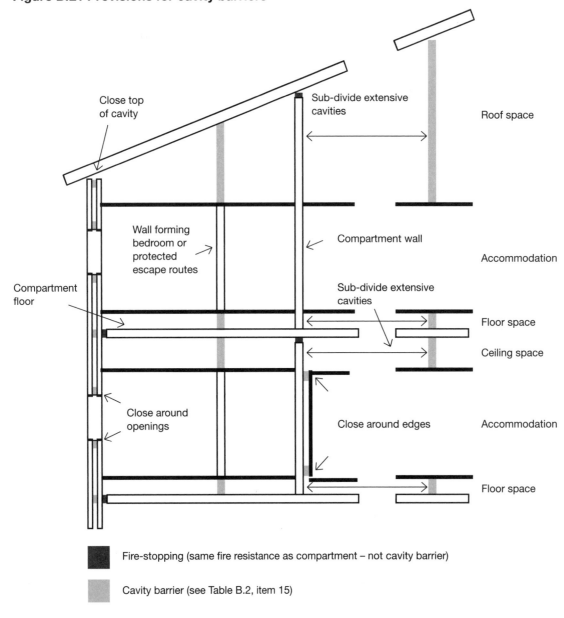

Fire-stopping (same fire resistance as compartment – not cavity barrier)

Cavity barrier (see Table B.2, item 15)

- doors with appropriate fire resistance (see AD vol 2, Table B1);
- pipes with protected openings (**B.5.4.1**);
- inlets, outlets and openings for ventilation ducts (**B.5.4.2**);
- lift cables to machine room – with openings as small as practicable.

There are no specific limitations on openings in external walls of protected shafts, however, openings may be restricted by the requirements for protected stairways and firefighting shafts.

B.5.3 Concealed spaces

Cavity barriers should be provided:

- to restrict the spread of smoke and flame through voids and concealed spaces in the construction;
- to seal pathways around fire-separating elements;
- to sub-divide extensive cavities.

B.5.3.1 Pathways around fire-separating elements

Junctions

Cavity barriers should be provided around the edges of cavities, including openings, and at junctions between:

- external cavity walls and every compartment floor and wall;
- internal cavity walls and every compartment floor and wall;
- internal cavity walls and wall or door assemblies which form a fire-resisting barrier.

Figure B.21 shows where cavity barriers generally are required, although cavity barriers are not required where the cavity wall complies with Figure B.22.

Protected escape routes

Where fire-resisting construction is not carried to full storey height, or to the underside of the roof coverings, any cavities formed above or below that construction should either:

- be fitted with cavity barriers on line of enclosure; or
- if it is a cavity above fire-resisting construction, be enclosed on its lower side by a fire-resisting ceiling which extends throughout the building, compartment or separated part (Figure B.23).

Cavity barriers may be required where corridors are sub-divided to prevent alternative escape routes being simultaneously affected by fire and/or smoke (**B.3.4.4**).

Separation of bedrooms

In institutional and other residential buildings where partitions between bedrooms are not carried to full storey height, or to the underside of the roof, cavities above or below the partitions should be protected in the same way as those above or below protected escape routes, as described above. (The limitations on openings do not apply.)

Figure B.22 Cavity wall which does not require cavity barriers

SECTION THROUGH CAVITY WALL

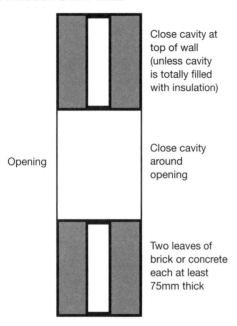

Opening

Close cavity at top of wall (unless cavity is totally filled with insulation)

Close cavity around opening

Two leaves of brick or concrete each at least 75mm thick

Notes:

1. Domestic meter cupboards may be installed provided that:
   a. there are no more than two cupboards per dwelling.
   b. the opening in the outer wall leaf is not more than 800 × 500mm for each cupboard.
   c. the inner leaf is not penetrated except by a sleeve not more than 80 × 80mm, which is fire stopped.
2. Combustible materials may be placed within the cavity.

Figure B.23 Fire-resisting ceiling below concealed space

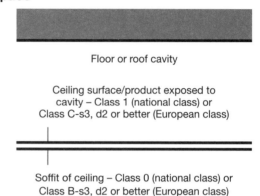

Floor or roof cavity

Ceiling surface/product exposed to cavity – Class 1 (national class) or Class C-s3, d2 or better (European class)

Soffit of ceiling – Class 0 (national class) or Class B-s3, d2 or better (European class)

Notes:

1. The ceiling should:
   a. have at least 30 minutes fire resistance;
   b. be imperforate, except for an opening described in **B.5.3.3**;
   c. extend throughout the building or compartment; and
   d. not be easily demountable.
2. The national classifications do not automatically equate with the equivalent classifications in the European column, therefore products cannot typically assume a European class unless they have been tested accordingly.
3. When a classification includes 's3, d2', this means that there is no limit set for smoke production and/or flaming droplets/particles.

Table B.27 Maximum dimensions of cavities in non-domestic buildings

Location of cavity	Maximum dimension (m)	Class of surface/product exposed in cavity	
		National class	European class
Between roof and a ceiling	20	Any	Any
Any other cavity	20	Class 0 or Class 1	Class A1, or Class A2-s3, d2, or Class B-s3, d2, or Class C-s3, d2
	10	Worse than Class 1	Worse than Class C-s3, d2
Ceiling cavity or underfloor void of a single room with cavity barriers at enclosing walls and/or partitions	40[1]	Class 0 or Class 1	No worse than Class C-s3,d2

[1] Concealed space may exceed 40m in any direction provided the following additional criteria are met: (i) the room and cavity are compartmented; (ii) the building has an automatic fire detection and alarm system to BS 5839-1:2002; (iii) a cavity used as a plenum has air circulation to BS 5588-9:1999; (iv) pipe insulation is Class 1 or Class C-s3, d2 or better; (v) electrical wiring is laid in metal trays or metal conduit; (vi) other materials are of limited combustibility or Class A2 or better.

Twin-skin roofing

Cavity barriers are not required between the inner and outer panels of twin-skin roofing, provided:

- the sheeting has limited combustibility; and

- the insulating layer has surface spread of flame Class 0 or Class 1 (European class C-s3,d2); and

- the insulating layer makes contact with the inner and outer panels.

B.5.3.2 Extensive cavities

Large cavities within building elements – including roof spaces – should be sub-divided with cavity barriers so that the distance between barriers does not exceed those in Table B.27. That requirement does not apply to a cavity:

- in a wall which should be fire-resisting only because it is loadbearing;

- in a masonry or concrete wall which complies with Figure B.22;

- in a floor or roof above a fire-resisting ceiling which extends throughout the building or compartment, and does not exceed 30m in any direction;

- formed behind the external skin of masonry cladding system with a masonry/concrete inner leaf at least 75mm thick, or formed by overcladding an existing masonry or concrete wall or an existing concrete roof (there must be no combustible insulation in cavity, and the building must not be residential or institutional);

- between the inner and outer sheets of twin-skin roofing which complies with **B.5.3.1**;

- below a floor which is next to the ground or oversite concrete, provided the cavity is either less than 1000mm high or is not normally accessible for persons.

B.5.3.3 Construction of cavity barriers

Cavity barriers should offer 30 minutes' fire resistance. They may be formed by construction for another purpose so long as it meets Table B.2 item 15: for example a window or door frame which meets the dimensions below may form a cavity barrier.

Cavity barriers in stud walls, partitions or around openings may be formed from:

- steel at least 0.5mm thick;

- timber at least 38mm thick;

- polyethylene sleeved mineral wool, or mineral wool slab, installed under compression;

- calcium silicate, cement-based or gypsum-based boards at least 12mm thick.

The material should be tightly fitted to rigid construction and mechanically fixed or, where that is not possible, the junction should be fire stopped (**B.5.4**). The fixing should ensure that the cavity barrier retains its function despite:

- building movement resulting from subsidence, shrinkage, temperature change or wind forces;

- fire collapse of services which penetrate it;

- failure of fixings (although roof members are not expected to have fire resistance, but only to support the cavity barrier);
- failure in a fire of any abutting material or construction.

Openings within cavity barriers are limited to:

- doors with 30 minutes' fire resistance;
- suitably fire-stopped pipes;
- openings with automatic fire dampers;
- fire-resisting ducts;
- ducts with automatic fire dampers at the barrier.

B.5.4 Protection of openings and fire stopping

In order to maintain the effectiveness of fire-separating elements, openings within them should be adequately protected by sealing or fire stopping. Although sealing and fire stopping are intended to delay passage of fire, the measures may also retard the spread of smoke. Designers of dwellinghouses should also consider any detrimental effects of service built into the construction.

B.5.4.1 Openings for pipes

Pipe openings should be protected by either:

- a proprietary seal which has been shown by test to maintain fire resistance; or
- fire stopping around the pipe, which does not exceed the dimensions in Table B.28; or
- sleeving a pipe of type (b) to Table B.28, with a maximum diameter of 160mm within a non-combustible pipe of type (a) (Figure B.24).

Figure B.24 Pipes penetrating structure

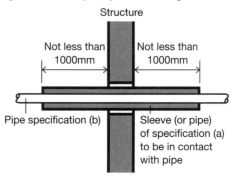

Notes:

1. Make the opening in the structure as small as possible and provide fire-stopping between pipe and structure.
2. See Table B.28 for materials specification.

Table B.28 Maximum internal diameters of pipes passing through compartment walls or floors			
Situation	Pipe material and nominal internal diameter (mm)		
	(a) Non-combustible material[1]	(b) Lead, aluminium, aluminium alloy, uPVC[2], fibre cement	(c) Any other material
1. Structure (but not wall separating buildings) enclosing a protected shaft which is not a stairway or lift shaft.	160	110	40
2. Compartment wall or compartment floor between flats.	160	Stack pipe[3]: 160 Branch pipe[3]: 110	40
3. Any other situation.	160	40	40

[1] A material such as cast iron, copper or steel which on exposure to a temperature of 800°C will not soften or fracture to allow flame or hot gas through the wall of the pipe.

[2] uPVC pipes to BS 4514:2001 or BS 5255:1989.

[3] Only apply to pipes in above ground drainage systems enclosed as **Figure B.25**: otherwise diameters for case 3 apply.

Figure B.25 Enclosure for drainage or water supply pipes

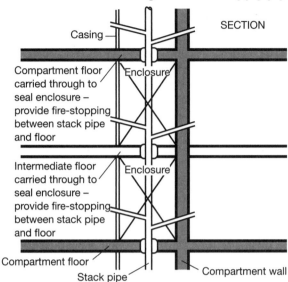

Notes:
1. The enclosure should:
   a. be bounded by a compartment wall or floor, an outside wall, an intermediate floor, or a casing (see specification at 2 below);
   b. have internal surfaces (except framing members) of Class 0 (national class) or Class B-s3, d2 or better (European class)
   Note: When a classification includes 's3, d2', this means that there is no limit set for smoke production and/or flaming droplets/particles);
   c. not have an access panel which opens into a circulation space or bedroom;
   d. be used only for drainage, or water supply, or vent pipes for a drainage system.
2. The casing should:
   a. be imperforate except for an opening for a pipe or an access panel;
   b. not be of sheet metal;
   c. have (including any access panel) not less than 30 minutes fire resistance.
3. The opening for a pipe, either in the structure or the casing, should be as small as possible and fire-stopped around the pipe.

B.5.4.2 Ventilation ducts

Air-handling ducts which penetrate fire-separating elements should be protected either by:

- fire-resisting ductwork; or
- fire-resisting enclosures; or
- fire dampers.

Fire dampers should be situated within the thickness of the fire-separating element and securely fixed, with adequate means of access for inspection and testing. They are not suitable for extract ductwork serving kitchens because built-up fat may prevent their closing. Fire dampers should attain at least Class E60, and fire and smoke dampers at least Class ES60 when tested to EN 1366:2:1999 and classified to BS EN 13501-3.

Where building occupants are likely to be sleeping, fire dampers should have automatic smoke actuation as well as thermal actuation. This requirement is relaxed if occupants can be expected to escape unaided and the building has an L1 alarm system which signals immediate evacuation. Where the building is divided into compartments and the alarm signals immediate evacuation of a compartment, then smoke-actuated dampers need only be provided where ductwork enters or leaves the fire compartment. Fusible link dampers are not suitable for escape routes.

B.5.4.3 Flues

Where a flue or a duct containing a flue passes through a compartment wall or floor, or is built into a wall, each wall of the flue or duct must have at least half the fire resistance of that wall or floor.

B.5.4.4 Fire stopping

Joints between fire-separating elements should be fire stopped, as should openings for pipes and ducts, with allowance made for thermal movement. Suitable materials include proprietary fire stopping and sealing systems, mortars, plasters and intumescent mastics.

Where non-rigid materials are used, or the unsupported span is greater than 100mm, the fire-stopping materials should be reinforced with materials of limited combustibility to prevent their displacement.

B.5.5 Car parks

The fire load of car parks is well defined, and in a well ventilated car park the probability for fire spread from one storey to another is low. Consequently, the fire resistance standards in Table B.2 are reduced for open-sided car parks which meet the criteria in Table B.29.

Further guidance

ASFP Blue Book – Fire-resisting ductwork. Association for Specialist Fire Protection. 2nd edition. [Now available in British Standards or European Standards versions.]

BS EN 1366-2:1999. Fire resistance tests for service installations. Fire dampers.

BS EN 13501-3:2005+A1:2009. Fire classification of construction products and building elements. Classification using data from fire resistance tests on products and elements used in building service installations: fire-resisting ducts and fire dampers.

ASFP Red Book – Fire stopping and penetration seals for the construction industry. Association for Specialist Fire Protection. 2nd edition. [3rd edition, 2010, revised 2011.]

Ensuring best practice for passive fire protection in buildings. Passive Fire Protection Federation. www.pfpf.org/pdf/publications/best_practice_guide.pdf

Table B.29 Requirements for open-sided car parks	
Feature	Requirement
Layout	No basement storeys.
Ventilation	Aggregate free vent area of permanent openings at least 1/20th of the floor area of each level, with 1/40th equally provided between two opposing walls.
Structure	A structural element supporting another to have no less than minimum fire resistance for the other element.
Other Purpose Groups	If building used for any other purpose then part forming car park is separated. Structural elements to have no less than minimum fire resistance of any element they support.
Construction	Materials to be non-combustible, except for: • a surface finish which meets Requirements B2 and B4 for internal and external fire spread; • any fire door; • an attendant's kiosk under 15m^2; • any shop mobility facility.

Car parks which do not meet the criteria for being open sided may be naturally ventilated, with permanent openings to each level equivalent to 1/40 (one-fortieth) floor area, with at least half of that split equally and provided between two opposing walls (1/160th on each side) (see also **F.4.4**).

Where that standard of natural ventilation is not achievable then mechanical ventilation should be provided. Such a system should:

- be independent of any ventilating system to the rest of the building;
- be designed to operate at 10 air changes per hour during fire;
- be split into two parts able to operate singly or together, each part providing 50% of the rating and having an independent power supply;
- have 50% of extract points at high level and 50% at low level;
- have fans rated to run at 300ºC for at least 60 minutes;
- have ductwork and fixings with melting points above 800ºC.

An alternative method for removing smoke is given in BS 7346-7:2006.

B.5.6 Shopping complexes

Although the provisions in the Approved Document will generally be applicable to individual shops, they may not be appropriate for shops in complexes such as covered malls. Designers should consult sections 5 and 6 of BS 5588-10:1991 and observe the relevant recommendations for alternative measures and compensatory features.

Further guidance
BS 5588-10:1991. Fire precautions in the design, construction and use of buildings. Code of practice for shopping complexes. [Withdrawn, replaced by BS 9999:2008. Code of practice for fire safety in the design, management and use of buildings. Annex E contains recommendations for shopping complexes.]

B.6 External fire spread (Requirement B4)

Buildings should resist the spread of fire over the exterior of the building and limit the spread of fire to other buildings. The risk of fire spreading depends on:

- the size and intensity of the fire;
- the distance between the buildings;
- the fire protection on the facing sides.

To limit the risk of fire spreading from a building to a building beyond the site boundary, or vice versa:

- external walls should have restricted risk of ignition from internal sources, low rate of fire spread and low rates of heat release;
- the amount of unprotected area on the sides of a building should be restricted to limit the amount of thermal radiation passing through the wall;
- roofs should be constructed to restrict the risk of spread of flame and/or ignition from an external fire source.

B.6.1 Construction of external walls

B.6.1.1 Fire resistance

External walls are elements of structure, and their required fire resistance depends on the use and height of the building. The level of fire resistance is also affected by the distance between the wall and the site boundary, as follows:

- Walls less than 1000mm from a relevant boundary must be fire-resistant from the inside and the outside.

- Walls more than 1000m from a relevant boundary need only be fire-resistant from inside.

External walls should have fire resistance to Table B.2, except for unprotected areas (**B.6.3.3**).

B.6.1.2 External surfaces

The external surfaces of external walls must be of restricted combustibility, meeting either the standards in Table B.30 or the performance criteria in BR 135.

In buildings with a storey that is more than 18m above the ground any insulation, filler or the like (but not gaskets or sealants) should be of limited combustibility (**B.2.3.2**); cavity walls complying with Figure B.22 are exempt.

Cavity barriers should be provided as **B.5.3**. Where cavity barriers are not provided between external cladding and masonry or concrete inner leaves (**B.5.3.2**) the surfaces facing the cavity should comply with Table B.30.

Further guidance

BR 135. *Fire performance of external thermal insulation for walls of multi-storey buildings*. BRE. 2003.

Table B.30 Requirements for external wall constructions			
Location	Distance from boundary (mm)	Height of building (m)	Performance of external surfaces of walls
Dwelling	Up to 1000	N/A	Class 0 or B-s3, d2 or better
Any building with an external wall facing a boundary	Up to 1000	18 or less	Class 0 or B-s3, d2 or better on wall facing boundary
Any building	Up to 1000	More than 18	All walls to be Class 0 or B-s3, d2 or better
All buildings except for assembly or recreation building of more than one storey	More than 1000	18 or less	None, but may be limited by criteria for space separation
Walls of assembly and recreation buildings up to 10m above the ground or a roof or any part of building to which public have access	More than 1000	18 or less	Material with Index I (to BS 476-6) of not more than 20, or European class C-s3, d2 or better (to BS EN 135011); timber cladding at least 9mm thick is also suitable
The portion of any external wall up to 18m above the ground	More than 1000	More than 18	
The portion of any external wall more than 18m above the ground	More than 1000	More than 18	Class 0 or B-s3, d2 or better

B.6.2 Portal frames

A portal frame, such as those frequently used in the construction of single-storey commercial and industrial buildings, acts as a single structural element. The failure in a fire of one element is likely to lead to significant failure of other elements. It may, therefore, be necessary to protect the columns and roof members of a portal frame building in order to protect the external wall.

The overturning moment caused by partial collapse of the roof can be overcome by designing the foundations and their connections to the frame in accordance with SCI P313. Alternatively, the installation of a sprinkler system (**B.1.8**) will provide an appropriate level of protection. Reinforced concrete portal frames can provide sufficient support to external walls without specific provisions to prevent overturning.

Existing portal frame buildings should perform to a satisfactory standard if:

- column members are fixed to a base which resists overturning; or
- columns are protected by brick, block, concrete up to a protected ring beam which provides lateral support; or
- there is some form of roof venting, such as PVC rooflights at 10% of floor area.

Further guidance

SCI P313. *Single storey steel framed buildings in fire boundary conditions*. Steel Construction Institute. 2002.

B.6.3 Space separation

Space separation is intended to prevent the spread of fire by limiting the extent of unprotected areas (such as openings) and areas of combustible surface on the sides of a building. The requirements apply to elements pitched more than 70° from the horizontal (walls, rather than roofs), although vertical elements within roofs – such as individual dormers – are generally excluded.

The requirements presume:

- The size of the fire depends on compartmentation. A fire in one compartment will not spread to another. Smaller compartments may allow reduced separation distances or a greater amount of unprotected area.
- The intensity of a fire is related to use of the building (Purpose Group). Intensity can be moderated by a sprinkler system.
- Buildings in Purpose Groups 'residential', and 'assembly and recreation' present the greatest risk to life.
- There is a building on the far side of the boundary which has similar elevation to the one in question, at the same distance from the common boundary.
- The amount of radiation passed through part of an external wall with fire resistance is discounted.

B.6.3.1 Requirements

- External walls on or within 1000mm of relevant boundary – the only permitted unprotected areas are those exclusions listed below and the wall must be fire-resisting from both sides.
- External walls 1000mm or more from relevant boundary – the unprotected area must not exceed that established by one of the calculating methods below and any remaining wall must be fire-resisting from the inside of the building.

B.6.3.2 Boundaries

Space separation is based on the distance between a building face and a relevant boundary (Figure B.26) which either:

- coincides with the face of the building;
- is parallel to the face of the building;
- is at an angle of less than 80° to the face of the building.

The relevant boundary may be:

- the site boundary;
- the centre line of a space adjoining the site, which is unlikely to be developed, for example a road, river, railway or canal;
- a notional boundary between two buildings on the same site, where:
  - the buildings are to be managed/operated by separate organisations, or
  - at least one of the buildings is in the 'residential' or 'assembly and recreation' Purpose Groups.

Figure B.27 sets out the rules for determining a notional boundary.

Figure B.26 Relevant boundary

For a boundary to be relevant it should:
a coincide with; or
b be parallel to; or
c be at an angle of not more than 80° to the side of the building

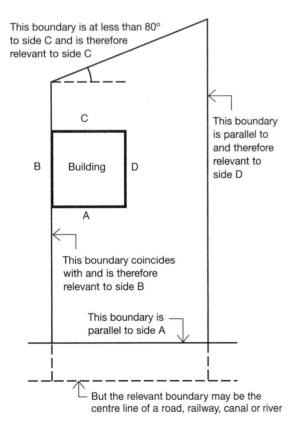

This boundary is at less than 80° to side C and is therefore relevant to side C

This boundary is parallel to and therefore relevant to side D

This boundary coincides with and is therefore relevant to side B

This boundary is parallel to side A

But the relevant boundary may be the centre line of a road, railway, canal or river

Figure B.27 Notional boundary

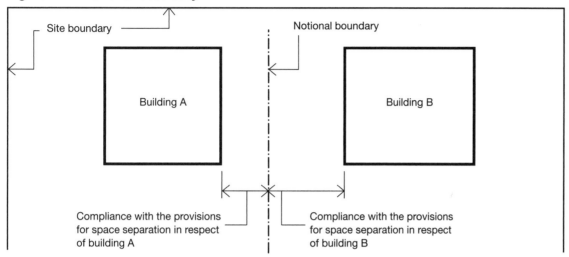

The notional boundary should be set in the area between the two buildings using the following rules:

1. The notional boundary is assumed to exist in the space between the buildings and is positioned so that one of the buildings would comply with the provisions for space separation having regard to the amount of its unprotected area. In practice, if one of the buildings is existing, the position of the boundary will be set by the space separation factors for that building.
2. The siting of the new building, or the second building if both are new, can then be checked to see that it also complies, using the notional boundary as the relevant boundary for the second building.

B.6.3.3 Unprotected areas

An unprotected area is one with less fire resistance than the appropriate amount in Table B.2. The total unprotected area on one face of a building must not exceed the maximum value calculated by one of the following methods:

Method 1 – for small residential buildings in Purpose Group 1, including dwellings and blocks of flats

The building must be:

- at least 1000mm from any point on a relevant boundary;
- not more than three storeys, including basements;
- not more than 24m in length.

The unprotected area should not exceed values in Table B.31 for the boundary distance; the rest of the side of the building should be fire-resisting.

Method 2 – for small buildings or compartments

The building or compartment must be:

- at least 1000mm from any point on a relevant boundary;
- not more than 10m in height – unless it is an open-sided car park.

Table B.31 Maximum total unprotected areas, method 1

Minimum distance (A) between side of building and relevant boundary (m)	Maximum total area of unprotected areas (m²)
1	5.6
2	12
3	18
4	24
5	30
6	No limit

Table B.32 Maximum total unprotected areas, method 2

Minimum distance between side of building and relevant boundary (m)		Maximum total percentage of unprotected areas (%)[1]
Residential, office, assembly, recreation, open-sided car parks	Shop, commercial, industrial, storage, other non-residential	
Not applicable	1	4
1	2	8
2.5	5	20
5	10	40
7.5	15	60
10	20	80
12.5	25	100

[1] = (total unprotected area / area of rectangle which encloses all unprotected areas) × 100.

The unprotected area should not exceed the values in Table B.32 for the boundary distance; the rest of the side of the building should be fire-resisting.

For both methods 1 or 2 the distances may be halved (but not reduced to less than 1m), or the permitted unprotected area doubled where the building has sprinklers.

Other methods for assessing unprotected areas for larger buildings, including the Enclosing Rectangle and Aggregate Notional Area methods, are described in BR 187.

When measuring unprotected areas, an area of wall which is fire-resistant but has combustible material more than 1mm thick on its surface should be included, but at half its actual area. The following may be excluded:

- any part of a stairway in a protected shaft (but see **B.3.3.4**);
- small unprotected areas in an otherwise protected wall (Figure B.28);
- parts of the wall of an uncompartmented building more than 30m above ground.

Further guidance
BR 187. *External fire spread: Building separation and boundary distances*. BRE. 1991.

Figure B.28 Unprotected areas which may be disregarded

The unprotected area of the external wall of a stairway forming a protected shaft may be disregarded for separation distance purposes

Compartment floor

Compartment wall

Unprotected areas which may be disregarded for separation distance purposes

Represents an unprotected area of not more than 1m² which may consist of two or more smaller areas within an area of 1000mm x 1000mm

Represents an area of not more than 0.1m²

Dimensional restrictions

4m minimum distance

1500mm minimum distance

Dimension unrestricted

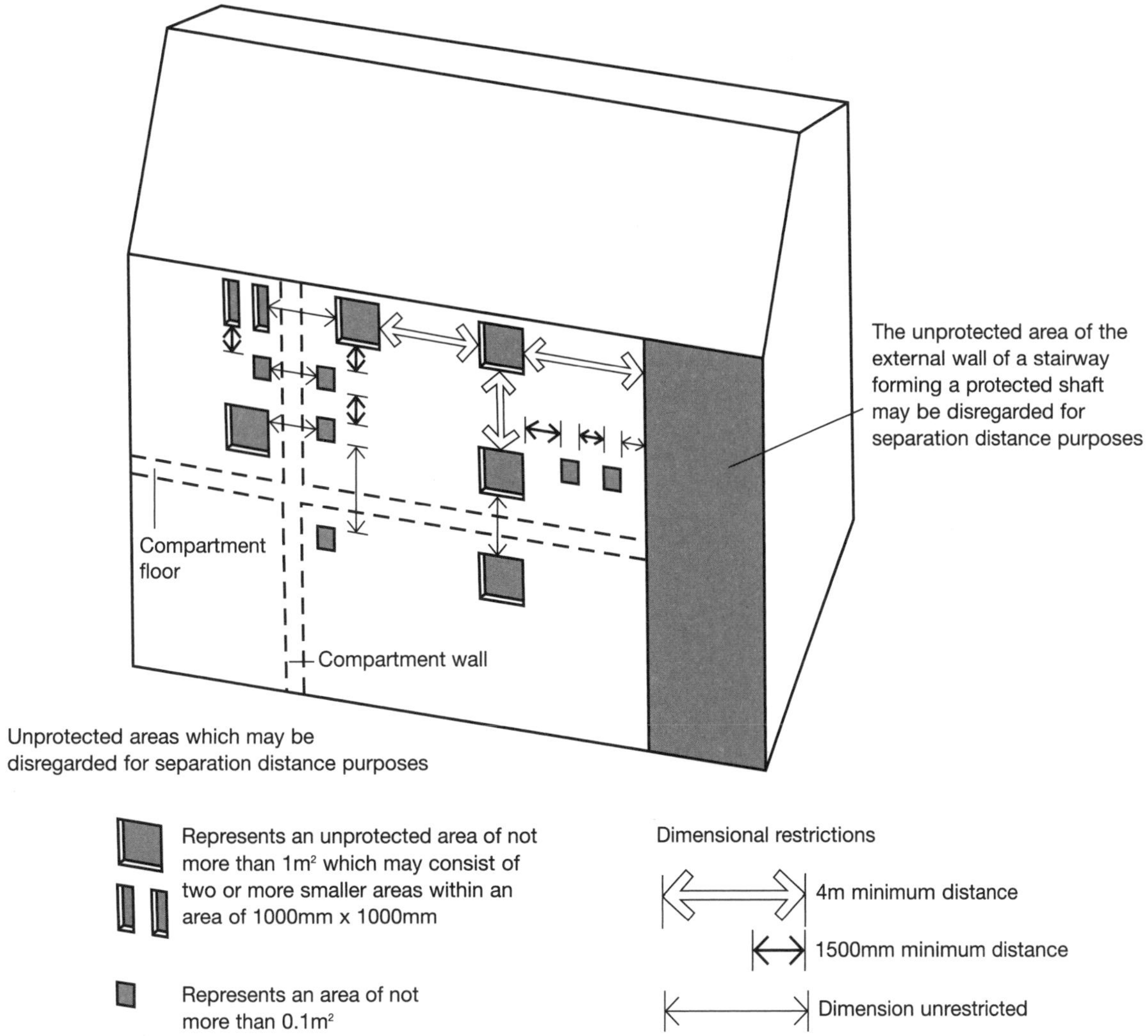

B.6.4 Roof coverings

The minimum distance between any roof covering and the relevant boundary should comply with the separation distance for a roof covering of that category shown in Table B.33. There are no restrictions on roof coverings classified as AA, AB, AC or $B_{ROOF}(t4)$, nor on roof coverings described by EU Commission Decision 2000/553/EC, which may be used without testing.

Thatch and shingles should be regarded as Class AD/BD/CD or $E_{ROOF}(t4)$ if they cannot be tested to BS 476-3:2004 or ENV 1187 (test 4). Unwired glass at least 4mm thick in rooflights may be considered as Class AA or $B_{ROOF}(t4)$.

Rigid thermoplastic sheets of polycarbonate or uPVC which achieve Class 1 surface spread of flame or Class C-s3,d2 can be regarded as AA or $B_{ROOF}(t4)$, but must still comply with the requirements for junctions between compartment walls and roofs (**B.5.2**). Other plastic rooflights must comply with separation distances in Table B.34 and the conditions in Figure B.29.

Further guidance
BS 476. Fire tests on building materials and structures. -3:2004. Classification and method of test for external fire exposure to roofs.

BS DD ENV 1187:2002+A1:2005. Test methods for external fire exposure to roofs. [Withdrawn, replaced by DD CEN/TS 1187:2012. Test methods for external fire exposure to roofs.]

Table B.33 Limitations on roof coverings

Description of roof covering		Minimum distance from any point on relevant boundary			
		Less than 6m	At least 6m	At least 12m	At least 20m
AA, AB or AC	B_{ROOF}(t4)	Y	Y	Y	Y
BA, BB or BC	C_{ROOF}(t4)	N	Y	Y	Y
CA, CB or CC	D_{ROOF}(t4)	N	Y[1][2]	Y[1]	Y
AD, BD or CD	E_{ROOF}(t4)	N	Y[1][2]	Y[1]	Y[1]
DA, DB, DC or DD	G_{ROOF}(t4)	N	N	N	Y[1][2]

Notes:

Separation distances do not apply to the boundary between roofs of a pair of semi-detached houses and to enclosed/covered walkways. However, see **Figure B.20** if the roof passes over the top of a compartment wall. Polycarbonate and PVC rooflights which achieve a Class 1 rating by test, see **B.6.4**, may be regarded as having an AA designation.

Openable polycarbonate and PVC rooflights which achieve a Class 1 (national class) or Class C-s3, d2 (European class) rating by test may be regarded as having an AA (national class) designation or B_{ROOF}(t4) (European class) classification.

[1] Not acceptable on any of the following buildings:

    a. houses in terraces of three or more houses;

    b. industrial, storage or other non-residential Purpose Group buildings of any size;

    c. any other buildings with a cubic capacity of more than 1500m³.

[2] Acceptable on buildings not listed in Note 1, if part of the roof is no more than 3m² in area and is at least 1500mm from any similar part, with the roof between the parts covered with a material of limited combustibility.

Table B.34 Separation distances for rooflights

	Minimum distance (m) from any point on relevant boundary to rooflight with external surface classification of:			
	AD BD CD CA CB CC E_{ROOF}(t4) D_{ROOF}(t4)	DA DB DC DD F_{ROOF}(t4)	TP(a)	TP(b)
Lower surface	*Class 3*	*Class 3*	*TP(a) rigid*	*TP(b)*
a. Balcony, verandah, carport, covered way or loading bay with at least one longer side permanently open. b. Detached swimming pool. c. Conservatory, garage or outbuilding with max. 40m² area.	6	20	6	6
d. Circulation space[1], except protected stairway. e. Room.	6[2]	20[2]	6	6[2]

[1] For a non-thermoplastic material, single skin rooflight only.

[2] Rooflight must comply with **Figure B.29**.

Figure B.29 Limitations on spacing and size of plastic rooflights with Class 3 or Class D-s3, d2 lower surface

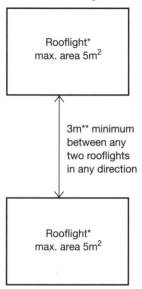

* Or group of rooflights amounting to no more than 5m^2

** Class 3 rooflights to rooms in industrial and other non-residential Purpose Groups may be spaced 1800mm apart provided the rooflights are evenly distributed and do not exceed 20% of the area of the room

Notes:

1. There are restrictions on the use of plastic rooflights in the guidance to Requirement B2 (**B.4.1**).
2. Surrounding roof covering to be a material of limited combustibility for at least 3m distance.
3. Where Figure B.20a or b applies, rooflights should be at least 1500mm from the compartment wall.

B.7 Access and facilities for the Fire Service (Requirement B5)

Buildings require reasonable facilities to assist firefighters in the protection of life, including external vehicle access for Fire and Rescue Service appliances. The size and use of the building may also require the provision of:

- fire mains and water supplies;
- firefighting shafts to improve internal access for firefighters; and
- smoke venting for basements.

Designers should also refer to **B.2.5** when insulating core panels are used internally.

B.7.1 Water supply

B.7.1.1 Fire mains

Fire mains have outlets to which the Fire and Rescue Service can connect hoses to obtain a water supply when inside a building to fight a fire:

- **Dry mains** are normally empty and, in the event of a fire, are supplied through a hose from a Fire and Rescue Service pumping appliance.
- **Wet mains** are kept full of water and supplied from tanks and pumps in the building, which should be replenishable from a pumping appliance.

Fire mains should be provided in:

- Buildings with firefighting shafts – There should be a fire main within each shaft. Additional fire mains should be provided within protected escape stairs where the position of the shafts does not meet the maximum hose distances of **B.7.3**.
- Buildings with inadequate vehicle access (**B.7.2**) – Fire mains should be sited to meet the maximum hose distances of **B.7.3**, but need not be within firefighting shafts.

Buildings with a floor more than 50m above Fire and Rescue Service vehicle access level require wet mains. Lower buildings may have wet or dry mains.

The outlets from fire mains should be located in a protected enclosure of a staircase or a protected lobby (Figure B.31) and the design of the mains should follow BS 9990:2006.

Further guidance
BS 9990:2006. Code of practice for non-automatic fire-fighting systems in buildings.

B.7.1.2 Private hydrants

Where a building with a compartment with an area of 280m² or more is to be built further than 100m from an existing fire hydrant then additional fire hydrants should be provided, as follows:

- Buildings with fire mains – hydrants to be within 90m of the inlets for the dry fire mains.
- Buildings without fire mains – hydrants should be provided within 90m of an entry point to a building and not more than 90m apart.

Each hydrant is to be clearly indicated by a conspicuous plate, which meets BS 3251:1976.

Alternative arrangements for water supply may be made (for example, where there is no piped water supply), such as:

- a charged static water tank of at least 45,000 litre capacity; or
- a spring, river, canal or pond capable of providing or storing at least 45,000 litres of water at all times of year, with access, space and hardstanding for a pumping appliance; or
- another source of water supply considered suitable by the fire and rescue authority.

Further guidance
BS 3251:1976. Specification. Indicator places for fire hydrants and emergency water supplies.

B.7.2 Vehicle access

Vehicle access is required to the exterior of a building for pumping appliances and high reach appliances, such as turntable ladders and hydraulic platforms. The extent of provision depends upon the size and height of the building and whether or not fire mains are provided.

B.7.2.1 Dwellinghouses and flats

There should be access for a pumping appliance to within 45m of all points within each dwelling, with suitable doors at least 750mm wide to each elevation to which access is provided. Where the 45m access distance is not met for flats, fire mains should be provided. The access distances for buildings with fire mains then apply.

B.7.2.2 Buildings with fire mains

Pumping appliances need access to the perimeter at points near fire mains so that firefighters can enter the building and, for dry mains, connect hose(s) to pump water in.

- Dry fire mains – pumping appliance access to within 18m of each fire main inlet connection point; and the inlet to be visible from an appliance.
- Wet fire mains – pumping appliance access to within 18m of suitable entrance giving access to the main, and within sight of main's replenishment inlet.

B.7.2.3 Buildings without fire mains

Vehicle access should be provided to the perimeter in accordance with Table B.35. The building perimeter is measured:

- excluding walls in common with other buildings; but
- including the vertical projection of any overhanging storey.

Where an elevation has vehicle access it should have suitable access doors to the interior, each at least 750mm wide, with no more than 60m between doors or the end of the elevation (so a 150m long elevation would require at least two doors).

Where the access requirement of Table B.35 is not met fire mains should be provided – the access distances for buildings with fire mains then apply.

Table B.35 Vehicle access to buildings without fire mains			
Floor area of building (m²)[1]	Height for floor of top storey above ground (m)	Provide vehicle access to	Type of appliance
Up to 2000	Up to 11	15% of perimeter[2]	Pump
	Over 11	15% of perimeter	High reach
2000–8000	Up to 11	15% of perimeter	Pump
	Over 11	50% of perimeter	High reach
8000–16,000	Up to 11	50% of perimeter	Pump
	Over 11	50% of perimeter	High reach
16,000–24,000	Up to 11	75% of perimeter	Pump
	Over 11	75% of perimeter	High reach
Over 24,000	Up to 11	100% of perimeter	Pump
	Over 11	100% of perimeter	High reach

[1] Aggregate area of all floors excluding basements.

[2] Or, if less onerous, to within 45m of all points on the building's projected plan.

Table B.36 Typical specifications for access routes

Requirement	Pump appliance	High reach appliance
Minimum width of road between kerbs	3.7m	3.7m
Minimum width of gateways	3.1m	3.1m
Minimum turning circle between kerbs	16.8m	26.0m
Minimum turning circle between walls	19.2m	29.0m
Minimum clearance height	3.7m	4.0m
Minimum carrying capacity	12.5 tonnes	17.0 tonnes

Figure B.30 Access requirements for high reach fire appliances

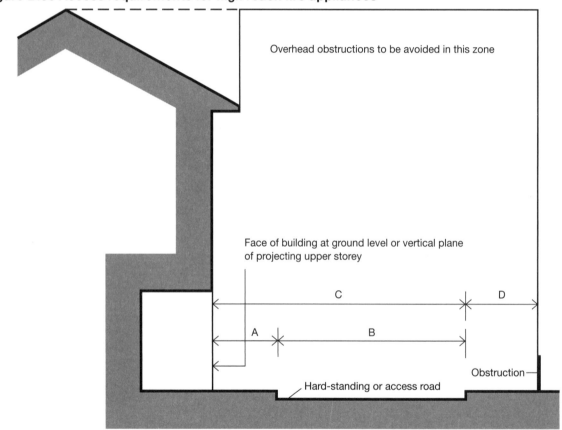

	Type of appliance	
	Turntable ladder dimension (m)	Hydraulic platform dimension (m)
A. Maximum distance of near edge of hard-standing from building	4.9	2.0
B. Minimum width of hard-standing	5.0	5.5
C. Minimum distance of further edge of hard-standing from building	10.0	7.5
D. Minimum width of unobstructed space (for swing of appliance platform)	NA	2.2

Notes:

1 Hard-standing for high reach appliances should be as level as possible and should not exceed a gradient of 1 in 12.

2 Fire appliances are not standardised. Some fire services have appliances with a greater weight or different size. In consultation with the Fire and Rescue Service, the Building Control Body should adopt the relevant dimensions and ground loading capacity.

B.7.2.4 Vehicle access routes

A vehicle access route may be a road or other route which meets standards in Table B.36. Additionally, access for high reach appliances should comply with Figure B.30, with overhead obstructions avoided in the marked zone. Any dead end access route that is more than 20m long should have a turning facility such as a hammerhead or turning circle to Table B.36 to prevent appliances having to reverse for more than 20m.

B.7.3 Access to buildings for personnel

B.7.3.1 Firefighting shafts

High-rise buildings and those with deep basements require additional provisions to enable firefighters to reach and fight the fire, including firefighting lifts, firefighting lobbies and firefighting stairs, which are combined in a protected shaft (**B.5.2.3**) known as a firefighting shaft. Table B.37 sets out the conditions in which buildings require firefighting shafts.

Table B.37 Provision of firefighting shafts	
Building	**Requirement**
Buildings with a floor at more than 18m above Fire and Rescue Service access level	One or more firefighting shafts with firefighting lifts
Buildings with a storey 900m² area with its floor at more than 18m above fire and rescue service access level	Two or more firefighting shafts with firefighting lifts
Buildings with a basement more than 10m below Fire and Rescue Service access level	One or more firefighting shafts with firefighting lifts
Buildings of Purpose Group 4, 5, and 6, with: • a storey of more than 900m² area, with • the floor more than 7.5m above Fire and Rescue Service access level	Two or more firefighting shafts
Buildings with two or more basement storeys, each more than 900m² area	One or more firefighting shafts
Shopping complexes	Provision to BS 5588-10:1991 section 3

Firefighting shafts should serve all the floors through which they pass. However, shafts to basements need not serve upper floors, nor those to upper floors serve basements unless they require shafts in their own right. They should be spaced so that every part of a storey required to be served by a shaft should be as follows:

- For buildings with automatic sprinklers throughout – a shaft should be within 60m hose-laying distance of a firefighting shaft.

- For buildings without automatic sprinklers – a shaft should be within 60m hose-laying distance of a firefighting shaft, and within 45m hose-laying distance of a fire main outlet in a protected stairway. (The escape stairs containing fire mains need not be designed as firefighting stairs.)

Every firefighting stair and firefighting lift should be approached through a firefighting lobby (Figure B.31). However, in blocks of flats which comply with the requirements for means of escape and compartmentation, the requirement for a firefighting lobby is relaxed. Both firefighting stairs and firefighting lifts may open directly onto a protected lobby or protected corridor, provided the doors of the lift are within 7.5m of the door to the firefighting stair.

Figure B.31 Components of a firefighting shaft

a. Any building

b. Shafts serving flats

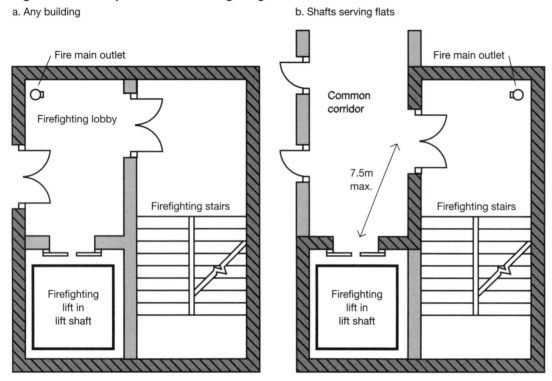

Minimum fire resistance 60 minutes from both sides with 30 minute fire doors

Minimum fire resistance 120 minutes from accommodation side and 60 minutes from inside the shaft with 60 minute fire doors

Firefighting shafts should be constructed to BS 5588-5:2004 clauses 7 and 8, while any lift installation (the lift car, lift well and machinery space as well as the control and communication systems) should follow the recommendations for firefighters' lifts in BS EN 81-72:2003, and either those for electric lifts (BS EN 81-1:1998) or hydraulic lifts (BS EN 81-2:1998). Provisions for smoke control should be made, in accordance with BS 5588-5:2004. For flats it will be sufficient to comply with **B.3.6.4**.

All shafts should be equipped with fire mains with outlet connections and valves at every level. Outlets should be located in the firefighting lobby or, for blocks of flats without a lobby, in the firefighting stairs.

B.7.3.2 Rolling shutters

Rolling shutters in compartment walls should be capable of being opened or closed manually by the Fire and Rescue Service without the use of a ladder.

B.7.4 Venting heat and smoke

Smoke outlets (or vents) to basements provide routes for heat and smoke to escape to the open air, facilitating rescue and firefighting operations. Smoke outlets are required for all basement storeys, except those with a floor area of less than 200m², or where the floor is not more than 3m below adjacent ground level.

Further guidance
BS 5588. Fire precautions in the design, construction and use of buildings.
-5:2004: Access and facilities for fire-fighting. [Withdrawn 2009. Replaced by BS 9999:2008. Code of practice for fire safety in the design, management and use of buildings. Section 6 covers access and facilities for fire-fighting.]

BS EN 81. Safety rules for the construction and installation of lifts
-1:1998. Electric lifts. [Amended: A3:2009.]
-2:1998. Hydraulic lifts. [Amended: A3:2009.]
-72:2003. Particular applications for passenger and goods passenger lifts. Firefighters lifts.

Each basement space should have a smoke outlet. However, where that is not feasible (for example, because of the basement plan and the presence of adjoining buildings) then a space may be vented indirectly by opening connecting doors to a directly vented space on the perimeter. In this case, each compartment of a basement should have direct access to venting. Strong rooms need not be provided with smoke outlets.

Basement compartments with external doors or windows do not need smoke outlets. The ventilation provisions for basement car parks are deemed also to satisfy the requirement for smoke venting.

B.7.4.1 Natural smoke outlets

Natural smoke outlets should:

- have combined clear cross-sectional area no less than 1/40 (one-fortieth) of the floor area of the storey they serve and be evenly distributed around the perimeter;
- be sited at high level, either in the ceiling or wall of the space they serve;
- be provided separately to areas of special fire hazard;
- not be placed where they would hinder escape from the building.

Outlets terminating at readily accessible points may be covered by panels, stallboards or pavement lights which can be open or broken, and their location should be clearly marked. Otherwise outlets should be covered only with a non-combustible grille or louvre.

B.7.4.2 Mechanical smoke extraction

Where a basement storey is fitted with a sprinkler system, mechanical smoke extraction may be used instead of natural venting. Such a mechanical system should:

- give at least 10 air changes per hour;
- be capable of handling gas temperatures of 300°C for at least an hour;
- be activated either by activation of the sprinkler system or by an automatic detection system (minimum Class L3 to BS 5839-1:2002).

B.7.4.3 Outlet ducts and shafts

Non-combustible, fire-resisting construction should be provided to:

- enclose ducts, shafts and their bulkheads;
- separate natural smoke outlets which serve different compartments and/or storeys.

Further guidance
BS 5839. Fire detection and fire alarm systems for buildings.
-1:2002. Code of practice for system design, installation, commissioning and maintenance. [Withdrawn, replaced by -1:2013. Code of practice for design, installation, commissioning and maintenance of systems in non-domestic premises.]

C. Site preparation and resistance to contaminants and moisture

C.1 General considerations

C.1.1 Scope

Part C is intended to protect the health and safety of building occupants from risks arising from site contamination and from moisture.

However, measures may not be required if:

- the building is to be used wholly for storing goods, or
- there would be no increase in the protection of the health and safety of anyone using the building.

2013 changes
Approved Document C has undergone only minor revisions in 2013:

- The provisions for radon protection have been updated to follow the latest radon maps and associated guidance.
- Annex A, which gave guidance on the assessment of contaminated land, has been withdrawn.
- Reference documents have been updated.

Part C: Site preparation and resistance to contaminants and moisture

Requirement	Limits on application
Preparation of site and resistance to contaminants	
C1 (1) The ground to be covered by the building shall be reasonably free from any material that might damage the building or affect its stability, including vegetable matter, topsoil and pre-existing foundations. (2) Reasonable precautions shall be taken to avoid danger to health and safety caused by contaminants on or in the ground covered, or to be covered by the building and any land associated with the building. (3) Adequate sub-soil drainage shall be provided, if it is needed to avoid – (a) the passage of ground moisture to the interior of the building; (b) damage to the building, including damage through the transport of water-borne contaminants to the foundations of the building. (4) For the purposes of this requirement, 'contaminant' means any substance, which is or may become harmful to persons or buildings including substances, which are corrosive, explosive, flammable, radioactive or toxic.	
Resistance to moisture	
C2 The walls, floors and roof of the building shall adequately protect the building and people who use the building from harmful effects caused by – (a) ground moisture; (b) precipitation including wind-driven spray; (c) interstitial and surface condensation; and (d) spillage of water from or associated with sanitary fittings or fixed appliances.	

C.1.2 Material change of use

Requirement C1(2), resistance to contaminants, applies at any material change of use. Requirement C2, resistance to moisture, applies when a building is used as a dwelling where previously it was not.

C.1.3 Definitions

Contaminant A substance which is or may become harmful to persons or buildings. It may be corrosive, explosive, flammable, radioactive or toxic, and solid, liquid, gaseous or a vapour.

Precipitation Includes wind-blown spray from the sea or any other body of water.

Wall An opaque part of the external envelope which is at an angle of 70° or more to the horizontal. A wall includes piers, columns, parapets and attached chimneys, and joints at openings, but not window and door components.

C.1.4 Historic buildings

Work to historic buildings should improve resistance to contaminants and moisture. Moisture transfer from the occupied spaces to the roof structure should be limited and adequate levels of ventilation maintained. Gas protection measures should not be excessively intrusive.

Further guidance
SPAB Information sheet 4. *The need for old buildings to 'breathe'*. SPAB. 1986.

BR 211 *Radon: Guidance on protective measures for new buildings* (including supplementary advice for extensions, conversions and refurbishment). BRE. 2007.

C.1.5 Flood risk

Where building takes place in flood-prone areas, some effects of flooding can be mitigated by:

- sub-soil drainage to lower groundwater levels (**C.4**);
- anti-flooding devices to prevent sewers surcharging (**H.2.2.2**);
- water-resisting construction to ground floors (**C.5.1**);
- access to sub-floor voids for cleaning (**C.5.1.3**).

Further guidance
National Planning Policy Framework. CLG. March 2012.

Technical Guidance to the National Planning Policy Framework. CLG. March 2012.

C.1.6 Contaminated land

Work on contaminated land may be subject to:

- Part IIA of the Environmental Protection Act 1990 and the Contaminated Land (England) Regulations 2006 (as amended 2012);
- Environmental Protection (Duty of Care (England)) Regulations 1991;
- Town and Country Planning Acts;
- Construction (Design and Management) Regulations 2007, for work on contaminated land.

Authorities with an interest in contaminated land include:

- district council environmental health departments;
- local planning authorities;
- the Environment Agency.

2013 changes
Annex A to Approved Document C – Guidance on the assessment of land affected by contaminants – has been withdrawn.

Further guidance
Environmental Protection (Duty of care (England)) Regulations 1991 as amended. SI 1991/2839 and SI 2003/63.

National Planning Policy Framework. CLG. March 2012.

Technical Guidance to the National Planning Policy Framework. CLG. March 2012.

Environmental Protection Act 1990: Part 2A: Contaminated Land Statutory Guidance. Defra. 2012 (www.defra.gov.uk).

C.2 Clearance or treatment of unsuitable material (Requirement C1(1))

C.2.1 Site investigation

The measures required to prepare the site should be determined from the results of a site investigation, which should comprise:

- Planning stage – Identification of the scope and requirements of the investigation.
- Desk study – Review of historical, geological and environmental information.
- Site reconnaissance – Identification of actual and potential physical hazards.
- Main investigation and reporting – Intrusive and non-intrusive sampling and testing.

The extent of the investigation should be guided by previous uses of the land, but it is likely to include a study of groundwater conditions, underlying geology, and ground and hydro-geological properties. Where contamination is expected, a combined geo-technical and geo-environmental investigation should be considered.

Further guidance
BS EN 1997-2:2007. Eurocode 7: Geotechnical design. Ground investigation and testing, with UK National Annex.

BS 5930:1999+A2:2010. Code of practice for site investigations.

BS 8103-1:2011. Structural design of low-rise buildings. Code of Practice for stability, site investigation, precast concrete floors and ground floor slabs for housing.

C.2.2 Unsuitable material

Vegetable material such as turf and roots should be removed from the ground to be covered by the building, to a depth sufficient to prevent later growth. Below-ground services, such as drains, should withstand the presence of tree roots and their joints should resist root penetration. Roots presenting a hazard to services should be removed.

On sites with shrinkable clays and mature trees (see Figure C.1 and Approved Document C Table 1) the risk of ground heave should be assessed, together with the likely extent of damage to services, floor slabs and oversite concrete. Preventative action may require the removal of trees or soil. The compressibility of any fill or made ground should be considered, together with its potential for collapse, and measures should be taken to prevent differential settlement.

The remains of previous buildings on a site, and their potential for hazard, should be evaluated and addressed.

Further guidance
BRE Digest 298. *Low-rise building foundations: the influence of trees in clay soils*. BRE. 1999.

NHBC Standards, Chapter 4.2 'Building near trees'. NHBC. 2003. [Latest edition 2013.]

BRE Digest 427 Low-rise buildings on fill.
-1. classification and load carrying characteristics. 1997.
-2. site investigation, ground movement and foundation design. 1998.
-3. engineered fill. 1998.

Figure C.1 Distribution of shrinkable clays and principal sulphate/sulphide-bearing strata in England and Wales

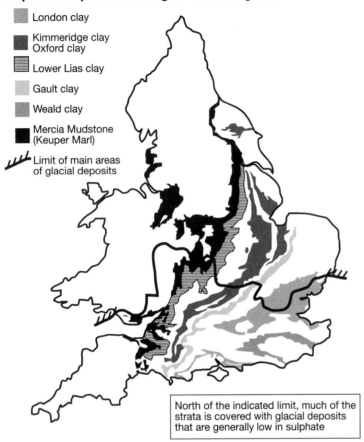

London clay

Kimmeridge clay
Oxford clay

Lower Lias clay

Gault clay

Weald clay

Mercia Mudstone
(Keuper Marl)

Limit of main areas
of glacial deposits

North of the indicated limit, much of the strata is covered with glacial deposits that are generally low in sulphate

C.3 Resistance to contaminants (Requirement C1(2))

The health and safety of building users may be adversely affected by:

- solid and liquid contaminants;
- methane and other gases from the ground;
- radon.

Sites may be contaminated as a result of the following:

- industrial use – contaminants will vary with previous use;
- agriculture or forestry – contaminants such as pesticides, fertiliser, fuels or decaying biological matter;
- landfill – biodegradable waste producing gas;
- naturally arising contaminants, including heavy metals such as cadmium and arsenic;
- sulphate, which can attack concrete floor slabs and oversite concrete (see Figure C.1 for distribution).

Further guidance
Department of the Environment. Industry Profiles. 1996.

P291 *Information on land quality in England: Sources of information*. Environment Agency. 2002.

C.3.1 Principles for addressing contamination

The methodology for preventing harm from on-site contaminants is based on the source–pathway–receptor model (Figure C.2), where:

- the source is the contaminant in the ground;
- the receptor may be a person, a building, a building material or service; and
- the pathway is the means by which the source contaminant reaches the receptor.

Pollution pathways between the source and receptors must be removed or conditioned so as not to pose a significant risk, by:

- treating the contaminant to eliminate or reduce its harmful properties;
- blocking or removing the pathway by isolating the contaminant;
- protecting or removing the receptor;
- removing the contaminant.

Figure C.2 Example of a conceptual model for a site showing source–pathway–receptor

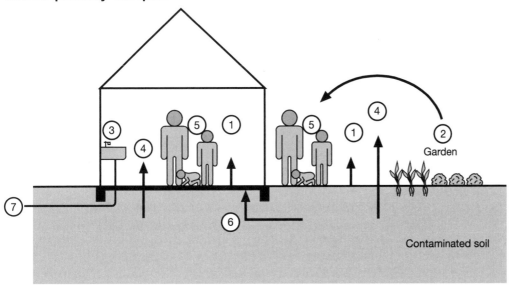

Possible pathways

Ingestion: of contaminants in soil/dust ①
           of contaminants in food ②
           of contaminants in water ③

Inhalation: of contaminants in soil particles/dust/vapours ④

Direct contact: with contaminants in soil/dust or water ⑤

Attack on building structures ⑥

Attack on services ⑦

Table C.1 Stages of risk assessment

Stage	Description	Actions
Hazard identification	Developing the conceptual model by establishing contaminant sources, pathways and receptors.	This is the preliminary site assessment which consists of a desk study and a site walk-over in order to obtain sufficient information to obtain an initial understanding of the potential risks. An initial conceptual model for the site can be based on this information.
Hazard assessment	Identifying what pollutant linkages may be present and analysing the potential for unacceptable risks.	Collect further information and undertake exploratory site investigation to refine understanding of risks and the likelihood of pollutant linkages. The results may be interpreted using generic criteria and assumptions.
Risk estimation	Establishing the scale of the possible consequences by considering the degree of harm that may result and to which receptors.	Undertake detailed ground investigation to collect sufficient data to estimate the risks the contaminants may pose to defined receptors under defined conditions of exposure.
Risk evaluation	Deciding whether the risks are acceptable or unacceptable.	Review all site data to decide whether estimated risks are unacceptable, taking into account the nature and scale of any uncertainties associated with the risk estimation process.

Note: Stages based on *Model procedures for the management of land contamination* (CLR 11), Environment Agency, 2004.

C.3.2 Risk assessment

Risk assessment should follow a tiered approach of increasing detail, consisting of:

- preliminary risk assessment;
- generic quantitative risk assessment (GQRA);
- detailed quantitative risk assessment (DQRA).

Once the need for a risk assessment has been established a preliminary risk assessment will always be required, but more detailed assessment may not be necessary. Each tier should follow the stages in Table C.1.

C.3.3 Solid and liquid contaminants

C.3.3.1 Hazard identification and assessment

A preliminary site assessment will provide information on the past and present uses of the site and its surroundings, while a site walk-over may produce signs of possible contaminants. The results will guide the design of detailed ground investigations to gather information for risk assessment and the design of any remedial works. Assessments should pay particular attention to those areas of the site where building operations will take place.

Some contaminants may constitute hazards to buildings, materials and services, including:

- aggressive substances, such as acids, alkalis, solvents and chlorides, which may affect the long-term durability of materials;
- combustible fill, such as domestic waste and colliery spoil, which may lead to subterranean fires;
- blast furnace and steel-making slag, which may expand after deposition;
- floodwater affected by ground contaminants.

Such hazards may ultimately become a hazard to health, particularly where hydrocarbons permeate polyethylene pipes for potable water.

Further guidance
BS 5930:1999+A2:2010 Code of practice for site investigations.

BS 10175:2011. Code of practice for investigation of potentially contaminated sites.

C.3.3.2 Remedial measures

Unacceptable risks must be managed through remedial measures to break pollutant linkages and reduce exposure, by:

- Treatment – Decreasing the mass, concentration, mobility, flux or toxicity of the contaminant by biological, chemical or physical techniques.

- Containment – Encapsulating the material that contains contaminants by cover systems and in-ground vertical barriers. The design of cover systems should take account of natural processes and human activity which may result in the soil cover mixing with ground contaminants.

- Removal – Excavation and safe disposal of contaminants and contaminated material. Excavation can remove concentrations of contaminants, or reduce site levels sufficiently to allow a cover system to be provided. Imported fill should be assessed for suitability at source.

The area to be occupied by the building together with areas accessible to building users should be remediated, but on larger sites there may be a case for limiting remediation and applying lower levels of treatment to less accessible areas. It is for the applicant to demonstrate that such a strategy is appropriate.

Treatment and containment may require a Waste Management Licence from the Environment Agency. Work on contaminated land should not introduce a risk to the health and safety of the public or of site workers.

C.3.4 Methane and other gases from the ground

The action of micro-organisms on biodegradable materials such as landfill waste and organic-rich soils and sediments can generate gases such as methane and carbon dioxide, together with small quantities of volatile organic compounds (VOCs) (for radon see **C.3.5**). Those gases can be harmful to health or compromise safety, being:

- explosive – methane;

- flammable – VOCs;

- asphyxiating – methane;

- toxic – carbon dioxide, VOCs;

- malodorous – VOCs.

C.3.4.1 Hazard identification and assessment

Risk assessment should be carried out for methane and other gases (see **C.3.2**). Further investigation may be required where the building and associated ground:

- is on or within 250m of a landfill site, or within its likely sphere of influence;

- has been subject to wide-scale distribution of biodegradable substances;

- has been subject to a use that could have given rise to spillages of petrol, oil or solvents;

- is in an area where methane, carbon dioxide and other hazardous gases occur naturally.

Assessment should be made of:

- the quantity of gas-generating materials;
- their rate of generation;
- gas movement below ground; and
- gas emissions from the surface.

Measurements should be taken over a period long enough to enable gas emissions to be characterised fully, including, for example, periods of falling atmospheric pressure when emissions are likely to be higher. The assessment should consider the possibility of the gas regime being altered by construction activities.

For conventional housing there are two pathways to human receptors:

- gas entering a dwelling through the sub-structure;
- householder exposure to gas in garden areas, including those where outbuildings and extensions are constructed, or excavations for garden features such as ponds.

For non-domestic buildings the same pathways apply, but the risk might be significant within the building only.

C.3.4.2 Remedial measures

Unacceptable risks should be managed by appropriate remedial measures, which may include:

- site-wide measures such as removing gas-generating material or installing a gas extraction system;
- for dwellings, installing a gas-resistant barrier over a permeable layer which vents gases to atmosphere;
- for non-domestic buildings, gas-resistant barriers which in larger buildings may be coupled to mechanical extraction systems.

C.3.5 Radon

Radon is a naturally occurring radioactive gas which is colourless and odourless. Long-term exposure to high levels of radon increase the risk of lung cancer. In areas that have high levels of radon – such as the West Country – protective measures are required to prevent concentrations of the gas within buildings.

Guidance on occurrence and practical protective measures in dwellings, such as radon resistant membranes, is given in BR 211.

The Ionising Radiations Regulations 1999 (SI 1999/3232) set a national reference level for radon gas in workplaces, and under these Regulations, the people responsible for a workplace are required to measure radon levels when directed. The Health and Safety Executive provides guidance on protection from radon in the workplace.

Further guidance
Waste Management Paper 27 *Landfill gas*. HMIP. 2nd edition. 1991. [Replaced by LFTGN 03 *Guidance on the management of landfill gas*. Environment Agency 2004.]

Monitoring of landfill gas. Chartered Institution of Wastes Management (CIWM). 2nd edition. 1998.

BGS Technical Report WP/95/1 *Methane, carbon dioxide and oil seeps from natural sources and mining areas: characteristics, extent and relevance to planning and development in Great Britain*. British Geological Survey. 1995.

CIRIA Report 130. *Methane: its occurrence and hazards in construction*. CIRIA.1993.

CIRIA Report 152. *Risk assessment for methane and other gases from the ground*. CIRIA. 1995.

GasSIM – Landfill gas assessment tool. Environment Agency.

Further guidance
CIRIA Report 149: *Protecting development from methane: methane and associated hazards to construction*. 1995.

BR 414 *Protective measures for housing on gas-contaminated land*. BRE/Environment Agency. 2001.

DETR/Arup Environmental PIT Research Report: *Passive venting of soil gases beneath buildings*. DETR/Arup. 1997.

2013 changes
Approved Document C now refers to the 2007 edition of BR 211, and to the updated radon maps which reflect improved knowledge on the prevalence of radon across the UK.

Further guidance
BR 211 *Radon: Guidance on protective measures for new buildings* (including supplementary advice for extensions, conversions and refurbishment). BRE. 2007.

FB 41 *Radon in the workplace: A guide for building owners and managers*. BRE. 2011.

www.hse.gov.uk/radiation/ionising/radon.htm [Guidance on radon in the workplace]

C.4 Sub-soil drainage (Requirement C1(3))

The following provisions presume the site is not subject to general flooding, or that appropriate mitigating measures are being undertaken (**C.1.5**).

Sub-soil drainage or other protective measures should be provided where:

- the water table can rise to within 0.25m of the lowest floor; or
- surface water could enter or adversely affect the building;
- groundwater beneath or around the building could affect the stability of the ground.

Excavation work for foundations and services can alter groundwater flows through the site. Where contaminants are present in the ground, sub-soil drainage should be considered in order to prevent contamination of the building, its foundations, or its services.

An active sub-soil drain which passes under the footprint of the building, and is cut during excavation, should be:

- re-laid in pipes with sealed joints and have access points provided outside the building; or
- re-routed around the building; or
- re-run to another outfall.

Localised flooding from surcharging drains and sewers should be prevented (**H.2.2.2**).

C.5 Resistance to moisture (Requirement C2)

C.5.1 Resistance to moisture from the ground – floors

Floors next to the ground should:

- resist the passage of ground moisture to the upper surface of the floor;
- not be damaged by moisture from the ground;
- not be damaged by groundwater;
- resist the passage of ground gases (**C.3.4** and **C.3.5**).

C.5.1.1 Ground supported floors

A groundbearing floor consisting of dense concrete laid on a hardcore bed, with a damp-proof membrane, will adequately resist the passage of moisture from the ground. Table C.2 and Figure C.3 describe one construction suitable for floors which are not subjected to water pressure. An alternative approach would be to follow the recommendations of Clause 11 of CP 102:1973. BS 8102:1990 includes recommendations for floors subject to water pressure, including those on permeable strata such as chalk, limestone or gravel.

Further guidance
CP 102:1973. Code of practice for protection of buildings against water from the ground.
[Partially replaced by BS 8102.]

BS 8102:1990. Code of practice for protection of structures against water from the ground.
[Replaced by 2009 edition.]

Table C.2 Groundbearing floor construction

Item	Requirement
Hardcore bed	Well-compacted, no greater than 600mm deep of clean, broken brick or similar inert material, free from materials including water-soluble sulphates in quantities which could damage the concrete (BRE Digest 276[1]).
Concrete	At least 100mm thick (thicker if the structural design requires) to mix ST2 in BS 8500[2] or, if there is embedded reinforcement, to mix ST4 in BS 8500.
Damp-proof membrane	Above or below the concrete, and continuous with the damp-proof courses in walls, piers and the like. If the ground could contain water-soluble sulphates, or there is any risk that sulphate or other deleterious matter could contaminate the hardcore, the membrane should be placed at the base of the concrete slab. A membrane below the concrete could be formed with a sheet of polyethylene (at least 300μm thick – 1200 gauge) with sealed joints and laid on a bed of material that will not damage the sheet. A membrane laid above the concrete may be either polyethylene sheet as described above (but without the bedding material) or three coats of cold applied bitumen solution or similar moisture and water vapour resisting material. In each case it should be protected by either a screed or a floor finish, unless the membrane is a material which will also serve as a floor finish.
Insulants	Those beneath floor slabs should have sufficient strength to resist the weight of the slab and the anticipated floor loading as well as any possible overloading during construction. In order to resist degradation insulation that is placed below the damp-proof membrane should have low water absorption. If necessary the insulant should be resistant to contaminants in the ground.
Floor finish	A timber floor finish laid directly on concrete may be bedded in a material which may also serve as a damp-proof membrane. Timber fillets laid in the concrete as a fixing for a floor finish should be treated with an effective preservative unless they are above the damp-proof membrane. Some preservative treatments are described in BS 1282:1999.

[1] BRE Digest 276, Hardcore, 1992. [Note: no longer current but cited in the Building Regulations]

[2] BS 8500-1:2002. Concrete. Complementary British Standard to BS EN 206-1 Method of specifying and guidance for the specifier. [Note: replaced by BS 8500-1:2006+A1:2012]

Figure C.3 Groundbearing floor construction

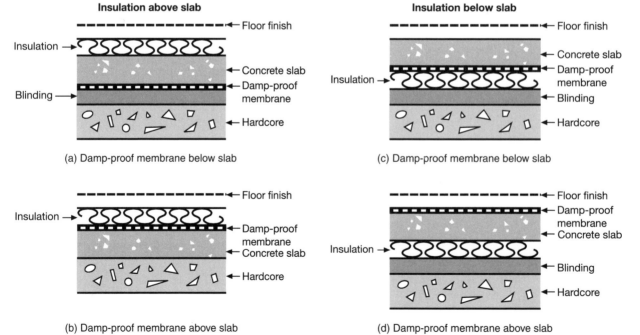

(a) Damp-proof membrane below slab

(b) Damp-proof membrane above slab

(c) Damp-proof membrane below slab

(d) Damp-proof membrane above slab

C.5.1.2 Suspended timber ground floors

A suspended timber floor will resist the passage of moisture from the ground if:

- the ground is covered to resist moisture and prevent plant growth;
- there is a ventilated air space between the ground covering and the timber;
- there are damp-proof courses between the timber and any material which can carry moisture from the ground.

Table C.3 and Figures C.4 and C.5 describe a construction suitable for suspended timber floors. Alternatively, the floor should meet the relevant recommendations of Clause 11 of CP 102:1973.

Table C.3 Suspended timber floor construction	
Item	**Requirement**
Ground covering	Either: • i. unreinforced concrete at least 100mm thick to mix ST 1 in BS 8500[1]. The concrete should be laid on a compacted hardcore bed of clean, broken brick or any other inert material free from materials including water-soluble sulphates in quantities which could damage the concrete; or • ii. concrete, composed as described above, or inert fine aggregate, in either case at least 50mm thick laid on at least 300μm (1200 gauge) polyethylene sheet with sealed joints, and itself laid on a bed of material which will not damage the sheet. In shrinkable clay soils, the depth of the air space may need to be increased to allow for heave. To prevent water collecting on the ground covering, either the top should be entirely above the highest level of the adjoining ground or, on sloping sites, consideration should be given to installing drainage on the outside of the up-slope side of the building (**Figure C.5**).
Ventilated air space	Ventilated air space measuring at least 75mm from the ground covering to the underside of any wall-plates and at least 150mm to the underside of the suspended timber floor (or insulation if provided). Two opposing external walls should have ventilation openings placed so that the ventilating air will have a free path between opposite sides and to all parts. Openings to be not less than the greatest of 1500mm^2/m run of external wall or 500mm^2/m^2 of floor area. Any pipes needed to carry ventilating air should have a diameter of at least 100mm. Ventilation openings should incorporate grilles which prevent the entry of vermin but do not resist the air flow unduly. Offset (periscope) ventilators may be used.
Damp-proof courses	Impervious sheet material, engineering brick or slates in cement mortar or other material which will prevent the passage of moisture. Guidance for choice of materials is given in BS 5628-3:2001[2].
Flooring	In areas such as kitchens, utility rooms and bathrooms where water may be spilled, any board used as a flooring, irrespective of the storey, should be moisture resistant. In the case of chipboard it should be of one of the grades with improved moisture resistance specified in BS 7331:1990[3] or BS EN 312-5:1997[4]. It should be laid, fixed and jointed in the manner recommended by the manufacturer. To demonstrate compliance the identification marks should be facing upwards. Any softwood boarding should be at least 20mm thick and from a durable species or treated with a suitable preservative.

[1] See **Table C.2**.

[2] BS 5628-3:2001. Code of practice for use of masonry. Materials and components, design and workmanship. [*Note: withdrawn, replaced by PD 6697:2010 Recommendations for the design of masonry structures to BS EN 1996-1-1 and BS EN 1996-2.*]

[3] BS 7331:1990. Specification for direct surfaced wood chipboard based on thermosetting. [*Note: withdrawn*]

[4] BS EN 312-5:1997. Particleboards. Specifications. Requirements for loadbearing boards for use in humid conditions. [*Note: withdrawn, replaced by BS EN 312:2010. Particleboards. Specifications.*]

Figure C.4 Suspended timber floor – construction

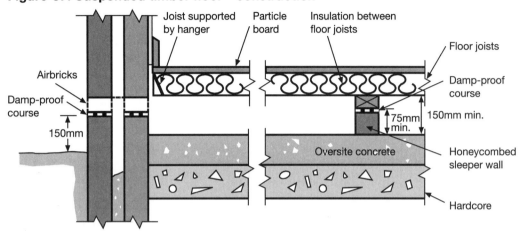

Figure C.5 Suspended floor – preventing water collection

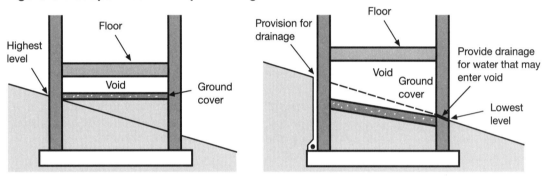

Note: Slope has been exaggerated for clarity.

C.5.1.3 Suspended concrete ground floors

A suspended floor of in situ or precast concrete, including beam and block floors, must prevent the passage of moisture to the upper surface and any reinforcement must be protected against moisture. Table C.4 describes one suitable construction.

C.5.2 Resistance to moisture from the ground – walls

Walls should:

- resist the passage of moisture from the ground to the inside of the building;
- not be damaged by moisture from the ground, nor carry moisture to any part of the structure which would be damaged by it.

Internal and external walls will resist moisture from the ground if a damp-proof course is provided. Table C.5 and Figures C.6 and C.7 describe damp-proof courses suitable for walls which are not subject to groundwater pressure: alternatively walls should comply with the relevant recommendations of Clauses 4 and 5 of BS 8215:1991. BS 8102:1990 includes guidance for walls subject to groundwater pressure, including basement walls.

Further guidance
BS 8215:1991. Code of practice for design and installation of damp-proof courses in masonry construction.

BS 8102:1990. See **C.5.1.1**.

Table C.4 Suspended concrete ground floor construction

Item	Requirement
Concrete deck	a. in situ concrete at least 100mm thick (but thicker if the structural design requires) containing at least 300kg of cement for each m³ of concrete; or b. precast concrete construction with or without infilling slabs; and c. reinforcing steel protected by concrete cover of at least 40mm if the concrete is in situ and at least the thickness required for a moderate exposure if the concrete is precast.
Damp-proof membrane	Required where the ground below the floor has been excavated below the lowest level of the surrounding ground and will not be effectively drained.
Ventilated air space	Ventilated air space measuring at least 150mm to the underside of the floor (or insulation if provided). Two opposing external walls should have ventilation openings placed so that the ventilating air will have a free path between opposite sides and to all parts. Openings to be not less than the greatest of 1500mm² per m run of external wall or 500mm² per m² of floor area. Any pipes needed to carry ventilating air should have a diameter of at least 100mm. Ventilation openings should incorporate grilles which prevent the entry of vermin but do not resist the air flow unduly. Offset (periscope) ventilators may be used.
Provision for flooding	Where flooding is likely, consideration may be given to including means of inspecting and clearing out the sub-floor voids beneath suspended floors.

Table C.5 Internal and external walls – damp-proof courses

Item	Requirement
Materials and construction	Bituminous material, polyethylene, engineering bricks or slates in cement mortar or any other material that will prevent the passage of moisture. The damp-proof course should be continuous with any damp-proof membrane in the floors.
Location	On external walls, the damp-proof course should be at least 150mm above the level of the adjoining ground (**Figure C.6**), unless the design is such that a part of the building will protect the wall.
	In external cavity walls (see **Figure C.7a**), the cavity should be taken down at least 225mm below the level of the lowest damp-proof course, or a damp-proof tray should be provided so as to prevent precipitation passing into the inner leaf (**Figure C.7b**), with weep holes every 900mm to assist in the transfer of moisture through the external leaf. Where the damp-proof tray does not extend the full length of the exposed wall, i.e. above an opening, stop ends and at least two weep holes should be provided.

Figure C.6 Damp-proof courses

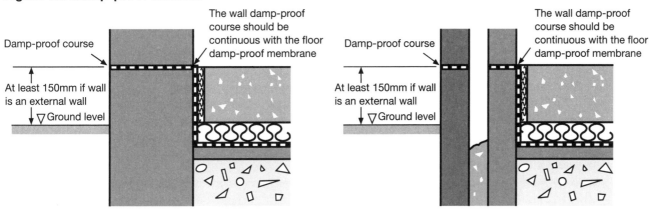

Figure C.7 Protecting the inner leaf

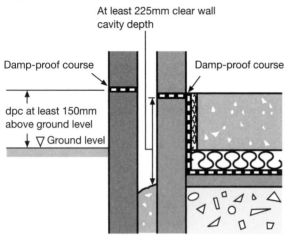

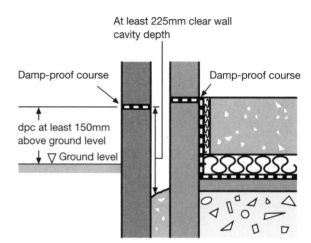

(a) Cavity carried down

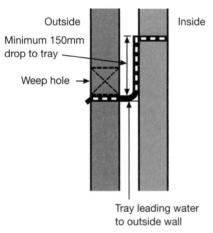

(b) Damp-proof (cavity) tray

C.5.3 Moisture from outside – external walls

External walls should resist penetration of precipitation to the inside of the building or components of a structure which might be damaged by moisture. Protection against precipitation may be provided by a solid wall, a cavity wall or an impervious or weather-resisting cladding.

C.5.3.1 Solid external walls

A solid wall should hold precipitation moisture – without it penetrating the inside of the building or causing damage – until it can be released in a dry period. The required wall thickness depends on the type of masonry and the severity of wind-driven rain.

Table C.6 and Figures C.8 and C.9 show wall constructions that will withstand severe exposure. An alternative approach would be to follow BS 5628-3:2001. In conditions of very severe exposure a solid wall will require impervious cladding.

Further guidance
BS 8104:1992. Code of practice for assessing exposure of walls to wind-driven rain.

BS 5628. Code of practice for the use of masonry. Part 3:2001. Materials and components, design and workmanship. [Withdrawn, replaced by BS EN 1996-2:2006 and PD 6697:2010. See **C.5.1.2**.]

Table C.6 Solid external walls – resistance to precipitation

Item	Requirement
Masonry	Brickwork or stonework at least 328mm thick; or Dense aggregate concrete blockwork at least 250mm thick; or Lightweight aggregate or aerated autoclaved concrete blockwork at least 215mm thick.
Mortar	Compatible with the strength of the bricks or blocks (BS EN 998-2:2003[1]). Joints raked out to a depth of at least 10mm if the wall is to be rendered.
Rendering	The exposed face of the bricks or blocks should be rendered or have equivalent protection. Rendering should be in two coats with a total thickness of at least 20mm and should have a scraped or textured finish. The rendering mix should be one part of cement, one part of lime and six parts of well graded sharp sand (nominal mix 1:1:6) unless the blocks are of dense concrete aggregate, in which case the mix may be 1:0.5:4 (see BS 5262:1991[2] for mixes for different severities and masonry types). Premixed and proprietary renders should be used in accordance with the manufacturer's instructions.
Protection	Wall tops should be protected and a damp-proof course provided unless the protection, including joints, forms a complete barrier to moisture (**Figure C.8**).
Damp-proof courses, cavity trays and closers	Installed to ensure water drains outwards: • where the downward flow will be interrupted by an obstruction, such as some types of lintel; • under openings, unless there is a sill and the sill and its joints will form a complete barrier; • at abutments between walls and roofs.
Insulation	Insulation on the inside should be separated from masonry by a cavity to break the path for moisture. Insulation on the outside should provide some resistance to the ingress of moisture to ensure the wall remains relatively dry (**Figure C.9**).

[1] BS EN 998-2:2003. Specification for mortar. Masonry mortar. [Withdrawn, replaced by 2010 edition.]

[2] BS 5262:1991. Code of practice for external renderings. [*Note: withdrawn, replaced by BS EN 13914-1:2005. Design, preparation and application of external rendering and internal plastering. External rendering.*]

Figure C.8 Protection of wall head from precipitation

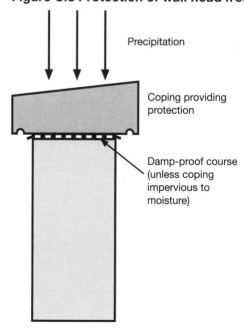

Precipitation

Coping providing protection

Damp-proof course (unless coping impervious to moisture)

Figure C.9 Insulated external walls: examples

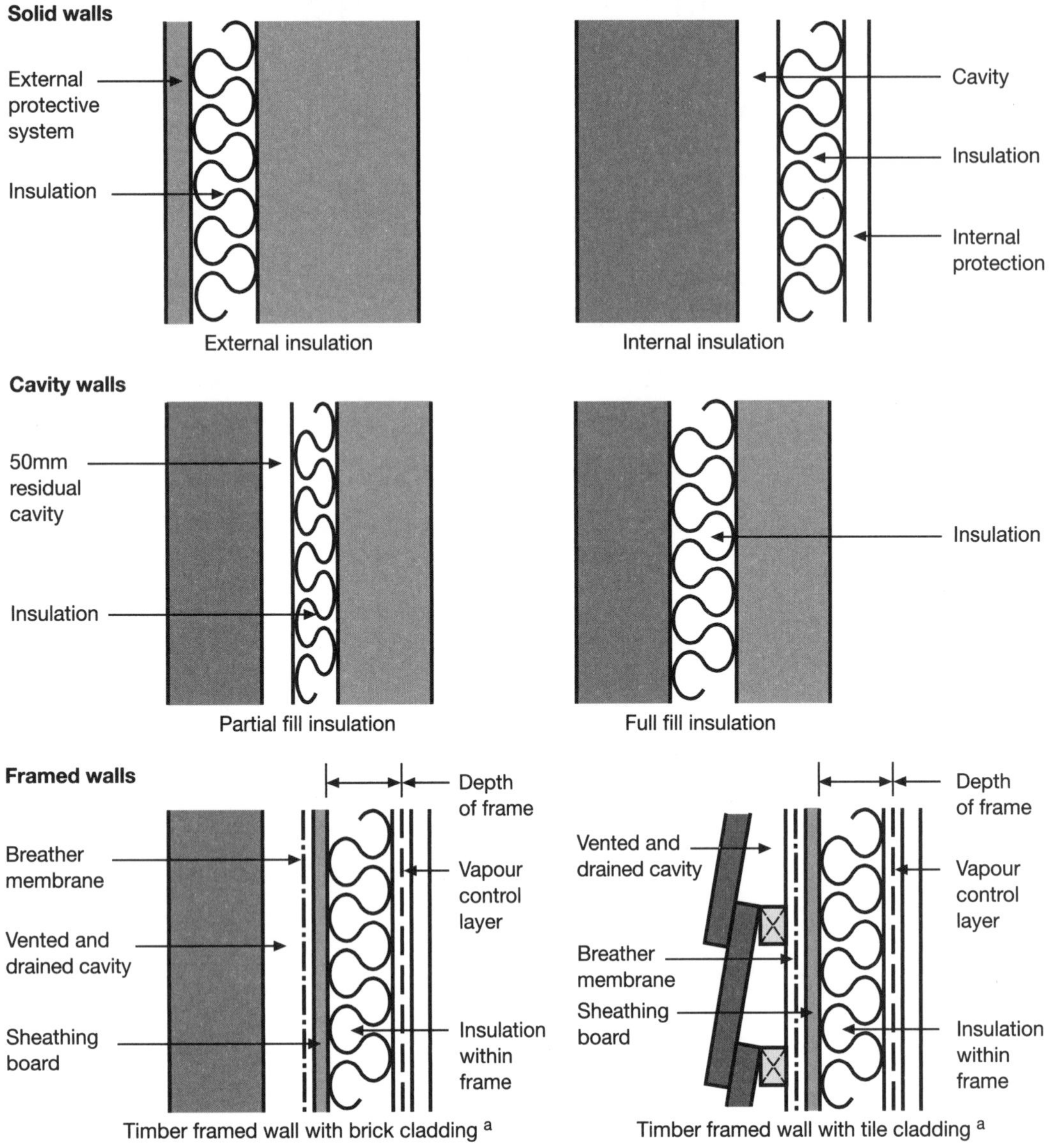

Solid walls

External insulation

Internal insulation

Cavity walls

Partial fill insulation

Full fill insulation

Framed walls

Timber framed wall with brick cladding [a]

Timber framed wall with tile cladding [a]

Note: a) In the case of light steel frame the insulation inside the cavity is placed over the frame.

C.5.3.2 Cavity external walls

The outer leaf must be separated from the inner leaf so as to prevent precipitation being carried to the inner leaf. Table C.7 and Figure C.9 describe a way of meeting that requirement. An alternative approach would be to follow BS 5628-3:2001.

Suitable wall constructions which include partial or full-fill cavity insulation should be determined by:

- taking the exposure zone from Figure C.10; and
  - adding 1 where local conditions accentuate wind effects, for example, open hillsides, or wind funnelled onto wall; or
  - subtracting 1 where walls do not face prevailing wind; and
- using constructions suitable for the modified zone from Table C.8.

Table C.7 Cavity external walls – resistance to precipitation

Item	Requirement
Outer leaf	Masonry: bricks, blocks, stone or manufactured stone.
Cavity	At least 50mm wide: the residual clear cavity in a partially filled cavity should not be less than 50mm. The cavity is to be bridged only by wall ties, cavity trays, cavity barriers, firestops and cavity closures.
Inner leaf	Masonry or frame with lining.
Masonry	Masonry units should be laid on a full bed of mortar with the cross joints substantially and continuously filled to ensure structural robustness and weather resistance.
Insulation	Rigid insulation built into the wall should be subject of a current technical approval and be installed in accordance with it. Other insulating material installed after construction should have certification and be installed in accordance with appropriate installation code. The state of repair and type of pointing of the external leaf of an existing dwelling should be assessed (see **D.2** for guidance).

Alternatively, the assessment methodology in current British or CEN Standards may be used.

For retrofitting insulation into existing buildings the exposure risk may be assessed by a method given in the third-party assessment of the insulation material. The condition of the outer leaf should be assessed to ensure that the wall's weather resistance will not be compromised.

C.5.3.3 Framed external walls

The cladding of a framed external wall should be separated from the insulation or sheathing by a vented and drained cavity lined on its inner side with a membrane that is both water resistant and vapour open (Figure C.9).

C.5.3.4 Cracking of external walls

Designers should take account of the possibility of rain penetration through cracks in external masonry caused by thermal movement in hot weather, or subsidence after droughts.

C.5.3.5 Impervious cladding systems for walls

Impervious cladding which is jointless or has sealed joints will prevent precipitation penetrating beyond the face of the building. Alternatively, cladding may be composed of impervious or weather-resisting units, with overlapped dry joints and a backing which drains precipitation from the back of the cladding towards the outer face. Table C.9 describes suitable cladding systems. Alternatively, systems should follow recommendations of the standards listed in Approved Document C paragraph 5.28.

Materials which deteriorate rapidly without special care should only be used as the weather-resisting part of cladding under strict conditions (**I.4.2**).

Further guidance

BS 8104:1992. Code of practice for assessing exposure to wind-driven rain. [For more accurate calculation of exposure zones.]

BR 262. *Thermal insulation: avoiding risks*. BRE. 2002. [For further guidance on use of the exposure table.]

BS 8208. Guide to assessment of suitability of external cavity walls for filling with thermal insulation.
-1:1985. Existing traditional cavity construction. [Withdrawn.]

BS 5628-3:2001. See **C.5.3.1**.

Further guidance

BRE *Building Elements: Walls, windows and doors*. 1998.

BRE Report 292 *Cracking in buildings*. 1995.

Figure C.10 UK zones for exposure to driving rain

Exposure zones		Approximate wind-driven rain* (litres/m^2 per spell)
	1 Sheltered	Less than 33
	2 Moderate	33 to less than 56.5
	3 Severe	56.5 to less than 100
	4 Very severe	100 or more

*Maximum wall spell index derived from BS 8104

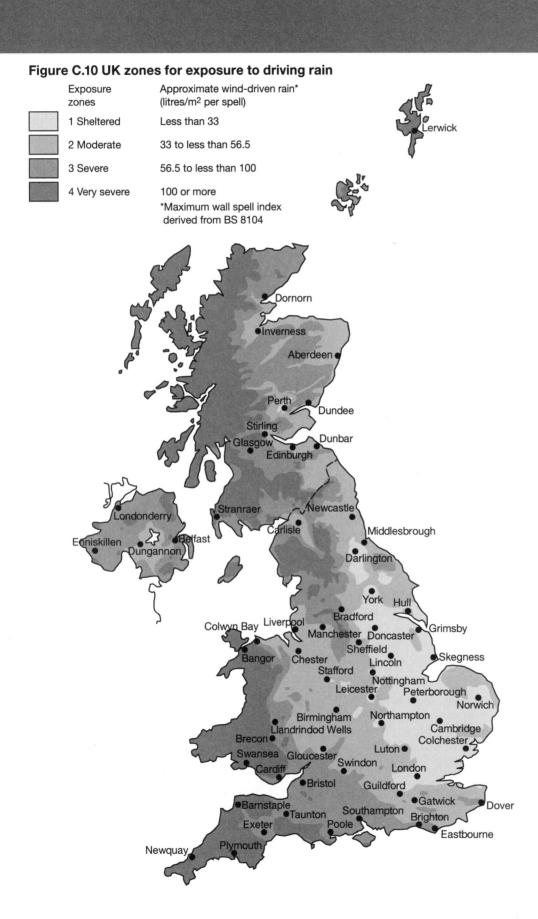

Table C.8 Maximum recommended exposure zones for insulated masonry walls

Wall construction		Maximum recommended exposure zone for each construction						
		Impervious cladding		Rendered finish		Facing masonry		
Insulation method	Minimum width of filled or clear cavity (mm)	Full height of wall	Above facing masonry	Full height of wall	Above facing masonry	Tooled flush joints	Recessed mortar joints	Flush sills and copings
Built-in full fill	50	4	3	3	3	2	1	1
	75	4	3	4	3	3	1	1
	100	4	4	4	3	3	1	2
	125	4	4	4	3	3	1	2
	150	4	4	4	4	4	1	2
Injected fill not UF foam	50	4	2	3	2	2	1	1
	75	4	3	4	3	3	1	1
	100	4	3	4	3	3	1	1
	125	4	4	4	3	3	1	2
	150	4	4	4	4	4	1	2
Injected fill UF foam	50	4	2	3	2	1	1	1
	75	4	2	3	2	2	1	1
	100	4	2	3	2	2	1	1
Partial fill, residual	50mm residual	4	4	4	4	3	1	1
	75mm residual	4	4	4	4	4	1	1
	100mm residual	4	4	4	4	4	2	1
Internal insulation – clear cavity	50	4	3	4	3	3	1	1
	100	4	4	4	4	4	2	2
Internal insulation – filled cavity	50	4	3	3	3	2	1	1
	100	4	4	4	3	3	1	2

C.5.3.6 Openings

A damp-proof course should be provided to direct moisture towards the outside of the wall where:

- the downward flow of moisture would be obstructed, for example, at a lintel;
- sill elements, including joints, do not prevent the transfer of precipitation;
- reveal elements, including joints, do not prevent the transfer of rain and snow.

Where a cavity is too wide to be covered by the door or window frame, the reveal may need to be lined with plasterboard, dry lining, support system or thermal backing board. Direct plastering should only be carried out on a backing of expanded metal lathing or similar.

In driving rain zone 4 all window and door reveals should have checked rebates (Figure C.11), or have an insulated finned cavity closer.

Table C.9 Impervious cladding systems for walls

Item	Requirement
Type of cladding	a. Impervious including metal, plastic, glass and bituminous products; or b. Weather resisting including natural stone or slate, cement based products, fired clay and wood; or c. Moisture resisting including bituminous and plastic products lapped at the joints, if used as a sheet material, and permeable to water vapour unless there is a ventilated space directly behind the material; or d. Jointless materials and sealed joints, which would allow for structural and thermal movement.
Joints	Dry joints between cladding units should be designed so that precipitation will not pass through them, or the cladding should be designed so that precipitation which enters the joints will be directed towards the exposed face without it penetrating beyond the back of the cladding. Note: Whether dry joints are suitable will depend on the design of the joint or the design of the cladding and the severity of the exposure to wind and rain.
Fixing	Each sheet, tile and section of cladding should be securely fixed. Guidance as to appropriate fixing methods is given in BS 8000-6:1990[1]. Particular care should be taken with detailing and workmanship at the junctions between cladding and window and door openings as they are vulnerable to moisture ingress.
Insulation	Insulation can be incorporated into the construction provided it is either protected from moisture or unaffected by it.
Timber components	Where cladding is supported by timber components or is on the façade of a timber framed building, the space between the cladding and the building should be ventilated to ensure rapid drying of any water that penetrates the cladding.

[1] BS 8000-6:1990. Workmanship on building sites. Code of practice for slating and tiling of roofs.

Accessible thresholds (Figure C.12) to Part M should have:

- an external landing laid to a fall of 1:40 – 1:60 in a single direction away from the doorway;
- a maximum slope of 15° on the sill leading up to the doorway.

Further guidance
BRE Good Building Guide 47. *Level external thresholds; reducing moisture penetration and thermal bridging*. 2001.

Accessible thresholds in new buildings: guidance for house builders and designers. TSO. 1999.

Figure C.11 Window reveals for use in areas of severe or very severe exposure to driving rain

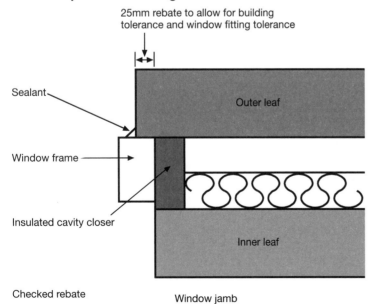

25mm rebate to allow for building tolerance and window fitting tolerance

Sealant

Outer leaf

Window frame

Insulated cavity closer

Inner leaf

Checked rebate

Window jamb

Figure C.12 Accessible threshold for use in exposed areas

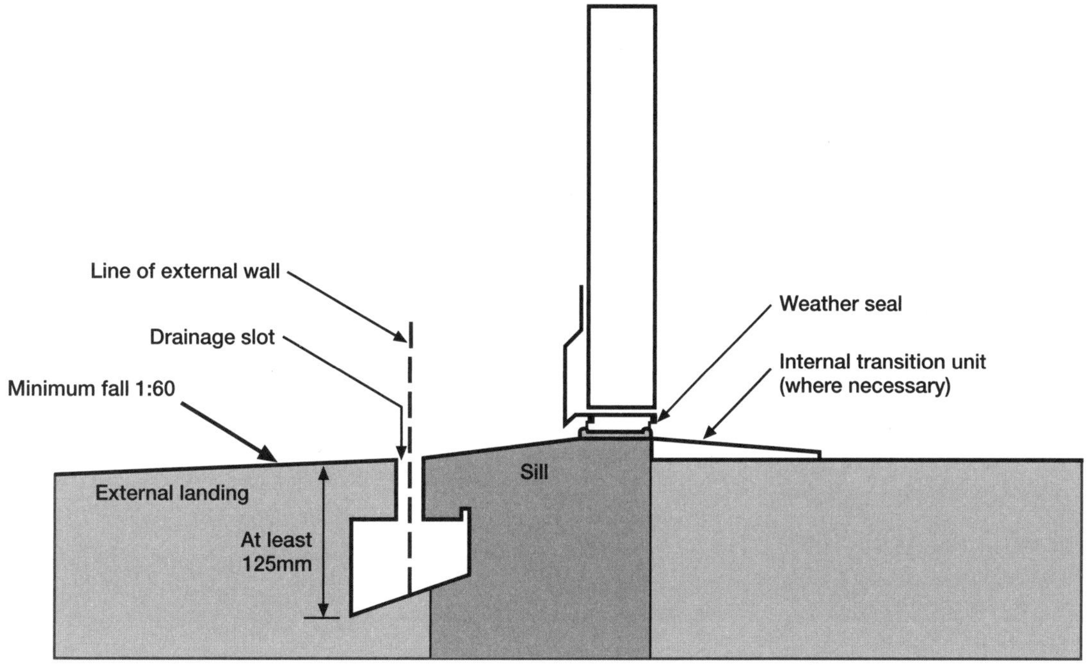

C.5.4 Resistance to moisture from outside – roofs

Roofs should:

- resist the penetration of precipitation to the inside of the building;
- not be damaged by precipitation;
- not carry precipitation to any part of the building which it would damage.

A roof should either hold precipitation at its outer face or prevent it penetrating beyond the back of the roofing system. The roof may be:

- impervious and jointless; or
- impervious with sealed joints; or
- impervious or weather resisting, with overlapping dry joints and backed with a material which will direct precipitation towards the outer face.

Roofing systems should comply with Table C.10 or meet the relevant recommendations of the standards in Approved Document C, paragraph 6.9.

Materials which require special care to avoid rapid deterioration should be used as the weather-resisting part of a roof only under certain conditions (see **I.4.2**).

Table C.10 Roofs – resistance to moisture from outside

Item	Requirement
Type of system	Impervious: including metal, plastic and bituminous products.
	Weather resisting: including natural stone or slate, cement based products, fired clay and wood.
	Moisture resisting: including bituminous and plastic products lapped at the joints, if used as a sheet material, and permeable to water vapour unless there is a ventilated space directly behind the material.
	Jointless materials and sealed joints which allow for structural and thermal movement.
Joints	Dry joints between roofing sheets should prevent precipitation passing, or the system should drain precipitation which enters the joints without it penetrating beyond the back of the roofing system. The suitability of dry joints depends on the exposure to wind and rain.
Fixing	Each sheet, tile and section of roof should be fixed in an appropriate manner (BS 8000-6:1990[1]).

[1] BS 8000-6:1990. Workmanship on building sites. Code of practice for slating and tiling of roofs.

C.5.5 Resistance to interstitial and surface condensation and mould growth

The structural and thermal performance of ground floors, exposed floors, external walls and roofs should not be adversely affected by interstitial condensation, nor should they promote surface condensation and mould growth, given reasonable occupancy conditions.

To avoid interstitial condensation the following elements should be designed and constructed to the following clauses of BS 5250:2002:

- ground floors and exposed floors – clause 8.5;
- external walls – clause 8.3;
- roofs – clause 8.4.

The excessive transfer of moisture to roof voids should be avoided by sealing gaps and penetrations and providing draught seals to loft hatches. Some cold deck roofs will require ventilation, although small roofs (such as those over porches or bay windows) may not.

To prevent surface condensation and mould growth the U-values of elements should not at any point exceed:

- Ground floors and exposed floors – 0.7 W/m^2 K;
- Walls – 0.7 W/m^2 K;
- Roofs – 0.35 W/m^2 K.

Junctions between elements and at openings within elements should follow the accredited construction details or BRE IP 17/01, or (for roofs) MRCMA Technical Paper 14.

Specialist advice should be sought when designing buildings with high levels of moisture, such as swimming pools.

2013 changes

Approved Document C refers to the 2002 edition of BS 5250, which has been replaced by the 2011 edition. Restructuring of the document means the relevant sections are:

- ground floors and exposed floors – Annex F;
- external walls – Annex G;
- roofs – Annex H.

Further guidance

BS 5250:2002. Code of practice for control of condensation in buildings. [Withdrawn and replaced by the 2011 edition.]

BR 262. *Thermal insulation: avoiding risks*. BRE. 2002.

Accredited Construction Details, available through www.planningportal.gov.uk

BRE IP 17/01. *Assessing the effects of thermal bridging at junctions around openings*. [Replaced by IP1/06. *Assessing the effects of thermal bridging at junctions and around openings*.]

MCRMA Technical Paper 14: *Guidance for the design of metal cladding and roofing to comply with Approved Document L2:2001*. The Metal Cladding and Roofing Manufacturers Association, www.mcrma.co.uk [MCRMA Technical Paper 17 gives updated guidance.]

D. Toxic substances

D.1 Scope

Part D is intended to protect the health and safety of building occupants from toxic fumes produced during and following the insertion of cavity wall insulation.

The guidance in Approved Document D considers only urea formaldehyde (UF) foam, which is no longer widely used. Most retrofit cavity wall insulation employs blown mineral fibre, polystyrene beads or polyurethane foam, which do not give off toxic fumes.

Part D: Toxic substances	
Requirement	**Limits on application**
Cavity insulation	
D1 If insulating material is inserted into a cavity in a cavity wall reasonable precautions shall be taken to prevent the subsequent permeation of any toxic fumes from that material into any part of the building occupied by people.	

D.2 Urea formaldehyde (UF) foam

The thermal performance of masonry cavity walls can be improved by filling the cavity with insulation, such as urea formaldehyde (UF) foam. However, UF foam gives off toxic formaldehyde fumes as it cures and dries. Should those fumes reach the interior of the building – through gaps in the wall's inner leaf – they can irritate the eyes and throat of the building occupants and cause breathing difficulties.

In order to prevent fumes reaching the building interior:

- The wall must be a cavity wall with an inner leaf of brickwork or blockwork and its suitability for foam filling must be assessed to BS 8208-1:1985. As a continuous inner leaf will usually be sufficient to prevent noticeable levels of formaldehyde within the building, the inner leaf must not have gaps or cracks. Any breaks should be sealed with mortar. Service penetrations and the perimeters of openings should also be sealed.

- The UF foam must comply with BS 5617:1985 and the installers must be operating under a Certificate of Registration of Assessed Capability issued by a certification body, such as BSI.

- The installation procedure should comply with BS 5618:1985.

Further guidance

BS 8208-1:1985. Guide to assessment of suitability of external cavity walls for filling with thermal insulants. Existing traditional cavity construction. [Withdrawn 2009.]

BS 5617:1985. Specification for urea formaldehyde (UF) foam systems suitable for thermal insulation of cavity walls with masonry or concrete inner and outer leaves.

BS 5618:1985. Code of practice for thermal insulation of cavity walls (with masonry or concrete inner and outer leaves) by filling with urea formaldehyde (UF) foam systems.

E. Resistance to the passage of sound

E.1 General considerations

E.1.1 Scope

Part E is intended to reduce the transmission of sound into, and between, the rooms of residential buildings. It also addresses the acoustic performance of school buildings.

Table E.1 sets out the application of E1 and E2 by element, type of building and type of building work.

Part E: Resistance to the passage of sound	
Requirement	**Limit on application**
Protection against sound from other parts of the building and adjoining buildings	
E1 Dwellinghouses, flats and rooms for residential purposes shall be designed and constructed in such a way that they provide reasonable resistance to sound from other parts of the same building and from adjoining buildings.	
Protection against sound within a dwellinghouse etc.	
E2 Dwellinghouses, flats and rooms for residential purposes shall be designed and constructed in such a way that – (a) internal walls between a bedroom or a room containing a water closet, and other rooms; and (b) internal floors provide reasonable resistance to sound.	Requirement E2 does not apply to – (a) an internal wall which contains a door; (b) an internal wall which separates an en suite toilet from the associated bedroom; (c) existing walls and floors in a building which is subject to a material change of use.
Reverberation in common internal parts of buildings containing flats or rooms for residential purposes	
E3 The common internal parts of buildings which contain flats or rooms for residential purposes shall be designed and constructed in such a way as to prevent more reverberation around the common parts than is reasonable.	Requirement E3 only applies to corridors, stairwells, hallways and entrance halls which give access to the flat or room for residential purposes.
Acoustic conditions in schools	
E4 (1) Each room or other space in a school building shall be designed and constructed in such a way that it has the acoustic conditions and the insulation against disturbance by noise appropriate to its intended use. (2) For the purposes of this Part – 'school' has the same meaning as in section 4 of the Education Act 1996; and 'school building' means any building forming a school or part of a school.	

Table E.1 Application of Requirements E1 and E2	Dwellings			Flats			Rooms for residential purpose		
	New	Change of use		New	Change of use		New	Change of use	
		New element	Existing element		New element	Existing element		New element	Existing element
Separating walls	✓	✓	✓	✓	✓	✓	✓	✓	✓
Separating floors	N/A	N/A	N/A	✓	✓	✓	✓	✓	✓
Internal floors	✓	✓	N/A	✓	✓	N/A	✓	✓	N/A
Internal walls to bedrooms	✓[1]	✓[1]	N/A	✓[1]	✓[1]	N/A	✓[1]	✓[1]	N/A
Internal walls to toilets	✓[2]	✓[2]	N/A	✓[2]	✓[2]	N/A	✓[2]	✓[2]	N/A

[1] Not applicable (N/A) if it contains a door.

[2] N/A if it separates an en suite toilet from the associated bedroom.

E.1.2 Other regulations

Noise in the workplace is addressed by the Control of Noise at Work Regulations 2005. Ambient environmental noise is addressed by the Environmental Noise (England) Regulations and Directive 2002/49/EC (the 'environmental noise directive').

E.1.3 Definitions

Adjoining Adjoining dwellinghouses, adjoining flats, adjoining rooms for residential purposes and adjoining buildings are those in direct physical contact with another dwellinghouse, flat, room for residential purposes or building.

Rooms for residential purposes Rooms or groups of rooms used by one or more people for living and sleeping, such as hotels, hostels, halls of residence or residential homes; but not patient accommodation.

E.1.4 The behaviour of sound in buildings

Sound consists of vibrations or pressure waves which travel through solids and fluids – including gases, such as air: it can be reflected or absorbed by surfaces. For Part E the significant mechanisms are:

- Airborne sound transmission – Sound generated within one space in a building reaches adjacent spaces:
  - directly, through the air through small gaps and spaces in the structure; or
  - indirectly, sound waves striking one side of a building element can cause it to vibrate, producing sound waves on the other side of the element.
- Impact sound transmission – An object which strikes a building element sets up vibrations within it, which in turn creates sound waves in an adjacent space. Impact sound is commonly generated by footfalls, but can also result from the shutting of doors and the use of electrical switches and sockets.
- Flanking transmission – The transmission of sound through walls or floors which adjoin elements which separate adjoining buildings or rooms. It can occur when impact sound on a floor also sets up vibrations in the supporting wall, or when vibrations are produced in wall cavities which by-pass separating walls. Pipework and ducting also provide routes for flanking transmission.

- Reverberation – The surfaces of building elements can reflect sound waves, effectively prolonging the duration of the initial sound. In some applications, for example concert halls, reverberation is beneficial, but in other contexts reverberation reduces audibility or makes sounds more intrusive.

E.1.5 Measuring sound

E.1.5.1 General measures

Frequency

The rate of vibration of a sound wave, measured in cycles per second and expressed in Hertz (Hz). The audible frequency range is 20Hz to 20,000Hz.

Loudness

The amount of energy in a sound wave is measured by the sound pressure level, measured in Pascals (Pa). In acoustics, loudness is measured in decibels (dB); the decibel scale is logarithmic (non-linear), which means a 20dB difference in loudness represents a tenfold difference in sound pressure level. For human hearing, the perceived loudness of a sound is not directly proportional to the decibel level.

E.1.5.2 Airborne sound

Airborne sound performance is expressed as the difference between the loudness of a sound generated on one side of an element and its loudness measured on the other side. Elements which transmit less sound produce higher differences; those that transmit most sound produce lower differences.

To measure the level of airborne sound, a standard noise source is used in the source room, while measurements are made in the receiving room using one or more microphones. Because sound transmission varies with the frequency of the sound, measurements are taken across multiple frequency bands and compared to a standard set of results to obtain an average performance figure.

The key measures are:

R_w – Weighted Sound Reduction Index. A laboratory measure of airborne sound insulation based on a standard test suite. Measured in decibels.

D_{nTw} – Weighted Standardised Level Difference. A site measure of airborne sound insulation, adjusted for reverberation. Measured in decibels.

C_{tr} – A correction factor which increases in contribution of low-frequency sound to the D_{nTw} figure.

Because airborne sound measurements record sound reduction, higher values for R_w and D_{nTw} are better.

E.1.5.3 Impact sound

Impact sound performance is expressed as the loudness of a sound generated by a standard impact on the building structure. Elements which generate less sound have lower sound levels; those that generate more sound have higher sound levels.

Measurements are made using a tapping machine (sound source), which strikes the floor surface in one room. The sound level is then measured with one or more microphones in the receiving room. Because sound generation varies across different frequencies, measurements are taken across multiple frequency bands and compared to a standard set of results to obtain an average performance figure. The key measures are:

L'_{nw} – Weighted Normalised Impact Sound Pressure Level. A laboratory measure of impact sound based on a standard test suite. Measured in decibels.

L'_{nTw} – Weighted Standardised Impact Sound Pressure Level. A site measure of impact sound performance, adjusted for reverberation time. Measured in decibels.

As both L'_{nw} and L'_{nTw} measure the level of sound transmission, lower values are better.

L_w – the change in impact sound level produced by a surface treatment. Measured in decibels. Higher values are better.

E.1.5.4 Reverberation

Reverberation is expressed as the length of time it takes for a sound to die away, once the source has stopped. The reverberation time is the time taken for a sound to decay by 60dB, measured in seconds.

E.1.5.5 Absorption

The absorption coefficient measures the proportion of sound a surface absorbs:

1 represents a surface which absorbs all sound falling on it

0 represents a surface which reflects all sound falling on it.

E.1.6 Reducing sound transmission

When designing building elements to reduce sound transmission between adjacent spaces there are four main physical attributes of the materials and structure to consider. Few constructions derive their performance from only one attribute; most depend on the combined effect of several attributes.

- Mass – The more mass a structure has, the more energy is required to set it vibrating, and the less sound will be transmitted through that structure. With enough mass, sound transmission can be stopped completely: although that is rarely a practical solution, the use of dense materials, such as concrete or masonry, can reduce sound transmission to acceptable levels. The performance of lightweight structures can be improved by adding mass; for example, plasterboard plank can be fitted in the voids between floor joists.

- Isolation – Components in direct contact transmit sound more effectively than those separated by cavities, with the degree of sound transmission being affected by the width of the cavity and the type and number of any connectors between the faces. Isolation is used in some separating wall constructions and also in independent ceilings beneath separating floors. However, open cavities in flanking structures can act as paths for airborne sound transmission.

- Stiffness – The rigidity, or dynamic stiffness, of components within building elements affects sound transmission. Components with high dynamic stiffness transmit more sound than those with low dynamic stiffness. Although dynamic stiffness is an important consideration for components such as wall ties in masonry cavity walls, and for resilient layers in floating floor constructions, acoustic considerations must be balanced with other performance requirements, particularly strength.

- Absorption – Porous materials, such as fibrous insulation or open-faced tiles, can dissipate sound within their networks of air spaces as friction turns the sound energy into heat. Absorptive materials may be used within constructions to reduce sound transmission, or may be used on surfaces to absorb sound and so reduce reverberation.

E.2 Separating walls and floors (Requirement E1)

Separating walls and floors must achieve the sound insulation performance requirements in Table E.2. Airborne sound transmission is addressed for both walls and floors, but impact sound transmission is addressed only for floors. The requirements for residential buildings formed by material change of use are less onerous than those for new build.

To ensure that the as-built performance of separating walls and floors meets the standards in Table E.2, elements must either

- undergo pre-completion testing, or
- be registered under the Robust Details scheme.

One project can include both methods of demonstrating compliance.

Table E.2 Sound insulation performance for separating walls and floors			Airborne sound reduction $D_{nTw} + C_{tr}$dB Minimum values	Impact sound transmission L'_{nTw}dB Maximum values
Dwellinghouses and flats	Purpose built	Walls	45	No requirement
		Floors and stairs	45	62
	Change of use	Walls	43	No requirement
		Floors and stairs	43	64
Rooms for residential purposes	Purpose built	Walls	43	No requirement
		Floors and stairs	45	62
	Change of use	Walls	43	No requirement
		Floor and stairs	43	64

Note: Levels to be achieved during on-site testing: they are not laboratory test levels.

E.2.1 Pre-completion testing

Pre-completion testing (PCT) is intended to ensure that appropriate performance standards are achieved, and it is the only method for demonstrating compliance for all rooms for residential purposes and for dwellinghouses and flats formed by material change of use. Acoustic tests are carried out when the buildings are substantially complete, but not necessarily decorated. Elements which fail testing must undergo remedial work and re-testing.

PCT offers considerable design flexibility, however, there is always the possibility an element will fail a test and require remedial measures, resulting in delays for the builder and purchaser.

E.2.1.1 Groups for testing

Only a sample of dwellings, flats and rooms for residential purposes need be tested, because the results for any type of construction on a project are taken to be indicative of other constructions of the same type. To establish test groups:

1. Treat dwellinghouses, flats and rooms for residential purpose as three separate groups. (If elements have the same construction and flanking construction, and room areas are roughly similar this step may be omitted.)

2. Subdivide groups where there are significant differences in construction (for example, some elements might be timber framed while others are masonry).

3. Subdivide again where flanking conditions vary significantly.

4. Atypical elements with unfavourable features, such as a flat with a large area of flanking wall at a gable, should be put into their own groups.

Developments based on material change of use are likely to require more sub-groups than new build developments.

At least one set of tests (see Table E.3) must be carried out for every ten dwellinghouses, flats or rooms for residential purposes in a group or sub-group: the first completed members of each group or sub-group must be tested. Wherever possible, each set of tests should include a test on a pair of living rooms and a test on a pair of bedrooms. If the layout of the rooms means the pairs on either side of an element are different then at least one room of one pair should be a bedroom, and one room in the other pair a living room. Where there is only one pair of rooms on each side of the separating wall then the number of tests can be reduced.

Test rooms should preferably have a volume greater than 25m³. If they are smaller, their volume should be included in reported results. Where the rooms in a pair are of a different size the sound source should be in the larger of the two rooms.

Table E.3 Definition of a set of tests	
Condition	**Tests required**
Dwellinghouse	1 airborne sound test between two rooms, preferably living rooms 1 airborne sound test between two rooms, preferably bedrooms
Flats (without separating walls) and rooms for residential purposes (RRP)	1 airborne and 1 impact sound test between two rooms, preferably living rooms 1 airborne and 1 impact sound test between two rooms, preferably bedrooms
Flats (separating walls and floors): and RRP	1 airborne sound test between two rooms, preferably living rooms 1 airborne sound test between two rooms, preferably bedrooms 1 airborne and 1 impact sound test between two rooms, preferably living rooms 1 airborne and 1 impact sound test between two rooms, preferably bedrooms

E.2.1.2 Testing procedure

After consultation with the developer on likely completion times, the Building Control Body (BCB) should require one set of tests for the first of each group or sub-group scheduled for completion or sale. Further tests should be carried out throughout the construction period, although with a weighting towards the early stage of the construction period.

Where flats are sold prior to fit-out, testing should follow the same principles, with precautions taken to ensure that fit-out does not worsen performance.

Airborne sound transmission should be tested to BS EN ISO 140-4:1998, and impact sound transmission to BS EN ISO 140-7:1998. Tests should be carried out by organisations that are:

- registered with UKAS (or a European equivalent) for on-site acoustic testing; or
- members of the Association of Noise Consultants (ANC) Registration Scheme.

However, if no such organisation is available when required then a non-registered organisation may be used.

Reports of testing must include details of:

- the testing organisation;
- element tested;
- the test results;
- the required standard;
- a pass/fail indication.

Further guidance
BS EN ISO 140. Acoustics. Measurement of sound insulation in buildings and of building elements.
-4:1998. Field measurements of airborne sound insulation between rooms.
-7:1998. Field measurements of impact sound insulation of floors.

E.2.1.3 Failed tests

An element which fails to achieve the required standard will need remedial treatment and must be re-tested. Where that failed element separates other pairs of rooms the developer must demonstrate the same problem does not occur, by:

- additional testing;
- remedial measures;
- demonstrating the initial cause of failure does not apply.

A test failure also brings into doubt the performance of untested properties in the same group. The developer must demonstrate that such properties meet the required standard. If such dwellings are occupied, the action taken must be agreed between developer, occupier and the BCB. The BCB should also increase the size of the test sample, until it is satisfied the problem has been solved.

Further guidance
IP 14/02 *Dealing with poor sound insulation between dwellings*. BRE. 2002. [Guidance on remedial measures.]

E.2.2 Robust Details

Robust Details offer an alternative method to site testing for demonstrating compliance with E1 for new build dwellinghouses and flats. The Robust Details themselves are separating wall and floor constructions which, in field testing, have been shown to provide better standards of sound insulation than required by E1.

Where a Robust Detail is adopted there is no need for pre-completion testing.

The major benefits of adopting Robust Details are: the avoidance of on-site testing; the absence of any risk of failure during pre-completion testing; and the avoidance of any need for remedial work. There is also no need to arrange and pay for pre-completion testing. However, the Robust Details scheme only includes a limited number of construction types, and the constructions are over-engineered to provide a safety margin against poorer standards of work.

E.2.2.1 The Robust Details Limited scheme

The Robust Details scheme is administered by Robust Details Limited (RDL), a non-profit-making organisation. Each plot which will rely on one or more Robust Details must be registered, in advance of construction, with RDL which will charge a fee. RDL then provides a Purchase Statement which lists the registered plots with their reference numbers and the list of Robust Details which will be used on that plot. The Purchase Statement must be submitted to the BCB to demonstrate that testing is not required.

Each registered Robust Detail comes with a specification sheet and site checklist, which must be completed as work on the separating floor or wall proceeds. RDL also provides a compliance certificate for each registered plot, which the developer must sign once the separating walls and floors have been completed. The certificate should be made available to the BCB on request.

Further guidance
Robust Details Limited. www.robustdetails.com

E.2.2.2 Performance

Each Robust Detail design has been assessed as:

- consistently exceeding the performance standards of E1;
- being practical to construct on site;
- being 'reasonably tolerant of workmanship'.

The performance of each type of Robust Detail is monitored by spot-check sound tests by acoustic consultants; site inspections also take place to ensure that construction proceeds correctly. Where a Robust Detail fails an acoustic test, RDL will inform the BCB, which can then require remedial work and pre-completion testing to be carried out. RDL will revise or even withdraw details that consistently fail acoustic testing on site.

Although the use of a Robust Detail enables compliance with E1, RDL offers no guarantee that the detail will comply with other parts of the Regulations.

E.2.3 Solutions

Approved Document E describes a number of construction solutions which, when built correctly, should comply with E1. There is, however, no obligation to adopt those designs. The details for the separating walls and floors must be considered in conjunction with those for flanking constructions and junctions with other elements.

E.2.3.1 General considerations

Calculating mass

The mass of walls, floors and the layers or leaves of which they are composed is expressed as the mass per unit surface area. The total mass of an element is calculated from the mass of all of the component layers (Annex A2 of Approved Document E gives a method for masonry leaves).

Cavity widths

Quoted figures represent minimum widths.

Finishes

Plasterboard/mineral wool laminates may be substituted where plasterboard is specified, or the finish is not specified.

Wall ties

Approved Document E defines two types of wall tie (derived from BS 1243:1978), based on the dynamic stiffness of the tie at a particular cavity width, k_{xmm}, and the number of ties per square metre, n:

- Type A: $n.k_{xmm} < 4.8 MN/m^3$. The most common example is a butterfly tie.
- Type B: $n.k_{xmm} < 113 MN/m^3$. The most common example is a double-triangle tie. This type is suitable for external masonry cavity walls where type A ties do not satisfy the requirements of Part A.

Corridor walls and doors

Rooms in flats should be separated from corridors by a separating wall to control flanking transmission, and to limit transmission of sound from the corridor. Door perimeters should be well sealed and the doors should have:

- mass greater than $25 kg/m^2$; or
- minimum sound reduction index R_w of 29dB.

Noisy parts of the building should be isolated by a lobby or double door, or flats near the noise should be isolated in the same way.

Refuse chutes

Walls separating refuse chutes from rooms should have a minimum mass of:

- $1320 kg/m^2$ for habitable rooms or kitchens;
- $220 kg/m^2$ for non-habitable rooms.

Pipes

Ducts should have mass of $15 kg/m^2$ and 25mm mineral wool lagging to either enclosure or pipe.

Further guidance
BS 1243:1978. Specification for metal ties for cavity wall construction. [Withdrawn and replaced by BS 845-1:2003+A1:2008. Specification for ancillary components of masonry. Ties, tension straps, hangers and brackets.]

E.2.3.2 Walls

There are four suggested wall constructions:

Wall type 1   Solid masonry wall (Table E.4). Performance depends on the mass of the wall.

Wall type 2   Cavity wall construction (Table E.5). Performance depends on a combination of the mass of masonry and the isolation of the leaves, which is affected by the connections between them and the width of the cavity.

Wall type 3 Masonry between independent panels (Table E.6). Performance depends on the type and mass of the masonry core, on the isolation between the panels and the core, and the mass of the panels.

Wall type 4 Framed timber walls with absorbent material (Table E.7). Performance depends on mass of leaves, isolation of frames and absorption in the cavity.

The field performance of all wall types is affected by the flanking walls and floors and their junctions, which should follow Table E.8.

Table E.4 Wall type 1 – Solid masonry wall

Type	Definition	Example	
1.1 Dense aggregate concrete block, with plaster on both room faces	Minimum mass, including plaster: 415kg/m² 13mm plaster to both faces Blocks laid flat to full wall thickness	215mm blockwork, density 1840kg/m³ laid flat with 110mm coursing 13mm plaster (min. 10kg/m²) to both faces	SECTION
1.2 Cast in situ dense aggregate concrete, with plaster on both room faces	Minimum mass, including plaster: 415kg/m² Plaster to both room faces	190mm concrete, density 2200kg/m³ 13mm plaster (min. 10kg/m²) to both faces	SECTION
1.3 Brick with plaster on both room faces	Minimum mass, including plaster: 375kg/m² Bricks laid frog up, coursed with headers 13mm plaster on both room faces	215mm brick, density 1610kg/m³ 75mm coursing 13mm plaster (min. 10kg/m²) to both faces	SECTION

Table E.5 Wall type 2 – Cavity wall construction

Type	Definition	Example	
2.1 Two leaves of dense aggregate concrete block with cavity and plaster on both faces	Minimum mass including plaster: 415kg/m^3 Minimum cavity width 50mm 13mm plaster both faces	100mm leaves of blockwork, density 1990kg/m^3 225mm coursing 13mm plaster (min. 10kg/m^2) to both faces	SECTION
2.2 Two leaves lightweight aggregate block with cavity and plaster on both faces	Minimum mass including plaster: 300kg/m^2 Minimum cavity width 75mm 13mm plaster both faces	100mm leaves of blockwork, density 1375kg/m^3 225mm coursing 13mm plaster (min. 10kg/m^2) to both faces	SECTION
2.3 Two leaves lightweight aggregate block with cavity and plasterboard on both faces[1]	Minimum mass including plasterboard: 290kg/m^2 Lightweight aggregate blocks, density 1350–1600kg/m^3 75mm minimum cavity Plasterboard, minimum mass 10kg/m^2	100mm leaves of blockwork, density 1375kg/m^3 225mm coursing Plasterboard (min. 10kg/m^2) to both faces	SECTION
2.4 Two leaves aircrete block with cavity and plasterboard or plaster on both faces[2]	Minimum mass including finish: 150kg/m^2 Minimum 75mm cavity Plasterboard, minimum mass 10kg/m^2 or 13mm plaster	100mm leaves of aircrete blockwork, density 650kg/m^3 225mm coursing Plasterboard (min. 10kg/m^2) to both faces	SECTION

Note: For all four walls, Type A wall ties are required and blocks are presumed to be without voids.

[1] Only suitable where there is a step/stagger of at least 300mm. Greater stagger or step will improve airborne sound insulation.

[2] Only suitable where there is a step/stagger of at least 300mm and no separating floors. Greater stagger or step will improve airborne sound insulation.

Table E.6 Wall type 3 – Masonry between independent panels

Type	Definition	Example	
Independent panels:	Minimum mass, excluding framing, 20kg/m² Panels not supported on a frame should be at least 35mm from the core Any frame should be at least 10mm from the core	Panels should consist of: • 2 or more layers of plasterboard with staggered joints; or • Composite panel with 2 sheets of plasterboard separated by a cellular core	
3.1 Solid masonry core of dense aggregate blocks	Minimum core mass 300kg/m² Core width – as determined by structural requirements Independent panels to both room faces	140mm blockwork, density 2200mg/m³ 110mm coursing Independent panels	SECTION
3.2 Solid masonry core of lightweight concrete blocks	Minimum core mass 150kg/m² Core width – as determined by structural requirements Independent panels to both room faces	140mm blockwork, density 1400kg/m³ 225mm coursing Independent panels	SECTION
3.3 Cavity masonry core	Core of any mass 50mm minimum cavity with type A ties Core width – as determined by structural requirements Independent panels to both room faces	Two leaves of 100mm concrete blockwork 50mm minimum cavity Independent panels	SECTION

Table E.7 Wall type 4 – Framed wall with absorbent material

Type	Definition	
4.1 Double-leaf frames with absorbent material	Minimum 200mm between inside lining faces Plywood sheathing in cavity A lining to each side consisting of: • two or more layers of plasterboard (each min. 10kg/m^2) with staggered joints; • absorbent material: unfaced mineral wool batts or quilt, minimum density 10kg/m^3. Thickness of absorbent material: • Suspended in cavity between frame: 25mm; • Fixed to one frame: 50mm; • One batt/quilt fixed to each frame: 25mm each side.	Socket detail →

Table E.8 Flanking walls, floors and junctions for separating walls

Element	Guidance
External cavity walls	The inner leaf must have sufficient mass (120kg/m^2 for masonry or 10kg/m^2 for timber – increased if there is a separating floor). The separating wall should either form the majority of the bond, or the inner leaf should be butted and tied to the separating wall. The cavity should be stopped with a flexible closer.
Internal masonry walls	Mass should exceed 120kg/m^2 (excluding finishes).
Internal timber floors	Supported on hangers, not built in.
Internal concrete floors	Solid slabs (minimum mass 375kg/m^2) can be carried through solid separating walls, but should not bridge cavity separating walls. Concrete planks should not be carried through solid separating walls and should not bridge cavity separating walls.
Ceilings and roofs	Separating walls should be continued to the underside of the roof and the junction sealed with a flexible fire stop. The mass of the wall may be reduced in a non-habitable loft, if the ceiling has minimum mass of 10kg/m^2. At eaves any cavity in an external wall should be sealed with flexible material.

E.2.3.3 Floors

The performance of floors depends on the floor construction and the type of ceiling. There are three floor types (1–3) and three ceiling treatments (A–C). Not all combinations will give the required level of performance. The ceiling treatments (Table E.9) are ranked in performance order, with A being better than C. The use of a better ceiling than that prescribed in the guidance should give better results.

Floor type 1 Concrete base with ceiling and soft floor covering (Table E.10). Airborne sound resistance depends mainly on the mass of the floor and partly on the mass of the ceiling. The soft floor covering reduces impact sound at source.

Floor type 2   Concrete base with ceiling and floating floor (Table E.11). Airborne sound resistance depends on the mass of the base, as well as the mass and isolation of the floating floor and the ceiling, while the floating floor reduces impact sound at source.

Floor type 3   Timber frame base with ceiling and platform floor (Table E.12). Airborne sound resistance depends on the structural floor base, the isolation of the platform floor and the ceiling. The platform floor reduces impact sound at source.

The performance of all floor types is affected by the flanking walls and their junctions, which should follow Table E.13.

Table E.9 Ceiling treatments	
Treatment	**Description**
A: Independent ceiling with absorbent material	Supported on independent joists fixed to the surrounding walls, with at least 100mm between plasterboard and underside of floor[1] The ceiling to consist of: • at least two layers of plasterboard laid with staggered joints; • minimum mass of 20kg/m²; • at least 100mm mineral wool, minimum density 10kg/m³.
B: Plasterboard on resilient bars with absorbent material	Supported on resilient metal bars, which on concrete floors should be fixed to timber battens The ceiling to consist of: • single layer of plasterboard (min.10kg/m²); • absorbent layer of mineral wool, minimum density 10kg/m³, which fills the ceiling void.
C: Plasterboard on timber battens or resilient channels	Ceiling fixed to floor with timber battens or resilient channels The ceiling to consist of: • single layer of plasterboard (min.10kg/m²); • for resilient channels fill void with mineral wool, minimum density 10kg/m³.

[1] On floor type 3 additional support may be provided by resilient hangers, but there should be at least 100mm between the top of the ceiling joists and the underside of the floor.

Table E.10 Floor type 1 – Concrete base and soft floor covering		
Type	**Requirement**	**Ceiling type**
1.1C Solid concrete slab	Concrete slab, minimum mass 365kg/m² (can include solid concrete or metal shuttering and a bonded screed) Soft floor covering[1]	C
1.2B Concrete planks	Hollow or solid planks, minimum mass, 365kg/m² (including bonded screed) All joints fully grouted Regulating floor screed Soft floor covering[1]	B

[1] Either a resilient material at least 4.5mm thick, or a floor covering with ΔL_w of at least 17dB.

Table E.11 Floor type 2 – Concrete base with floating floor

Type	Requirement	Ceiling
2.1C – Solid concrete slab	Minimum mass 300kg/m² including bonded screed and shuttering of metal or concrete Any floating floor	A, B or C
2.2B – Concrete planks	Minimum mass 300kg/m² All joints fully grouted with regulating floor screed Any floating floor	A or B
Floating floors		
A – Timber raft	Timber board material (min. 12kg/m² mass) with edges sealed 45 × 45mm battens Resilient layer of 25mm mineral wool, min. 36kg/m³	
B – Cement: sand screed	65mm of minimum 80kg/m² sand:cement or proprietary screed Resilient layer of 25mm mineral wool, min. 36kg/m³ (or any layer with maximum dynamic stiffness of 15MN/m³, and at least 5mm thick under load)	
C – Performance based approach	Rigid boarding above a resilient layer which gives a reduction in impact sound pressure level ΔL_w of at least 29dB	

Table E.12 Floor type 3 – Timber frame base with platform floor and resilient layer

Type	Requirement	Ceiling type
3.1A Timber frame base	Structural floor: timber joists with a deck of min. 20kg/m² Platform floor, min. 25kg/m², consisting of two layers of board material, each min. 8mm thick, fixed together with staggered joints Resilient layer of 25mm mineral wool (density 60–100kg/m³)	A

Table E.13 Flanking walls and junctions for separating floors

Element	Guidance
External masonry cavity walls	The cavity should be stopped with a flexible closer. The mass of the inner leaf should exceed 120kg/m², excluding finish. Concrete floor bases must be built into the wall, but must not bridge the cavity. In concrete plank floors the first plank junction should be at least 300mm from the cavity face of the inner leaf.
External timber framed walls	The cavity should be stopped with a flexible closer. The inner leaf should be finished with two layers of plasterboard, each with minimum mass 10kg/m².
Internal masonry walls	Rigidly connected walls need a minimum mass of 120kg/m², excluding finishes.
Separating walls	Concrete slab floors should be carried through solid masonry walls: other floors should not be continuous. With cavity masonry walls floors should not extend beyond the cavity face of a masonry leaf. Timber floors should be built off hangers, and at timber framed walls there should be full depth timber blocking between joists.
Recessed light fittings	These can impair the performance of a ceiling by providing a route for airborne sound transmission.

E.2.3.4 Material change of use

Where dwellinghouses, flats and rooms for residential purposes are formed by material change of use, the acoustic performance levels necessary for an existing wall, floor and stair may be achieved in one of four ways:

1. Performance may achieve the required standard without remedial work if the existing construction is similar to one of the standard solutions, with, for example, mass within 15% of the standard solution.

2. The standard solutions may be used as guidance to the remedial work required to reach the required performance.

3. Proprietary solutions may be used to improve performance. Consultation with the manufacturer is essential.

4. The remedial measures shown in Table E.14 may be applied.

Floors may require preparatory treatment before applying other remedial measures.

Flanking transmission must be addressed, particularly where flanking walls or floors are continuous across separating floors or walls. Masonry walls may need to be upgraded with independent panels of plasterboard or plasterboard laminate, and penetrations will require careful detailing. Designers should consider the effect on the structure of increased loadings produced by remedial work.

The performance of elements in historic buildings should be improved as much as is practically possible, although it may not reach the standards in Table E.1.

Table E.14 Remedial measures for material change of use	
Type	**Description**
Wall treatment 1 Independent panels with absorbent material [*Note: Resistance depends on existing construction, mass of panels, their isolation and the absorbent material.*]	Independent panel, min. 20kg/m² excluding frame. At least two layers of plasterboard with joints staggered. Free-standing panels at least 35mm from core, or framed panels 10mm between frame and wall. Minimum 35mm mineral wool, min. density 10kg/m³ in cavity between panel and wall.
Floor treatment 1 Independent ceiling with absorbent material [*Note: Resistance depends on mass of existing floor and independent ceiling, absorbent material, isolation and airtightness. Suitable for locations where loss of ceiling height not an issue.*]	Independent joists – clearing 25mm below existing ceiling, or independent joists with resilient hangers. At least two layers of plasterboard laid with staggered joints, giving at least 20kg/m². Minimum 100mm mineral wool, min. density 10kg/m³.
Floor treatment 2 Platform floor with absorbent material [*Note: Resistance depends on mass of floor, effectiveness of resilient layer and the absorbent material.*]	100mm of min. 10kg/m³ mineral wool laid between joists of existing floor. Floating layer, two layers board material each min. 8mm thick fixed together, giving min. 25kg/m² mass. Resilient layer min. 25mm of mineral wool 60–100kg/m³ density.
Stair treatment 1 Stair covering and independent ceiling with absorbent material [*Note: Resistance to airborne sound depends on the mass of stair and ceiling, isolation of the ceiling and airtightness of any enclosure under stairs. The floor covering reduces impact sound at source.*]	6mm thick soft covering securely fixed over stair treads. Under-stair cupboard: line with min. 10kg/m² plasterboard with min. 10kg/m³ density mineral wool behind, and form cupboard walls with two layers of 10kg/m² plasterboard and fit a heavy door. No cupboard: fit independent ceiling below the stairs, as floor treatment 1.

E.2.3.5 Rooms for residential purpose

Sound transmission between new-build rooms for residential purposes can be controlled with several of the standard solutions. Walls may be:

Wall type 1 – Solid masonry wall (Table E.4):

- 1.1 Dense aggregate block with plaster;
- 1.2 Dense in-situ aggregate concrete, plaster;
- 1.3 Brick, plaster.

Wall type 3 – Masonry with independent panels (Table E.6):

- 3.1 Solid masonry core – dense aggregate block;
- 3.2 Solid masonry core – lightweight concrete block.

Wall types 2 and 4 may also be used, provided isolation between the leaves is maintained.

Where type 1 walls join a roof, there is no need to carry the wall to the underside of the roof, provided the ceiling consists of two layers of plasterboard with a total mass of at least 20kg/m^2, with 200mm of mineral wool (minimum density 10kg/m^3) above, and joists and sheets are not continuous between rooms.

Doors opening onto corridors should follow the guidance given for doors to flats in **E.2.3.1**.

Floors may be type 1 – Concrete base with soft covering (Table E.10):

- Type 1.1C Solid concrete slab with ceiling treatment C;
- Type 1.2B Concrete planks with ceiling treatment B.

Floor types 2 and 3 may be used, provided floating floors and ceilings are not continuous between rooms.

E.3 Internal walls and floors (Requirement E2)

Internal walls within dwellinghouses, flats or rooms for residential purpose must meet the performance standards in Table E.15, where they separate:

- a bedroom from another room;
- a room containing a toilet from another room.

All internal floors must meet the standards in Table E.15.

Table E.15 Sound insulation standards for internal walls and floors	
	Airborne sound insulation, R_w dB (minimum values)
Walls	40
Floors	40

Table E.16 Example constructions for internal walls and floors	
Type	**Description**
Internal walls	
A: Timber or metal frames with plasterboard linings	Two layers of plasterboard to each side, each layer min. 10kg/m^2 Linings 75mm apart on timber frame, or 45mm apart on steel frame All joints well sealed
B: Timber or metal frames with plasterboard lining and absorbent material	One layer of plasterboard to each side, each sheet min. 10kg/m^2 Linings 75mm apart on timber frame, or 45mm apart on steel frame Minimum 25mm of min. 10kg/m^3 mineral wool suspended in cavity All joints well sealed
C: Concrete block wall	Minimum mass of core 120kg/m^2 excluding finish Plaster or plasterboard finish to both sides All joints well sealed
D: Aircrete block wall	Minimum mass 90kg/m^2 including plaster finish Minimum mass 75kg/m^2 including plasterboard finish All joints well sealed
Internal floors	
A: Concrete planks	Minimum mass 180kg/m^2 Optional regulating screed Optional ceiling finish
B: Concrete beams	Beam and block deck, minimum mass 220kg/m^2 Bonded screed, min. 40mm sand cement, or equivalent proprietary screed Ceiling treatment A, B or C
C: Timber or metal joists	Timber deck – wood based board min. 15kg/m^2 Minimum 100mm mineral wool, min. density 10kg/m^3, laid between joists One layer of plasterboard, min. 10kg/m^2

The requirements do not apply to:

- a wall which contains a door;
- a wall separating an en suite toilet from the associated bedroom;
- existing walls or floors in buildings subject to material change of use.

Designers may meet the requirement by adopting one or more of the example constructions for walls and floors (Table E.16), or by using constructions which laboratory testing has shown to meet the standards. Junctions should be treated in the same way as those for separating walls and floors, with gaps around internal walls and floors filled to avoid air paths.

E.4 Reverberation in common areas (Requirement E3)

Excessive reverberation times in common areas which contain doors to flats and rooms for residential purposes will increase the disturbance residents experience from traffic in those common areas. Reverberation must be controlled by providing surface finishes which have good sound absorption properties (classified to BS EN ISO 11654:1997). There are two methods of determining the amount and type of sound absorber required.

Method A is a simple method which takes no account of the existing absorption characteristics of the volume:

- for entrance halls, hallways or corridors – provide a Class C sound absorber to an area equal to or greater than the floor area;
- for stairwells – calculate the area of stair treads, upper surfaces of landings, and ceiling area of top floor and either:
  - cover a comparable area with Class D absorber or better; or
  - cover 50% of area with Class C absorber or better.

The absorber may be a suspended ceiling system or absorptive tiles/material.

Method B is a more complex method which allows for the existing absorption characteristics of the volume. The method requires the provision of the minimum amount of absorption material which will raise the total absorption area, A_T, to the performance standard for the type of space.

Because method B takes account of the absorption capacity of the rest of the surfaces it will usually require less absorber than method A. Method B is not suitable for stairwells.

Further guidance
BS EN ISO 11654:1997. Acoustics. Sound absorbers for use in buildings. Rating of sound absorption.

Approved Document E. 2003. Section 7. [Calculation method B and absorption coefficient data for common materials in buildings.]

E.5 Acoustic conditions in schools (Requirement E4)

The acoustic performance of new school buildings should comply with the standards set out in Section 1 of Building Bulletin 93 (BB93). Material alterations should also comply with these standards. Institutes of Further Education, including most sixth form colleges, are not defined as schools and so need not comply with Requirement E4.

The standards in BB93 cover:

- indoor ambient noise levels in unoccupied spaces;
- airborne sound insulation between spaces;
- impact sound insulation of floors;
- reverberation in teaching and study space;
- sound absorption in circulation spaces;
- intelligibility of speech in open-plan spaces.

Acoustic conditions in administration and ancillary spaces are covered by the guidance only if they affect conditions in adjacent spaces for teaching and learning.

BB93 recommends the building contract include a requirement for on-site testing to ensure that as-built performance matches the design performance.

Further guidance
Building Bulletin 93. *Acoustic design of schools*. DfES. 2003.

Ventilation

F.1 General considerations

F.1.1 Scope

Part F is intended to ensure that buildings have adequate ventilation for their occupants. The changes to Part F introduced in 2010 address two main concerns:

- The ventilation provisions previously set in Part F were based on the expectation that deliberate ventilation would be augmented by the infiltration of air through the building fabric. However, the better standards of airtightness required by Part L (to reduce heat loss) will also reduce the contribution of 'adventitious ventilation', which may result in some dwellings being inadequately ventilated. To prevent that, the levels of deliberate ventilation have been adjusted to ensure that even dwellings with little air infiltration will be adequately ventilated.

- Research suggests that, in many cases, design ventilation rates are not being achieved in finished dwellings. In order to address this, mechanical ventilation systems must now be commissioned, and their air flow rate must be tested and reported to the Building Control Body (BCB).

Part F: Ventilation	
Requirement	**Limit on application**
Means of ventilation	
F1 (1) There shall be adequate means of ventilation provided. (2) Fixed systems for mechanical ventilation and any associated controls must be commissioned by testing and adjusting as necessary to secure that the objective referred to in sub-paragraph (1) is met.	Requirement F1 does not apply to a building or space within a building – (a) into which people do not normally go; or (b) which is used solely for storage; or (c) which is a garage used solely in connection with a single dwelling.

The ventilation system should limit the accumulation of:

- moisture, which could lead to mould growth;
- pollutants originating within the building, which would otherwise be hazardous to health for its occupants (**F.2.2**).

The ventilation system should:

- extract water vapour from areas with high rates of generation (e.g. kitchens, utility rooms and bathrooms) before it can spread widely;
- extract hazardous pollutants from areas where they are produced in significant quantities, before they can spread widely;
- rapidly dilute pollutants and water vapour in habitable rooms, occupiable rooms and sanitary accommodation;
- provide a minimum supply of outdoor air for occupants and disperse residual pollutants and water vapour;
- perform in a way which is not detrimental to the health of people in the building;
- facilitate maintenance, where necessary.

The provisions do not address the products of tobacco smoking.

F.1.2 Other requirements

Ventilation systems may also need to comply with other parts of the Regulations:

B   Ducting which passes through a fire-resisting or compartment wall/floor must maintain the effectiveness of fire-separating elements (**B.5.4**).

C   Inlets and outlets should not result in rain penetration (**C.5.3.6**).

E   Ventilation ductwork should not increase sound transmission through certain walls and floors (**E.2**).

J   To prevent ventilation systems causing combustion products from open-flued appliances from spilling into the room the guidance on installation and testing of such appliances should be observed (**J.2.1.2**).

L   Ventilation systems affect energy consumption directly, in their operation, and also indirectly, through the heating of air drawn from outside (**L.3** and **L.4**): those energy requirements may be mitigated by heat recovery devices and energy-efficient equipment.

P   Electrical work in dwellings may come under Part P (**P.2**).

F.1.3 Commissioning and testing

Any fixed mechanical ventilation system which can be tested and adjusted must be commissioned to ensure that it provides adequate ventilation. Commissioning must follow an approved procedure:

* for dwellings – *Domestic ventilation compliance guide*;
* for other buildings – CIBSE Code M.

The BCB must be provided with a commissioning notice, which may also constitute the commissioning notice required by Part L (**L.1.5**).

The air flow rates of mechanical ventilation systems in new dwellings must also be measured, and a notice given to the BCB.

Further guidance
Domestic ventilation compliance guide. CLG. 2010. [Sections 2 and 3 cover commissioning, and section 5 air flow rate testing.]

Commissioning Code M: Commissioning management. CIBSE. 2003.

DW143 Practical guide to ductwork leakage testing. HVCA. 2000.

DW144 Specification for sheet metal ductwork: low, medium and high pressure/velocity air systems. HVCA. 1998.

DW154 Specification for plastics ductwork. HVCA. 2000. [Guidance on commissioning ductwork.]

HVCA has changed its name to Building & Engineering Services Association. HVCA publications are now available from www.b-espublications.co.uk

F.1.4 Provision of information

Building owners must be given sufficient information to enable them to operate the ventilation system to provide adequate air flow:

* For dwellings, section 4 of the *Domestic ventilation compliance guide* lists the documents which should be provided; and it includes the inspection checklist, and air flow measurement test and commissioning sheet from section 5.
* For other buildings, follow CIBSE TM 31.

Further guidance
TM 31. Building log book toolkit. CIBSE. 2006.

[See also **F.1.3**.]

F.2 Ventilation principles

F.2.1 Ventilation

Ventilation is the removal of stale indoor air and its replacement with fresh outside air (which is assumed to be of reasonable quality), to:

* provide air for breathing;
* dilute and remove airborne pollutants;
* control excess humidity;

- provide for fuel-burning appliances (**J.2.1**);
- maintain thermal comfort (**L.3.1.3**).

Airborne pollutants may be released by materials and products used in the construction and furnishing of a building, or be generated by the activities of the building's occupants. Common pollutants include:

- combustion products from unflued appliances;
- chemical emissions from consumer products;
- chemical emissions from furnishings, printers and photocopiers.

F.2.2 Moisture levels and air quality

Ventilation should prevent moisture and pollutants in buildings from exceeding acceptable levels. Moisture levels should be controlled so that there is no visible mould on the internal surfaces of the external walls of a properly heated dwelling with typical moisture generation. That is likely to be the case if the average surface water activity (a measure of dryness) and relative humidity are maintained below the levels in Approved Document F Tables A1 and A2.

Pollutant levels should not exceed those in Approved Document F Appendix A. Control of bio-effluents (body odours) requires an air supply rate of 3.5l/s in dwellings (where perception is reduced due to a period of exposure) and 8l/s in other buildings.

The required ventilation provision intended to control moisture and pollutants may not be sufficient to remove pollutants generated by flueless combustion space heaters or occupant-controlled events such as painting, smoking or cleaning.

F.2.3 Source control

Indoor air quality can also be improved by reducing the release of water vapour and pollutants. However, Approved Document F makes no recommendations for source control, because there is only limited knowledge about the emission of pollutants from construction and consumer products.

Further guidance
BRE Digest 464 *VOC emissions from building products: sources, testing and emissions data*. BRE. 2002. [Information about control of emissions from construction products.]

F.2.4 Ventilation strategies

Air exchange between inside and outside can be:

- uncontrolled – **infiltration** through air leakage paths in the building structure;
- controlled – **purpose-provided ventilation** by means of natural and/or mechanical devices.

In principle, ventilation should be purpose-provided, and infiltration minimised.

Ventilation systems generally involve three complementary strategies:

- Extract ventilation – provided in rooms where the most water vapour and/or pollutants are released, to remove contaminated air and to prevent its spread to the rest of the building. It may be intermittent or continuous.
- Whole building ventilation – provides a continuous air exchange in order to supply fresh air to the building occupants and remove water vapour and pollutants not dealt with by extract ventilation, as well as those released

throughout the building. Ventilation may be reduced, or ceased, when the building is not occupied.

- Purge ventilation – intermittent air exchange for removing high concentrations of pollutants and water vapour released from occasional activities.

Ventilation can be provided by natural, mechanical or mixed-mode systems. Naturally ventilated buildings will often use intermittent extract fans for extract ventilation, trickle ventilators for whole building ventilation and windows for purge ventilation. For mechanically ventilated and air-conditioned buildings the same system may provide all three types of ventilation.

The assessment of the suitability of a ventilation system should take account of the design air permeability of the building.

F.2.5 Control systems

Ventilation must be controllable by manual or automatic means. Demand-controlled systems adjust the ventilation rate to the level of occupancy to avoid over-ventilation.

Manually controlled trickle ventilators for background ventilation can be located over window frames, in window frames, just above the glass or through the wall (Figure F.1). They may incorporate a flap allowing users to shut off ventilation, but are usually left open in occupied rooms in dwellings.

Humidity-controlled devices can control the level of water vapour and so minimise condensation and mould growth. They are best suited to extract ventilation in moisture-generating areas, but are not suitable for sanitary accommodation where odour is usually the main pollutant.

Automatic control systems should be matched to the ventilation requirement of the room. Trickle ventilators with automatic controls should have manual over-ride. Some trickle vents can reduce the ventilation flow passages according to the pressure difference across the ventilator to reduce draughts in windy weather. Where such ventilators are fully open in typical conditions (e.g. 1Pa pressure difference), only a manual close option is recommended.

Figure F.1 Provision for background ventilation

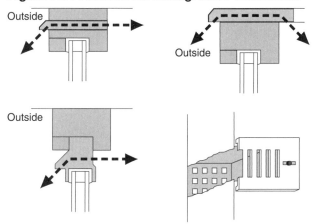

Buildings other than dwellings may have more sophisticated automatic control systems incorporating occupancy sensors or indoor carbon dioxide concentration sensors.

F.2.6 Noise

Noise caused by ventilation systems is not controlled under the Building Regulations. However, it is recommended that measures are taken to minimise such noise to reduce disturbance to building occupants.

Where external noise levels are high the use of sound-attenuating ventilation products may be beneficial. Designers should also consider disturbance that noise from the ventilation system might cause outside the building.

A ventilation system can radiate noise from extract or supply ducts, fan units and terminals (grilles). High noise levels may discourage the building occupants from using the system. Noise levels may be minimised by careful design and the use of quieter products.

It is recommended that noise levels (measured by the noise index $L_{Aeq,T}$ to BS 8233:1999, over an appropriate time period, T) not exceed:

- noise sensitive rooms (such as bedrooms and living rooms) – 30 dB;
- less sensitive rooms (such as kitchens and bathrooms) – 35 dB.

Further guidance
BS 8233:1999. Sound insulation and noise reduction for buildings. Code of practice.

F.2.7 Minimising ingress of pollutants

Ventilation systems should be designed to minimise the introduction of pollutants into the building interior. The intake of pollutants depends on factors such as the relative location of pollutant sources (such as road traffic, combustion plant and industrial processes), the physical characteristics of the building, the ventilation strategy and the location of air intakes.

More detailed guidance on the placement of ventilation intakes and exhaust outlets is given in Approved Document F Appendix D.

Further guidance
UK Air Quality Strategy: 2007. Defra. 2007. [Describes typical urban pollutants that need to be considered. Available at https://www.gov.uk/government/uploads/system/uploads/attachment_data/file/69336/pb12654-air-quality-strategy-vol1-070712.pdf

TM21 Minimising pollution at air intakes. CIBSE. 1999.

F.2.8 Purge ventilation

Purge ventilation may be provided by openable windows and/or external doors. The required opening areas for different window and door configurations are given in Table F.1 and Figure F.2. Windows which are emergency egress windows (**B.3.6.1**) should comply with the larger of the provisions of Approved Documents B or F.

Table F.1 Purge ventilation

	Configuration	Minimum area of opening part (h × w) as proportion of floor area of room
Windows	For a hinged or pivot window that opens 30° or more, or for sliding sash windows	1/20
	For a hinged or pivot window that opens between 15° and 30°	1/10
	Window opens less than 15°	Not suitable for purge ventilation
	More than one openable window	Combined opening area at least 1/20 or 1/10, based on opening angle of the largest window
External doors (including patio doors)	One external door	1/20
	If the room contains more than one external door, the areas of all the opening parts	Combined opening area at least 1/20
Windows and doors	At least one external door and at least one openable window	Combined opening area at least 1/20

Figure F.2 Window dimensions for purge ventilation

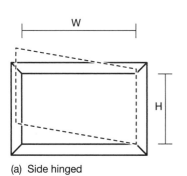

(a) Side hinged

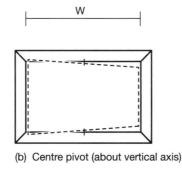

(b) Centre pivot (about vertical axis)

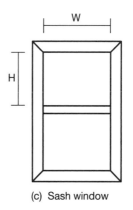

(c) Sash window

F.2.9 Equivalent area of ventilators

The air flow performance of a background ventilator is expressed as its equivalent area, and is measured to BS EN 13141-1:2004 (clause 4). As equivalent area cannot be measured on site it is preferable to use ventilators with the equivalent area marked in an easily visible location. Where a ventilator is used in conjunction with other components some form of temporary marking would be acceptable to the BCB.

Further guidance
BS EN 13141-1:2004. Ventilation in Buildings. Performance testing of components/products for residential ventilation. Externally and internally mounted air transfer devices.

F.3 Dwellings

Ventilation systems should either:

- provide the ventilation rates given in **F.3.1**;
- follow the system guidance in **F.3.2** and **F.3.3**; or
- be demonstrated to meet the moisture and air quality criteria in **F.2.2**.

There should be reasonable access for maintenance work, such as changing filters, replacing components and cleaning ductwork. All systems should be fully commissioned and have the air flow rate measured (**F.1.3**).

Table F.2 Extract ventilation rates

| Room | Intermittent extract Minimum rate (l/s) | Continuous extract | |
		Minimum high rate (l/s)	Minimum low rate
Kitchen	30 (adjacent to hob), or 60 (elsewhere)	13	Total extract rate as **Table F.3**
Utility room	30	8	
Bathroom	15	8	
Sanitary accommodation	6	6	

F.3.1 Ventilation rates for dwellings

Each dwelling requires:

- Extract ventilation to outside in each kitchen, utility room and bathroom; and in all sanitary accommodation. The extract, which can be intermittent or continuous, should provide minimum airflow rates as Table F.2.

- Whole building ventilation for the supply of air to habitable rooms, with minimum flow rate as Table F.3.

- Purge ventilation to each habitable room which is capable of extracting to outside a minimum of 4 air changes per hour (ach) per room. This can usually be provided by openable windows and doors (**F.2.8**), otherwise a mechanical extract should be provided. In other rooms (kitchens and bathrooms) the mechanical or passive extract provision should suffice.

The performance of systems should comply with Table F.4, taking account of the additional resistance imposed by ducts, terminals and filters.

Table F.3 Whole building ventilation rates

| | Number of bedrooms in dwelling | | | | |
	1	2	3	4	5
Whole building ventilation rate (l/s)[1][2]	13	17	21	25	29

[1] Minimum ventilation rate to be not less than 0.3l/s per m² of total internal floor area (all storeys).

[2] Based on a default of 2 occupants in the main bedroom and 1 in each other bedroom. If greater occupancy is expected add 4l/s per occupant.

Further guidance
BS EN 13141. Ventilation for buildings. Performance testing of components/products for residential ventilation.
-1:2004. Externally and internally mounted air transfer devices.
-3:2004. Range hoods for residential use.
-4:2004. Fans used in residential ventilation systems. [Withdrawn, replaced by 2011 edition.]
-6:2004. Exhaust ventilation system packages used in a single dwelling.
-7:2004. Performance testing of a mechanical supply and exhaust ventilation units (including heat recovery) for mechanical ventilation systems intended for single family dwellings. [Withdrawn, replaced by 2010 edition.]
-8:2006. Performance testing of un-ducted mechanical supply and exhaust ventilation units (including heat recovery) for mechanical ventilation systems intended for a single room.

Performance testing of products for residential ventilation. EST, BRE, TEHVA and RVA. [Now listed as test methods for different ventilation systems, and available at www.ncm-pcdb.org.uk/sap/page.jsp?id=24

Approved Document F 2010: Appendix C [Worked examples of the four ventilation systems.]

Table F.4 Performance test methods

System	Test methods
Intermittent extract fans	BS EN 13141-4 clause 4 Performance testing of aerodynamic characteristics. All sub-clauses are relevant.
Range hoods	BS EN 13141-3 clause 4 Performance testing of aerodynamic characteristics. All sub-clauses are relevant.
Background ventilators (non-RH controlled)[1]	BS EN 13141-4 clause 4 Performance testing of aerodynamic characteristics. Only the following sub-clauses are relevant: 4.1 Flow rate/pressure; and 4.2 Non-reverse flow ability.
Passive stack ventilators	Domestic ventilation compliance guide.
Continuous mechanical extract (MEV) systems	BS EN 13141-6 clause 4 Performance testing of aerodynamic characteristics.[2]
Continuous supply and extract ventilation MVHR units	BS EN 13141-7 clause 6 Test methods.[2]
Single room heat recovery ventilators	BS EN 13141-8 clause 6 Test methods. Only the following sub-clauses are relevant: 6.1 General; 6.2 Performance testing of aerodynamic characteristics, sub-clauses 6.2.1 Leakage and mixing and 6.2.2 Airflow. For internal and external leakage and for mixing, the unit should meet at least Class U4 to clause 3.2 classification.

[1] The performance requirements should normally be met for both airflow into and out of the dwelling. To ensure the installed performance matches tested performance ventilators should be installed in accordance with manufacturers' instructions.

[2] Further guidance in *Performance testing of products for residential ventilation*.

F.3.2 Dwellings without basements

The required ventilation provision could be achieved by using one of four ventilation systems:

System 1   Background ventilators and intermittent extract fans. Tables F.5, F.6, F.7 and F.9 and Figures F.3 and F.4;

System 2   Passive stack ventilation (PSV). Tables F.5, F.6, F.7, F.8 and F.10 and Figure F.5;

System 3   Continuous mechanical extract (MEV). Tables F.5 and F.11, and Figure F.6;

System 4   Continuous mechanical supply and extract with heat recovery (MVHR). Tables F.5 and F.12, and Figure F.7.

Each system has guidance for dwellings to cover all designed air permeabilities. The guidance is therefore suitable for all dwellings, and for ventilation purposes, the as-built permeability need not be close to the design permeability. There is also guidance for as-built permeabilities greater than $3m^3/(h.m^2)$ @ 50Pa. It is recommended that this guidance be followed only if the design air permeability is greater than $5m^3/(h.m^2)$ @ 50Pa, and the person carrying out the building work has experience of closely matching design and as-built air permeabilities.

If the alternative guidance is followed and the dwelling, or another dwelling of the same type (**L.3.2.4**, see Air permeability and pressure testing) has a tested air permeability equal to or lower than $3m^3/(h.m^2)$ @ 50Pa, the BCB may ask for more air permeability testing to ensure that all dwellings in the sample have adequate ventilation.

Figure F.3 Background ventilators and intermittent extract fans

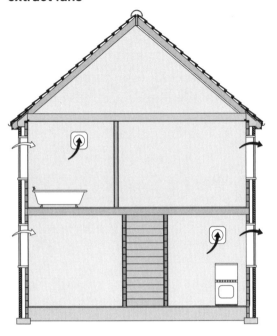

Figure F.4 Single-sided ventilation

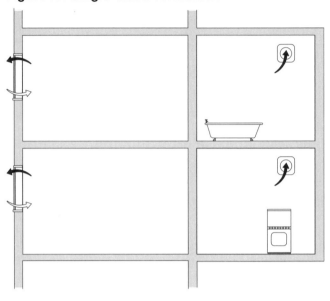

Figure F.5 Passive stack ventilation

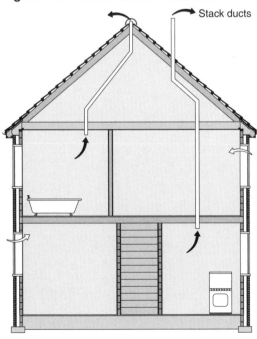

Figure F.6 Continuous mechanical extract

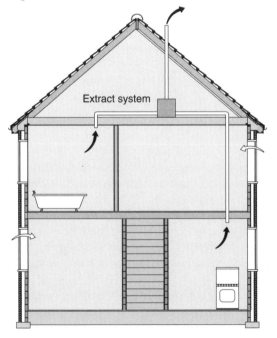

Figure F.7 Continuous mechanical supply and extract with heat recovery

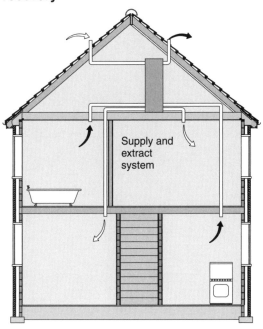

Table F.5 Common provisions for ventilation systems 1–4	
Requirement	**Guidance**
Design assumptions	Systems have been sized for the winter period. Additional ventilation may be required during warmer months and it has been assumed that the provisions for purge ventilation (e.g. openable windows) could be used.
Purge ventilation	For each habitable room with: • external walls, see **F.2.8** for window or external door (including patio door) sizing; • no external walls, see **F.3.4**. There may be practical difficulties in achieving this (e.g. if unable to open a window due to excessive noise from outside). In such situations, seek expert advice. For each wet room with: • external walls, install an openable window (no minimum size); • no external walls, the normal extract provisions will suffice, although it will take longer to purge the room. As an alternative to the provisions given above for habitable and wet rooms, a mechanical fan extracting at 4ach to outside could be used. Devices used for purge ventilation should be manually controlled: their location is not critical.
Air transfer	To ensure good transfer of air throughout the dwelling, there should be an undercut of minimum area 7600mm² in all internal doors above the floor finish. This is equivalent to an undercut of 10mm for a standard 760mm width door. This should be achieved by making an undercut of 10mm above the floor finish if the floor finish is fitted, or by a 20mm undercut above the floorboards, or other surface, if the finish has not been fitted.
Location of manual controls	Any manual controls should be within reasonable reach of the occupants. It is recommended that they are located in accordance with the requirements for safe opening and closing of windows in **K.8**.
Noise	Intermittent and continuously running fans should be quiet, so as not to discourage their use by occupants.

Table F.6 Total equivalent ventilator areas (mm²) for dwellings with any design air permeability

Total floor area (m²)	Number of bedrooms				
	1	2	3	4	5
≤50	35000	40000	50000	60000	65000
51–60	35000	40000	50000	60000	65000
61–70	45000	45000	50000	60000	65000
71–80	50000	50000	50000	60000	65000
81–90	55000	60000	60000	60000	65000
91–100	65000	65000	65000	65000	65000
>100	Add 7000mm² for every additional 10m² floor area				

Note: Based on two occupants in main bedroom and one in each of other bedrooms. For greater level of occupancy, assume a greater number of bedrooms. For more than 5 bedrooms add 10000mm² per bedroom.

Table F.7 Total equivalent ventilator areas (mm²) for dwellings with design air permeability ≥5m³/(h.m²) @ 50Pa

Total floor area (m²)	Number of bedrooms				
	1	2	3	4	5
≤50	25000	35000	45000	45000	55000
51–60	25000	30000	40000	45000	55000
61–70	30000	30000	30000	45000	55000
71–80	35000	35000	35000	45000	55000
81–90	40000	40000	40000	45000	55000
91–100	45000	45000	45000	45000	55000
>100	Add 5000mm² for every additional 10m² floor area				

Note: Based on two occupants in main bedroom and one in each of the other bedrooms. For greater level of occupancy, assume a greater number of bedrooms. For more than 5 bedrooms add 10000mm² per bedroom.

Table F.8 Sizing of passive stack ventilators

Room	Internal duct diameter (mm)	Internal cross-sectional area (mm²)
Kitchen	125	12000
Utility room	125	12000
Bathroom	125	12000
Sanitary accommodation[1]	125	12000

[1] The purge ventilation provision of **F.2.8** can be used where security is not an issue.

Table F.9 System 1 – Background ventilators and intermittent extract fans

	Guidance
Intermittent extract	Intermittent extract rates to **Table F.2**. Alternatively, for sanitary accommodation follow the purge ventilation provisions in **F.2.8** if security is not an issue. Instead of a conventional intermittent fan, a continuously running single room heat recovery ventilator could be used in wet rooms. It should use the minimum high rate given in **Table F.2** and 50% of this value as the minimum low rate. No background ventilator is required in the same room as the single room heat recovery ventilator. Furthermore, the total equivalent background ventilator area described below can be reduced by 2500mm² for each room containing a single room heat recovery ventilator.
Location of intermittent extract fans	Intermittent extract fans should be installed in each wet room. Cooker hoods should be 650mm to 750mm above the hob surface (or follow manufacturer instructions). Mechanical extract fans should be installed as high as is practical and preferably less than 400mm below the ceiling. Where fans and background ventilators are fitted in the same room they should be a minimum of 0.5m apart.
Background ventilators	Step 1 – For dwellings with more than one exposed façade, select **Table F.6** or **F.7** according to the design air permeability; Step 2 – Depending on the number of storeys: • for multi-storey dwellings, and single-storey dwellings more than four storeys above ground level, use the total equivalent area for the dwelling given in the table; or • for single-storey dwellings up to and including the fourth storey above ground level, add a further 10000mm² to the value given in the table, preferably shared between several rooms. Step 3 – For a dwelling with only a single exposed façade, cross ventilation is not possible with this system and an alternative is required. In this case, background ventilators should be located at both high and low positions in the façade to provide enhanced single-sided ventilation. The total equivalent area should be determined as described in Steps 1 and 2 above, and should be provided at the high position (typically 1.7m above floor level) for all dwelling types and all storey heights. In addition, ventilators having the same total equivalent area should be provided at least 1.0m below the high ventilators as shown in **Figure F.4**. Single-sided ventilation is most effective if the dwelling is designed so that the habitable rooms are on the exposed façade, and these rooms are no greater than 6m in depth.
Location of background ventilators	Background ventilators should be located to avoid draughts, e.g. typically 1.7m above floor level (except in the single-sided case described above). Background ventilators should be located in all rooms with external walls with at least 5000mm² equivalent area in each habitable room and 2500mm² in each wet room. If a habitable room has no external walls follow **F.3.4**. If a wet room has no external walls follow the guidance for intermittent extract given for Purge ventilation and Controls. If the dwelling has more than one exposed façade, locate similar equivalent areas of background ventilators on opposite (or adjacent) sides of the dwelling.
Purge ventilation	As **Table F.5**
Air transfer	As **Table F.5**
Controls	Intermittent extracts: • May be operated manually and/or automatically by a sensor. Humidity controls should not be used for sanitary accommodation. • In kitchens, any automatic control must provide sufficient flow during cooking with fossil fuel (e.g. gas) to avoid build-up of combustion products. • Automatic controls should have a manual override. • In a room with no openable window (i.e. an internal room) an intermittent extract fan should have a 15 minute overrun, for example controlled via the main room light switch. Background ventilators may be either manually adjustable or automatically controlled (**F.2.5**).
Location of manual controls	As **Table F.5**
Noise	As **Table F.5**

Table F.10 System 2 – Passive stack ventilation (PSV)

	Guidance
Design	Ceiling extract grilles should have a free area of not less than the duct cross-sectional area (when in the fully open position if adjustable). If a dwelling in which PSV is proposed is situated near a building more than 50% taller, it should be at least five times the difference in height away from the taller building (e.g. if the difference in height is 10m, PSV should not be installed in a dwelling within 50m of the taller building). The roof terminal design should be as specified by the PSV manufacturer.
Size of PSV	As **Table F.8**
Location of PSV	For a dwelling with only a single exposed façade, the dwelling should be designed such that the habitable rooms are on the exposed façade so as to achieve cross ventilation. PSV extract terminals should be located in the ceiling or on a wall less than 400mm below the ceiling. Instead of PSV, an open-flued appliance may provide sufficient extract ventilation for the room in which it is located when in operation, and can be arranged to provide sufficient ventilation when not firing. For instance, the provisions would be adequate if: • the solid fuel open-flued appliance is a primary source of heating, cooking or hot water production; or • the open-flued appliance has a flue of free area at least equivalent to a 125mm diameter duct and the appliance's combustion air inlet and dilution inlet are permanently open, i.e. there is a path with no control dampers which could block the flow, or the ventilation path can be left open when the appliance is not in use.
Background ventilators	Step 1 – Determine the equivalent ventilator area for the dwelling from **Table F.6** or **F.7** as appropriate. Step 2 – Make an allowance for the total air flow through all PSV units. As an approximation, assume each PSV unit provides an equivalent area of 3000mm^2. Step 3 – The actual equivalent ventilator area required for the dwelling is the value found in Step 1 and Step 2. In addition, the total equivalent area of the background ventilators must be at least equal to the total cross-sectional area of all the PSV ducts.
Location of background ventilators	Background ventilators should be located in all rooms with external walls except the rooms where a PSV is located, but open-flued combustion appliances will still require an air supply as **J.2.1**. At least 5000mm^2 equivalent area in each habitable room and 2500mm^2 in each wet room. If a habitable room has no external walls, follow **F.3.4**. Background ventilators should be located to avoid draughts, e.g. typically 1.7m above floor level. If the dwelling has more than one exposed façade, locate similar equivalent areas of background ventilators on opposite (or adjacent) sides of the dwelling.
Purge ventilation	As **Table F.5**
Air transfer	As **Table F.5**
Controls	Should be set up to operate without occupant intervention and may have automatic controls. Humidity controls should not be used for sanitary accommodation. In kitchens, any automatic control must provide sufficient flow during cooking with fossil fuel (e.g. gas) to avoid build-up of combustion products. Ensure the system always provides the minimum whole building ventilation rate specified in **Table F.3** in the heating season. Background ventilators may be either manually adjustable or automatically controlled (**F.2.5**).
Location of manual controls	As **Table F.5**

Table F.11 System 3 – Continuous mechanical extract ventilation (MEV)

	Guidance
Design	Step 1 – Determine the whole dwelling air supply rate from **Table F.3**. (Note: no allowance is made for infiltration as the extract system lowers the pressure in the dwelling and all airflow through infiltration paths does not increase the overall ventilation rate.) Step 2 – Calculate the whole dwelling air extract rate at maximum operation by summing the individual room rates for 'minimum high rate' from **Table F.2**. (For sanitary accommodation only, the purge ventilation provisions in **F.2.8** can be used where security is not an issue. In this case the 'minimum high extract rate' for the sanitary accommodation should be omitted from the calculation.) Step 3 – The required extract rates are as follows: • The maximum rate (i.e. 'boost') should be at least the greater of Step 1 and Step 2 (the maximum individual room extract rates should be at least those given in **Table F.2** for minimum high rate). • The minimum rate should be at least the whole building rate in Step 1. The system could comprise either a central extract system or individual room fans (or a combination of both). To ensure that the system provides the intended ventilation rate, measures should be taken to minimise likely wind effects when any extract terminal is located on the prevailing windward façade. Possible solutions include ducting to another façade, use of constant volume flow rate units or, for central extract systems, follow *Performance testing of products for residential ventilation*. If a single room heat recovery ventilator (SRHRV) is used to ventilate a habitable room, with the rest of the dwelling provided by continuous mechanical extract, the air flow rates are determined as follows: • determine the whole building ventilation rate from **Table F.3**; • calculate the room supply rate required for the SRHRV from (Whole building ventilation rate × Room volume)/(Total volume of all habitable rooms); • undertake Steps 1 to 3 above for sizing the continuous mechanical extract for the rest of the dwelling, but subtract the SRHRV supply rate from the **Table F.3** value.
Background ventilators	For any design air permeability, controllable background ventilators having a minimum equivalent area of 2500mm² should be fitted in each room, except wet rooms, from which air is extracted. Where the design air permeability is leakier than 5m³/(h.m²) at 50Pa background ventilators are not necessary. Where this approach causes difficulties (e.g. on a noisy site) seek expert advice. Where background ventilators are fitted: • they should be located to avoid draughts, e.g. typically 1.7m above floor level; • fans and background ventilators fitted in the same room should be a minimum of 0.5m apart; • background ventilators may be either manually adjustable or automatically controlled (**F.2.5**).
Purge ventilation	As **Table F.5**
Location of ventilation devices	Extract should be from each wet room. Cooker hoods should be 650mm to 750mm above the hob surface (or follow manufacturer's instructions). Mechanical extract terminals and fans should be installed as high as is practical and preferably less than 400mm below the ceiling. Where ducts etc. are provided in a dwelling with a protected stairway, precautions may be necessary to prevent smoke or fire spreading into the stairway (**B.3.6.1**).
Air transfer	As **Table F.5**
Controls	Should be set up to operate without occupant intervention, but may have manual or automatic controls to select the boost rate. Any manual boost controls should be provided locally to the spaces being served. Humidity controls should not be used for sanitary accommodation. In kitchens, any automatic control must provide sufficient flow during cooking with fossil fuel (e.g. gas) to avoid build-up of combustion products. Ensure the system always provides the minimum whole building ventilation rate specified in **Table F.3**.
Location of manual controls	As **Table F.5**
Noise	As **Table F.5**

Table F.12 System 4 – Continuous mechanical supply and extract with heat recovery (MVHR)	
	Guidance
Design	Step 1 – Determine the whole dwelling air supply rate from **Table F.3**. Where the design air permeability exceeds 5m³/(h.m²) at 50Pa allow for infiltration for all dwelling types by subtracting from this value: 0.04 l/(s.m³) × gross internal volume of the dwelling heated space (m³). Step 2 – Calculate the whole dwelling air extract rate at maximum operation by summing the individual room rates for 'minimum high rate' from **Table F.2**. (For sanitary accommodation only, as an alternative, the purge ventilation provisions given in **Table F.1** can be used where security is not an issue. In this case the 'minimum high extract rate' for sanitary accommodation should be omitted from the Step 2 calculation.) Step 3 – The required air flow rates are as follows: • The maximum extract rate (e.g. 'boost') should be at least the greater of Step 1 and Step 2. Note that the individual room extract rates should be at least those given in **Table F.2** for 'minimum high rate'. • The minimum air supply rate should be at least the whole dwelling ventilation rate in Step 1.
Purge ventilation	As **Table F.5**
Location of ventilation devices	• Extract should be from each wet room. Air should normally be supplied to each habitable room. The total supply airflow should usually be distributed in proportion to the habitable room volumes. Avoid recirculation of moist air from the wet rooms to the habitable rooms. • Cooker hoods should be 650mm to 750mm above the hob surface (or follow the manufacturer's instructions). • Mechanical extract terminals and fans should be installed as high as is practical and preferably less than 400mm below the ceiling. • Mechanical supply terminals should be located and directed to avoid draughts. • Where ducts etc. are provided in a dwelling with a protected stairway, precautions may be necessary to prevent smoke or fire spreading into the stairway (**B.3.6.1**). • Background ventilators are not required.
Air transfer	As **Table F.5**
Controls	• Should be set up to operate without occupant intervention, but may have manual or automatic controls to select the boost rate. Any manual boost controls should be provided locally to the spaces being served. Humidity controls should not be used for sanitary accommodation. • In kitchens, any automatic control must provide sufficient flow during cooking with fossil fuel (e.g. gas) to avoid build-up of combustion products. • Ensure the system always provides the minimum whole building ventilation rate specified in **Table F.3**.
Location of manual controls	As **Table F.5**
Noise	As **Table F.5**

F.3.3 Dwellings with basements

Where a basement is connected to the rest of the dwelling above ground level by a large permanent opening (such as an open stairway) the whole dwelling, including the basement, should be ventilated as a multi-storey dwelling (**F.3.2**). If the basement has only one exposed façade, while the rest of the building has more than one façade, then systems 3 and 4 are preferred; expert advice should be sought before using systems 1 or 2.

Where the basement is not connected to the rest of the dwelling by a large permanent opening:

- the above-ground part of the building should be ventilated as **F.3.2**, and if that part has no bedrooms, then one bedroom should be presumed; and

- the basement should be treated separately as a single-storey dwelling above ground as **F.3.2**, and if the basement has no bedrooms then one bedroom should be presumed.

Where the dwelling comprises only a basement it should be treated as a single-storey dwelling above ground in accordance with **F.3.2** and expert advice sought.

F.3.4 Ventilation through another room

A habitable room without openable windows (an internal room) can be ventilated through another habitable room if:

- there is, from the habitable rooms to outside, provision for both:
  - purge ventilation by one or more ventilation openings with total area shown in Figure F.8, based on the combined floor area of the habitable rooms; and
  - background ventilation of at least 8000mm^2 equivalent area;
- and there is a permanent opening between the two rooms as illustrated in Figure F.8, based on the combined area of the habitable rooms.

A habitable room without openable windows (an internal room) can be ventilated through a conservatory if:

- there is, from the conservatory to outside, provision for both:
  - purge ventilation by one or more ventilation openings with total area as shown in Figure F.9, based on the combined floor area of the habitable room and the conservatory; and
  - background ventilation of at least 8000mm^2 equivalent area;
- and there are openings (which must be closable) between the habitable room and the conservatory for:

Figure F.8 Two habitable rooms treated as a single room for ventilation purposes

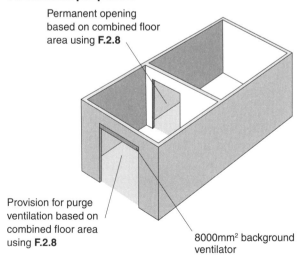

Permanent opening based on combined floor area using **F.2.8**

Provision for purge ventilation based on combined floor area using **F.2.8**

8000mm^2 background ventilator

Figure F.9 Habitable room ventilated through a conservatory

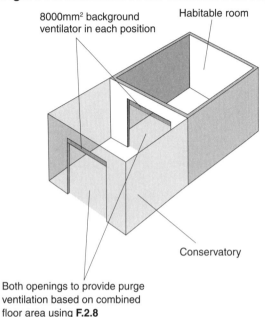

8000mm² background ventilator in each position

Habitable room

Conservatory

Both openings to provide purge ventilation based on combined floor area using **F.2.8**

– purge ventilation by one or more ventilation openings with total area shown in Figure F.9, based on the combined floor area of the habitable room and conservatory; and

– background ventilation of at least 8000mm² equivalent area, with the opening typically at least 1.7m above floor level.

F.4 Buildings other than dwellings

In addition to the requirements below, designers should bear in mind that:

• the ventilation provisions below will not necessarily meet cooling needs (**L.3.3.4**);

• fresh air supplies should be protected from contaminants injurious to health (**F.2.7**);

• measures may be required to avoid legionella contamination.

F.4.1 Access for maintenance

There should be:

• access to enable replacement of filters, fans and coils; and

• access points for cleaning ductwork.

Central plant rooms should have adequate space for maintenance. Where there are no special requirements, 600mm wide access routes and 1100mm wide work spaces for routine cleaning would be sufficient (Figure F.10). Additional space may be required for opening access doors and withdrawing filters, etc.

Further guidance
L8 Legionnaires Disease: the control of legionella bacteria in water systems. Approved code of practice and guidance. HSE. 2000. [See Paragraphs 79 to 144.]

TM13 Minimising the risk of Legionnaires' disease. CIBSE. 2002.

BSRIA Application Guides AG19/2000, AG20/2000, AG21/2000.

L24 Workplace (Health, Safety and Welfare) Regulations 1992. Approved code of practice and guidance. HSE. 12th edition. 2004. [Guidance on re-circulated air in air-conditioning and mechanical ventilation systems.]

Further guidance
Defence Works Functional Standard, Design & Maintenance Guide 08: Space requirements for plant access operation and maintenance. Defence Estates. 1996. [Available at http://webarchive.nationalarchives.gov. uk/+/http://www.defence-estates.mod.uk/publications/ dmg/dmg_08.pdf]

Ventilation hygiene toolkit: BSRIA Facilities Management Specification 1: Guidance to the standard specification for ventilation hygiene. BSRIA. 2002.

TR/19 Guide to good practice: Internal cleanliness of ventilation systems. HVCA. 2005. [HVCA has changed its name to Building & Engineering Services Association. HVCA publications are now available from www.b-espublications.co.uk.]

Figure F.10 Spaces for access

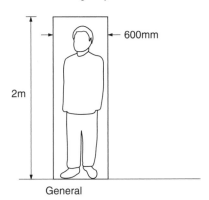

Passageway

600mm

2m

General

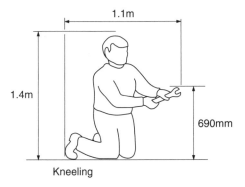

1.1m

1.4m

690mm

Kneeling

F.4.2 Offices

A ventilation system will comply if it:

- provides the airflow rates in **F.4.2.1**; or
- follows the system guidance in **F.4.2.2**; or
- follows the alternative approach in **F.4.2.3**; or
- can be demonstrated to provide the moisture and air quality criteria in **F.2.2**.

F.4.2.1 Ventilation rates

The ventilation system should meet the following requirements:

- Extract to outside from all office sanitary accommodation, washrooms and food and beverage preparation areas. Printers and photocopiers used for more than 30 minutes per hour should be located in a separate room with its own extract provision. Extract flow rates to meet Table F.13.
- A whole building ventilation rate of at least 10l/s per person; where there are significant levels of pollutants the required air supply should be determined from CIBSE Guide A.
- Purge ventilation should be provided in each office. Purged air should be taken directly to outside and not recirculated within the building.

Table F.13 Extract ventilation rates

Room	Extract rate
Rooms containing printers and photocopiers in substantial use (>30 minutes per hour)	20l/s per machine during use. If the operators are in the room continuously use the greater of the extract and whole building ventilation rates.
Office sanitary accommodation and washrooms	Intermittent air extract rate of: • 15l/s per shower/bath; • 6l/s per WC/urinal.
Food and beverage preparation areas (excluding commercial kitchens)	Intermittent air extract rate of: • 15l/s with microwave and beverages only; • 30l/s adjacent to the hob with cookers; • 60l/s elsewhere with cookers. All to operate while food and beverage preparation is in progress.

Note: For specialist buildings and spaces see references in Approved Document F Table 6.3.

F.4.2.2 Ventilation systems

Natural ventilation systems as set out in Table F.14 can provide the air flow rates required by **F.4.2.1**. Mechanical ventilation systems will be satisfactory if they provide the air flow rates in **F.4.2.1** and if the location of, and controls for, extract ventilation comply with Table F.14.

Further guidance
Applications Manual AM10: Natural ventilation in non-domestic buildings. CIBSE. 2005.

Table F.14 Ventilation for offices with natural air supply

	Guidance
Ventilation provisions	
Extract	Rates as Table F.13 Notes: PSV can be used as an alternative to mechanical extract for office sanitary, washroom and food preparation areas. Open-flued appliances must operate safely without spillage of flue gases resulting from extraction. See **J.2.1.2**.
Whole building ventilation	CIBSE Applications Manual AM 10: *Natural ventilation in non-domestic buildings.*
Purge ventilation	CIBSE Applications Manual AM 10: *Natural ventilation in non-domestic buildings.*
Location of ventilators in rooms	
Extract	• Extract ventilators should be located as high as practicable and preferably less than 400mm below the ceiling. This will tend to remove pollutants from the breathing zone of the occupants as well as increase the effectiveness of extracting buoyant pollutants and water vapour. • For PSV, extract terminals should be located in the ceiling of the room.
Whole building ventilation	CIBSE Applications Manual AM 10: *Natural ventilation in non-domestic buildings.*
Purge ventilation	CIBSE Applications Manual AM 10: *Natural ventilation in non-domestic buildings.*
Controls for ventilators in rooms	
Extract	• Extract fans can be controlled either manually or automatically. For a room with no openable window (i.e. an internal room), the extract should have a 15 minute overrun. • For PSV, either operated manually and/or automatically by a sensor or controller.
Whole building ventilation	See CIBSE Applications Manual AM 10: *Natural ventilation in non-domestic buildings.*
Purge ventilation	See CIBSE Applications Manual AM 10: *Natural ventilation in non-domestic buildings.*
Accessible controls	Readily accessible override controls should be provided for the occupants.

F.4.2.3 Alternative approaches

The requirement will be satisfied by following the recommendations of:

- CIBSE Applications Manual AM13. Mixed mode ventilation;
- CIBSE Guides A and B.

F.4.3 Other types of building

For other types of buildings follow the appropriate guidance in Approved Document F Table 6.3. Provision in workplaces must also satisfy the Workplace (Health, Safety and Welfare) Regulations 1992.

F.4.4 Car parks

Car parks below ground level, enclosed car parks and multi-storey car parks should have ventilation which limits carbon monoxide levels to:

- an average concentration of not more than 30 parts per million (ppm) over an eight-hour period;
- peak concentrations, such as by ramps and exits, of not more than 90ppm for periods not exceeding 15 minutes.

This may be achieved in naturally ventilated car parks by the provision of well-distributed permanent natural ventilation, for example, openings at each car parking level with an aggregate equivalent area equal to at least 1/20 (one-twentieth) of the floor area at that level, of which at least 25% should be on each of two opposing walls.

Mechanically ventilated car parks should have either:

- permanent natural ventilation openings of equivalent area not less than 1/40 (one-fortieth) of the floor area and a mechanical ventilation system capable of at least three air changes per hour (ach); or
- for basement car parks, a mechanical ventilation system capable of at least six air changes per hour (ach).

In addition, at exits and ramps, where cars queue inside the building with engines running, provisions should be made to ensure a local ventilation rate of at least 10ach.

Car parks will also require ventilation for fire risk management (**B.5.5**).

F.5 Existing buildings

F.5.1 General provisions

Trickle ventilators should be fitted to replacement windows if the original windows had such vents. Where the original windows were not fitted with trickle ventilators, but the room is not adequately ventilated, it would be good practice to fit trickle vents (or equivalent means of ventilation) to help control of condensation and improve indoor air quality.

Further guidance
Applications Manual AM13. Mixed mode ventilation. CIBSE. 2000.

CIBSE Guide A: Environmental design. CIBSE. 2006.

CIBSE Guide B: Heating, ventilating, air-conditioning and refrigeration. CIBSE. 2005.

Further guidance
INDG244. Workplace health, safety and welfare. A short guide for managers. HSE. 2007. [www.hse.gov.uk/pubns/indg244.pdf]

Further guidance
Code of practice for ground floor, multi-storey and underground car parks. Association for Petroleum and Explosives Administration. 1995. [www.apea.org.uk]

CIBSE Guide B Heating, ventilating, air conditioning and refrigeration. CIBSE. 2005. [Section 2.3.23.3.]

EH40: Occupational exposure limits for limiting concentration of exhaust pollutants. [Now: *EH40. Workplace exposure limits.* HSE. 2005. Available at www.hse.gov.uk/pubns/priced/eh40.pdf]

In all cases where trickle ventilators (or equivalent) are to be fitted, the new ventilation opening should be no smaller than that originally provided, and should be controllable. Otherwise they should meet the following minimum sizes:

- Dwellings:
  - habitable rooms: 5000mm^2 equivalent area;
  - kitchen, utility room and bathroom (with or without WC): 2500mm^2 equivalent area.

- Other buildings:
  - occupiable rooms with floor areas up to 10m^2: 2500mm^2 equivalent area;
  - occupiable rooms greater than 10m^2: 250mm^2 equivalent area per m^2 of floor area;
  - kitchens (domestic type): 2500mm^2 equivalent area;
  - bathrooms and shower rooms: 2500mm^2 equivalent area per bath or shower;
  - sanitary accommodation (and/or washing facilities): 2500mm^2 equivalent area per WC.

Where windows are replaced as part of a material change of use the requirements for new buildings apply (**F.3** and **F.4**).

During refurbishment work, existing extract fans and passive stack ventilators should either be retained or replaced with an equivalent or better system; but no system need be provided where one does not already exist.

F.5.2 Addition of a habitable room to an existing dwelling

The general ventilation rate for the additional room and, if necessary, adjoining rooms could be achieved by background ventilators.

If the additional room is connected to an existing habitable room that still has windows opening to outside and has a total background ventilator equivalent area of at least 5000mm^2, then there should be:

- background ventilators of at least 8000mm^2 equivalent area between the two rooms; and
- background ventilators of at least 8000mm^2 equivalent areas between the additional room and outside.

Otherwise provision should meet **F.3.4**.

Alternatively, the additional habitable room could be ventilated by a single heat recovery ventilator sized by:

- taking the whole building ventilation rate from Table F.3;
- calculating the room supply rate required from:
  (whole building ventilation × room volume)/(total volume of all habitable rooms).

Provisions for purge ventilation, location and controls should follow Table F.5; systems should be tested to Table F.4.

Further guidance
A guide to trickle ventilators. Glass and Glazing Federation. 2010.

F.5.3 Addition of a wet room to an existing dwelling

Whole building and extract ventilation should be provided by:

- intermittent extract as given in Table F.9, and a background ventilator of at least 2500mm^2 equivalent area; or

- single room heat recovery ventilator as Table F.9; or

- passive stack ventilator as Table F.10; or

- continuous extract fan as Table F.11.

Purge ventilation and controls should meet the appropriate system in Table F.5, and air transfer provided by undercutting the internal door to the wet room as Table F.5.

F.5.4 Addition of a conservatory to an existing building

Background ventilators may be used to achieve the required ventilation level in **F.3.4**. Purge ventilation, location and controls should follow Table F.5.

F.5.5 Historic buildings

Work to a historic building should improve the ventilation of the building, without prejudicing its character, or increasing the risk of long-term deterioration of its fabric or fittings. It would be appropriate to seek the advice of the local authority's conservation officer when a ventilation system is being considered.

Further guidance
BS 7913:1998. Principles of the conservation of historic buildings.

SPAB Information Sheet No. 4. *The need for old buildings to breathe*. SPAB. 1986. [Guidance on enabling the fabric to 'breathe' to control moisture and long term decay problems.]

G. Sanitation, hot water safety and water efficiency

G.1 General considerations

G.1.1 Scope

Part G is intended to ensure that buildings have wholesome and safe hot and cold water supplies, and have adequate sanitary arrangements. The 2010 revision of Part G and Approved Document G was a thorough overhaul of the 1992 requirements and guidance. The revision introduced new requirements and extended and re-ordered existing ones. There were major changes to address:

- Safety – The requirements for hot water systems were extended, to take account of fatalities caused by malfunctioning hot water systems, and to prevent scalding by hot water when bathing.
- Sanitation – Provisions for sanitary conveniences and bathrooms were updated and extended to cover residential accommodation other than dwellings.
- Sustainability – There is now a requirement for water efficiency in dwellings. The predicted usage of wholesome water in a new dwelling must be calculated, and be within a stated limit. The locations where wholesome water must be supplied are defined. The use of non-wholesome water (such as harvested rainwater and recycled greywater) for other functions is permitted as a means of reducing the unnecessary consumption of wholesome water.

Part G: Sanitation, hot water safety and water efficiency	
Requirement	**Limit on application**
Cold water supply	

G1 (1) There must be a suitable installation for the provision of –
    (a) wholesome water to any place where drinking water is drawn off;
    (b) wholesome water or softened wholesome water to any washbasin or bidet provided in or adjacent to a room containing a sanitary convenience;
    (c) wholesome water or softened wholesome water to any washbasin, bidet, fixed bath or shower in a bathroom; and
    (d) wholesome water to any sink provided in any area where food is prepared.
 (2) There must be a suitable installation for the provision of water of suitable quality to any sanitary convenience fitted with a flushing device.	

Water efficiency	
G2 Reasonable provision must be made by the installation of fittings and fixed appliances that use water efficiently for the prevention of undue consumption of water.	Requirement G2 applies only when a dwelling is – (a) erected; or (b) formed by a material change of use of a building within the meaning of Regulation 5(a) or (b).

Hot water supply and systems

G3 (1) There must be a suitable installation for the provision of heated wholesome water or heated softened wholesome water to:

(a) any washbasin or bidet provided in or adjacent to a room containing a sanitary convenience;

(b) any washbasin, bidet, fixed bath and shower in a bathroom; and

(c) any sink provided in any area where food is prepared.

(2) A hot water system, including any cistern or other vessel that supplies water to or receives expansion water from a hot water system, shall be designed, constructed and installed so as to resist the effects of temperature and pressure that may occur either in normal use or in the event of such malfunctions as may reasonably be anticipated, and must be adequately supported.

(3) A hot water system that has a hot water storage vessel shall incorporate precautions to:

(a) prevent the temperature of the water stored in the vessel at any time exceeding 100°C; and

(b) ensure that any discharge from safety devices is safely conveyed to where it is visible but will not cause a danger to persons in or about the building.

(4) The hot water supply to any fixed bath must be so designed and installed as to incorporate measures to ensure that the temperature of the water that can be delivered to that bath does not exceed 48°C.

Requirement G3(3) does not apply to a system which heats or stores water for the purposes only of an industrial process.

Requirement G3(4) applies only when a dwelling is –
(a) erected;
(b) formed by a material change of use within the meaning of regulation 5(a) or (b).

Sanitary conveniences and washing facilities

G4 (1) Adequate and suitable sanitary conveniences must be provided in rooms provided to accommodate them or in bathrooms.

(2) Adequate handwashing facilities must be provided in:

(a) rooms containing sanitary conveniences; or

(b) rooms or spaces adjacent to rooms containing sanitary conveniences.

(3) Any room containing a sanitary convenience, a bidet, or any facility for washing hands provided in accordance with paragraph (2)(b), must be separated from any kitchen or any area where food is prepared.

Bathrooms

G5 A bathroom must be provided containing a washbasin and either a fixed bath or a shower.

Requirement G5 applies only to dwellings and to buildings containing one or more rooms for residential purposes.

Kitchens and food preparation areas

G6 A suitable sink must be provided in any area where food is prepared.

The requirements apply on:
- the erection and extension of a building;
- the provision or extension of a controlled service or fitting;
- the material alteration of a building, controlled service or fitting.

Controlled services include:
- heating boilers and fuel tanks;
- hot water vessels;
- controls to boilers and hot water storage systems.

In the event of the material change of use of a building or part of a building:
- for a dwelling, Requirements G1–G6 apply;
- for other buildings Requirements G1, G3(1–3), G4, G5 and G6 apply.

G.1.1.1 Exempt buildings

Buildings exempt from the Building Regulations under Schedule 2 (see **I.3.2**) have that exemption removed where they share hot and cold water supplies with other buildings. An otherwise exempt building must comply with Requirements G1 and G2(2 and 3) if it is:

- a greenhouse receiving a hot or cold water supply from a dwelling;
- a small detached building (Class VI) or extension (Class VII – including a conservatory under 30m²) which receives or shares a supply from any building subject to the Building Regulations.

However, there is no requirement to provide any water supply.

Work covered by Part G must be notified to the Building Control Body (BCB); minor work (see Table I.2) need not be notified, but should still comply with Part G.

G.1.2 Other Regulations

Other Regulations also impose requirements for water supply and sanitation:

- **The Water Supply (Water Fittings) Regulations 1999** – address contamination, waste, undue consumption and misuse;
- **The Workplace (Health, Safety and Welfare) Regulations 1992** – address space requirements, cleaning and provision of sanitary conveniences;
- **Food Hygiene (England) Regulations 2006** – address food preparation and the provision of washbasins and sinks;
- **Gas Safety (Installation and Use) Regulations 1998** – address the use of gas conveyed from a gas storage vessel.

Electrical work to hot water systems should comply with BS 7671:2008 and, for dwellings, Approved Document P.

Further guidance
BS 7671:2008+A1:2011. Requirements for electrical installations. IEE Wiring Regulations. Seventeenth edition.

G.1.3 Definitions

Non-self-resetting energy cut-out A device which interrupts the supply of heat to a hot water storage vessel when a fixed, factory-set temperature is exceeded and, if actuated, must be reset manually.

Pressure relief valve A mechanically operated valve which opens to discharge water when a fixed, factory-set pressure is exceeded.

Sanitary accommodation A room containing a water closet (WC) or urinal; one or more cubicles counts as a single space if there is free circulation of air.

Sanitary appliance A WC, urinal, bath, shower, washbasin, sink, bidet and drinking fountain, including appliances not connected to a water supply (e.g. waterless urinal) and those not connected to a drain (e.g. composting toilet).

Sanitary convenience A closet (WC) or urinal.

Softened wholesome water Water which would be regarded as wholesome, but for the presence of an excessive level of sodium which results from softening of the water to reduce the concentrations of calcium and magnesium.

Temperature relief valve A mechanically operated valve which opens to discharge water when a fixed, factory-set temperature is exceeded.

Tundish A device installed in a discharge pipe from a valve that provides an air break. It prevents backflow and gives a visible indication of discharge.

Wholesome water Water which protects the lifelong health of the population, and meets parameters for its biological, chemical and physical qualities (Section 67 (Standards of wholesomeness) of Water Act 1991).

G.1.4 Discharge to drains

Drains should comply with Requirement H.1 (see **H.2**), and be adequate to accept discharge from:

- any WC fitted with a flushing apparatus;
- a urinal fitted with a flushing apparatus, which should discharge through a grating, a trap or mechanical seal and a branch pipe to a discharge stack or drain;
- any sanitary appliance used for personal washing, which should discharge through a grating, a trap and a branch discharge pipe;
- any sink, which should discharge through a grating, a trap and a branch discharge pipe.

A macerator and pump connected to a small-bore drainage system discharging to a discharge stack may be used to discharge:

- a WC, provided there is also access to a WC discharging directly to a gravity system; or
- a sanitary appliance used for personal washing, provided there is access to washing facilities discharging directly to a gravity system.

The macerator and pump should meet BS EN 12050-1:2001 or BS EN 12050-3:2001.

Greywater recycling will result in lower flow rates, which should be taken into account when designing drains, particularly at the head of a drain where only one building is connected.

G.2 Cold water supply (Requirement G1)

There must be a supply of:

- wholesome water to any place where drinking water is drawn off;

- wholesome water or softened wholesome water to any washbasin or bidet provided in or adjacent to a room containing a sanitary convenience;

- wholesome water or softened wholesome water to any washbasin, bidet, fixed bath or shower in a bathroom;

- wholesome water to any sink provided in any area where food is prepared;

- water of suitable quality to any sanitary convenience fitted with a flushing device, although that supply need not be wholesome water, but may be non-wholesome water such as harvested rainwater or greywater.

Water supplies must be at a pressure and flow rate sufficient for sanitary appliances and must be reliable. Installations must convey:

- wholesome water, without waste, misuse, undue consumption or contamination of water;

- water to sanitary appliances, without waste, misuse, undue consumption or contamination of wholesome water.

G.2.1 Wholesome water

Wholesome water can be:

- mains water supplied by a statutory water undertaker, or a licenced water supplier; or

- water from a source which complies with Private Water Supplies Regulations 1991 (SI 1991/2790 as amended) or the Private Water Supplies (Wales) Regulations (SI 2010/66).

G.2.2 Alternative sources of water

Some functions, such as toilet flushing or irrigation, do not require wholesome water. Such functions may be carried out using:

- water drawn from wells, springs, boreholes, watercourses;

- harvested rainwater;

- reclaimed greywater;

- reclaimed industrial process water.

A risk assessment should be carried out to ensure that the source of supply and method of treatment are appropriate, and that the use of water from alternative sources is not likely to cause the waste, misuse, undue consumption or contamination of wholesome water.

Treatment systems for water from alternative sources should be designed to minimise the impact on water quality of:

Further guidance
BS EN 12050 Wastewater lifting plants for buildings and sites. Principles of construction and testing.
-1:2001. Lifting plants for wastewater containing faecal matter.
-3:2001. Lifting plants for wastewater containing faecal matter for limited applications.

- component failure;
- failure of the maintenance regime;
- power failure;
- any other measures noted in the risk assessment.

Systems or units used to supply dwellings should undergo a risk assessment to determine the effect on water quality of such failures. The assessment should be conducted by the system designer and manufacturer, and should include appropriate testing to demonstrate any risks have been suitably addressed.

To avoid contamination, pipes conveying water from alternative sources should be clearly marked to distinguish them from those conveying wholesome water.

Further guidance
WRAS Information and Guidance Note 9-02-05 Marking and identification of pipework for reclaimed (greywater) systems. Water Regulations Advisory Scheme. 2005.

WRAS Information and Guidance Note 9-02-04 Reclaimed water systems. WRAS. 2004. [Guidance on the design, maintenance and installation of systems.]

BS 8515:2009 Rainwater harvesting systems. Code of practice.

G.3 Water efficiency (Requirement G2 and Regulation 36)

To ensure the water efficiency of new dwellings, the potential consumption of wholesome water for hot and cold water systems should not exceed 125 litres/person/day. The calculation should be carried out using the 'Water Efficiency Calculator for New Dwellings' and should take account of consumption from all installed fittings and fixed appliances.

Requirement G2 applies to each new dwelling, including those formed by material change of use. Individual dwellings in blocks of flats should *each* comply with the requirement. A dwelling which complies with the minimum water efficiency standards of the Code for Sustainable Homes is presumed to meet Requirement G2.

A notification of the calculated potential consumption must be given to the BCB not later than 5 days after completion of the building work or – where the BCB is an Approved Inspector – not later than the day on which the initial notice ceases to be in force.

Further guidance
The Water Efficiency Calculator for new dwellings. CLG. 2009. [Available at www.planningportal.gov.uk/uploads/br/water_efficiency_calculator.pdf]

G.3.1 Water efficiency calculator for new dwellings

In determining the potential wholesome water consumption the calculation method takes account of:

- manufacturers' declared values for water consumption for sanitary appliances and white goods (washing machines and dishwashers);
- any alternative sources of non-wholesome water to be used in the dwelling (e.g. harvested rainwater for flushing toilets), which will reduce the consumption of wholesome water;
- an outdoor usage allowance of 5 litres/person/day, which covers water for washing cars or gardening (that allowance is not used in the water use calculation for the Code for Sustainable Homes).

The sanitary appliances, white goods and systems for non-wholesome water that are used in the calculation must be supplied and installed. A record of those appliances and systems should be provided, together with sufficient information for the building owners or occupiers to maintain the building's water efficiency.

The consumption calculation is based on standardised usage patterns and will therefore not be an accurate prediction of actual water use.

G.4 Hot water supply and systems (Requirement G3)

There must be a suitable installation for the provision of heated wholesome water, or heated softened wholesome water, to:

- any washbasin or bidet in or adjacent to a room containing a sanitary convenience;
- any washbasin, bidet, fixed bath or shower in a bathroom;
- any sink provided in areas where food is prepared.

A heated water supply may be required elsewhere for workplace heath and safety, or food hygiene purposes.

Heated wholesome water requires:

- a wholesome cold water supply (**G.2.1**); and
- an installation which complies with the Water Supply (Water Fittings) Regulations 1999.

Hot water systems (including cisterns and other storage, supply and expansion vessels) must resist the pressures and temperature arising:

- during normal operation;
- following failure of any thermostat;
- during operation of any safety device that prevents the temperature from exceeding 100°C.

Where a dwelling is erected or formed by material change of use, the water supply to any fixed bath must have measures to prevent the temperature of water delivered to the bath exceeding 48°C.

G.4.1 Hot water storage systems

Hot water storage systems and storage vessels must comply with the standards in Table G.1. Storage vessels (excluding those used for industrial purposes) must have:

- a device to prevent the water temperature exceeding 100°C; and
- any discharge must be carried safely away, but still be visible.

To avoid waste, pipework should be designed to minimise the transfer time between the hot water storage system and outlets.

Further guidance
Water Regulations Guide. WRAS. 2000. [Guidance on the requirements of the Water Supply (Water Fittings) Regulations.]

Table G.1 Standards for hot water systems and components

Group	System or component	Standard or requirement
Hot water storage systems	General	BS 6700:2006 + A1:2009. Specification for design, installation, testing and maintenance of services supplying water for domestic use within buildings and their curtilages. [*Withdrawn, replaced by BS 8558:2011. Guide to the design, installation, testing and maintenance of services supplying water for domestic use within buildings and their curtilages. Complementary guidance to BS EN 806.*] Or BS EN 12897:2006. Water supply. Specification for indirectly heated unvented (closed) storage water heaters.
	Storage vessels	BS 853-1:1990+A3:2011. Specification for vessels for use in heating systems. Calorifiers and storage vessels for central heating and hot water supply. BS 1566-1:2002+A1:2011. Copper indirect cylinders for domestic purposes. Open vented copper cylinders. Requirements and test methods. BS 3198:1981. Specification for copper hot water storage combination units for domestic purposes. [*Note: Or other relevant national standard.*]
	Cold water storage cistern	BS 417-2:1987. Specification for galvanized low carbon steel cisterns, cistern lids, tanks and cylinders. Metric units. Or BS 4213:2004. Cisterns for domestic use. Cold water storage and combined feed and expansion (thermoplastic) cisterns up to 500 litres. Specification.
Safety devices	Non-resetting energy cut-outs	BS EN 60335-2-73:2003+A2:2009. Household and similar electrical appliances. Safety. Particular requirements for fixed immersion heaters. *And* BS EN 60730-2-9:2002. Automatic electrical controls for household and similar user. Particular requirements for temperature sensing control. [Replaced by 2010 edition.] Or BE EN 257:1992. Mechanical thermostats for gas-burning appliances.
	Temperature relief valves	BS 6283-2:1991. Safety and control devices for use in hot water systems. Specifications for temperature relief valves for pressures from 1 bar to 10 bar.
	Combined temperature and pressure relief valves	BS EN 1490:2000. Building valves. Combined temperature and pressure relief valves. Tests and requirements.
Electric water heating	Fixed immersion heaters	BS EN 60335-2-73:2003+A2:2009. Household and similar electrical appliances. Safety. Particular requirements for fixed immersion heaters.
	Instantaneous water heaters	BS EN 60335-2-35:2002+A2:2011. Household and similar electrical appliances. Safety. Particular requirements for instantaneous water heaters.
	Storage water heaters	BS EN 60335-2-21:2003+A2:2008. Household and similar electrical appliances. Safety. Particular requirements for storage water heaters.
Solar water heating	Factory-made solar water heating systems	BS EN 12976-1:2006. Thermal solar systems and components. Factory-made systems. General requirements.
	Other systems	BS EN 12977-1:2012. Thermal solar systems and components. Custom built systems. General requirements for solar water heaters and combi systems. [*Note: replaces preEN/TS 12977-1:2008.*] Or BS 5918:1989 Code of practice for solar heating systems for domestic hot water.
Water supply temperature limiting devices	Thermostatic mixing valves	BS EN 1111:1999. Sanitary tapware. Thermostatic mixing valves (PN10). General technical specification. Or BS EN 1287:1999. Sanitary tapware. Low pressure thermostatic mixing valves. General technical specifications.
	Thermostatic mixing valves – care homes	As above and NHS Estates Model Specification D 08.

G.4.1.1 Vented hot water storage systems

Any build-up of pressure caused by the expansion of water within the storage vessel is relieved through a vent pipe which runs from the top of the vessel and terminates over the top of the cold water storage cistern, above the level of the water. The pipe should have a minimum internal diameter of 19mm.

In addition there should be **either**:

- a device to disconnect the supply of heat to the storage vessel in the event of storage system overheating;
  - for direct heat sources, a non-self-resetting energy cut-out;
  - for indirect heat sources an overheating cut-out which prevents the temperature of the stored water exceeding 100ºC;
- **or** a temperature relief valve, or combined temperature and pressure relief valve which will safely discharge water in the event of significant overheating.

The cold water storage cistern must:

- conform to the standards in Table G.1; and
- be supported on a flat level rigid platform capable of supporting the weight of the cistern when full, and which extends 150mm in all directions beyond the widest dimensions of the cistern; and
- be accessible for maintenance, cleaning and replacement.

G.4.1.2 Unvented hot water storage systems

Unvented hot water storage systems require additional safety devices to relieve any build-up of pressure from water expansion and so prevent bursting or explosion. In addition to any control for setting the desired temperature, any system requires at least two temperature-activated safety devices, such as:

- a non-self-resetting cut-out to disconnect the supply of heat to the storage vessel; and
- a temperature relief valve or combined temperature and pressure relief valve to safely discharge water in the event of serious overheating.

Alternative approaches which provide an equivalent degree of safety will be acceptable.

Water heaters with a capacity of 15 litres or less

Such heaters will be satisfactory, provided they have appropriate safety devices for temperature and pressure.

Systems up to 500 litres capacity and 45kW power input

In addition to the requirements above, the hot water storage system should comprise a proprietary unit or package, and the package and its components should be appropriate to the circumstances of use and satisfy appropriate standards (see Table G.1: Hot water storage systems – General). In an indirectly heated system the energy cut-out may be on the boiler.

The unit or package should be indelibly marked with the:

- manufacturer's name and contact details;

Figure G.1 Warning notice for hot water storage units or packages

WARNING TO USER

a. Do not remove or adjust any component part of this unvented water heater; contact the installer.

b. If this unvented water heater develops a fault, such as a flow of hot water from the discharge pipe, switch the heater off and contact the installer.

WARNING TO INSTALLER

a. This installation is subject to the Building Regulations.

b. Use only appropriate components for installation or maintenance.

Installed by:

Name ....

Address ....

Tel. No. ....

Completion date..

- model reference;
- rated storage capacity of storage water heater;
- operating pressure of system and of the expansion valve;
- relevant operating data on each of the safety devices fitted; and
- maximum primary circuit pressure and flow temperature of indicated hot water storage system units or packages.

There should also be an indelibly marked warning (Figure G.1) which is visible after installation.

Systems over 500 litres or 45kW power input

Such systems will generally be bespoke designs and are unlikely to be suitable for third party accreditation. They should be designed by an appropriately qualified engineer to meet the requirements above.

Systems with a capacity of less than 500 litres but with an input of more than 45kW should be in the form of a package; and both the package and the components should be appropriate to the circumstances of use and satisfy an appropriate standard (e.g. Table G.1: Hot water storage systems – General).

Installation

The safety and performance of an unvented system depends on correct installation. Building owners and occupiers should take care to choose installers with the necessary skills, which can be demonstrated by:

- registration with an appropriate competent persons scheme;
- holding a current registered operative skills certification card for unvented hot water systems.

The BCB must be given prior notification of the installation of an unvented hot water storage system, unless the installer is registered with an appropriate competent persons scheme.

G.4.1.3 Safety devices

Non-self-resetting energy cut-outs

These are only suitable where they would instantly disconnect supply of energy to a storage vessel. They should comply with the standards in Table G.1. In addition:

- any cut-out which operates indirectly (for example, being wired up to a motorised valve) should either comply with the standards in Table G.1, or the supplier or installer must be able to demonstrate it has equivalent performance;

- an electrical device such as a relay or motorised valve connected to the cut-out should interrupt the supply of energy if the electrical power supply is disconnected;

- multiple cut-outs should be independent (for example, with separate motorised valves and temperature sensors);

- each heat source should have a separate non-self-resetting cut-out.

Temperature and pressure relief devices

Temperature relief valves and combined temperature and pressure relief valves should comply with the standards in Table G.1, and should be configured to ensure that the temperature of stored water does not exceed 100°C. Temperature relief valves should have a discharge rating at least equal to the total power input to the hot water storage system, measured to either BS 6283-2:1991 or BS EN 1490:2000.

Relief valves should be located directly on the storage vessel. In hot water storage system units and packages, the temperature relief valves should be:

- factory fitted and not disconnected other than for replacement; and

- not relocated in any other device or fitting.

Temperature and/or pressure relief valves should not be used in systems which have no provision to replenish stored water automatically (for example, unvented primary storage vessels). Such systems should have a second, non-self-resetting energy cut-out independent of the first one.

G.4.1.4 Discharge pipes from safety devices

Requirements for discharge pipes are given in Tables G.2 and G.3 and Figure G.2. Each temperature relief valve or combined temperature and relief valve should discharge, as shown in Figure G.2, by a short length of metal pipe (D1) into a tundish and from there into a further discharge pipe (D2), which should discharge into a safe place where there is no risk to persons.

Further guidance

BS 6283-2:1991. Safety and control devices for use in hot water systems. Specifications for temperature relief values for pressures from 1 bar to 10 bar.

BS EN 1490:2000. Building valves. Combined temperature and pressure relief valves. Tests and requirements.

Table G.2 Requirements for discharge pipes

Component	Attribute	Requirement
Discharge pipe D1	Diameter	Not less than nominal outlet size of temperature relief valve.
	Manifold	Any manifold sized to accept and discharge total discharge from all connected pipes.
		Factory fitted where several valves from a single system discharge into the same manifold.
Tundish	Compliance	Complies with Water Supply (Water Fittings) Regulations 1999.
	Construction	Incorporates a suitable air gap.
	Location	• Vertical, in the same space as the unvented hot water system. • As close as possible to the valve outlet (600mm maximum). • Lower than the safety device.
	Visibility	• Discharge should be visible at the tundish. • A warning device which operates on discharge should be considered where discharge may not be apparent (e.g. dwellings occupied by people with impaired vision or mobility).
Discharge pipe D2	Arrangement	• 300mm (minimum) vertical section immediately below tundish before any elbows or bends. • 1 in 200 (minimum) fall thereafter.
	Construction	Metal, or another material demonstrated to be capable of receiving water at discharge temperature: clearly and permanently marked to identify product and discharge standards (e.g. BS 7291-1:2006).
	Diameter	• Appropriately sized for the valve outlet size and equivalent hydraulic resistance, which depends on the length of the pipe and the resistance produced by bends. (**Table G.3** or Annex D of BS 6700:2006). • A single discharge pipe serving more than one system should be at least one pipe size larger than the largest discharge pipe (D2) connected to it.
	Termination	• To a trapped gully with the end of the pipe below a fixed grating and above the water seal; or • To a low level downward discharge: up to 100mm above external surfaces such as car parks or grassed areas, provided with a wire cage or similar guard to prevent contact and maintain visibility; or • To high level discharge, e.g. into metal hopper and metal downpipe, with end of discharge pipe clearly visible, or onto a roof capable of withstanding high temperature water discharges and at least 3m from any plastic guttering systems which would collect discharges; or • To a soil discharge stack which: – can safely withstand water at the discharge temperature (plastics branch pipes to be polybutylene (PB) to Class S of BS 7291-2:2006 or cross-linked polyethylene (PE-X) to Class S of BS 7291-3:2006); and, – contains a mechanical seal, not incorporating a water trap which allows water into the branch pipe but does not permit foul air to be ventilated through the tundish; and, – is a separate branch pipe with no sanitary appliances connected to it; and – is continuously marked with a warning that no sanitary appliances should be connected to it.

BS 7291. Thermostatic pipes and fittings for hot and cold water for domestic purposes and heating installations in buildings.

-1:2006. General requirements. [*Withdrawn, replaced by 2010 edition*]

-2:2006. Specification for polybutylene (PB) pipe and associated fittings. [*Withdrawn, replaced by 2010 edition*]

-3:2006. Specification for cross-linked polyethylene (PE-X) pipes and associated fittings. [*Withdrawn, replaced by 2010 edition*]

BS 6700:2006 + A1:2009 Specification for design, installation, testing and maintenance of services supplying water for domestic use within buildings and their curtilages. [*Withdrawn, replaced by BS 8558:2011. Guide to the design, installation, testing and maintenance of services supplying water for domestic use within buildings and their curtilages. Complementary guidance to BS EN 806.*]

Table G.3 Sizing of copper discharge pipe 'D2' for common temperature relief valve outlet sizes				
Valve outlet size	Minimum size of discharge pipe 'D1' (mm)	Minimum size of discharge pipe 'D2' (mm)	Resistance created by each elbow or bend (m)	Maximum resistance allowed (expressed as length of straight pipe) (m)
G½	15	22	0.8	9
		28	1.0	18
		35	1.4	27
G¾	22	28	1.0	9
		35	1.4	18
		42	1.7	27
G1	28	35	1.4	9
		42	1.7	18
		54	2.3	27

Note: The table is based on copper tube. Sizing and maximum lengths of plastic pipe should be based on data for the type of pipe being used.

Figure G.2 Typical discharge pipe arrangement

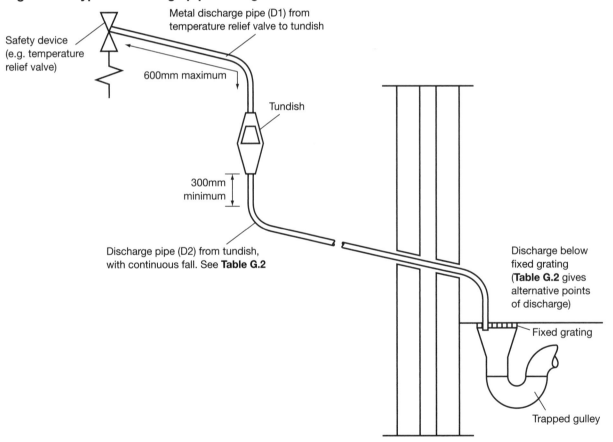

Metal discharge pipe (D1) from temperature relief valve to tundish

Safety device (e.g. temperature relief valve)

600mm maximum

Tundish

300mm minimum

Discharge pipe (D2) from tundish, with continuous fall. See **Table G.2**

Discharge below fixed grating (**Table G.2** gives alternative points of discharge)

Fixed grating

Trapped gulley

G.4.2 Electric water heating

Electric water heating systems should comply with Table G.1.

G.4.3 Solar water heating

Solar water heating systems should comply with Table G.1. Those operating at elevated temperatures and pressures require appropriately rated components. An additional heat source will be required to maintain water temperature and prevent microbial growth.

Further guidance
CIBSE Guide G: Public health engineering. CIBSE. 2004. [Covers solar water heating.]

CIBSE technical guide. *Solar heating design and installation.* CIBSE. 2007.

G.4.4 Prevention of excessive temperatures

Where the operating temperature of domestic hot water in a storage vessel in a dwelling is likely to exceed 80°C under normal conditions, the outlets from the vessel should be fitted with a device to ensure that the temperature of domestic hot water supplied does not exceed 60°C. An in-line hot water supply tempering valve to BS EN 15092 would be suitable.

The Water Supply (Water Fittings) Regulations 1999 require water to be stored at not less than 60°C and distributed at a temperature of not less than 55°C to prevent contamination with pathogens such as legionella.

Further guidance
L8 Legionnaires Disease: the control of legionella bacteria in water systems. Approved code of practice and guidance. HSE. 2000.

BS EN 15092:2008. Building valves. In-line hot water tempering valves.

G.4.5 Supply to baths

To prevent scalding, the hot water supply to a bath should not exceed 48°C. The temperature should be limited by an in-line blending valve or other appropriate temperature control device with a maximum temperature stop (such as thermostatic mixing values to Table G.1), which will not allow water temperatures above 48°C and will failsafe.

To prevent colonisation of waterborne pathogens, pipework between blending valves and final outlets should be kept to a minimum. Baths expected to have intermittent use should have provision for high temperature flushing.

Further guidance
IP 14/03 Preventing hot water scalding in bathrooms: using TMVs. BRE. 2003.

G.4.6 Installation and commissioning

Water heaters must be properly installed (see BS 8000-15:1990) and should be commissioned to ensure efficient functioning (**L.1.5**) with the BCB being notified of that commissioning. However, commissioning is not required for systems which are not capable of adjustment (for example, those that have only on/off controls) or for those where the process of commissioning would make little difference to performance. The commissioning process must not compromise any relevant health and safety requirements.

Further guidance
BS 8000-15:1990. Workmanship on Building Sites. Code of practice for hot and cold water services (domestic scale).

G.5 Sanitary conveniences and washing facilities (Requirement G4)

Any building must have:

- sufficient, suitable sanitary conveniences, appropriate for the sex and age and number of persons using a building, and which are in rooms provided for that purpose, or in bathrooms; and

- adequate handwashing facilities, either in rooms containing sanitary conveniences or in adjacent rooms or spaces.

Any room or space containing a sanitary convenience, bidet or associated handwashing facility must be separated from any kitchen or area where food is prepared.

Sanitary conveniences should also comply with:

- accessibility requirements of Part M;
- ventilation requirements of Part F;
- the regulator's performance specification for WC suites made under the Water Supply (Water Fittings) Regulations 1999.

Where hot and cold taps are provided, the hot tap should be to the left.

G.5.1 Dwellings

Any dwellinghouse or flat should have at least one sanitary convenience with a WC and handwashing facilities, located on the principal or entrance storey (**M.8.5**). Any additional sanitary conveniences should have handwashing facilities.

Handwashing facilities may either be in the room containing the sanitary convenience or be in an adjacent room or place that provides the sole means of access to that room (provided the room or place is not used for food preparation). There is no need to provide a separation lobby between a kitchen and a room containing a sanitary convenience and a handwashing basin (Figure G.3). However, where the room contains *only* the sanitary convenience then the room or space with handwashing facilities should be accessed before the food preparation area, and be separated from it by a door (Figure G.4).

Figure G.3 Separation between hand washbasin/WC and food preparation area (single room)

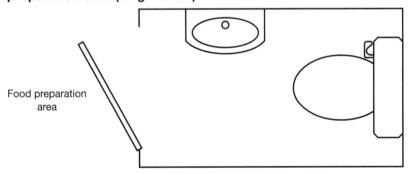

Food preparation area

Further guidance

BS 6465. Sanitary installations.
-1:2006 +A1:2009. Code of practice for the design of sanitary facilities and scale of provision for sanitary and associated appliances. [Guidance on provision of sanitary appliances beyond the scope of the ACOP, and for where a level of provision beyond the minimum is required.]
-2:1996. Code practice for space requirements for sanitary appliances. [Guidance on provision of activity space around sanitary appliances in dwellings and buildings other than dwellings.]
-3:2006. Code of practice for the selection, installation and maintenance of sanitary and associated appliances.

Figure G.4 Separation between hand washbasin/WC and food preparation area (two rooms)

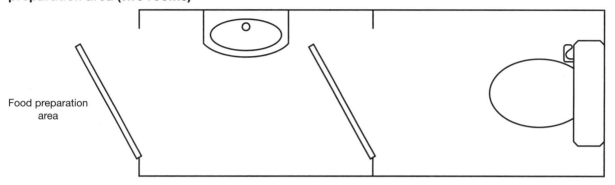

Food preparation area

G.5.2 Buildings other than dwellings

The provision of sanitary conveniences should meet the Approved Code of Practice (ACOP) for Workplaces to Workplace (Health, Safety and Welfare) Regulations 1992, and should include sanitary accommodation to satisfy Part M (**M.7**). HSE document L24 sets out the provision necessary for each group of workers. BS 6465-1 gives further guidance on levels of provision.

A sanitary convenience may be provided in:

- a self-contained washroom with handwashing facilities;

- a self-contained room with handwashing facilities in an adjacent room;

- a cubicle, with shared handwashing facilities located in a room containing a number of cubicles (urinals, WC cubicles and handwashing facilities may be in the same room).

A room containing a sanitary convenience and/or associated handwashing facilities should be separated by a door from any place used for food preparation, including a kitchen.

G.5.3 Chemical and composting toilets

Chemical toilets or composting toilets may be used where:

- suitable arrangements can be made for the disposal of waste either on or off the premises; and

- waste can be removed without carrying it through any living spaces or food preparation areas (including kitchens); and

- no part of the installation would be affected by flood water.

Composting toilets may only be connected to an energy source in order to ventilate the composting chamber, or to sustain the composting process.

Further guidance
L24. Workplace, health, safety and welfare. Workplace (Health, Safety and Welfare) Regulations 1992 Approved code of practice. HSE. 2004.

Food hygiene – a guide for businesses. Food Standards Agency. 2006. [Guidance on washbasins associated with sanitary conveniences. Available via www.food.gov.uk]

Further guidance
ANSI/NSF 41:2005. Amended by Addendum 1:2007. Non-liquid saturated treatment systems. American National Standards Institute (ANSI). 2007. [Withdrawn, replaced by 2011 edition. Guidance on composting toilets.]

G.6 Bathrooms (Requirement G5)

A dwelling must have at least one bathroom. A building containing at least one room for residential purposes must have at least one bathroom, with the number of fixed baths or showers determined from BS 6465-1:2006.

Every bathroom must contain a fixed bath or shower and a washbasin, and have appropriate provision for:

- backflow protection on taps, mixer fittings and hose connections – Water Supply (Water Fittings) Regulations 1999;
- ventilation – Part F (**F.3**);
- electrical safety – Part P (**P.2**).

Where hot and cold taps are provided, the hot tap should be on the left.

Further guidance
BS 6465-1, -2, -3. [See **G.5**.]

G.7 Food preparation areas (Requirement G6)

Any area where food is prepared, including a kitchen, must have a suitable sink. In dwellings, a room with a dishwasher which is separate from the principal food preparation area does not require an additional sink.

In buildings where the Food Hygiene (England) Regulations 2006 apply, separate handwashing facilities may be required, in addition to any handwashing facilities required by Requirement G4 (see **G.5**).

H. Drainage and waste disposal

H.1 General considerations

H.1.1 Scope

Part H is intended to ensure that buildings have adequate drainage systems for foul water and rainwater, and have provision for the storage of solid waste.

Part H: Drainage and waste disposal	
Requirement	**Limit on application**
Foul water drainage	
H1 (1) An adequate system of drainage shall be provided to carry foul water from appliances within the building to one of the following, listed in order of priority – (a) a public sewer; or, where that is not reasonably practicable; (b) a private sewer communicating with a public sewer; or, where that is not reasonably practicable; (c) either a septic tank which has an appropriate form of secondary treatment or another wastewater treatment system; or, where that is not reasonably practicable; (d) a cesspool. (2) In this Part 'foul water' means waste water which comprises or includes – (a) waste from a sanitary convenience, bidet or appliance used for washing receptacles for foul waste; or (b) water which has been used for food preparation, cooking or washing.	Requirement H1 does not apply to the diversion of water which has been used for personal washing or for the washing of clothes, linen or other articles to collection systems for reuse.
Wastewater treatment systems and cesspools	
H2 (1) Any septic tank and its form of secondary treatment, other wastewater treatment system or cesspool, shall be so sited and constructed that – (a) it is not prejudicial to the health of any person; (b) it will not contaminate any watercourse, underground water or water supply; (c) there are adequate means of access for emptying and maintenance; and (d) where relevant, it will function to a sufficient standard for the protection of health in the event of a power failure. (2) Any septic tank, holding tank which is part of a wastewater treatment system or cesspool shall be – (a) of adequate capacity; (b) so constructed that it is impermeable to liquids; and (c) adequately ventilated. (3) Where a foul water drainage system from a building discharges to a septic tank, wastewater treatment system or cesspool, a durable notice shall be affixed in a suitable place in the building containing information on any continuing maintenance required to avoid risks to health.	

H. Drainage and waste disposal

Rainwater drainage

H3 (1) Adequate provision shall be made for rainwater to be carried from the roof of the building.

(2) Paved areas around the building shall be so constructed as to be adequately drained.

(3) Rainwater from a system provided pursuant to sub-paragraphs (1) or (2) shall discharge to one of the following, listed in order of priority –

    (a) an adequate soakaway or some other adequate infiltration system; or; where that is not reasonably practicable;

    (b) a watercourse; or, where that is not reasonably practicable;

    (c) a sewer.

Requirement H3(2) applies only to paved areas –

(a) which provide access to the building pursuant to Requirement M1 (access and use), or Requirement M2 (access to extensions to buildings other than dwellings);

(b) which provide access to or from a place of storage pursuant to Requirement H6(2) (solid waste storage); or

(c) in any passage giving access to the building, where this is intended to be used in common by the occupiers of one or more other buildings.

Requirement H3(3) does not apply to the gathering of rainwater for reuse.

Building over sewers

H4 (1) The erection or extension of a building or work involving the underpinning of a building shall be carried out in a way that is not detrimental to the building or building extension or to the continued maintenance of the drain, sewer or disposal main.

(2) In this paragraph 'disposal main' means any pipe, tunnel or conduit used for the conveyance of effluent to or from a sewage disposal works, which is not a public sewer.

(3) In this paragraph and paragraph H5 'map of sewers' means any records kept by a sewerage undertaker under section 199 of the Water Industry Act 1991.

Requirement H4 applies only to work carried out –
(a) over a drain, sewer or disposal main which is shown on any map of sewers; or
(b) on any site or in such a manner as may result in interference with the use of, or obstruction of the access of any person to, any drain, sewer or disposal main which is shown on any map of sewers.

Separate systems of drainage

H5 Any system for discharging water to a sewer which is provided pursuant to paragraph H3 shall be separate from that provided for the conveyance of foul water from the building.

Requirement H5 applies only to a system provided in connection with the erection or extension of a building where it is reasonably practicable for the system to discharge directly or indirectly to a sewer for the separate conveyance of surface water which is –
(a) shown on a map of sewers; or
(b) under construction either by the sewerage undertaker or by some other person (where the sewer is the subject of an agreement to make a declaration of vesting pursuant to section 104 of the Water Industry Act 1991).

Solid waste storage

H6 (1) Adequate provision shall be made for storage of solid waste.

(2) Adequate means of access shall be provided –

    (a) for people in the building to the place of storage; and

    (b) from the place of storage to a collection point (where one has been specified by the waste collection authority under section 46 (household waste) or section 47 (commercial waste) of the Environmental Protection Act 1990) or to a street (where no collection point has been specified).

H.1.2 Definitions

Disposal mains Pipes, conduits or tunnels which convey effluent to or from sewage disposal works, but are not public sewers.

Drains Carry surface water or foul water from a single property or premises to a sewer or to an outfall such as a septic tank.

Sewers Carry surface water or foul water from more than one property or premises; they may be private or public.

H.1.3 Sewerage undertakers

Under the Water Industry Act 1991 the sewerage undertaker has general duties to:

- provide and maintain a system of public sewers, and deal with the connection and adoption of drains and sewers;
- maintain records of drains, public sewers and disposal mains, including the location and functions of sewers.

In much of England and Wales the companies which act as water undertakers also act as sewerage undertakers.

H.1.4 Safe working

Laying and maintaining drains is hazardous. Any work should comply with:

- the Construction (Design and Management) Regulations 2007;
- the Confined Spaces Regulations 1997.

Further guidance
HSG 185. *Health and safety in excavation – be safe and shore.* Health and Safety Executive. 1999.

L101. *Safe work in confined spaces. Confined Spaces Regulations 1997 – Approved code of practice, regulations and guidance.* HSE Books. 1997. [Second edition, 2009.]

H.2 Foul water drainage (Requirement H1)

There should be an adequate system for carrying foul water from appliances within the building to (in order of preference):

- a public sewer;
- a private sewer;
- a septic tank with secondary treatment, or another wastewater treatment system;
- a cesspool.

The system should take waste from sanitary conveniences, bidets and appliances for washing receptacles for foul waste, and water used in food preparation or washing. It should have sufficient capacity for the expected flow and should be designed:

- to minimise the risk of blockage/leakage;
- to prevent foul air from the drainage system entering buildings;
- to be ventilated;
- to be accessible for clearing blockages;
- so as not to increase vulnerability of a building to flooding.

H. Drainage and waste disposal

The requirement does not apply to the recycling of greywater from personal washing or the washing of clothes.

The following guidance is applicable for domestic and small non-domestic systems with WCs with a major flush volume of five litres or more. Larger or more complex systems, and those WCs with major flush volume down to four litres should comply with the recommendations of BS EN 12056.

Further guidance
BS EN 12056 Gravity drainage systems inside buildings.
-1:2000. General and performance requirements.
-2:2000. Sanitary pipework. Layout and calculation.
-4:2000. Wastewater lifting plants. Layout and calculation.
-5:2000. Installation and testing, instructions for operation, maintenance and use.

H.2.1 Sanitary pipework

H.2.1.1 Traps

Traps, such as water seal traps, prevent foul air from drainage systems reaching the inside of a building. All points of discharge into the system should have a trap with a minimum seal of 25mm of water, or equivalent. Traps should comply with the minimum sizes and depths shown in Table H.1.

To enable the clearing of blockages, an appliance with an integral trap should be removable; otherwise, traps should be fitted directly after the appliance, and be removable or have a cleaning eye.

Table H.1 Minimum trap sizes and seal depths		
Appliance	**Diameter of trap (mm)**	**Depth of seal (mm of water or equivalent)**
Washbasin[1] Bidet	32	75
Bath[2] Shower[2]	40	50
Food waste disposal unit Urinal bowl Sink Washing machine[2] Dishwashing machine[2]	40	75
WC pan – outlet <80mm – outlet >80mm	75 100	50 50
Sanitary towel macerator	40	75
Food waste disposal unit (industrial type)	50	75
Urinal stall (1–6 person position)	65	50

[1] Depth of seal may be reduced to 50mm for flush grated wastes without plugs on spray tap basins.

[2] Where these appliances discharge directly into a gully the depth of seal may be reduced to not less than 38mm.

[3] Traps used on appliances with flat bottom (trailing waste discharge) and discharging to a gully with a grating may have a reduced water seal of not less than 38mm.

H.2.1.2 Branch discharge pipes

Appliances should discharge into branch pipes or discharge stacks. On the ground floor they may also discharge:

- to a stub stack – subject to **H.2.1.3**;
- directly to a drain – for a ground floor closet the depth from floor level to drain invert should not exceed 1.3m (Figure H.1);
- into a gully, provided the pipe carries only wastewater and terminates between the grating or sealing plate and the top of the water seal.

Figure H.1 Direct connection of ground floor WC to a drain

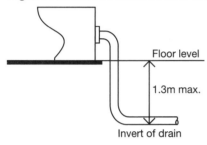

Floor level

1.3m max.

Invert of drain

Branch pipes should discharge into another branch pipe or into a discharge stack, but should not discharge:

- into a stack in a way which could cause cross-flow into another branch pipe (Figure H.2);
- into open hoppers;
- too close to the base of the stack (Table H.2).

A branch pipe to a single appliance should have the same diameter as the appliance trap. Unventilated pipes to more than one appliance should be sized to Table H.3.

Table H.2 Branch connections to stacks – limiting conditions	
Building	**Connection limits**
Dwellings of up to three storeys	450mm minimum between the stack invert and any branch pipe.
Buildings up to five storeys	<ul><li>750mm minimum between the stack invert and any branch pipe; and</li><li>a branch pipe serving any ground floor appliance can discharge directly to a drain or into its own stack.</li></ul>
Buildings of more than five storeys	Ground floor appliances not discharging to a gully or drain should discharge into their own stacks.
Buildings of more than 20 storeys	Ground floor appliances not discharging to a gully or drain and all first floor appliances should discharge to their own stacks.

Figure H.2 Branch connection to stacks – cross-flow prevention

A branch creates a no connection zone on a stack
No other branch may be fitted such that its centre
line falls inside a zone but its centre line may be
on the boundary of the zone

Opposed branch connection in the
horizontal plane should be avoided

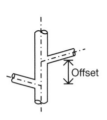

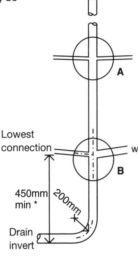

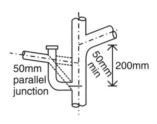

50mm parallel junction

50mm min   200mm

Lowest connection — WC

450mm min *   200mm

Drain invert

Key

A opposed connections without
swept entries not exceeding 65mm
should be offset
110mm on a 100mm diameter stack
250mm on a 150mm diameter stack

Opposed connections larger than 65mm
(without swept entries) should be offset at
least 200mm irrespective of stack diameter
Unopposed connections may be at any position

B Angled connection or 50mm diameter
parallel junction where a branch discharge
pipe would enter the WC no connection
zone

NB A waste (branch discharge pipe)
manifold may be a suitable alternative

* This should be increased in buildings
over 3 storeys

Table H.3 Common branch discharge pipes (unventilated)

Appliance	Max. no. to be connected	Max. length of branch pipe (m)	Min. size of pipe (mm)	Gradient limits (mm fall per metre)
WC outlet >80mm	8	15	100	18[2] to 90
WC outlet <80mm	1	15	75[3]	18 to 90
Urinal – bowl – trough – slab[4]		3[1] 3[1] 3[1]	50 65	18 to 90
Washbasin or bidet	3 4	1.7 1.1 0.7 3.0 4.0	30 30 30 40 50	18–22 18–44 18–87 18–44 18–44

[1] Should be as short as possible to prevent deposition.

[2] May be reduced to 9mm on long runs where space is restricted, but only if more than 1 WC is connected.

[3] Not recommended where disposal of sanitary towels may take place via the WC, as there is an increased risk of blockage.

[4] Slab urinals longer than seven persons should have more than one outlet.

Configuration

- Bends should be avoided wherever possible and, where unavoidable, should be as large as possible.

- Junctions between branch pipes of similar diameter should have a sweep of 25mm radius, or be at 45°.

- The junction of a branch pipe of a diameter of 75mm or more to a stack of equal diameter should have a sweep of 50mm radius, or be at 45°.

- Branch pipes up to 40mm diameter joining branch pipes of 100mm diameter or greater should, if practicable, join to the upper part of the wall of the larger branch.

- Rodding points are required for any length of discharge pipe which cannot be reached by removing traps or appliances with integral traps.

Ventilation

Branch discharge pipes should be designed to prevent the water seal in any trap being broken by pressure in the system. A branch pipe which exceeds the length and slope limits of Table H.3 and Figure H.3 should be ventilated to prevent pressures breaking the water seal. It may be ventilated by means of a branch ventilating pipe which runs to:

- external air – terminating at least 900mm above any opening in the building nearer than 3m (see Figure H.5, at **H.2.1.3** Discharge stacks);

- a ventilated discharge stack;

- a separate ventilating stack (if a large number of sanitary appliances are sited a long distance from the discharge stack); or

- be ventilated from the building interior by an air admittance valve.

Branch ventilating pipes should be connected to the discharge pipe within 750mm of the trap and should connect with the ventilating stack or stack vent above the highest spillover level of the appliances served. There should be a continuous incline from the discharge pipe to the ventilating stack (Figure H.4).

Figure H.3 Branch connections

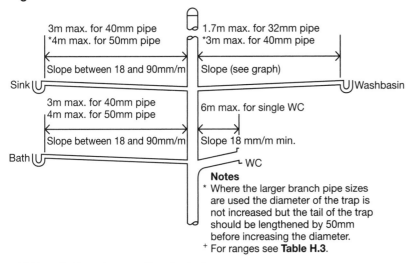

3m max. for 40mm pipe
*4m max. for 50mm pipe

1.7m max. for 32mm pipe
*3m max. for 40mm pipe

Slope between 18 and 90mm/m

Slope (see graph)

Sink

Washbasin

3m max. for 40mm pipe
4m max. for 50mm pipe

6m max. for single WC

Slope between 18 and 90mm/m

Slope 18 mm/m min.

Bath

WC

Notes
* Where the larger branch pipe sizes are used the diameter of the trap is not increased but the tail of the trap should be lengthened by 50mm before increasing the diameter.
+ For ranges see **Table H.3**.

(a) Unvented branch connections to stacks

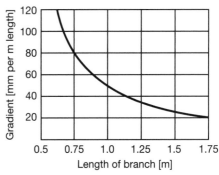

(b) Design curve for 32mm washbasin waste pipes

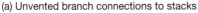

Figure H.4 Branch ventilation pipes

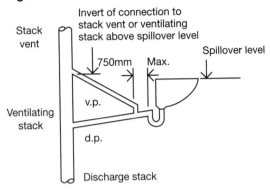

A branch ventilating pipe serving one appliance should have a minimum diameter of 25mm, or 32mm where the branch is 15m or has more than five bends.

In larger buildings, branch ventilation pipes may be connected to dry ventilation stacks. The lower end of a ventilating stack may be connected directly to a ventilated discharge stack – between the lowest branch discharge pipe and the bend at the foot of the pipe – or to the crown of the lowest branch discharge pipe (provided its diameter is at least 75mm). Ventilating stacks serving buildings with not more than 10 storeys and containing only dwellings should be at least 32mm diameter.

Condensate

Condensate from boilers may be discharged to sanitary pipework through a 75mm trap, which should be separated from a boiler by an air gap. Although the connection should preferably be to an internal stack, any connection to a branch pipe should be downstream of any sink waste connection. Pipework should:

- have 22mm minimum diameter; and
- resist pH values of 6.5 and lower; and
- be installed to BS 6798.

Further guidance
BS 6798:2000 (2005). Specification for installation of gas-fired hot water boilers of rated input not exceeding 70kW. [Withdrawn, replaced by BS 6798:2009 Specification for installation and maintenance of gas-fired boilers of rated input not exceeding 70kW net.]

H.2.1.3 Discharge stacks

Stacks discharging to drains should comply either with the following guidance, or with the relevant requirements of BS EN 12056-1, -2 and 5, and BS EN 12109. In buildings over three storeys the discharge stack should be within the building.

Size

Stacks should be sized as given in Table H.4 and should be no smaller than the largest branch or discharge pipe. For larger buildings, stacks should be sized for the maximum flow (see AD H Annex H1A, Table A2). The size should not be reduced in the direction of flow, although in one- and two-storey houses a stack ventilation pipe may be reduced to 75mm above the highest branch pipe.

Table H.4 Minimum diameters for discharge stacks		
Stack size (mm)	Maximum capacity (l/s)	Notes
50	1.2	Minimum diameter for stack serving urinals: no WCs
65	2.1	No WCs
75	3.4	Not more than one WC with outlet size less than 80mm WCs with outlets greater than 80mm require outlets of min. 80mm
90	5.3	–
100	7.2	–

Layout

The bend at the foot of the stack should have as large a radius as possible, at least 200mm at the centre line. Offsets in the 'wet' portion of the stack should be avoided wherever possible, otherwise:

- in buildings of no more than three storeys there should be no branch connection within 750mm of the offset;
- in buildings over three storeys a ventilation stack may be needed with connections above and below the offset.

Ventilation

Stacks should be ventilated to prevent pressures in the system breaking water seals in traps. Ventilating pipes opening to outside air should:

- terminate at least 900mm above any opening within 3m (Figure H.5); and
- have a cage or cover which does not restrict the flow of air; and
- in areas where rodent control is an issue, be metallic.

Figure H.5 Termination of ventilation stacks or ventilation part of discharge

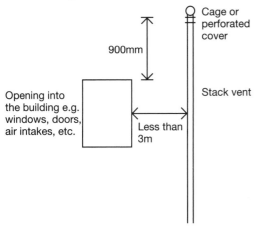

Alternatively, ventilating discharge stacks may terminate inside the building. They should be fitted with air admittance valves to BS EN 12380:2002, and should be:

- in areas with adequate ventilation; and
- accessible for maintenance; and
- removable to give access to blockages.

Air admittance valves should not be used:

- where ventilation of the below ground system would be impaired;
- in dust-laden atmospheres;
- outside buildings.

Discharge stacks connected to drains liable to surcharging, or near an intercepting trap, require a ventilating pipe of not less than 50mm diameter connected to the base of the stack above the likely flood level.

Stub stacks

A stub stack may be used if:

- it connects to a ventilated discharge stack or ventilated drain not subject to surcharging; and
- no connected WC has a floor level more than 1.3m above the invert of the drain connection; and
- no branch has a centre line more than 2m above the invert (Figure H.6).

Figure H.6 Stub stack

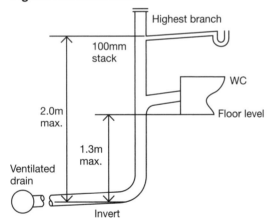

Access for blockages

Discharge stacks should have rodding points above the spillover level of appliances to give access to otherwise inaccessible lengths of pipe. Pipes should be reasonably accessible for repair.

Materials and installation

Materials should comply with the standards in Table H.5. To discourage rodent damage, pipework connected to WCs should be opaque. Connections between two metals should be isolated to avoid electrolytic corrosion, but any electrical earth bonding should be maintained.

Table H.5 Materials for sanitary pipework

Category	Material	Sanitary pipework	Below ground drainage[1]
Rigid pipes	Cast iron	BS 416[2], BS EN 877	–
	Grey iron	–	BS 437
	Ductile iron	–	BS EN 598
	Galvanised steel	BS 3868	–
	Copper	BS EN 1254, BS EN 1057	–
	Vitrified clay	–	BS 65, BS EN 295
	Concrete	–	BS 5911
Flexible pipes	uPVC	BS EN 1329	BS EN 1401[3]
	PVC-C	BS EN 1566	–
	Polypropylene (PP)	BS EN 1451	BS EN 1852[3]
	Polyethylene (PE)	BS EN 1519	–
	ABS	BS EN 1455	–
	Styrene copolymer blends (PVC + SAN)	BS EN 1565	–
	Structure walled plastic pipes	–	BS EN 13476
Traps		BS EN 274 BS 3943[4]	–

[1] Some materials may not be suitable for conveying trade effluent.

[2] Part 2:1990 withdrawn, replaced by BS EN 877:1999+A1:2006.

[3] Application code UD should normally be specified.

[4] Withdrawn, replaced by BS EN 274.

Pipes should be firmly supported without restricting thermal movement, and should comply with requirements for compartmentation and fire stopping (**B.5.2.2** and **B.5.4.1**). Workmanship should comply with BS 8000-13.

Airtightness

Pipes, fittings and joints should be air tested:

- a positive pressure of at least 38mm water gauge should be maintained for at least 3 minutes; and
- every trap should maintain a water seal of at least 25mm.

H.2.1.4 Greywater recovery

Sanitary pipework and underground drainage used for greywater collection for recovery and reuse should be designed in accordance with the preceding guidance, and should be clearly marked 'GREYWATER'.

Further guidance
BS EN 12109:1999. Vacuum drainage systems inside buildings.

BS EN 12380:2002. Air admittance valves for drainage systems. Requirements, test methods and evaluation of conformity.

BS 8000-13:1989. Workmanship on building sites. Code of practice for above ground drainage and sanitary appliances.

Further guidance
WRAS Information Guidance Note 09-02-05 *Marking and identification of pipework for reclaimed and greywater systems*. Water Regulations Advisory Scheme (WRAS). 2005.

H.2.2 Foul drainage

The requirements for foul drainage address the construction of underground drains and sewers from buildings to the point of connection with an existing sewer or cesspool or wastewater treatment system, even beyond the curtilage of the building. Drainage systems should follow either the guidance below or the recommendations in BS EN 752-3, -4, -6, BS EN 1091 or BS EN 1671.

H.2.2.1 Outlets

Foul drainage should connect to a public foul or combined sewer wherever reasonably practicable. Small developments within 30m of a public sewer should be connected to it, provided the developer has the right to construct drainage over intervening private land. A pumping installation should be provided where levels do not allow gravity drainage.

For developments with more than one curtilage, the developer may requisition a sewer from the sewerage undertaker, who has powers to construct sewers over private land. Otherwise, connection may be made to a private sewer which in turn connects to a public sewer, subject to the consent of the sewer owner. The sewer should be in satisfactory condition and large enough for the additional flows.

If a sewer connection is not practicable then a wastewater treatment system or cesspool should be provided (**H.3**).

H.2.2.2 Surcharging

Combined and rainwater sewers which surcharge during heavy rainfall (the water level in a manhole rising above the top of the pipe), bring a risk of flooding to low-lying sites, where the ground or basement level is below that of the connection to the public sewer. The sewerage undertaker should be consulted regarding the extent and frequency of surcharging.

Where the risk of flooding is low:

- basement drainage should have an anti-flooding valve; and
- buildings without basements should have an external gully at least 75mm below floor level, positioned so any flooding from the gully will not damage any buildings.

Where the risk of flooding is high:

- basements should have pumped drainage; and
- buildings without basements should have pumped drainage or an anti-flooding valve.

Anti-flooding values should comply with EN 13564, be suitable for foul water and have a manual closure device. There should be a notice which indicates the system is drained through a valve, and should give the location of any manual override together with advice on maintenance.

Drainage unaffected by surcharge should by-pass protective measures and discharge by gravity.

Further guidance
BS EN 752. Drain and sewer systems outside buildings.
-3:1997 (2001). Planning.
-4:1998 (2005). Hydraulic design and environmental considerations.
-6:1998. Pumped installations. [Individual parts have been withdrawn and replaced by BS EN 752:2008. Drain and sewer systems outside buildings.]

BS EN 1091:1997. Vacuum sewerage systems outside buildings.

BS EN 1671:1997. Pressure sewerage systems outside buildings.

Further guidance
BS EN 13564. Anti-flooding devices for buildings.
-1. 2002. Requirements.
-2. 2002. Test methods.
-3. 2003. Quality assurance.

H.2.2.3 Pumped installations

Packaged pumping installations for internal use should comply with BS EN 12050 and BS EN 12056-4; and those for external use should comply with BS EN 752-6. The effluent receiving chamber should be sized to accept 24-hour inflow to allow for disruption in service. For domestic use, the inflow should be taken as 150 litres/head/day; for other buildings the flow rate should be based on water intake. The capacity can be reduced pro rata if only a proportion is to be pumped.

H.2.2.4 Rodent control

On previously developed sites the local authority should be consulted regarding any special requirements for rodent control, such as sealed drainage, intercepting traps or rodent barriers.

H.2.2.5 Layout

The layout of the system should be simple, with pipes laid to even gradients and in straight lines (slight curves are permissible so long as they can still be cleared). Sewers should avoid locations where an extension might be sited, such as the rear or side of the building. Bends should only occur near inspection chambers and manholes and at the foot of discharge and ventilating stacks. Access points should be provided only at changes in gradient and where blockages could not otherwise be cleared.

The system should be ventilated, with a ventilating pipe to the head of each main drain and to any drain fitted with an intercepting trap or subject to surcharge. Ventilated discharge stacks may be used (**H.2.1.3**). Drainage to kitchens in commercial hot food premises require a means of grease removal, such as grease separators to BS EN 1825-1:2004 and -2:2002.

Connections to other drains and sewers should be made with pre-fabricated components, and be oblique and in the direction of flow. Where connections to existing drains/sewers require the replacement of pipes, repair couplings should be used and care taken to avoid differential settlement.

H.2.2.6 Protection from settlement

A pipe running under a building should be protected with at least 100mm of granular or flexible fill. Further measures, such as flexible joints, may be desirable where excessive settlement is expected. A pipe with its crown within 300mm of the underside of a concrete slab should be protected as described at **H.2.2.10**.

Pipes built into the structure – at inspection chambers, manholes, footings, groundbeams or walls – should be protected against misalignment or damage as shown in Figure H.7. To protect foundations, drain trenches excavated close to buildings should be treated as shown in Figure H.8. For other conditions, including pipes laid on piles or beams, consult *A guide to the design loadings for buried rigid pipes*.

Further guidance

BS EN 12050. Wastewater lifting plants for buildings and sites. Principles of construction and testing.

BS EN 12056-4:2000. Gravity drainage systems inside buildings. Wastewater lifting plants. Layout and calculation.

BS EN 752-6:1998. Drain and sewer systems outside buildings. Pumping installations. [Withdrawn, replaced by BS EN 752:2008. Drain and sewer systems outside buildings.]

Further guidance

BS EN 1825. Grease separators.
-1:2004. Principles of design, performance and testing, marking and quality control.
-2:2002. Selection of nominal size, installation and maintenance.

Further guidance

O C Young and M P O'Reilly. *A guide to the design loadings for buried rigid pipes*. Transport and Road Research Laboratory (TRL). HMSO, 1983.

Figure H.7 Pipes penetrating walls

(a) Short length of pipe bedded in wall, joints formed within 150mm of either wall face. Adjacent rocker pipes of max. length 600mm with flexible joints

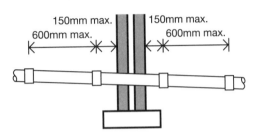

(b) Arch or lintelled opening to give 50mm space all round the pipe

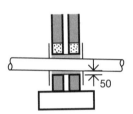

Mask opening both sides with rigid sheet material to prevent entry of fill or vermin

Important Fill void with compressible sealant to prevent entry of gas

Figure H.8 Pipe runs near buildings

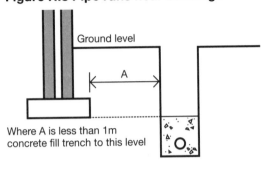

Ground level

Where A is less than 1m concrete fill trench to this level

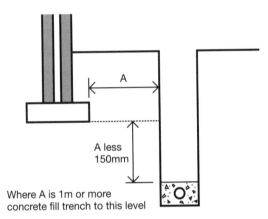

A less 150mm

Where A is 1m or more concrete fill trench to this level

H.2.2.7 Depth of cover

The depth of cover is determined by the levels of connections to the system, the required pipe gradients and the ground levels. Where the available cover is insufficient to protect a pipe from damage another pipe strength and bedding should be specified or special protection provided (**H.2.2.10**).

Further guidance
BS EN 1295. Structural design of buried pipelines under various conditions of loading.
-1:General requirements. [Guidance on choice of pipe strength and bedding. See in particular the national annex NA.]

H.2.2.8 Pipe gradients and sizes

Pipes should have sufficient capacity to carry the flow, which depends on the number, type and grouping of appliances; although, appliances are seldom in use simultaneously and minimum pipe sizes can carry the flow from large numbers of appliances. Table H.6 gives approximate flow rates for dwellings.

Table H.6 Flow rates from dwellings	
Number of dwellings	Flow rate (l/s)
1	2.5
5	3.5
10	4.1
15	4.6
20	5.1
25	5.4
30	5.8

Note: Based on 1 WC, 1 bath, 1–2 washbasins, 1 sink and 1 washing machine, to BS EN 12056.

Table H.7 Recommended minimum gradients for foul drains

Peak flow (litres/second)	Pipe size (mm)	Minimum gradient (1 in ...)	Maximum capacity (litres/second)
<1	75	1:40	4.1
	100	1:40	9.2
>1	75	1:80	2.8
	100	1:80[1]	6.3
	150	1:150[2]	15.0

[1] Minimum of 1 WC.

[2] Minimum of 5 WCs.

Pipe capacity depends on size and gradient (Figure H.9). Table H.7 shows the flattest gradient to which pipes should be laid and the resultant capacity. The minimum internal diameter of a drain is 75mm for one carrying foul water, and 100mm for one carrying effluent from WCs or trade effluent. The minimum diameter for a sewer is 100mm for one serving no more than 10 dwellings and 150mm for one serving more than 10 dwellings.

Combined systems should be sized to accept the peak flow of rainwater (**H.4.3**).

Figure H.9 Discharge capacities of foul drains running 0.75 proportional depth

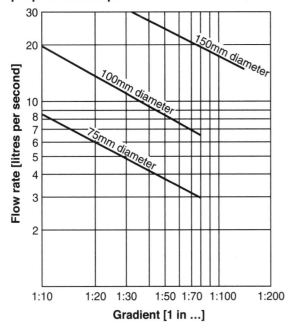

H.2.2.9 Materials

Materials should comply with standards in Table H.5. Joints should be flexible to minimise the effects of differential settlement and should be watertight under working and test conditions. There should be nothing in the pipe to project into the pipeline or cause an obstruction.

Figure H.10 Bedding for pipes

a) Rigid pipes

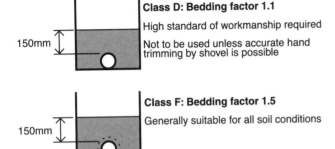

Class D: Bedding factor 1.1

High standard of workmanship required

Not to be used unless accurate hand trimming by shovel is possible

150mm

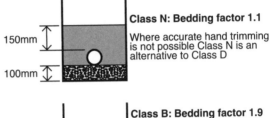

Class N: Bedding factor 1.1

Where accurate hand trimming is not possible Class N is an alternative to Class D

150mm
100mm

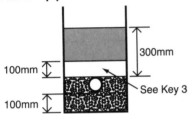

150mm
100mm

Class F: Bedding factor 1.5

Generally suitable for all soil conditions

See Note 2

45° min.

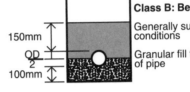

Class B: Bedding factor 1.9

Generally suitable in all soil conditions

Granular fill to half depth of pipe

150mm
$\frac{OD}{2}$
100mm

b) Flexible pipes

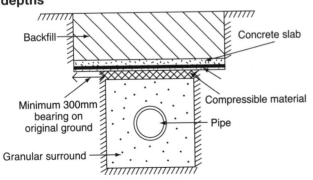

300mm
100mm
100mm
See Key 3

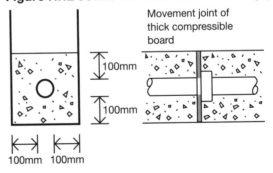

300mm
100mm
100mm
See Key 3

Detail for vee trench

Key

1   Selected fill: free from stones larger than 40mm, lumps of clay over 100mm, timber, frozen material, vegetable matter.

2   Granular material – For rigid pipes the granular material should conform to BS EN 1610 Annex B Table B.15 and should be single size material or graded material from 5mm up to a maximum size of 10mm for 100mm pipes, 14mm for 150mm pipes, 20mm for pipes from 150mm up to 600mm diameter and 40mm for pipes more than 600mm diameter. Compaction fraction maximum 0.3 for Class N or B and 0.15 for Class F.

3   Selected fill or granular fill free from stones larger than 40mm.

Notes:
1. Provision may be required to prevent groundwater flow in trenches with Class N, F or B type bedding.
2. Where the pipe has sockets and Class D bedding is used, holes which should be as short as is practicable should be prepared in the trench bottom to give a clearance of 50mm beneath the socket.
3. Where the pipe has sockets and Class F or N bedding is used, the sockets should be not less than 50mm above the floor of the trench.
4. All dimensions are in mm.

Figure H.11 Protection for pipes laid at shallow depths

Backfill

Concrete slab

Minimum 300mm bearing on original ground

Compressible material

Pipe

Granular surround

Figure H.12 Joints for concrete encased pipes

Movement joint of thick compressible board

100mm
100mm

100mm   100mm

H.2.2.10 Bedding and backfilling

Suitable types of bedding for rigid and flexible pipes are shown in Figure H.10, while Table H.8 gives limits of cover for standard pipe specifications. Where the minimum depth of cover is not available pipes can be protected with a reinforced concrete slab with flexible filler and 75mm (minimum) granular material between the top of the pipe and the filler (Figure H.11).

Where a trench is backfilled with concrete to protect foundations (**H.2.2.6**), movement joints should be formed in the concrete by compressible board at each socket or sleeve joint face (Figure H.12).

Table H.8 Limits of cover for pipes in any width of trench				
Pipe specification	Nominal size (mm)	Laid in fields (m)	Laid in light roads (m)	Laid in main roads (m)
Class 120 clayware[1] to BS EN 295	100	0.6–8+	1.2–8+	1.2–8
	225	0.6–5	1.2–5	1.2–4.5
	400	0.6–4.5	1.2–4.5	1.2–4
	600	0.6–4.5	1.2–4.5	1.2–4
Class M concrete pipes[1] to BS 5991	300	0.6–3	1.2–3	1.2–2.5
	450	0.6–3.5	1.2–3.5	1.2–2.5
	600	0.6–3.5	1.2–3.5	1.2–3
Thermoplastics pipes[2][3] (nominal ring stiffness SN4)	100–300	0.6–7	0.9–7	0.9–7

[1] Bedding assumed to be Class B with bedding factor of 1.9. Minimum depth in roads is 1.2m, irrespective of pipe strength.

[2] Bedding assumed to be Class S2 with 80% compaction and average soil conditions. Calculation to BS EN 1295 required where drains and sewers are less than 1.5 m deep and there is a risk of excavation close to the drain.

[3] Minimum depth set to 1.5 m, irrespective of pipe strength to cover loss of strength from parallel excavations.

H.2.2.11 Clearance of blockages

Drains and sewers should have access points for clearing blockages by rodding:

- on or near the head of a drain run;
- at a bend or change in gradient;
- at a change of pipe size (but see below);
- at a junction, unless each run can be cleared from an access point;
- on long runs as Table H.9.

The access points should be accessible and apparent for use in emergency, and may be:

- rodding eyes – capped extensions of pipes;
- access fittings – small chambers on (or an extension of) a pipe, but without an open channel;
- inspection chambers – chambers with working space at ground level;
- manholes – deep chambers with working space at drain level.

Access points should be sized to Tables H.10 and H.11, and be constructed of materials to Table H.12. They should be able to contain foul water under working and test conditions, and to resist the entry of groundwater and rainwater.

Table H.9 Maximum spacing of access points (metres)

From	Maximum spacing of access points (m)				
	To access fitting		To junction	To inspection chamber	To manhole
	Small	Large			
Start of external drain[1]	12	12	–	22	45
Rodding eye	22	22	22	45	45
Access fitting: Small (150mm diameter or 150mm × 100mm) Large (225mm × 100mm)	– –	– –	12 22	22 45	22 45
Shallow inspection chamber	22	45	22	45	45
Deep inspection chamber Manhole	–	–	–	45	90[2]

[1] Stack or ground floor appliances.

[2] Up to 200m for man-entry size drains and sewers.

Table H.10 Minimum dimensions for access fittings and inspection chambers

	Type	Depth to invert from cover level (m)	Internal sizes		Cover sizes	
			Length × width (mm × mm)	Circular (mm)	Length × width (mm × mm)	Circular (mm)
Rodding eye		–	As drain but min. 100			Same size as pipework[1]
Access fitting (mm)	Small – 150 diameter – 150 × 100	0.6 or less, except where situated in a chamber	150 × 100	150	150 × 100[1]	Same size as access fitting
	Large – 225 × 100		225 × 100	225	225 × 100[1]	
Inspection chamber	Shallow	0.6 or less	225 × 100	190[2]	–	190[1]
		1.2 or less	450 × 450	450	Min. 430 × 430	430
	Deep	>1.2	450 × 450	450	Max. 300 × 300[3]	Access restricted to max. 350[3]

[1] Clear opening may be reduced by 20mm in order to provide proper support for the cover and frame.

[2] Drains up to 150mm.

[3] A larger clear opening may be used in conjunction with restricted access. Size is restricted for health and safety reasons to deter entry.

In inspection chambers and manholes with half-round channels:

- branches up to and including 150mm diameter should discharge in the channel in the direction of flow at or above the widest part of the main drain;
- a branch of more than 150mm diameter should have its soffit at the same level as the main drain;
- a three-quarter section branch pipe should be used where the angle to the drain exceeds 45°;
- channels and branches should be benched up at least to the top of the outgoing pipe and at a slope of 1:12; and at the channel the benching should be rounded with radius of at least 25mm.

Table H.11 Minimum dimensions for manholes

Type	Size of largest pipe (DN)	Minimum internal dimensions (mm)[1]		Minimum clear opening size(mm)[1]	
		Rectangular length and width	Circular diameter	Rectangular length and width	Circular diameter
Manhole					
<1.5m deep to soffit	≤150	750 × 675[7]	1000[7]	750 × 675[2]	n/a[3]
	225	1200 × 675	1200	1200 × 675[2]	
	300	1200 × 750	1200		
	>300	1800 × (DN+450)	Largest of 1800 or (DN+450)		
>1.5m deep to soffit	≤225	1200 × 1000	1200	600 × 600	600
	300	1200 × 1075	1200		
	375–450	1350 × 1225	1200		
	>450	1800 × (DN+775)	Largest of 1800 or (DN+775)		
Manhole shaft[4]					
>3.0m deep to soffit of pipe	Steps[5]	1050 × 800	1050	600 × 600	600
	Ladder[5]	1200 × 800	1200	–	–
	Winch[6]	900 × 800	900	600 × 600	600

[1] Larger sizes may be required for manholes on bends or where there are junctions.

[2] May be reduced to 600 × 600 where required by highway loading considerations, subject to a safe system of work being specified.

[3] Not applicable due to working space needed.

[4] Minimum height of chamber in shafted manhole 2m from benching to underside of reducing slab.

[5] Min. clear space between ladder or steps and the opposite face of the shaft should be approximately 900mm.

[6] Winch only – no steps or ladders, permanent or removable.

[7] The minimum size of any manhole serving a sewer (i.e. any drain serving more than one property) should be 200mm × 675mm rectangular or 200mm diameter.

Table H.12 Materials for access points

Item	Material	British Standard
Inspection chambers and manholes	Clay, bricks and blocks Vitrified clay Concrete – pre-cast Concrete – in situ Plastics	BS 3921 [Withdrawn, replaced by BS EN 771-1.] BS EN 295, BS 65 BS 5911 BS 8110 [Withdrawn, replaced by BS EN 1992-1-1.] BS 7158 [Withdrawn, replaced by BS EN 13598.]
Rodding eyes and access fittings (excluding covers and frames)	As pipes	See **Table H.5** European Technical Approval (ETA) Certificates

Inspection chambers should have durable, removable non-ventilating covers of suitable strength. Small lightweight covers should be secured to deter unauthorised access. In buildings, covers should be airtight and mechanically fixed (unless the drain itself has watertight access covers). Manholes deeper than 1m require metal step irons or fixed ladders.

H.2.2.12 Workmanship

Workmanship should comply with BS 8000-14. During construction, drains and sewers should be protected against entry by rats, and the precautions in **H.5.3** should be observed.

Further guidance

BS 8000-14:1989. Workmanship on building sites. Code of practice for below ground drainage.

H.2.2.13 Testing

After laying, pipes should be tested for watertightness, either by air or water testing. Pipes greater than 300mm diameter should be tested by methods in BS 8000-14 or BS EN 1610, smaller pipes as described below.

Air test

The system should be pressurised to 110mm water gauge and kept there for approximately 5 minutes before testing. It should then be able to hold 100mm pressure, with maximum loss of head of 25mm over 7 minutes.

Water test

The system should be filled to 5m above the lowest invert, and at least 1m above the highest invert and left for about an hour to condition the pipe. The test pressure should then be maintained for 30 minutes by topping up the water level, so it is within 100mm of the required level throughout the test. The losses per square metre of surface area should not exceed:

- 0.15 litres for lengths of pipeline only;
- 0.20 litres for lengths including pipelines and manholes;
- 0.40 litres for inspection chambers and manholes alone.

Connectivity

Where separate rainwater and foul water drainage are provided, connections should be tested to ensure that they are correct.

Further guidance
BS EN 1610:1998. Construction and testing of drains and sewers.

H.3 Wastewater treatment systems and cesspools (Requirement H2)

Non-mains foul drainage systems – such as septic tanks, packaged treatment works or cesspools – may be used where connection to mains drainage is impractical. Such systems must:

- not present a risk to health, where necessary continuing to function in the event of power failure;
- not contaminate water sources or resources;
- have adequate means of access for emptying and maintenance;
- have a durable notice containing information on maintenance.

Any tanks and cesspools must:

- have adequate capacity;
- be impermeable to liquids;
- be ventilated.

Discharge from a wastewater treatment system is likely to require a consent from the Environment Agency, which should be obtained early in the design process as it may restrict wastewater treatment options.

Designers should observe the guidance below or, alternatively, follow the recommendations of BS 6297:1983.

Further guidance
BS 6297:1983. Code of practice for design and installation of small sewage treatment works and cesspools. [Withdrawn, replaced by BS 6297:2007+A1:2008. Code of practice for the design and installation of drainage fields for use in wastewater treatment.]

H.3.1 Wastewater treatment or storage systems

When any of the wastewater treatment systems described below are installed, a notice setting out the maintenance requirements should be fixed within the building.

H.3.1.1 Septic tanks

Septic tanks provide for the settlement, storage and partial decomposition of solids (which then require removal), and are generally the most economic option for small developments (1–3 dwellings). Septic tanks should comply with Table H.13.

Table H.13 Requirements for septic tanks	
Condition	**Requirement**
Siting	At least 7m from habitable parts of building, preferably down slope.
Vehicle access	Within 30m of vehicle access, provided invert level of tank no more than 3m below level of vehicle access. Deeper invert level may require the tank to be closer. Access should not require the hose to be taken through a dwelling or place of work.
Capacity	At least 2700 litres (2.7m³) capacity below level of inlet for up to four users. Increased by 180 litres for each additional user.
Construction	Factory-made tanks of GRP, polyethylene or steel should meet BS EN 12566-1. Tanks may be constructed on site from min. 220mm thick engineering brick with 1:3 cement-sand mortar, or 150mm thick C/25/P mix concrete, in both cases roofed with heavy concrete slabs.
Performance	Septic tanks should prevent leakage of contents and ingress of sub-soil water.
Ventilation	Ventilation is required, and outlets should be kept away from buildings.
Inlets and outlets	Inlets and outlets should be designed to prevent disturbance of the surface scum or settled sludge, should incorporate at least two chambers/compartments in series. For tanks up to 1200mm wide the inlet should be via a dip pipe. Flow rates of incoming foul water should be limited: velocity in steeply laid drains up to 150mm wide may be limited by laying the last 12m of drain at 1:50 or flatter. Inlet and outlets should have access for sampling and inspection.
Access	There should be access for cleaning and emptying. Access covers should be durable, with regard to contents of tank. Should be lockable, or otherwise engineered to prevent personnel entry.

Discharge from the tank is still harmful and requires further treatment, usually from:

- Drainage fields – sub-surface irrigation pipes which allow effluent to percolate into surrounding soil where it breaks down naturally (Figure H.13 and Table H.14). They require free-draining sub-soil which is not prone to waterlogging or flooding at any time of year.

- Drainage mounds – effectively, drainage fields placed above the natural soil surface to provide an aerated layer of ground to treat the discharge (Figure H.14 and Table H.14). They may be used where sub-soil is occasionally waterlogged, but is otherwise suitable for a drainage field.

- Constructed wetlands – man-made systems which rely on the natural treatment capacity of wetland plants such as the common reed, reed maces and rushes. Wetlands may be:
  - Horizontal flow systems – continuously fed with water from one end.
  - Vertical flow systems – intermittently fed with water which floods the surface. Two or more beds are frequently required for rotation.

Figure H.13 Drainage field

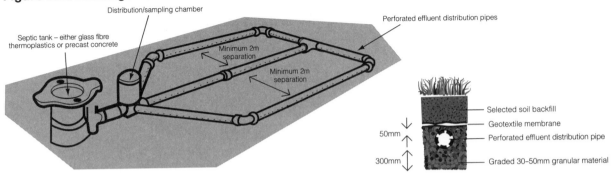

Figure H.14 Drainage mound

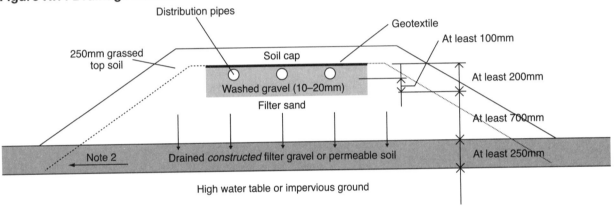

Notes:
1. To provide venting of the filter, the upstream ends of the distribution pipes may be extended vertically above mound level and capped with a cowl or grille.

2. Surface water runoff and uncontaminated seepage from the surrounding soil may be cut off by shallow interceptor drains and diverted away from the mound. There must be no seepage of wastewater to such an interceptor drain.

3. Where the permeable soil is slow draining and overlaid on an impervious layer, the mound filter system should be constructed on a gently sloping site.

H.3.1.2 Packaged treatment works

There are a wide range of systems with pre-fabricated components that can treat effluent to a higher standard than septic tanks, so permitting direct discharge into a watercourse. They are normally more cost-effective for larger developments, and are also suitable where space is limited. They should be designed and type tested to BS 7781. Powered units should be able to operate adequately without power for at least 6 hours. They should be sited at least 10m from watercourses and other buildings.

H.3.1.3 Cesspools

These are watertight underground tanks for storage of sewage which carry out no treatment and must be regularly emptied (Table H.15). They may be acceptable where no other option is feasible and must have sufficient capacity to store foul water until emptied.

Further guidance
BRE Good Building Guide 42. *Reed beds*. -1. Application and specification.
-2. Design, construction. BRE. 2000.

BS 7781:1994. Procedure for type testing of small biological domestic wastewater treatment plants. [Withdrawn, replaced by BS EN 12566-3:2005+A1:2009. Small wastewater treatment systems for up to 50 PT. Packaged and/or site assembled domestic wastewater treatment plants.]

Table H.14 Requirements for drainage fields and mounds

	Requirement
Siting	Not in a Zone 1 groundwater protection zone At least: • 10m from any watercourse or permeable drain; • 50m from point of abstraction of groundwater supply; • 15m from any building. Sufficiently far from other drainage fields/mounds so as not to exceed the soakage capacity of the ground. Downslope of groundwater sources in disposal area.
Disposal area	To contain: • No water supply pipes or underground services; • No access roads, driveways or paved areas.
Ground conditions	Requires a well drained, aerated sub-soil with good percolation in summer and winter. A 1m² by 2m deep trial hole (or min. 1.5m below invert of proposed pipework) to be dug and groundwater table not to be within 1m of invert level of proposed pipework. Percolation test (as AD H: H2 1.34–1.37) should give a value V_p of 12–100.
Capacity	Floor area of drainage field, $A_t = p \times V_p \times 0.25$, where p is number of people and V_p is result of percolation test.
Layout	Set out in continuous loop, with inspection chamber between the septic tank and drainage field. Trenches 300–900mm wide with at least 2m undisturbed ground between parallel pipes.
Construction	Constructed using perforated pipe at uniform gradient, not steeper than 1:200 and min. 500mm below surface. Pipes laid on 300mm layer of clean shingle, or 20–50mm graded broken stone. Filled to 50mm above pipe and covered with geotextile filled with soil.

Table H.15 Requirements for cesspools

	Requirement
Siting	Preferably on ground sloping away from and lower down than any existing building in immediate vicinity. At least 7m away from habitable parts of buildings.
Vehicle access	Within 30m of vehicle access, and at levels which enables them to be emptied and cleaned without hazard to building occupants, or the contents being taken through a dwelling or place of work. Access may be through a lockable covered space.
Capacity	At least 18,000 litres (18m³) for two users, increased by 6800 (6.8m³) for each additional user.
Construction	Factory-made tanks of GRP, polyethylene or steel should meet BS EN 12566-1. Tanks may be constructed on site from min. 220mm thick engineering brick with 1:3 cement-sand mortar, or 150mm thick C/25/P mix concrete, in both cases roofed with heavy concrete slabs.
Performance	Septic tanks should prevent leakage of contents and ingress of sub-soil water.
Access	No openings except the inlet, an opening for emptying, and ventilation. Access covers should be durable, having regard for corrosive material involved. Lockable or otherwise engineered to prevent personnel entry. Inlet to have access for inspection.

H.3.1.4 Remedial measures

Local authorities have powers under Section 50 of the Public Health Act 1936 and Section 59 of the Building Act 1984 to require remedial measures from owners/occupiers of buildings with leaking, inadequate, poorly maintained or disused septic tanks and cesspools.

H.3.2 Greywater and rainwater

Greywater and rainwater storage tanks should:

- prevent leakage of the contents and ingress of groundwater;

- be ventilated;

- have an anti-backflow device on any overflow connected to a drain or sewer to prevent contamination in the event of surcharge;

- have access for emptying and cleaning, with covers to the same standard as septic tanks.

Further guidance
WRAS leaflet 09-02-04 *Reclaimed water systems. Information about installing, modifying or maintaining reclaimed water systems*. WRAS. 2004.

H.4 Rainwater drainage (Requirement H3)

Rainwater must be carried from the roof of the building by a system which:

- can carry it to an outfall;

- minimises the risk of blockage or leakage;

- is accessible for clearing blockages.

Paved areas must be adequately drained where they:

- provide access for people with disabilities;

- give access to a solid waste store; or

- form part of an access passage used in common by occupants of two or more buildings.

Rainwater from roofs and paved areas should discharge (in order of priority) into:

- a soakaway or infiltration system;

- a watercourse;

- a sewer.

Rainfall intensities:

- For gutters and rainwater pipes the design rainwater intensity should be taken from Figure H.15.

- For paved areas and surface water drainage the design rainwater intensity may generally be taken as 0.014 litres/second per m^2.

- Where ponding is undesirable the intensity should be taken from Figure H.16.

Designers should follow either the guidance below or the recommendations of BS EN 12056, in particular Parts 3 and 5. Designs which include valley gutters, parapet gutters, siphonic drainage or drainage systems from flat roofs, or where over-topping would have serious consequences, should follow BS EN 12056.

Further guidance
BS EN 12056 Gravity drainage systems inside buildings.
-3:2000. Roof drainage, layout and calculation.
-5:2000. Installation and testing, instructions for operation, maintenance and use.

Figure H.15 Rainfall intensities for design of gutter and rainfall pipes

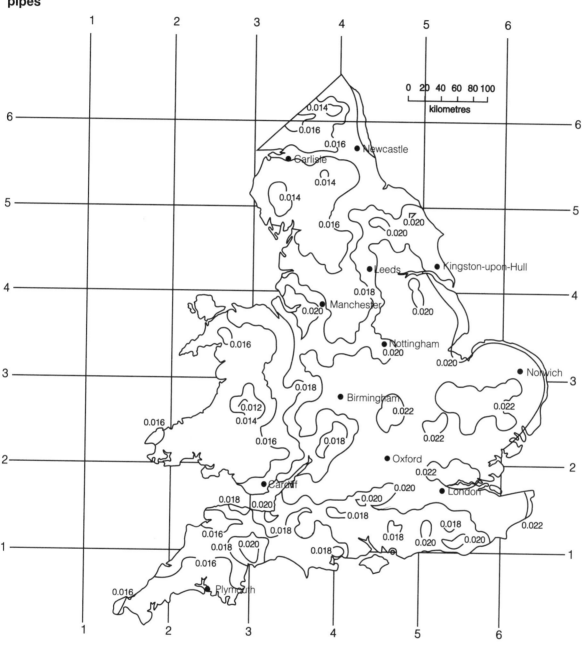

Figure H.16 Rainfall intensities for paved areas and underground rainwater drainage

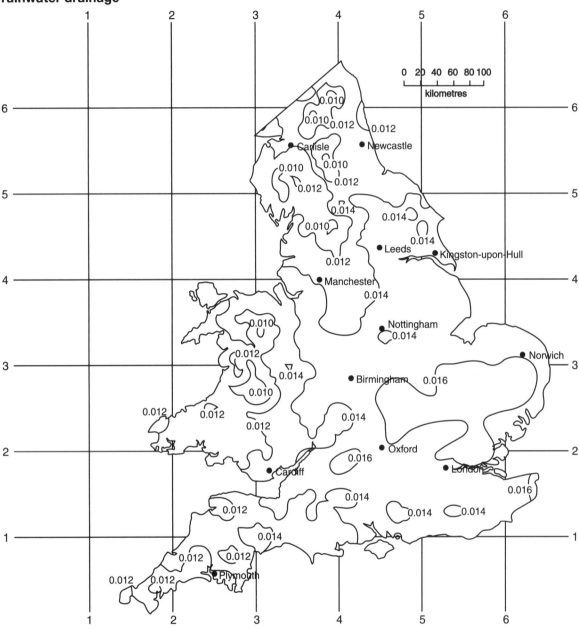

H.4.1 Gutters and rainwater pipes

H.4.1.1 Gutters

The rate of flow into a gutter depends on the effective area of the surface being drained (Table H.16). Table H.17 shows the largest effective areas which should be drained by standard gutter sizes, together with the smallest size of outlet which may be used. The size of gutter and rainwater pipe may be reduced for:

- gutters laid to falls;

- gutter sections with greater capacity than half-round sections;

Table H.16 Calculation of drained areas

Type of surface	Effective design area
Flat roof	Plan area of relevant portion
Pitched roof at: 30° 45° 60°	 1.29 × plan area of relevant portion 1.50 × plan area of relevant portion 1.87 × plan area of relevant portion
Pitched roof over 70° or any wall	0.5 × elevational area

Table H.17 Gutter and outlet sizes

Maximum effective roof area (m²)	Gutter size (mm diameter)	Outlet size (mm diameter)	Flow capacity (litres/second)
6.0	–	–	–
18.0	75	50	0.38
37.0	100	63	0.78
53.0	115	63	1.11
65.0	125	75	1.37
103.0	150	89	2.16

Note: Refers to nominal half-round eaves gutters laid level with sharp-edged outlets at one end and distance from stop end to outlet of not more than 50 × water depth. Round-edged outlets allow smaller downpipe sizes. Capacity reduced for greater distances. When the outlet is not at the end of the gutter, the gutter should be sized to the larger of the two areas drained.

- round-edged outlets;
- gutters with two outlets, which may be 100 × water depth apart.

Gutters should be laid with any fall towards the nearest outlet, and so any overflow will discharge clear of the building.

H.4.1.2 Rainwater pipes

A rainwater pipe should be at least as large as the outlet. A downpipe serving more than one gutter should be sized to the largest contributing outlet, and should be of sufficient size to take the flow from the whole contributing area.

Rainwater pipes should discharge into a drain or gully, or into another gutter or another drained surface. A pipe discharging onto a lower roof or paved area requires a pipe shoe to divert water away from the building. Where the pipe drains a roof with an effective area in excess of 25m² then a distributor pipe should be fitted to the shoe to prevent over-topping of the receiving gutter.

Any rainwater pipe which discharges into a combined system should do so through a trap.

H.4.1.3 Siphonic drainage systems

Siphonic systems should be designed to BS EN 12056-3, taking particular account of:

- reduced flow in the downpipe owing to surcharge in the downstream drainage system;
- the risk of overflow in long gutters while the siphonic system is priming.

H.4.1.4 Eaves drop systems

Eaves drop systems allow rainwater to drop freely to the ground without a gutter. Their design should prevent water from entering the building or damaging the building fabric and should protect people from falling water or splashing.

H.4.1.5 Rainwater recovery systems

Guidance on the recovery of rainwater is given in WRAS leaflet 09-02-04. Pipework, washouts and valves should be clearly identified on marker plates and storage tanks should comply with **H.3.2**.

H.4.1.6 Construction

Materials should be of adequate strength and durability, with different metals isolated to prevent electrolytic corrosion.

- Gutters and rainwater pipes should be firmly supported, without restricting thermal movement.
- Gutter joints should be watertight under working conditions.
- Pipes in buildings should be airtight when tested to the method in **H.2.1.3**.
- Pipework in siphonic drainage systems should be able to resist the predicted negative pressures.

Further guidance
WRAS Leaflet 09-02-04 [See **H.3.2**.]

SR 463 Performance of siphonic drainage systems for roof gutters. HR Wallingford. 1996.

H.4.2 Drainage of paved areas

The following recommendations are suitable for paved areas around buildings and car parks up to 4000m². An alternative approach, which is also appropriate for larger catchments, or high-risk areas where ponding could cause flooding, is given in BS EN 752-4.

Further guidance
BS EN 752-4 [See **H.2.2**.]

H.4.2.1 Gradients

Surfaces should direct water away from buildings, with a minimum gradient of 1:60, although gradients across paths should not exceed 1:40 (see **M.2.1** and **M.3.2**). Where a surface slopes towards a building a reverse gradient extending 500mm from the wall should be formed to divert water away.

H.4.2.2 Free-draining surfaces

Paths, driveways and other narrow areas of paving should be free-draining to pervious areas such as grassland, provided:

- the water is not discharged adjacent to buildings where it could damage the foundations;
- the soakage capacity of the ground is not exceeded.

Where the ground is not sufficiently permeable, filter drains may be provided. To allow for run-off, paving should finish above or flush with the ground surface.

H.4.2.3 Pervious paving

Pervious paving consists of a porous or permeable surface overlaying a granular layer, which acts as a storage reservoir and retains the peak flow while water soaks into underlying sub-soil. The storage layer should be designed on the same basis as that of the storage volume in soakaways (**H.4.3**).

On steeply sloping surfaces pervious paving will only be suitable if the water level can rise sufficiently within the granular layer.

Pervious paving should not be used:

- where ground conditions are unsuitable (**H.4.3.2**);
- where large amounts of sediment are likely to block pores;
- where stored water may accumulate around the foundations of the building;
- in oil storage areas or where run-off may be contaminated.

Where infiltration is not possible it may be used with an impermeable barrier below the storage area to act as a detention tank prior to flows discharging to a drainage system.

H.4.2.4 Drainage systems

Where free-draining surfaces or pervious paving are not practicable, impervious paving should be used with gullies or channels discharging to the drainage system.

Gullies should be provided at low points where water would otherwise pond, with intermediate gullies at intervals to prevent overloading and to restrict the depth of flow.

Gratings should sit approximately 5mm below the level of paved areas to allow for settlement and gully pots or catch pits should be provided to prevent silt and grit entering the system.

H.4.3 Surface water drainage

Wherever practicable, surface water drainage should discharge to a soakaway or other infiltration system. Discharge may be made to a watercourse, subject to obtaining the consent of the Environment Agency and, as a last resort, to a sewer. The sewerage operator may permit surface water to be discharged to a combined foul and surface water sewer; in such a system all surface water drainage should have traps.

The following guidance is appropriate for up to 2 hectares of impervious surface; for larger areas, or as an alternative approach, designers may follow the guidance in BS EN 752-4. Where there is evidence of surcharging from sewers, or where levels make gravity connection impossible, surface water lifting equipment will be required (**H.2.2.2**).

H.4.3.1 Pipes

Pipes should have sufficient capacity to carry the predicted flow. Surface water drains should have a minimum 75mm diameter and sewers a minimum 100mm diameter. Capacity can be increased by increasing gradient or using larger pipes (Figure H.17 and Table H.18). In all other respects pipes should follow **H.2.2.8**.

Further guidance
CIRIA C522 *Sustainable urban drainage systems – A design manual for England and Wales*. CIRIA. 2000. [For information on pervious paving.]

Figure H.17 Drainage capacities for different gradients

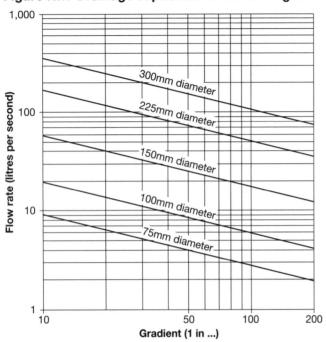

Table H.18 Minimum gradients for rainwater drains and sewers

Pipe diameter (mm)	Minimum gradient
75	1:100
100	1:100
150	1:150
225	1:225

Note: For larger pipes see BS EN 752-4.

H.4.3.2 Infiltration drainage systems

Infiltration drainage systems include:

- Soakaways – For areas less than 100m² these usually consist of square or circular pits filled with rubble, or lined with dry-jointed masonry or perforated ring units. Soakaways for larger areas are usually lined pits or trenches. Larger ones should be designed to BS EN 752-4 and BRE Digest 365.

- Swales – Grass-lined channels intended to transport rainwater from the site and control the flow and quality of surface run-off, which are good for run-off from small residential developments, parking areas and roads.

- Infiltration basins – Dry grass-lined basins designed to promote infiltration of surface water into the ground.

- Filter drains (French drains) – A geotextile membrane-lined trench filled with gravel. Much of the flow infiltrates to ground. A perforated pipe is often laid through the gravel to attenuate the flow.

- Detention ponds – Limit the peak rate for flow into a sewer system or watercourse.

Infiltration drainage systems should not be built:

- within 5m of buildings or roads;

- in areas of unstable land;

- in ground where the water table reaches the bottom of the device at any time of year;

- so close to other drainage fields, mounds or soakaways that their effectiveness is impeded or the storage capacity of the ground is exceeded;

- where contamination in the run-off could pollute a groundwater source or resource.

Soakaways should be sized to contain the water from the worst storm in a ten-year return period. For the duration of a storm the soakaway should be able to contain the difference between the inflow volume and the outflow volume (overflow drains may be acceptable on marginal ground):

- Inflow volume is determined from the area drained and the rainfall depth. For small soakaways (draining areas of 25m^2 or less) use 10mm of rain in 5 minutes. For larger soakaways refer to BS EN 752-4 or BRE Digest 365.

- Outflow volume, O, is determined from $O = a_{s50} \times f \times D$ where:
  f is the soil infiltration rate, derived from $f = 10^{-3}/3V_p$, where V_p is the result of the percolation test
  a_{s50} is the area of the side of the storage volume when filled to 50% of effective depth
  and D is the storm duration in minutes.

Further guidance
CIRIA Report 156 *Infiltration drainage – manual of good practice*. CIRIA. 1996.

BRE Digest 365. *Soakaway design*. BRE. 1991. [Revised 2003.]

BS EN 752-4 [See **H.2.2**.]

H.5 Building over sewers (Requirement H4)

When building work is to take place within 3m of the centre of any existing drain, sewer or disposal main shown on the sewerage undertaker's sewer records, the work:

- must not damage or overload existing drains, sewers or disposal mains, either during construction work, or after completion;

- must allow the drain, sewer or disposal main to be replaced on its existing alignment, or offer a satisfactory diversionary route;

- must not present an excessive risk to the building in the event of the collapse of the drain, sewer or disposal main, taking account of:
  - the nature of the ground;
  - the condition, location and construction of the drain, sewer or disposal main;
  - the nature, volume and pressure of the flow within it; and
  - the design and construction of the building's foundations.

The requirement applies to the erection of new buildings, and to the extension or underpinning of existing buildings. Where such work is proposed the developer should consult with the owner of the drain, sewer or disposal main. The Building Control Body (BCB) is required to consult with the sewerage undertaker (**I.5.1.3**).

H.5.1 Undue risk of failure

To prevent undue risk to a building in the event of failure of a drain or sewer, special measures should be taken in the design and construction of the foundations of any building that is to be constructed within 3m of:

- any rising main (except one used solely to drain the building);
- a drain or sewer constructed in brick or masonry;
- a drain or sewer in poor condition.

The same restriction applies to any drain laid in easily eroded soil (such as fine sands, silty sands or peat), unless special measures are taken, or the invert of the drain or sewer is:

- above the level of the foundations; and
- above groundwater level; and
- no more than 1m deep.

H.5.2 Maintaining access

There should be no more than 6m length of drain or sewer running under a building. Where a drain or sewer is more than 3m deep, or more than 225mm in diameter, no building or extension should be constructed within 3m. The owner of the drain or sewer may relax those requirements.

To allow for the subsequent reconstruction of a drain or sewer, there should be a satisfactory diversionary route that does not pass within 3m of the building. Where the drain or sewer is more than 1.5m deep, and has access for mechanical excavators, the diversionary route should also have such access.

Buildings or extensions should not be constructed over manholes, inspection chambers or other access fittings on sewers. Requirement H1 requires access points to be apparent and accessible in an emergency. Buildings or extensions should not remove existing provision, unless alternative access is provided at a location suitable to the owner.

H.5.3 Protection during construction

Drains and sewers should be protected from damage by construction traffic and plant, and heavy materials should not be stored over them.

Before piling is undertaken, the position of a drain or sewer should be determined by a survey. If the drain or sewer lies within 1m of the piling, trial holes should be dug to determine its exact line and the location of any connections. Piling should not be carried out if the distance from the outside of the pile to the outside of the drain is less than twice the diameter of the pile.

H.5.4 Protection from settlement

Drains and sewers should be protected from settlement, with:

- 100mm of granular or flexible filling provided around the pipe; and
- additional flexible joints or other protective measures (on sites where excessive subsidence is possible); and

- special protection where the crown of the pipe is within 300mm of the underside of the slab (**H.2.2.10**).

Where a drain or sewer is less than 2m deep the foundation should be extended so the pipe runs through the wall (**H.2.2.6**). For deeper pipes, the foundations should be designed as a lintel, spanning at least 1.5m either side of the pipe and transmitting no load to it.

H.6 Separate systems of drainage (Requirement H5)

In order to reduce the risk of flooding caused by rainwater overloading foul sewers, a system which discharges rainwater from a building or paved area to a sewer (**H.4**) should, where practicable, be separate from that which conveys foul water from the building. The requirement applies if:

- the rainwater is not contaminated; and
- drainage is to a public sewer system where separate systems for foul and surface water exist or are under construction.

Contaminated rainwater should be discharged into a foul sewer, with the consent of the sewerage undertaker.

H.7 Solid waste storage (Requirement H6)

There should be adequate storage provision for solid waste, taking account of the use of the building and the collection arrangements. Storage areas should be readily accessible to building occupiers and to the waste collection authority. Storage facilities should allow for the separation of recyclable waste and should be hygienic.

H.7.1 Waste storage for dwellings

Each dwelling requires a minimum 0.25m³ storage for separated waste (recyclable waste being stored separate from non-recyclable). That requirement may be increased in consultation with the waste collection authority.

Low-rise dwellings, including flats up to fourth floor, should have access to a location where at least two individual or communal movable waste containers can be stored. Individual storage areas should be at least 1.2 × 1.2 m. Consult the waste collection authority for sizing of communal storage areas.

High-rise dwellings may share a single container for non-recyclable waste fed by chutes, with separate storage for recyclable waste. Chutes should have at least 450mm diameter, have smooth, non-absorbent surfaces, have close-fitting access doors at every floor that has a dwelling, and should be ventilated at top and bottom. Alternative arrangements will be acceptable, provided a satisfactory management system exists for conveying refuse to the storage area.

Further guidance
BS 5906:1980. Code of practice for the storage and on-site treatment of solid waste from buildings. [Withdrawn, replaced by BS 5906:2005. Waste management in buildings. Code of practice.]

Storage areas and chutes should be sited so that householders do not have to carry waste more than 30m horizontally, and waste containers should be within 25m of the specified waste collection point. Wherever possible, the route to the collection point should not require containers to be taken through the building (passage through a porch or garage is acceptable). Any extension or conversion work should not remove such a facility where it already exists.

Where waste containers are larger than 250 litres the route should not have steps. For smaller containers, routes may have up to three steps. Slopes should not exceed 1:12, although short steeper sections are permitted, provided they are not part of a series of slopes (**K.2.3**).

External storage areas should be sited away from windows and ventilators, preferably in shade or under shelter. Where a storage area is in a publicly accessible area, or at the front of the building, an enclosure or shelter should be considered. Waste storage should not interfere with pedestrian or vehicle access.

Enclosures for individual containers should allow the lid to be opened for filling, should have a paved impervious floor and should be permanently ventilated at top and bottom. Communal enclosures, compounds or storage rooms should provide enough room for filling and emptying containers, with at least 150mm clear space between and around containers, and should have a minimum 2m headroom.

Communal waste storage areas should have impervious floors, with provision for washing down and drainage into a system suitable for polluted effluent. Gullies should have traps which maintain their seal even during prolonged periods of disuse. Rooms for open storage of waste should be secured against vermin. Compounds for waste storage should also be secured, unless waste is stored in secure containers with close-fitting lids. There should be separate rooms for recyclable and non-recyclable waste.

H.7.2 Waste storage for non-domestic buildings

For non-domestic developments the waste collection authority should be consulted regarding:

- the volume and nature of waste and the storage capacity required;
- requirements for waste segregation for recycling;
- the method of waste storage and any on-site treatment;
- the location of waste storage and/or treatment areas and waste collection areas, taking account of access for operatives and vehicles;
- hygiene arrangements;
- fire hazards and protective measures (**B.3.3.8**).

Waste storage areas and rooms for open storage of waste should be designed and constructed to the same specification as communal domestic ones.

Combustion appliances and fuel storage systems

J.1 General considerations

J.1.1 Scope

Part J is intended to ensure the safe operation of combustion appliances and to reduce the risk of fire presented by liquid fuels. Part J also addresses the risk of pollution from liquid fuels. The 2010 revision to Part J introduced a requirement for provision of carbon monoxide alarms where solid fuel appliances are being installed. The guidance in Approved Document J was also updated in 2010, with significant changes to address:

- the reduction of 'adventitious ventilation' in airtight dwellings, which may result in inadequate air supply for combustion appliances – recommended sizes of ventilation openings have been increased for such dwellings;
- access for visual inspection of concealed flues;
- the use of liquid biofuel and mineral oil/liquid biofuel mixes;
- the provision of secondary containment within Zone 1 of a groundwater Source Protection Zone.

The principal requirements are as follows.

Part J: Combustion appliances and fuel storage systems	
Requirement	**Limit on application**
Air supply	
J1 Combustion appliances shall be so installed that there is an adequate supply of air to them for combustion, to prevent over-heating and for the efficient working of any flue.	Requirements J1 and J2 apply only to fixed combustion appliances (including incinerators).
Discharge of products of combustion	
J2 Combustion appliances shall have adequate provision for the discharge of products of combustion to the outside air.	
Warning of release of carbon monoxide	
J3 Where a combustion appliance is provided, appropriate provision having regard to the design and location of the appliance shall be made to detect and give early warning of the release of carbon monoxide at levels harmful to persons.	Requirement J3 applies only to fixed combustion appliances located in dwellings.
Protection of building	
J4 Combustion appliances and flue pipes shall be so installed, and fireplaces and chimneys shall be so constructed and installed, as to reduce to a reasonable level the risk of people suffering burns or the building catching fire in consequence of their use.	Requirement J4 applies only to fixed combustion appliances (including incinerators).
Provision of information	
J5 Where a hearth, fireplace, flue or chimney is provided or extended, a durable notice containing information on the performance capabilities of the hearth, fireplace, flue or chimney shall be affixed in a suitable place in the building for the purpose of enabling combustion appliances to be safely installed.	

Protection of liquid fuel storage systems

J6 Liquid fuel storage systems and the pipes connecting them to combustion appliances shall be so constructed and separated from buildings and the boundary of the premises as to reduce to a reasonable level the risk of the fuel igniting in the event of fire in adjacent buildings or premises.	Requirement J6 applies only to – (a) fixed oil storage tanks with capacities greater than 90 litres and connecting pipes; and (b) fixed liquefied petroleum gas storage installations with capacities greater than 150 litres and connecting pipes, which are located outside the building and which serve fixed combustion appliances (including incinerators) in the building.

Protection against pollution

J7 Oil storage tanks and the pipes connecting them to combustion appliances shall – (a) be so constructed and protected as to reduce to a reasonable level the risk of the oil escaping and causing pollution; and (b) have affixed in a prominent position a durable notice containing information on how to respond to an oil escape so as to reduce to a reasonable level the risk of pollution.	Requirement J7 applies only to fixed oil storage tanks with capacities of 3500 litres or less, and connecting pipes, which are – (a) located outside the building; and (b) serve fixed combustion appliances (including incinerators) in a building used wholly or mainly as a private dwelling, but does not apply to buried systems.

The guidance in Approved Document J is applicable for:

- solid fuel installations up to 50kW rated output;
- gas installations up to 70kW net (77.7kW gross) rated input;
- oil installations up to 45kW rated heat output.

Installations with larger rating, or specialist ones such as incinerators, will need specialist guidance.

Further guidance
CIBSE Guide B: Heating, ventilating, air-conditioning and refrigeration. CIBSE. 2005. [Information on larger appliances.]

J.1.2 Other Regulations

- **The Gas Safety (Installation and Use) Regulations 1998** – Control the installation of gas fittings, appliances and gas storage vessels. These may be installed only by a person who holds a current certificate of competence and is registered with Gas Safe Register. Consequently, where work comprises only the installation of a gas appliance, the work need not be notified to the Building Control Body (BCB). The Regulations make other requirements which are described in **J.4.1**.

- **The Control of Pollution (Oil Storage) (England) Regulations 2001** – Apply to oil storage tanks to buildings other than private dwellings, and to tanks with a capacity greater than 3500 litres storing oil for private dwellings. Requirement J6 does not apply to such tanks.

- **The Clean Air Act (1993)** – Gives a local authority the power to declare a smoke control zone. Within such a zone it is an offence to emit smoke from the chimney of a building, a furnace or any fixed boiler; or to acquire an unauthorised fuel for use, unless in an exempt appliance. Authorised fuels are those which have been tested to confirm they can be burned in an open fire without producing smoke. Exempt appliances are those which have been tested to confirm they can burn unauthorised or smoky fuel without emitting smoke.

Further guidance
L56. Safety in the installation and use of gas systems and appliances. Approved code of practice. HSE. 1998. [Third edition, 2011.]

Pollution Prevention Guide 2 (PPG2) *Above ground oil storage tanks.* environment agency. 2004. [Revised, 2011.]

http://smokecontrol.defra.gov.uk [Information on authorised fuels and exempt appliances.]

J.1.3 Definitions

Appliance compartment An enclosed compartment constructed or adapted to accommodate one or more combustion appliances.

Balanced compartment A compartment with an open-flued appliance, which is sealed from the rest of the building and ventilated in such a way as to achieve a balanced flue effect.

Balanced flue appliance A room-sealed appliance which draws combustion air from a point outside the building, adjacent to where combustion products are discharged. The inlet and outlet are arranged so wind effects are substantially balanced.

Boundary The effective perimeter of land or buildings under control of the building owner, which may follow the perimeter of the land, or may extend to the centre line of adjacent routes or waterways (Figure J.1).

Figure J.1 Boundaries for Part J

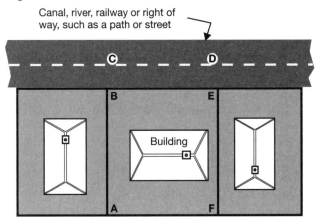

The boundary for the purposes of:	
See **J.2.2.9** Figures J.27 and J.34	is ACDF
See **J.6** and **J.6.3** Figure J.36 Tables J.17 and J.18	is ABEF

Chimney A structure consisting of a wall or walls enclosing one or more flues. A chimney for a gas appliance is commonly called a flue.

Combustion appliance (or appliance) Apparatus where fuel is burned to generate heat for space heating, water heating, cooking or similar purpose (excluding systems to deliver fuel to it and to distribute heat).

Designation The performance characteristics of chimneys and flues are designated in accordance with the system described in BS EN 1443:2003, following testing to an appropriate European product standard.

Draught breaks/diverters/stabilisers Factory-formed components providing breaks in the flue to prevent combustion being adversely affected by conditions in the flue.

Fanned draught An arrangement where the discharge of flue gases depends upon a fan (Figure J.2).

Figure J.2 Types of installation

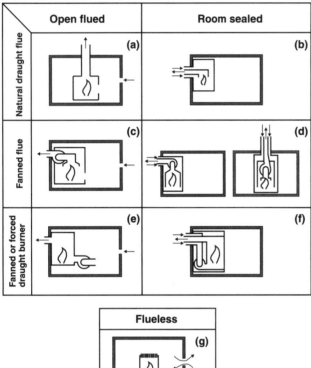

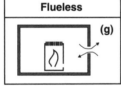

Note – For gas appliances only:	CEN TR1749 classifies gas appliances according to their method of evacuating the products of combustion:
	Type A – Flueless appliances
	Type B – Open flued
	Type C – Room sealed

The letters A, B and C are further qualified by numbers to identify the existence and mode of use of fans and draught diverters, as applicable (e.g. B_{11} for an open-flued natural draught appliance with draught diverter).

Fireplace recess A structural opening in a wall or chimney breast which leads to a chimney and has a hearth at its base. The finished fireplace opening area determines the size of flue required for an open fire.

Fire wall A means of shielding a fuel tank from thermal radiation from a fire. For LPG tanks it must also enable leaking gas to disperse safely before reaching a potential ignition source.

Flue Passage conveying products of combustion from an appliance to outside. Connected to a combustion appliance by a fluepipe. The flue liner is the wall of a chimney in contact with products of combustion.

Hearth A base which safely isolates a combustion appliance from people, combustible parts of the building fabric and soft furnishings. Its exposed surface provides a region which must be kept clear of anything at risk of fire.

Natural draught The flow of combustion products into the flue is a result of buoyancy force produced by different temperatures of flue gases and ambient air (Figure J.2).

Non-combustible materials See **B.2.3.1**.

Notified body One approved under the Gas Appliances (Safety) Regulations (1995) for carrying out certification of gas appliances, or similarly approved by another European Community member state.

Open-flued appliance One which draws combustion air from the space within which it is installed and requires a flue to discharge its products of combustion.

Rated heat input Maximum rate of energy flow into a gas appliance that could be provided by the prevailing rate of fuel flow. Now generally quoted as the net value: kW (net).

Rated heat output For an oil appliance, the maximum declared energy output rate (kW), as given on the appliance data plate. For solid fuel appliances, the maximum manufacturer's declared energy output rate.

Room-sealed appliance A combustion system which is sealed from the room in which it is located and draws air for combustion from outside (or from a ventilated uninhabited space in the building) and vents products of combustion directly to outside.

J.1.4 Measurement of flues and ducts

The size of a flue or duct is measured at right angles to the direction in which gases flow. Offset components should not reduce the flue area to less than the required minimum.

J.1.5 Maintenance

It is essential for the safe working of combustion appliances that they be adequately and regularly maintained.

J.2 Common provisions

Building provisions for combustion appliances must:

- allow sufficient supply of air for the proper combustion of fuel and operation of flue and cooling of appliances where necessary;
- enable normal operation without the products of combustion forming a hazard to health;
- incorporate an appropriate warning of a release of carbon monoxide for solid fuel appliances;
- enable normal operation without appliances causing danger through damage by heat or fire to the fabric of the building;
- be inspected and tested to establish suitability;
- be labelled to indicate performance capabilities.

Further guidance
BS EN 1443:2003. Chimneys. General requirements.

Approved Document J:2002 Edition: Supplementary guidance on the UK implementation of European standards for chimneys and flues. ODMP. 2004.
[Describes the designation system for chimneys and flues.]

Figure J.3 General air supply to a combustion appliance

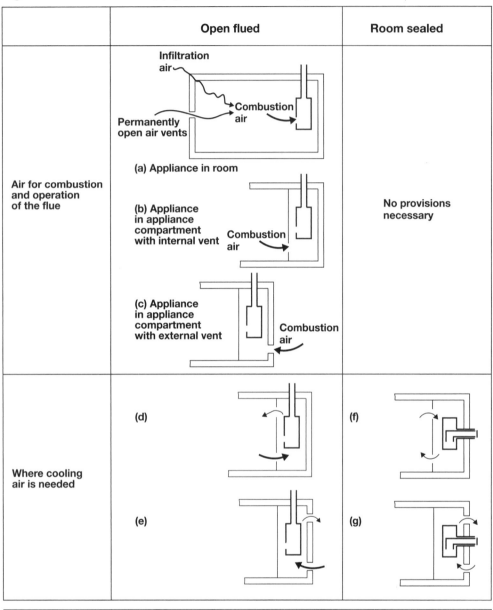

	Open flued	Room sealed
Air for combustion and operation of the flue	(a) Appliance in room (b) Appliance in appliance compartment with internal vent (c) Appliance in appliance compartment with external vent	No provisions necessary
Where cooling air is needed	(d) (e)	(f) (g)

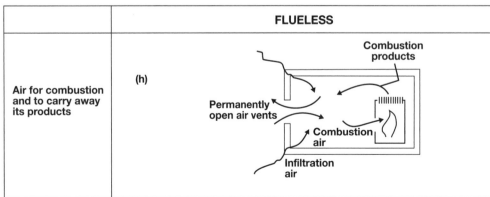

	FLUELESS
Air for combustion and to carry away its products	(h)

J.2.1 Air supply

Combustion appliances require an air supply to enable proper operation of flues or – for flueless appliances – to ensure that the products of combustion are safely dispersed. Some appliances require air for cooling to ensure that their cases remain safe to touch (Figure J.3).

Vent sizes depend on the type of fuel burned. The sizes given are for single appliances, and must be increased for multiple appliances. Open-flued appliances must receive some of their combustion air from outside; for some appliances, air infiltration through the fabric may be sufficient, but higher rated appliances will require permanent ventilation openings.

Appliance compartments with open-flued appliances should have vents large enough to admit all the air required by the appliance, whether from the room or directly from outside. The compartment should be large enough to enable air to circulate, and should have high- and low-level vents. Appliances installed within balanced compartments will require special provisions; manufacturer's instructions should be observed.

Where a room-sealed appliance takes air from another space in the building, or the flue has a permanent opening to another space in the building (for example, if it feeds to a secondary flue in a roof void), that space should have ventilation that opens directly to outside. The openings to outside should be at least as big as those opening to the room with the appliance. Air vents for flueless appliances should open directly to outside air.

J.2.1.1 Permanently open vents

Permanently open vents should be non-adjustable and positioned where they are unlikely to be blocked. They should be sized to provide the appropriate equivalent free area (Figure J.4), which may be the aggregate of individual apertures for airbricks and grilles. Grilles or meshes preventing the entry of animals or birds should not have aperture dimensions smaller than 5mm.

Figure J.4 Ventilator-free areas

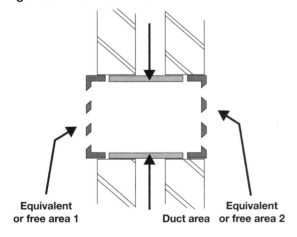

**Equivalent
or free area 1**

Duct area **Equivalent
or free area 2**

(a) Ventilator assembled on site from components

**The ventilator area is the smaller of equivalent area (1 or 2)
(as declared by manufacturer), free area (1 or 2)
(as measured in (b)) or the duct area.**

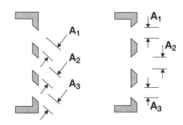

(b) Measuring the free area of components on site
Free area = $A_1 + A_2 + A_3$

Figure J.5 Example locations for permanent air vent openings

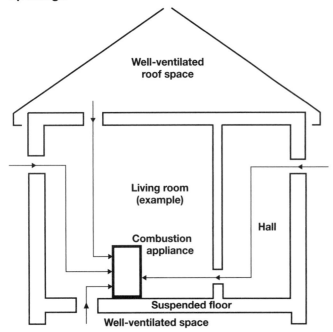

Figure J.6 Permanent vent openings in a solid floor

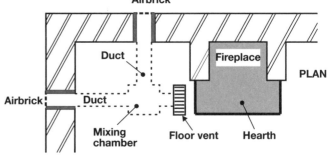

Airbrick, duct and grille should have an equivalent free area of at least that recommended in **J.3**, **J.4** or **J.5**, as relevant

To avoid discomfort from draughts, vents should:

- be placed close to appliances (e.g. floor vents); or
- draw air from intermediate areas such as hallways; or
- be located near the ceiling to ensure a good mix of air (Figures J.5 and J.6).

Vents should not be located in fire-resisting walls, other than external walls. Floor vents should not interfere with airtight membranes in the floor.

Permanently open vents to Part J can count towards the background ventilation requirement for Part F (**F.2.4**). However, adjustable vents to Part F cannot count towards the requirement for Part J.

For flueless appliances, the permanent ventilation to Part J can count towards the adjustable vent provision of Part F, and the purge ventilation provision for Part F may be acceptable for the rapid ventilation required for Part J.

J.2.1.2 Interaction between mechanical extract ventilation and open-flued combustion appliances

The operation of extract fans must not result in combustion products spilling from open-flued appliances as a result of lowered air pressure. To ensure safe operation:

- For gas appliances – in a kitchen with an open-flued appliance, the extract rate should not exceed 20l/s (72m^3 per hour).
- For oil appliances – the extract rate should be limited to 40l/s for pressure jet burners and 20l/s for vaporising burners.

Further guidance

BR 414. *Protective measures for housing on gas contaminated land*. BRE. 2001.

BR 211. *Radon: guidance on protective measures for new buildings (including supplementary advice for extensions, conversions and refurbishment*. BRE 2007. [Guidance on service penetrations for sub-floor vents and floors with gas barriers.]

- For solid fuel appliances – extract ventilation should not be installed in the same room. Seek specialist advice if mechanical extract is unavoidable.

- For commercial and industrial installations – specialist advice may be required regarding interlocking gas heaters and mechanical ventilation systems.

The effect of fans such as those for radon extract (**C.3.5**) or in tumble-dryers should also be considered.

Testing for gas appliances should be carried out to BS 5440-1:2008 or to manufacturer's instructions. Oil appliances should be shown to operate satisfactorily with and without fans running. Testing should show no spillage at conditions of greatest depressurisation; several tests may be required with different internal conditions.

J.2.2 Flues

Appliances other than flueless appliances should incorporate or be connected to flues which discharge to outside air. Although the following guidance applies to flues serving one appliance, flues may serve more than one oil or gas appliance, but each solid fuel appliance should have its own flue.

J.2.2.1 Condensate

To control condensate:

- chimneys to non-condensing appliances should have insulated flues so that flue gases do not condense in normal operation; and

- chimneys to condensing appliances should have linings that are impervious to condensates and resistant to corrosion (designation 'W' to BS EN 1443:2003) together with provision for disposal of condensate from the appliances.

J.2.2.2 Connecting fluepipes

Connecting fluepipes should be made of suitable materials, as follows:

- cast iron fluepipes to BS 41:1972(1998);

- metal fluepipes with designation to BS EN 1856-2:2004 for the appliance and fuel type;

- vitreous enamelled steel pipe to BS 6999:1989(1996);

- other fluepipes independently certified as having the necessary performance designation for the combustion appliance.

Spigot and socket joints should have the socket facing upwards to contain moisture and other condensates in the flue. Joints should be gas-tight either by use of proprietary jointing accessories or by packing with non-combustible rope and fire cement.

J.2.2.3 Masonry chimneys

New masonry chimneys should be constructed as set out in Table J.1, from bricks, medium weight concrete blocks or stone, with suitable joints and supported and caulked liners.

Further guidance
BS 5440-1:2008. Installation and maintenance of flues and ventilation for gas appliances of rated input not exceeding 70kW net (1st, 2nd and 3rd family gases). Specification for Installation and maintenance of flues.

OFTEC Technical books 2, 4 and 5. [Guidance on spillage testing.]

Further guidance
BS 5410-1:1997. Code of practice for oil firing. Installations up to 44kW output capacity for space heating and hot water supply purposes. AMD 3637.

BS 5440-1:2008. [See **J.2.1.2**.] [Guidance for flues serving more than one oil or gas appliance.]

Further guidance
BS EN 1443:2003. Chimneys. General requirements.

Further guidance
BS 41:1973(2010). Specification for cast iron spigot and socket flue or smoke pipes and fittings.

BS EN 1856-2:2004. Chimneys. Requirements for metal chimneys. Metal liners and connecting fluepipes.

BS 6999:1989 (1996). Specification for vitreous-enamelled low-carbon-steel fluepipes, other components and accessories for solid-fuel-burning appliances with a maximum rated output of 45kW.

Table J.1 Requirements for masonry chimneys

Feature	Requirement
Standards	Performance equal to BS EN 1443 designation T400 N2 D 3 G, such as: • rebated or socketed clay liners to BS EN 1457 Classes A1 N2 or A1 N1; • concrete flue liners to BS EN 1857 types A1, A2, B1, B2; • other independently certified products.
Installation	Liners should be constructed following manufacturer's instructions. Components selected to avoid cutting and minimise joints: bend offsets formed with pre-formed components. Sockets and rebated joints to go uppermost. Joints sealed with fire cement, refractory mortar, or as manufacturer's instructions.

Space between lining and masonry	Observe manufacturer's instructions or use weak, insulating concrete:
	    1:20 OPC: lightweight expanded clay aggregate, slightly wetted
	    1:6 OPC: vermiculite
	    1:10 OPC: perlite

J.2.2.4 Flueblock chimneys

Flueblock chimneys should be constructed of suitable factory-made components, including:

• flue blocks equivalent to BS EN 1443:2003, designation T400 N2 D 3 G, such as clay flue blocks to BS EN 1806:2006, Class FB1 N2 or other independently certified products;

• blocks lined in accordance with **J.2.2.3** and independently certified.

Blocks should be installed in accordance with the manufacturer's instructions, with bends and offsets formed with factory-made components.

J.2.2.5 Plastic fluepipes

Plastic flues and liners should be of a designation to BS EN 14471:2005 which is appropriate to the appliance, fuel and flue. They may be used with condensing boilers where the appliance manufacturer supplies the fluepipes, or specifies them as suitable.

Further guidance
BS EN 14471:2005. Chimneys. System chimneys with plastic flue liners. Requirements and test methods.

J.2.2.6 Factory-made metal chimneys

Factory-made metal chimneys should comply with Table J.2 and Figure J.7.

J.2.2.7 Configuration of natural draught flues

Flues should offer the least possible resistance to flue gases. They should be straight and vertical, with bends angled at no more than 45° to vertical, and the only horizontal section being a length of no more than 150mm at the outlet of at rear outlet appliances (Figure J.8).

To facilitate sweeping and inspection, there should be no more than four changes of direction between the appliance outlet and flue outlet, with no more than two of those being between an intended access point or the flue outlet; and 90° factory-made elbows, bends or tee-pieces should be treated as two 45° bends.

Table J.2 Requirements for factory-made metal chimneys

Feature	Requirement
Construction	• Independently certified component system to BS 1856-1:2003 installed to BS EN 15287-1:2007. • Gas and oil where temperatures will not normally exceed 250°C, twin wall (or, for gas, single wall) component systems to BS EN 1856-1:2003 installed to BS 5440-1:2008. • Other system, independently certified as suitable, installed to BS 15287-1:2007 or BS 54401:2008 as appropriate.
Arrangement	• Chimney to be sleeved where it passes through a wall to prevent damage to the flue or building through thermal expansion. • Joints not to be concealed in ceiling joist spaces or within thickness of walls, without access being provided. • It should be possible to withdraw the appliance without having to dismantle the chimney.
Separation from combustible materials	At least XXmm as **Figure J.7**, where XX is the separation distance in the chimney designation to BS EN 1856-1:2003. Where it passes through a cupboard, storage space or roof space provide a guard no closer to outer wall than XX.
Compartment walls and floors	Maintain fire separation, by: • using chimney of appropriate level of fire resistance installed to BS EN 1856-1:2003 Annex NA • casing the chimney in non-combustible material with at least half fire resistance required for the fire compartment wall or floor (**B.5.4**).

Note: BS 1856-1:2003 superseded by 2009 edition. BS 15287-1:2007 now +A1:2010.

Figure J.7 Separation of combustible material from a factory-made metal chimney to BS EN 1856-1

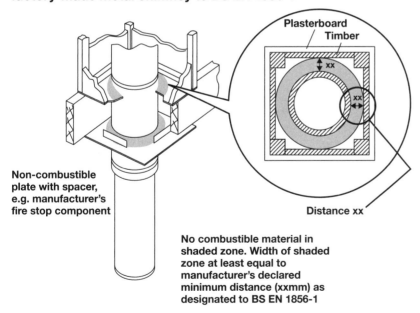

Plasterboard
Timber

XX

XX

Non-combustible plate with spacer, e.g. manufacturer's fire stop component

Distance xx

No combustible material in shaded zone. Width of shaded zone at least equal to manufacturer's declared minimum distance (xxmm) as designated to BS EN 1856-1

Figure J.8 Bends in flues

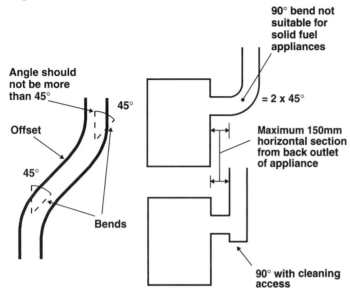

J.2.2.8 Inspection and cleaning openings in flues

A flue should not have openings into more than one room or space except for:

- inspection or cleaning;
- fitting an explosion door, draught break, draught stabiliser or draught diverter.

Inspection and cleaning openings should be formed with purpose factory-made components, with the same level of non-combustibility, gas-tightness and thermal insulation as the flue system. Openings for cleaning should allow easy passage of the cleaning brush; it should be possible to sweep the whole flue.

There should be a permanent means of safe access to appliances for maintenance; and the installation of gas-fired appliances in roof space walkways should comply with BS 6798:2009.

Further guidance
BS 6798:2009. Specification for installation and maintenance of gas-fire boilers of rated input not to exceed 70kW net.

J.2.2.9 Flues discharging at low level near boundaries

Low-level flues near boundaries are permitted, provided the building owner will always be able to ensure safe flue gas disposal. Where owners of adjacent land could build up to the boundary wall, the layouts in Figures J.27 and J.34 (see **J.4.6** and **J.5.3** respectively) may be adopted.

J.2.2.10 Concealed flues

Where a flue runs within a void there must be access for visual inspection to ensure that:

- the flue is continuous throughout the length of the void;
- the flue is adequately supported throughout the length;
- joints appear correctly assembled and sealed; and
- the fallback gradient to the boiler for draining condensate is correct and any drain point has been provided.

Figure J.9 Locations of access panels for concealed flues

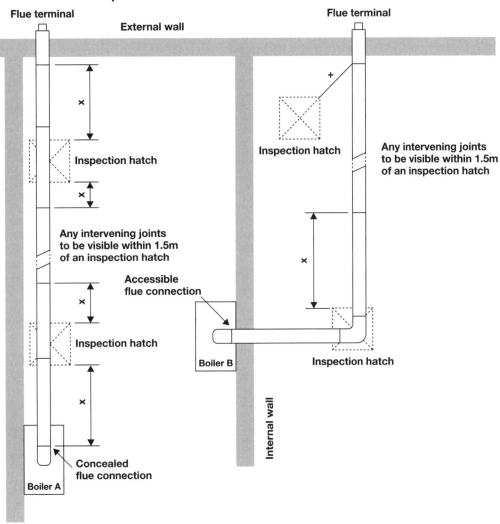

All voids containing concealed flues should have at least one inspection hatch measuring at least 300mm square.

No flue joint within the void should be more than 1.5m distant from the edge of the nearest inspection hatch, i.e. dimension x in the diagram should be less than 1.5m.

Where possible inspection hatches should be located at changes of direction. Where this is not possible then bends should be viewable from both directions.

A minimum 300mm × 300mm opening will be sufficient to allow an operator to look along the length of the chimney (Figure J.9). Panels or hatches should be permanent and available for the life of the appliance and should not impair compliance with other requirements of the Building Regulations.

Flues should not pass through another dwelling, but may pass through communal areas including purpose-designed ducts with inspection access.

J.2.2.11 Dry lining around fireplace openings

Any gaps between a fireplace opening and a decorative surround should be sealed to prevent flue gases reaching the void behind the decorative treatment. The sealing should withstand any differential movement between components.

J.2.2.12 Completion of installation

Where the work includes installation of a combustion appliance, tests should cover fluepipes and the gas-tightness of the connections between combustion appliances, outlets and fluepipes. Flues should be checked to show they are:

- free from obstructions;
- satisfactorily gas-tight;
- constructed with suitable materials.

A spillage test for Requirement J2 should be carried out as part of the commissioning to Part L and, for gas appliances, to the Gas Safety (Installation and Use) Regulations. A report should be provided which shows that materials and components used are appropriate to the intended application and that flues have passed appropriate tests.

Hearths should be constructed of materials and components of sizes to suit the application and should show where combustible materials should not intrude.

J.2.2.13 Notice plates for hearths and flues

When a hearth, fireplace, flue or chimney is provided or extended (including as part of refurbishment work), essential information on its correction application and use should be provided. This may be done by securely fixing a notice plate in an unobtrusive but obvious position, such as next to the:

- electricity or consumer unit;
- chimney or hearth described;
- water supply stop-cock.

The plate should be robust, and indelibly marked with:

- the location of the hearth or fireplace, or beginning of the flue;
- the category of flue and generic type of appliances that can be safely accommodated;
- the type and size of flue (or liner) and manufacturer's name;
- the installation date;
- optionally, the designation, for appliances tested to a European Standard (EN).

J.2.3 Flues in existing buildings

J.2.3.1 Material change of use

The fire resistance of existing chimneys may need to be upgraded at a material change of use (Figure J.10).

Further guidance

Approved Document J: Appendix A. [Checklist and report format for checking and testing installations.]

Approved Document J: Appendix E. [Guidance on testing to requirement J2.]

Figure J.10 Material change of use: fire protection of chimneys passing through other dwellings

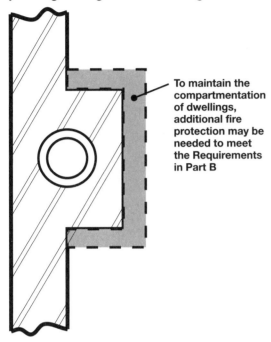

To maintain the compartmentation of dwellings, additional fire protection may be needed to meet the Requirements in Part B

J.2.3.2 Repair of flues

The renovation, repair or refurbishment of flue liners should result in flues that comply with Requirements J2, J4 and J5. Flues are controlled services, so the local authority must be notified of work to provide a new or replacement flue liner, including:

- relining, to form new flue walls;
- installing a cast in situ liner that significantly alters the flue's internal dimensions.

J.2.3.3 Reuse of existing flues

Where a flue in an existing chimney is to be brought back into use, or re-used with a different type or rating of appliance, the flue and chimney should be checked and, if necessary, altered:

- A defective flue could be relined, following sweeping to remove deposits.
- The flue may need to be reduced in size because over-sized flues can be dangerous.

An existing metal lining should be replaced, unless it can be demonstrated that it was recently installed and is visibly in good condition.

Flexible metal flue liners may be used to reline existing chimneys, but should not be used as the primary liner of a new chimney; they may be used to connect a gas back boiler to a chimney where the appliance is in the fireplace recess.

Further guidance
Approved Document J: Appendix E. [Guidance on testing flues.]

J.3 Solid fuel (including solid biofuel) appliances to 50kW rated output

The installation of solid fuel appliances should either follow the guidance in this section, or achieve the equivalent level of performance by following the relevant recommendations in BS EN 15287-1:2007 and BS 8303-1, -2, -3:1994.

J.3.1 Air supply

Permanent air vent openings should comply with Table J.3 or manufacturer's recommendations if greater.

Further guidance
BS EN 15287-1:2007 Chimneys. Design, installation and commissioning of chimneys. Chimneys for non-roomsealed heating appliances. [Now +A1:2010.]

BS 8303: Installation of domestic heating and cooking appliances burning solid mineral fuels.
-1:1994. Specification for the design of installations.
-2:1994. Specification for installing and commissioning on site.
-3:1994. Recommendations for design and on site installation.

Table J.3 Air supply to solid fuel appliances

Type of appliance	Type and amount of ventilation			
Open appliance, such as an open fire with no throat e.g. fire under a canopy as **Figure J.16**	Permanently open air vent(s) with a total equivalent area of at least 50% of the cross-sectional area of the flue			
Open appliance such as an open fire with a throat as in **Figure J.15** and AD J, Diagram 29	Permanently open air vent(s) with a total equivalent area of at least 50% of the throat opening area[1]			
Other appliance, such as a stove, cooker or boiler with a flue draught stabiliser	Permanently open vents Design air permeability $>5.0 m^3/(h.m^2)$: • $300 mm^2/kW$ for first 5kW of appliance rated output; • $850 mm^2/kW$ for balance of appliance rated output. Design air permeability $\leq 5.0 m^3/(h.m^2)$: • $850 mm^2/kW$ of appliance rated output.			
Other appliance such as a stove, cooker or boiler with no flue draught stabiliser	Permanently open vents Design air permeability $>5.0 m^3/(h.m^2)$: • $550 mm^2/kW$ for appliance rated output above 5kW. Design air permeability $\leq 5.0 m^3/(h.m^2)$: • $550 mm^2/kW$ of appliance rated output.			
[1] For simple open fires as **Figure J.7**, the requirement can be met as follows:				
Nominal fire size (fireplace opening size)	500mm	450mm	400mm	350mm
Total equivalent area of permanently open air vents	$20,500 mm^2$	$18,500 mm^2$	$16,500 mm^2$	$14,500 mm^2$
Example: an appliance with a flue draught stabiliser and a rated output of 7kW would require an equivalent area of $[5 \times 300] + [2 \times 850] = 3200 mm^2$				

J.3.2 Connecting fluepipes

Fluepipes should have the same diameter or equivalent cross-sectional area as the appliance flue outlet and should not be smaller than the size recommended by the appliance manufacturer. They should be used only to connect appliances to their chimneys and should not pass through a roof space, partition, internal wall or floor except to pass directly into a chimney through its wall, or the floor supporting the chimney. They should be guarded if they present a hazard which is not immediately apparent.

To avoid fluepipes igniting combustible material, they should be:
• shielded in accordance with Figure J.11; or

Figure J.11 Protecting combustible material from uninsulated fluepipes for solid fuel

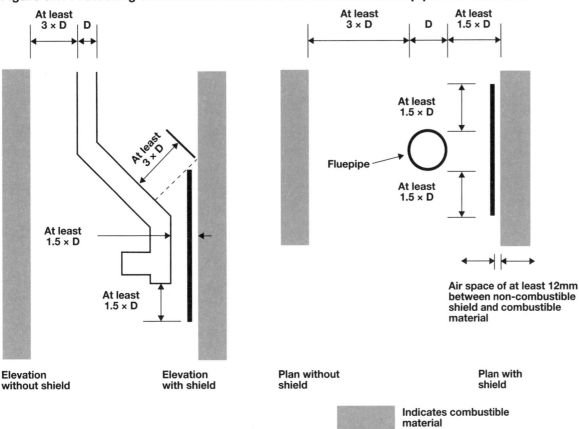

Elevation
without shield

Elevation
with shield

Plan without
shield

Plan with
shield

Fluepipe

At least
1.5 × D

At least
1.5 × D

Air space of at least 12mm
between non-combustible
shield and combustible
material

Indicates combustible
material

Shields should either:
  a) **extend beyond the fluepipe by at least 1.5 × D; or**
  b) **make any path between fluepipes and combustible material at least 3 × D long.**

- for fluepipes which are factory-made metal chimneys of designation T400 N2 D3 G to BS EN 1856-1:2003 or BS EN 1856-2:2004 separated as Table J.2.

J.3.3 Flues

Flues should be at least the size shown in Table J.4, and not less than the size of the appliance flue outlet or the manufacturer's recommended size. For multi-fuel appliances the flue should be sized to the fuel which requires the largest flue. For fireplaces with openings larger than 500mm × 500mm, or those exposed on both sides, a flue with cross-sectional area equal to 15% of the total face area of the opening would be sufficient, although specialist advice should be sought for flue areas greater than 15% of the face area, or more than 120,000mm² (0.12m²).

Flues should be high enough to generate sufficient draught to clear the products of combustion. The required height may be assessed using the calculation method in BS EN 13384-1:2002, although a height of 4.5m will be sufficient for a flue which follows **J.3.4**. The height is measured vertically from the highest point at which air can enter the fireplace to the level at which the flue discharges into outside air.

Further guidance
BS EN 1856-1:2003. Chimneys. Requirements for metal chimneys. System chimney products. [Withdrawn, replaced by 2009 edition.]

BS EN 1856-2:2004. Chimneys. Requirements for metal chimneys. Metal liners and connecting fluepipes. [Withdrawn, replaced by 2009 edition.]

Further guidance
BS EN 13384-1:2002+A2:2008. Chimneys. Thermal and fluid dynamic calculation methods. Chimneys serving one appliance.

Table J.4 Sizes of flues in chimneys

Installation[1]	Minimum flue size
Fireplace with an opening of up to 500mm × 550mm.	200mm diameter or rectangular/square flues having the same cross-sectional area and a minimum dimension not less than 175mm.
Fireplace with an opening in excess of 500mm × 550mm or a fireplace exposed on two or more sides.	See **J.3.3**. If rectangular/square flues are used the minimum dimension should not be less than 200mm.
Closed appliance of up to 20kW rated output which: a) burns smokeless or low volatiles fuel[2] or b) is an appliance which meets the requirements of the Clean Air Act when burning an appropriate bituminous coal or wood.[3]	125mm diameter or rectangular/square flues having the same cross-sectional area and minimum dimension not less than 100mm for straight flues or 125mm for flues with bends or offsets.
Pellet burner or pellet boiler complying with the Clean Air Act.	Minimum 100mm diameter. Less than 125mm diameter only when permitted by the appliance manufacturer and supported by calculation according to BS EN 13384-1:2002.[4]
Other closed appliance of up to 30kW rated output burning any fuel.	150mm diameter or rectangular/square flues having the same cross-sectional area and a minimum dimension not less than 125mm.
Closed appliance of above 30kW and up to 50kW rated output burning any fuel.	175mm diameter or rectangular/square flues having the same cross-sectional area and a minimum dimension not less than 150mm.

[1] Closed appliances include cookers, stoves, room heaters and boilers.

[2] Fuels such as bituminous coal, untreated wood or compressed paper are not smokeless or low volatiles fuels.

[3] These appliances are known as 'exempted fireplaces'.

[4] BS EN 13384-1:2002+A2:2008. Chimneys. Thermal and fluid dynamic calculation methods. Chimneys serving one appliance.

J.3.4 Outlets from flues

The outlet from a flue should be above the roof, in a location where products of combustion can discharge freely and not present a fire hazard, whatever the wind conditions. Figure J.12 shows positions which, in common circumstances, would meet that requirement, although heights might have to be increased where conditions, such as wind exposure, surrounding buildings, trees or high ground might have an adverse effect on flue draught.

Where flues discharge on or close to roofs with readily ignitable surfaces (e.g. thatch or shingles) the clearances in Figure J.13 should be adopted.

J.3.5 Debris collection space

Where a chimney cannot be cleaned through the appliance, a debris collecting space which is accessible for emptying should be provided, together with suitably sized openings for cleaning.

J.3.6 Chimneys

Masonry chimneys should be built to **J.2.2.3**, and flueblock chimneys to **J.2.2.4**. The thickness of the walls around the flues, excluding the thickness of the liners, should be in accordance with Figure J.14. Factory-made metal chimneys should comply with Table J.2. Minimum performance designations are given in Table J.5.

Further guidance
HETAS Information paper 1/007. *Chimneys in thatched properties*. HETAS. 2009.

Figure J.12 Flue outlet positions for solid fuel appliances

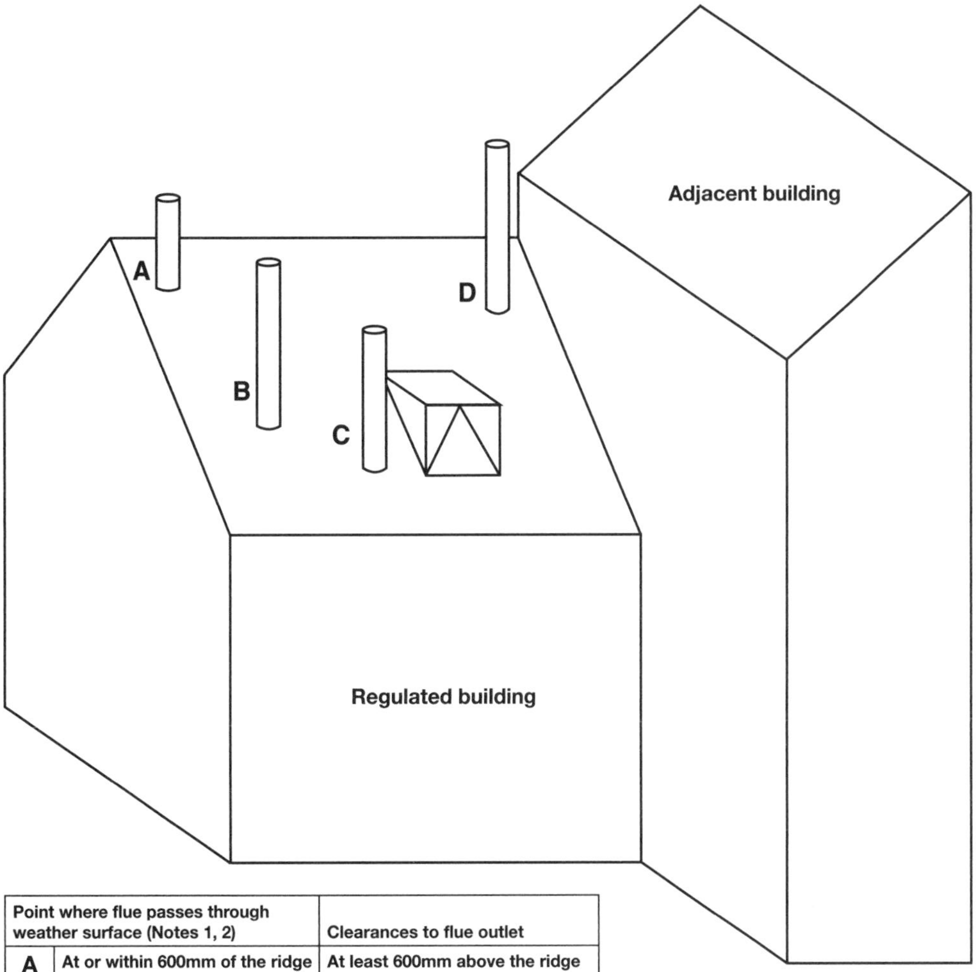

Adjacent building

Regulated building

Point where flue passes through weather surface (Notes 1, 2)		Clearances to flue outlet
A	At or within 600mm of the ridge	At least 600mm above the ridge
B	Elsewhere on a roof (whether pitched or flat)	At least 2300mm horizontally from the nearest point on the weather surface and: a) at least 1000mm above the highest point of intersection of the chimney and the weather surface; or b) at least as high as the ridge.
C	Below (on a pitched roof) or within 2300mm horizontally to an openable rooflight, dormer window or other opening (Note 3)	At least 1000mm above the top of the opening.
D	Within 2300mm of an adjoining or adjacent building, whether or not beyond the boundary (Note 3)	At least 600mm above any part of the adjacent building within 2300mm.

Notes

1) The weather surface is the building external surface, such as its roof, tiles or external walls.

2) A flat roof has a pitch less than 10°.

3) The clearances given for A or B, as appropriate, will also apply.

4) A vertical flue fixed to an outside wall should be treated as equivalent to an inside flue emerging at the nearest edge of the roof.

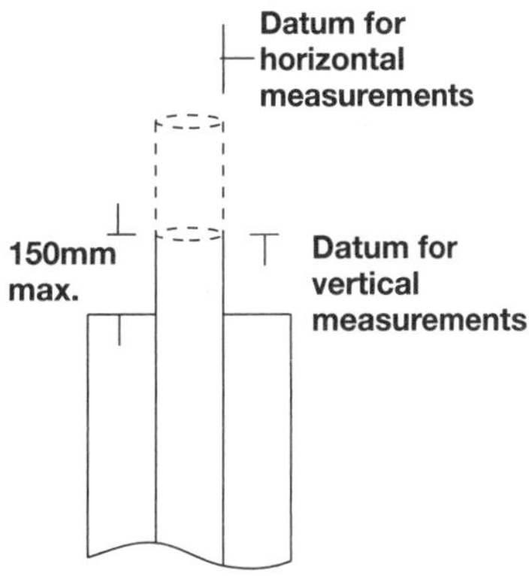

Datum for horizontal measurements

150mm max.

Datum for vertical measurements

The datum for vertical measurements is the point of discharge of the flue, or 150mm above the insulation, whichever is the lower

287

Figure J.13 Flue positions for solid fuel appliances – clearances to easily ignited roof coverings

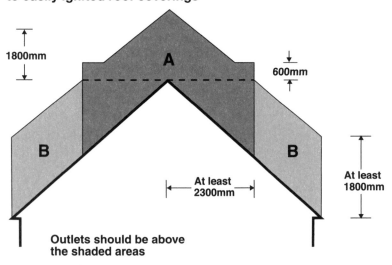

1800mm

600mm

A

B   B

At least
2300mm

At least
1800mm

**Outlets should be above
the shaded areas**

Area	Location of flue outlet
A	At least 1800mm vertically above the weather surface and at least 600mm above the ridge.
B	At least 1800mm vertically above the weather surface and at least 2300mm horizontally from the weather surface.

Table J.5 Minimum performance designations for chimney and fluepipe components for use with new solid fuel fired appliances		
Appliance type	**Component**	**Minimum designation**
All solid fuel appliances burning coal, smokeless fuel, peat wood and other biomass	Masonry or flueblock flue with liner	T400 N2 D3 Gxx
	Clay flue blocks	FB1N2
	Clay/ceramic liners	B1N2
	Concrete liners	B2
	Factory-made metal chimneys	T400 N2 D3 Gxx

Figure J.14 Wall thickness for masonry and flueblock chimneys

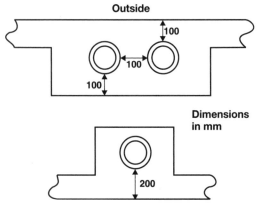

Outside

100

100

100

Dimensions
in mm

200

Another fire compartment of another dwelling

J.3.7 Lining and relining of flues in chimneys

Chimney flues may be lined or relined using liners whose performance has been independently certified as at least equal to designation T400 N2 D3 G to BS EN 1443:2003, such as:

- factory-made flue lining systems manufactured to BS EN 1856-1:2003 or BS EN 1856-2:2004;

- cast in situ flue relining systems to BS EN 1857:2003+A1:2008 where material and installation procedures are suitable for use with solid fuel burning appliances;

- other systems independently certified as being suitable for use with solid fuel appliances.

Alternatively, liners to **J.2.2.3** may be used.

J.3.8 Formation of gathers

To minimise resistance to the proper working of flues, tapered gathers should be provided in fireplaces for open fires. Gathers may be formed:

- using prefabricated gather components built into a fireplace recess, as Figure J.15(a);

- corbelling masonry, as Figure J.15(b);

- using a suitable canopy, as Figure J.16; or

- using a prefabricated appliance chamber incorporating a gather.

J.3.9 Separation of combustible material from fireplaces and flues

Combustible material should not be subject to heat dissipating through the walls of fireplaces or flues (Figure J.17). It should be at least:

- 200mm from the inside surface of a flue or fireplace recess; or

- at least *xx*mm from a flue product, where *xx* is the separation distance given in the product designation (G*xx*);

- 40mm from the outer surface of a masonry chimney or fireplace recess, unless it is a floorboard, skirting board, dado, picture rail, mantel-shelf or architrave.

Metal fixings in contact with combustible materials should be at least 50mm from the inside surface of the flue.

Further guidance

BS EN 1856-1:2003 and BS EN 1856-2:2004 [See **J.3.2.**]

BS EN 1857:2003+A1:2008. Chimneys. Components. Concrete flue liners. [Withdrawn, replaced by 2010 edition.]

Figure J.15 Construction of fireplace gathers

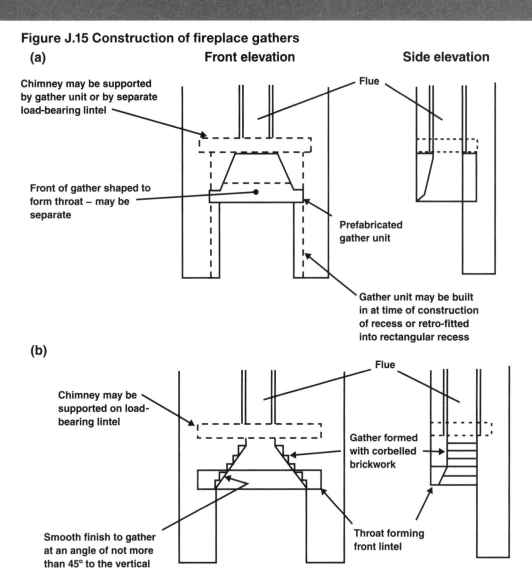

(a)

Front elevation   Side elevation

Chimney may be supported by gather unit or by separate load-bearing lintel

Flue

Front of gather shaped to form throat – may be separate

Prefabricated gather unit

Gather unit may be built in at time of construction of recess or retro-fitted into rectangular recess

(b)

Flue

Chimney may be supported on load-bearing lintel

Gather formed with corbelled brickwork

Smooth finish to gather at an angle of not more than 45° to the vertical

Throat forming front lintel

Figure J.16 Canopy for an open solid fuel fire

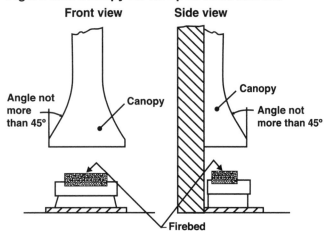

Front view   Side view

Angle not more than 45°

Canopy

Canopy

Angle not more than 45°

Firebed

Figure J.17 Minimum separation distances from combustible material in or near a chimney

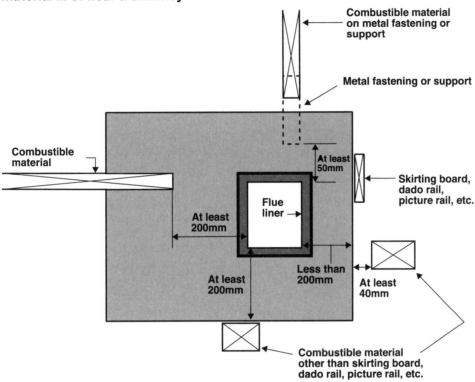

J.3.10 Hearths

A hearth should be able to accommodate the weight of the appliance and that of the chimney, if the chimney is not independently supported.

Appliances should stand wholly above a constructional hearth to Table J.6 and Figures J.18–J.20. Where the appliance is not to stand in an appliance recess, and has been independently certified that it cannot cause the temperature of the hearth to exceed 100°C, the hearth may be made of non-combustible board/sheet or tiles at least 12mm thick (Figure J.21(a)).

Table J.6 Hearths for solid fuel appliances (including open fires)	
Item	**Requirement**
Constructional hearth	Solid non-combustible material, such as concrete or masonry, at least 125mm thick, including the thickness of any non-combustible floor and/or decorative surface; to plan dimensions in **Figure J.18**.
Combustible material	Not beneath constructional hearths, unless 50mm between underside of hearth and the combustible material, or 250mm below top of hearth (**Figure J.19**). Combustible material placed on or besides a constructional hearth should not extend under superimposed hearth by more than 25mm or closer than 150mm to the appliance, measured horizontally (**Figure J.21**).
Hearth surface	Free of combustible material (**Figure J.20**), and with edges marked (e.g. a change of level) to warn occupants and to discourage combustible floor finishes being laid too close.

Figure J.18 Constructional hearth suitable for a solid fuel appliance (including open fires) plan view

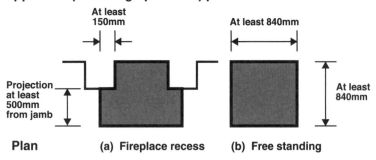

Plan   (a) Fireplace recess   (b) Free standing

Figure J.19 Constructional hearths suitable for solid fuel appliances (including open fires) cross-section

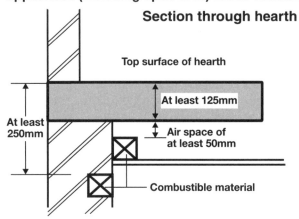

Figure J.20 Non-combustible hearth surface surrounding a solid fuel appliance

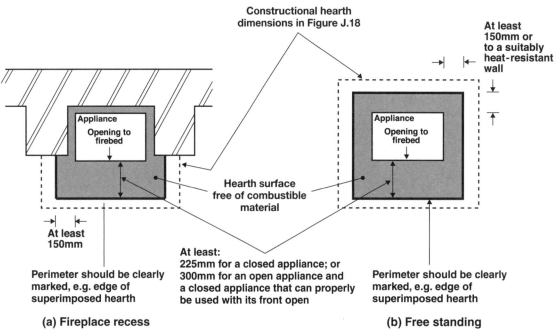

(a) Fireplace recess   (b) Free standing

Figure J.21 Ways of providing hearths

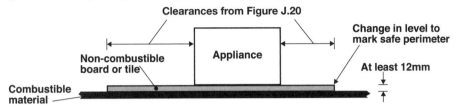

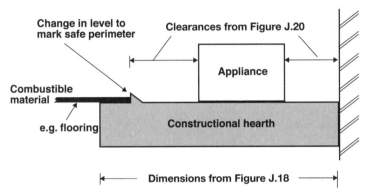

(a) Appliance that cannot cause hearth temperature to exceed 100°C

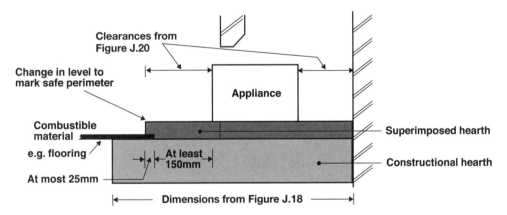

(b) Any appliance standing directly on a constructional hearth

(c) Any appliance in a fireplace recess with a superimposed hearth

J.3.11 Fireplace recesses and appliance chambers

Fireplaces should be constructed so as to protect the building fabric from catching fire. That may be achieved as follows:

- Prefabricated, factory-made appliance chambers of components of insulating concrete with a density of 1200–1700kg/m³, and minimum thickness as given in Table J.7. Components should be supplied as sets for assembly and jointing in accordance with the manufacturer's instructions.

- A fireplace recess of masonry or concrete, as shown in Figure J.22. The recess may need to be protected from heat if it is to be used with appliances such as inset open fires; it may be lined with firebricks or lining components.

Table J.7 Prefabricated appliance chambers: minimum thickness

Component	Minimum thickness (mm)
Base	50
Side section, forming wall on either side of chamber	75
Back section, forming rear of chamber	100
Top slab, lintel or gather, forming top of chamber	100

Figure J.22 Fireplace recesses

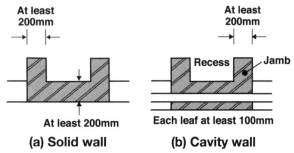

(a) Solid wall **(b) Cavity wall**

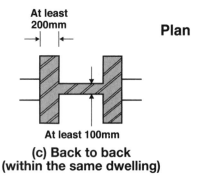

Plan

(c) Back to back (within the same dwelling)

Walls adjacent to hearths, which do not form part of the fireplace recess or appliance chamber, also need to protect the building from catching fire. This may be achieved by the methods shown in Figure J.23 and Table J.8, although thinner material could be used if it would give the same level of protection as solid non-combustible material.

Table J.8 Non-combustible materials adjacent to hearths

Location of hearth or appliance	Solid, non-combustible material	
	Thickness (T)	Height (H)
Hearth abuts a wall, appliance not more than 50mm from the wall	200mm	At least 300mm above the appliance and 1.2m above the hearth
Hearth abuts a wall, appliance is 50–300mm from the wall	75mm	At least 300mm above the appliance and 1.2m above the hearth
Hearth does not abut a wall and is within 150mm of the wall	75mm	At least 1.2m above the hearth
Hearth does not abut a wall and is more than 150mm from the wall	No requirement	No requirement

Figure J.23 Walls adjacent to hearths

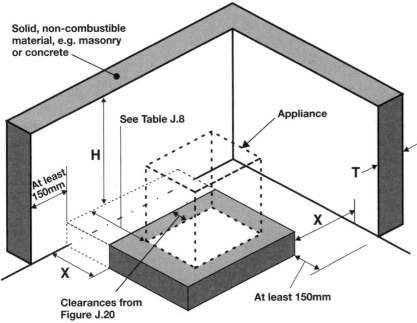

Solid, non-combustible material, e.g. masonry or concrete

See Table J.8

Appliance

H

T

At least 150mm

X

X

Clearances from Figure J.20

At least 150mm

Note: Where X >150mm, there is no requirement for protection of the wall

J.3.12 Carbon monoxide alarms

When a new or replacement solid fuel appliance is installed a carbon monoxide alarm should be provided in the same room. The alarm should comply with BS EN 50291, be powered by a battery with the same working life as the alarm, and have a warning device to alert users when working life is due to expire. BS EN 50291 Type A alarms with fixed mains wiring may be used, providing they have a sensor failure warning device.

The alarm should be located on the ceiling at least 300mm from a wall, or on a wall as high up as possible (above doors and windows) but not within 150mm of the ceiling, and 1–3m horizontally from the appliance.

Further guidance
BS EN 50291:2001. Electrical apparatus for the detection of carbon monoxide in domestic premises. Test methods and performance requirements. [Withdrawn, replaced by BS EN 50291-1:2010+A1:2012. Electrical apparatus for the detection of carbon monoxide in domestic premises. Test methods and performance requirements.]

BS EN 50292:2002. Electrical apparatus for the detection of carbon monoxide in domestic premises. Guide on the selection, installation, use and maintenance.

J.4 Gas-burning appliances to 70kW rated input

The installation of gas appliances should either follow the guidance in this section, or achieve the equivalent level of performance by following the relevant recommendations in:

- BS 5440: Flueing and ventilation for gas appliances of rated input not exceeding 70 kW net (1st, 2nd and 3rd family gases):
  - Part 1:2008. Specification for installation of gas appliances to chimneys and for maintenance of chimneys;
  - Part 2:2009. Specification for the installation and maintenance of ventilation provision for gas appliances;

- BS 5546:2000 Specification for installation of hot water supplies for domestic purposes, using gas-fired appliances of rated input not exceeding 70kW [Withdrawn, replaced by BS 5546:2010];
- BS 5864:2004 Specification for installation in domestic premises of gas-fired ducted-air heaters of rated input not exceeding 60kW [Withdrawn, replaced by BS 5864:2010];
- BS 5871: Specification for installation of gas fires, convector heaters, fire/back boilers and decorative fuel effect gas appliances:
  - Part 1:2005 Gas fires, convector heaters and fire/back boilers and heating stoves (1st, 2nd and 3rd family gases);
  - Part 2:2005 Inset live fuel effect gas fires of heat input not exceeding 15kW and fire/back boilers (2nd and 3rd family gases);
  - Part 3:2005 Decorative fuel effect gas appliances of heat input not exceeding 20kW (2nd and 3rd family gases);
- BS 6172:2004 Specification for installation of domestic gas cooking appliances (1st, 2nd and 3rd family gases) [Withdrawn, replaced by BS 6172:2010];
- BS 6173:2001 Specification for installation of gas-fired catering appliances for use in all types of catering establishments (2nd and 3rd family gases) [Withdrawn, replaced by BS 6173:2009];
- BS 6798:2009 Specification for installation of gas-fired boilers of rated input not exceeding 70kW net.

Further guidance
BS 5546:2010. Specification for installation and maintenance of gas-fired water-heating appliances of rated input not exceeding 70kW net.
BS 5864:2010. Installation and maintenance of gas-fired ducted air heaters of rated heat input not exceeding 70kW net (2nd and 3rd family gases). Specification.
BS 6172:2010. Specification for installation, servicing and maintenance of domestic gas cooking appliances (2nd and 3rd family gases).
BS 6173:2009. Specification for installation and maintenance of gas-fired catering appliances for use in all types of catering establishments (2nd and 3rd family gases).

J.4.1 The Gas Safety (Installation and Use) Regulations

The Gas Safety (Installation and Use) Regulations control all aspects of the installation, maintenance and use of gas combustion systems in domestic and commercial premises. There are particular requirements which affect gas installations covered by Part J of the Building Regulations:

- An appliance installed in a room used or intended to be used as a bath or shower room must be room-sealed.
- A gas fire, other gas space heater or gas water heater up to 14kW (gross) heat input (12.7kW (net) heat input) must not be installed in a room used or intended to be used as sleeping accommodation unless it is room-sealed or has a device to shut down the appliance before there is a dangerous build-up of products of combustion. A larger appliance may only be used if it is room-sealed. Those restrictions apply to any cupboard or compartment within the room or an adjacent space with an air vent into the room.
- Instantaneous water heaters (in any room) must be room-sealed or have a shut-down device as above.
- Any flue must be installed in a safe position.
- LPG storage vessels and LPG-fired appliances with automatic ignition or pilot lights must not be installed in cellars or basements.
- On installation, gas appliances must be checked to ensure their safe functioning.
- No alteration is allowed to premises where a gas fitting or storage vessel is fitted, which would adversely affect the safety of that fitting or vessel, so that it would no longer comply with the Regulations.

J.4.2 Gas fires

Categories of gas fires are shown in Figure J.24; the provisions for each type differ.

Figure J.24 Types of gas fire

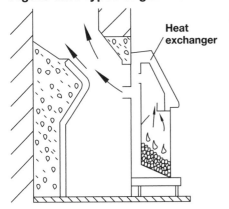

(a) **Radiant convector gas fires, convector heaters and fire/back boilers, as described in BS 5871: Part 1**

These stand in front of a closure plate which is fitted to the fireplace opening of a fireplace recess or suitable fluebox. The appliance covers the full height of the fireplace opening so that air enters only through purpose-designed openings and the flue gases discharge only through the flue spigot.

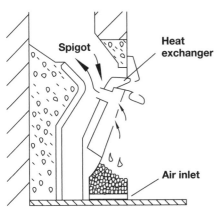

(b) **Inset live fuel effect (ILFE) fires, as described in BS 5871: Part 2**

These stand fully or partially within a fireplace recess or suitable fluebox and give the impression of an open fire. The appliance covers the full height of the fireplace opening so that air enters only through purpose-designed openings and the flue gases discharge only through the flue spigot.

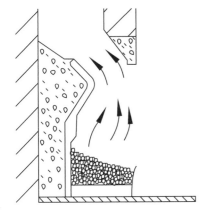

(c) **Decorative fuel effect (DFE) fires, as described in BS 5871: Part 3**

These are gas-fire imitations which can be substituted for the solid fuel appliances in open fires. Where suitable, they can also be used in flueboxes designed for gas appliances only.

Common designs include beds of artificial coals shaped to fit into a fireplace recess or baskets of artificial logs for use in larger fireplaces or under canopies.

Note: For illustration purposes, this diagram shows gas fires installed at or within a fireplace recess formed by fireplace components within a builder's opening. The actual setting for an appliance depends upon its type and manufacturer's installation instructions.

Provided it can be shown to be safe, a gas fire may be installed in a fireplace intended for solid fuel appliances; certain gas fires may also be installed in fireplaces with flues designed specifically for gas appliances. The Gas Appliances (Safety) Regulations 1995 require the particular combinations of appliance, flue box (where required) and flue to have been selected from those stated in the manufacturer's instructions to have being shown to be safe by a Notified Body.

Flueless gas appliances require ventilation as **J.4.3**, but a flueless instantaneous water heater must not be installed in a room or space having a volume less than 5m³.

J.4.3 Air supply

In addition to the guidance in **J.2.1**, the following provisions for air supply should be met.

A room or space intended to contain a flued decorative fuel-effect (DFE) fire requires permanently open air vents:

- a DFE fire in a fireplace recess with a throat having an equivalent free area of at least 10,000mm²;
- a DFE fire in a fireplace with no throat (for example, under a canopy), and the vent area should be sized to Table J.3.

In dwellings with an air permeability worse than 5.0m³/(h.m²), permanently open vents may not be necessary for DFE fires not exceeding 7kW (net) rating, which have a flue gas clearance rate (without spilling) not exceeding 70m³ per hour.

Other flued appliances – such as inset live fuel effect (ILFE) fires, radiant convector fires and boilers, in both room-sealed and open-flued configurations – should have vents sized as shown in Figure J.25.

Flueless appliances may require permanently open air vents or provision for rapid ventilation as BS 5440-2:2009 or equivalent. For appliances such as flueless cookers, water heaters and space heaters, see Figure J.26 and Table J.9. The ventilation provision for a room with a gas point intended for use with a flueless appliance should be based on the largest rated appliance which could be installed.

Further guidance
BS 5440-2:2009. Flueing and ventilation for gas appliances of rated input not exceeding 70kW net (1st, 2nd and 3rd family gases). Specification for the installation and maintenance of ventilation provisions for gas appliances.

Table J.9 Free areas of permanently open air vents for flueless gas appliances

Flueless appliance	Maximum appliance rated heat input	Volume of room or space (m³)	Free areas of permanently open vent (mm²)[1]
Cooker, oven hotplate or grill or a combination	Not applicable	<5	10,000
		5–10	5000[2]
		>10	none required
Instantaneous water heater	11kW (net)	5–10	10,000
		10–20	5000
		>20	none required
Space heater not in an internal space[3][4]	0.045kW (net)/m³ volume of room or space[2]	all cases	10,000 plus 5500 per kW input (net) over 2.7kW (net)
Space heater in an internal space[3][4]	0.090kW (net)/m³ volume of room or space	all cases	10,000 plus 2750 per kW input (net) over 5.4kW (net)

[1] The permanent ventilation provisions listed in this table are additional to the openable elements or extract ventilation in Approved Document F.

[2] No permanently open vent is needed if the room or space has a door direct to outside.

[3] An internal space here means one which communicates with several other rooms or spaces. An example would be a hallway or landing.

[4] For LPG fired space heaters conforming to BS EN 449:2002+A1:2007, follow the guidance in BS 5440-2:2009.

Figure J.25 Free area of permanently open air vents for gas appliance installations (other than DFE fires for flueless appliances)

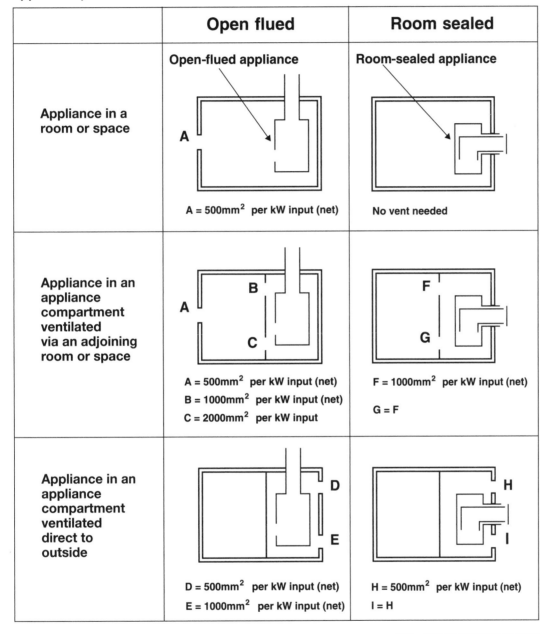

	Open flued	Room sealed
Appliance in a room or space	Open-flued appliance A A = 500mm² per kW input (net)	Room-sealed appliance No vent needed
Appliance in an appliance compartment ventilated via an adjoining room or space	A B C A = 500mm² per kW input (net) B = 1000mm² per kW input (net) C = 2000mm² per kW input	F G F = 1000mm² per kW input (net) G = F
Appliance in an appliance compartment ventilated direct to outside	D E D = 500mm² per kW input (net) E = 1000mm² per kW input (net)	H I H = 500mm² per kW input (net) I = H

Notes:

1. A, D, E, H and I are permanently open vents on the outside. B, C, F and G are permanently open vents between an appliance compartment and a room or a space.
2. Calculations employ the appliance rated net heat input as described in J.1.3 Definitions.
3. The area given above is the free area of the vent(s) or the equivalent free area for ventilators of more complex design.
4. Divide the area given above in mm² by 100 to find the corresponding area in cm².
5. In older dwellings with an air permeability which is more than 5.0m³/(h.m²) the first 7kW(net) can be ignored.

Figure J.26 Ventilation for flueless gas appliances

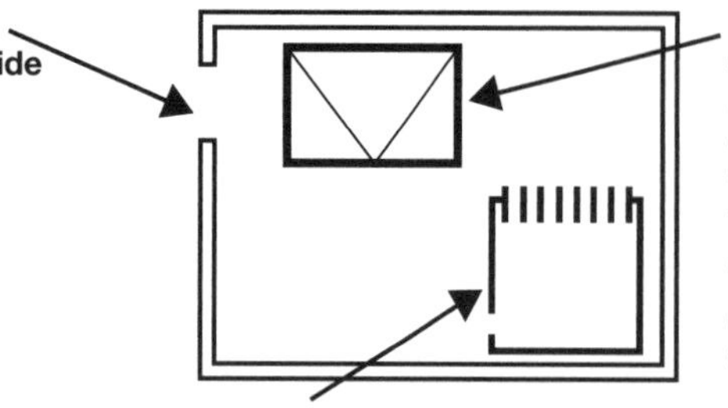

Permanently open vent opening directly to outside with free area not less than that given in Column 4 of Table J.9

In accordance with Approved Document F:

(a) openable window, door or similar form of controllable ventilation opening directly to outside;

or

(b) for a kitchen, mechanical extract ventilation

Flueless appliance with a rating not exceeding that given in Column 2 of Table J.9

J.4.4 Flues

Connecting fluepipes should be of the same diameter and/or cross-sectional area as the appliance flue outlet and the chimney flue should have the same cross-sectional area as that of the appliance flue outlet.

For CE-marked appliances, flues should be sized as per the manufacturer's installation instructions. Where builders wish to provide or refurbish flues for gas appliances but do not intend to fit them, then flues should be sized to Table J.10.

Table J.10 Size of flues for gas-fired appliances			
Intended installation	**Flue**		**Minimum flue size**
Radiant/gas convector fire	New flue:	Circular	125mm diameter
		Rectangular	16,500mm² cross-sectional area, with minimum dimension of 90mm
	Existing flue:	Circular	125mm diameter
		Rectangular	12,000mm² cross-sectional area, with a minimum dimension of 63mm
ILFE or DFE fire within a fireplace with opening up to 500mm × 550mm	Circular or rectangular		Minimum flue dimension of 175mm[1]
DFE fire installed in a fireplace with opening larger than 500mm × 550mm	Calculate as for a comparable solid fuel fireplace as **J.3.3**.		

[1] Some ILFE and DFE appliances require a circular flue of at least 125mm diameter.

J.4.5 Height of flues

For CE-marked appliances the flue height should match that given in the manufacturer's instructions. For older, non-CE-marked appliances:

- for DFE fires – follow guidance in BS 5871-3:2005;
- for other appliances – follow calculation procedures in BS 5440-1:2008.

J.4.6 Outlets from flues

Outlets from flues should be situated to allow dispersal of products of combustion and, for balanced flues, the intake of air, and should follow Figures J.27 and J.28 and Table J.11. To avoid the plume of wet flue products from a condensing boiler being a nuisance, installers should adopt the guidance in chapter 6 of the *Guide to Condensing Boiler Installation Assessment Procedure for Dwellings*.

Further guidance
BS 5871-3:2005 Specification for the installation and maintenance of gas fires, convector heaters, fire/back boilers and decorative fuel effect gas appliances. Decorative fuel effect gas appliances of heat input not exceeding 20kW (2nd and 3rd family gases).

BS 5440-1:2008. [See **J.2.1.2**.]

Figure J.27 Location of outlets from flues serving gas appliances

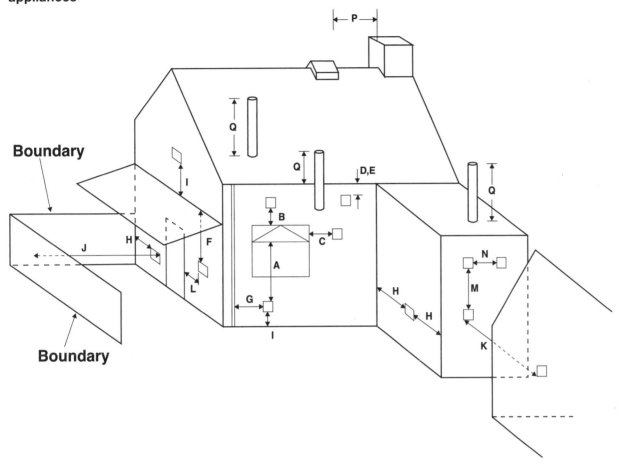

Figure J.28 Location of outlets near roof windows from flues serving gas appliances

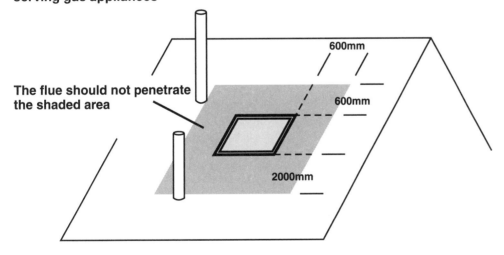

**Terminals adjacent to windows
or openings on pitched and flat roofs**

Table J.11 Minimum separation distances for terminals in Figure J.27

Location		Balanced flue			Open flue	
		Natural draught		Fanned draught	Natural draught	Fanned draught
		Appliance rated heat input (net)				
A	Below an opening[1]	0–7kW	300	300	[3]	300
		>7–14kW	600			
		>14–23kW	1500			
		>32kW	2000			
B	Above an opening[1]	0–32kW	300	300	[3]	300
		>32kW	600			
C	Horizontally to an opening[1]	0–7kW	300	300	[3]	300
		>7–14kW	400			
		>14kW	600			
D	Below gutters, soil pipes or drainpipes	300		75	[3]	75
E	Below eaves	300		200	[3]	200
F	Below balcony or carport roof	600		200	[3]	200
G	From a vertical drainpipe or soil pipe	300		150[4]	[3]	150
H	From an internal or external corner or to a boundary alongside the terminal[2]	600		300	[3]	200
I	Above ground, roof or balcony level	300		300	[3]	300
J	From a surface or boundary facing the terminal[2]	600		600	[3]	600
K	From a terminal facing the terminal	600		1200	[3]	1200
L	From an opening in the carport into the building	1200		1200	[3]	1200
M	Vertically from a terminal on the same wall	1200		1500	[3]	1500
N	Horizontally from a terminal on the same wall	300		300	[3]	300
P	From a structure on the roof	Not applicable		N/A	1500mm if a ridge terminal. Any other terminal as BS 5440-1:2008	N/A
Q	Above the highest point of intersection with the roof	Not applicable		Manufacturer's instructions	Sites as BS 5440-1:2008	150

[1] Opening means an openable element such as a window or fixed opening such as an air vent. The outlet should not be within 150mm (fanned draught) or 300mm (natural draught) to an opening into the building fabric formed for the purpose of accommodating a built-in element, such as a window frame.

[2] Boundary as **J.1.3**. Smaller separations may be acceptable for appliances shown to operate safely in such circumstances.

[3] Should not be used.

[4] Dimension may be reduced to 75mm for appliances up to 5kW input (net).

Flue outlets should be protected where there is a significant risk of blockage, as follows:

- Flues serving natural draught open-flued appliances should be fitted with outlet terminals if the flue diameter is no greater than 170mm, e.g. to BS EN 1856-1:2003 and BS EN 13502:2002.

- Flues more than 170mm require individual assessment. Where nests of squirrels or jackdaws are likely, a protective cage designed for solid fuel use with a mesh of 6–25mm, provided the total equivalent area of its openings is at least twice the cross-sectional area of the flue.

The flue outlet should be protected with a guard if people could come into contact with it or if it could be damaged. In vulnerable areas (for example, near ground) the outlet should be designed to avoid entry of matter which could obstruct the flow of flue gases.

J.4.7 Provision of flues

Connecting fluepipes should be:

- any of the options in **J.2.2.2**;
- sheet metal fluepipes to BS EN 1856-2:2004;
- fibre cement pipes as BS EN 857:2003+A1:2008; or
- any other material or component which has been certified as suitable.

Chimneys and fluepipes should be provided either by following the guidance on selection and installation of components below, or (if the intended appliance is new and of a known type) using factory-made components independently certified to appropriate performance class in Table J.12 and then installed as described below.

Further guidance

BS EN 1856-1:2003. Chimneys. Requirements for metal chimneys. System chimney products. [Withdrawn, replaced by 2009 edition.]

BS EN 13502:2002. Chimneys. Requirements and test methods for clay/ceramic flue terminals.

Guide to condensing boiler installation assessment procedure for dwellings. ODPM. 2005.

Table J.12 Minimum performance designations for chimney and fluepipe components for use with new gas appliances

Appliance type		Minimum designation[1]
Boiler: open flued	Natural draught	T250 N2 D 1 O
	Fanned draught	T250 P2 D 1 O
	Condensing	T140 P2 W 1 O
Boiler: room sealed	Natural draught	T250 N2 D 1 O
	Fanned draught	T250 P2 D 1 O
	Condensing	T140 P2 W 1 O
Gas fire – radiant/convector, ILFE or DFE		T250 N2 D 1 O
Air heater	Natural draught	T250 N2 D 1 O
	Fanned draught	T250 P2 D 1 O
	SE – duct	T250 N2 D 1 O

[1] Default designations. Follow appliance manufacturer's instructions if a higher designation is specified.

Masonry chimneys should follow **J.2.2.3**; flueblock chimneys should be as **J.2.2.4**, or be factory-made flueblock systems which comply with:

- BS EN 1858-1:2003 for concrete flueblocks of at least Class D2; or
- BS EN 1806:2006 for clay/ceramic flueblocks with performance class at least FB4 N2.

Flues should be installed with sealed joints to the manufacturer's instructions. Bends and offsets should be formed with matching factory-made components, appropriately supported and restrained. Factory-made metal chimneys should meet **J.2.2.6** and should be guarded if they would present a burn hazard.

Combustible materials should be protected from heat from flues, as Table J.13.

Further guidance
BS EN 1856-1:2003. Chimneys. Requirements for metal chimneys. System chimney products. [Withdrawn, replaced by 2009 edition.]

BS EN 1856-2:2004. Chimneys. Requirements for metal chimneys. Metal liners and connecting fluepipes. [Withdrawn, replaced by 2009 edition.]

BS EN 1857:2003+A1:2008. Chimneys. Components. Concrete flue liners. [Withdrawn, replaced by 2010 edition.]

BS EN 1806:2006. Chimneys. Clay/ceramic flue blocks for single wall chimneys. Requirements and test methods.

Table J.13 Protecting buildings from hot flues

Flues within	Protecting measures
Connecting fluepipes	Flues at least 25mm from any combustible surface. When passing through a combustible wall, floor or roof (other than a compartment wall, floor or roof) this separation can be achieved by enclosing the fluepipe or chimney with a 25mm air-space to the relevant flue wall).
Factory-made chimney appropriately designated to BS EN 1856-1:2003	
Factory-made chimney appropriately designated to BS EN 1856-1:2003 and BS EN 1856-2:2004	Install in accordance with **Table J.2** with separation distances according to flue designation.
Masonry chimney	Provide at least 25mm of masonry between flues and any combustible material.
Flue block chimney	Provide flueblock walls at least 25mm thick.

J.4.8 Relining of flues in chimneys

Relining of flues may be carried out using:

- liners as Table J.1;
- liners as **J.3.7**;
- flexible stainless steel liners to BS EN 1856-1:2003;
- other independently certified systems.

Flexible metal liners should be installed in one complete length without joints, and the space between chimney and liner left empty (unless the manufacturer's instructions say otherwise). Double-skin flexible liners should be installed in accordance with the manufacturer's instructions. BS 715 liners should be installed as BS 5440-1:2008.

Further guidance
BS EN 1856-1:2003. [See **J.4.7**.]

BS 715:2005. Specification for metal flue boxes for gas-fired appliances not exceeding 20kW. [The 1993 edition of BS 715 contained guidance on chimneys and flues, but the 2005 edition addresses only metal flue boxes. All other requirements and recommendations are now in BS EN 1856-1 and -2. The text of Approved Document J 2010 does not reflect those changes.]

BS 5440-1:2008. [See **J.2.1.2**.]

J.4.9 Debris collection space

A debris collection space should be provided at the base of the flue, unless it is lined, or constructed of flue blocks, or is a factory-made chimney with a flue box. The debris collection should have a minimum volume of 12 litres and a depth of at least 250mm below the point where flue gases discharge into the chimney. The space should be readily accessible for the clearance of debris, for example by removal of the appliance.

For gas fires as those shown in Figure J.24 (a) and (b) there should be 50mm clearance between the end of the appliance flue outlet and any surface.

Figure J.29 Bases for back boilers showing proprietary back boiler enclosure

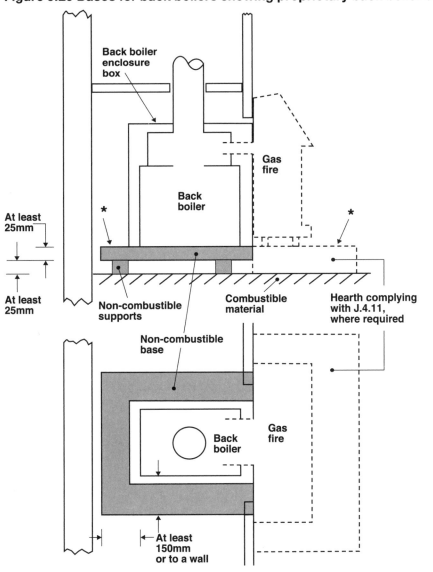

Back boiler
enclosure
box

Gas
fire

Back
boiler

*

At least
25mm

*

At least
25mm

Non-combustible
supports

Combustible
material

Hearth complying
with J.4.11,
where required

Non-combustible
base

Gas
fire

Back
boiler

◄── At least
150mm
or to a wall

* Where the gas fire requires a hearth, the
back boiler base should be level with it

J.4.10 Bases for back boilers

To protect the building fabric from heat, back boilers should either stand on a
hearth intended for solid fuel appliances, or on a base complying with Figure J.29.

J.4.11 Hearths

An appliance should be installed on a hearth unless:

- the manufacturer's instructions state none is required; or
- it is installed so that every part of the flame or incandescent material is at least
  225mm above the floor.

Figure J.30 Hearths for DFE and ILFE fires: minimum plan dimensions for non-combustible surfaces

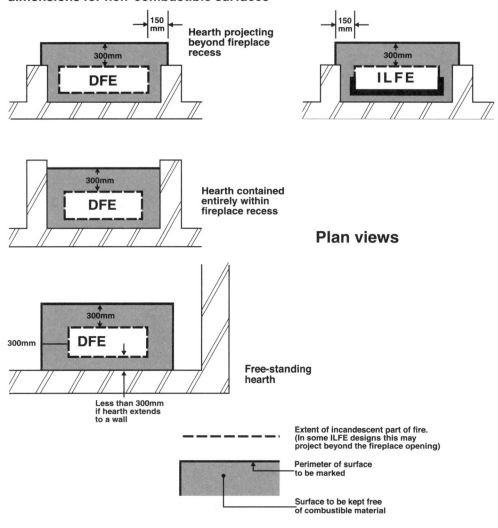

Plan views

Figure J.31 Hearths for other appliances: plan dimensions of non-combustible surfaces

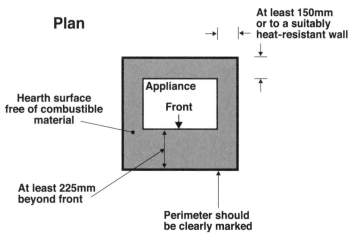

Hearths should be dimensioned as Figures J.30 and J.31 and, as a minimum, should have a top layer of 12mm non-friable non-combustible material. The edge should be marked – for example by a change of level – to warn occupants and to discourage combustible floor finishes from being set too close.

J.4.12 Shielding of appliances

Appliances should be located where accidental contact is unlikely, and should be surrounded by a non-combustible surface which protects combustible materials. That may be provided by:

- following the manufacturer's instructions; or
- a shield of non-combustible material at least 25mm thick, with a fire-resistant surface; or
- an airspace of at least 75mm (Figure J.32).

Figure J.32 Shielding of appliances

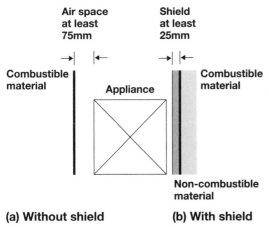

Air space at least 75mm

Shield at least 25mm

Combustible material

Appliance

Combustible material

Non-combustible material

(a) Without shield   (b) With shield

J.5 Oil-burning appliances up to 45kW rated output

The guidance covers combustion installations designed to burn:

- oils to BS 2869:2006 Class C2 (Kerosene) and Class D (Gas oil), or equivalent;
- liquid biofuel to EN 14213:2003;
- blends of mineral oil and liquid biofuels.

The installation of oil-burning appliances should either follow the guidance in this section, or achieve the equivalent level of performance by following the relevant recommendations in BS 5410-1:1997.

J.5.1 Appliances in bathrooms and bedrooms

Open-flued oil-fired appliances are not to be installed in rooms such as bathrooms and bedrooms; room-sealed appliances should be used if an appliance is required.

Further guidance
BS 2869:2006. Fuel oils for agricultural, domestic and industrial engines and boilers. Specification. [Withdrawn, replaced by BS 2869:2010+A1:2011.]

BS EN 14213:2003. Heating fuels. Fatty acid methyl esters (FAME). Requirements and test methods. [Withdrawn, replaced by BS EN 14214:2012. Liquid petroleum products. Fatty acid methyl esters (FAME) for use in diesel engines and heating applications. Requirements and test methods.]

BS 5410-1:1997. Code of practice for oil firing. Installations up to 45kW output capacity for space heating and hot water supply purposes.

Figure J.33 Free areas of permanently open air vents for oil-fired appliance installations

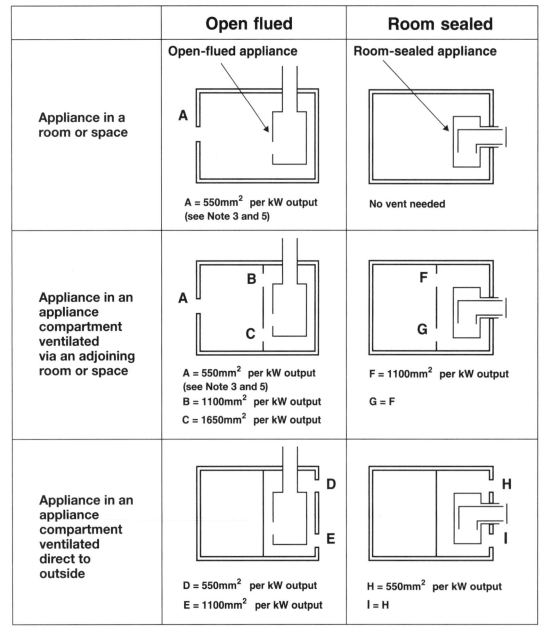

Notes:

1. A, D, E, H and I are permanently open vents on the outside. B, C, F and G are permanently open vents between an appliance compartment and a room or space.

2. The area given above is the free area of the vent(s) or the equivalent free area for ventilators of more complex design.

3. Vent A should be increased by a further 550mm^2 per kW output if the appliance is fitted with a draught break.

4. Divide the area given above in mm^2 by 100 to find the corresponding area in cm^2.

5. In older dwellings with an air permeability which is more than 5.0m^3/(h.m^2) the first 5kW(net) can be ignored.

J.5.2 Air supply

The air supply should be as **J.2.1** with permanently open vents as Figure J.33, or greater if specified in the manufacturer's instructions.

J.5.3 Flues

Connecting fluepipes should have the same size as the appliance flue outlet. Flues in chimneys should have the same cross-sectional area as the appliance outlet flue, which may be achieved in masonry or flueblock chimneys by:

- making the flue the same size as the appliance flue outlet; or
- making the flue larger so a flexible flue liner could later be installed.

In some cases the manufacturer's instructions may require larger flues.

Flue outlets should be located as shown in Figure J.34 and Table J.14 to disperse the products of combustion effectively and provide a suitable air intake for balanced flues. Flue outlets should be protected with terminal guards to avoid harm to persons and damage to the outlet.

Figure J.34 Location of outlets from flues serving oil-fired appliances

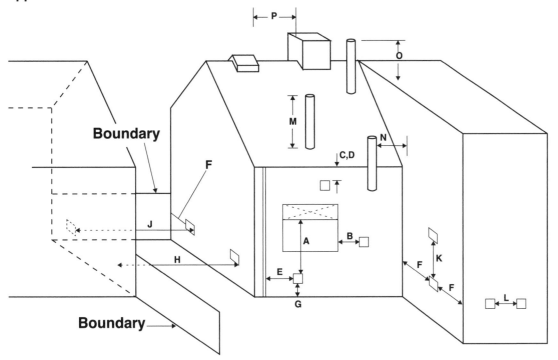

Table J.14 Minimum separation distances for terminals in Figure J.34

Location of outlet[1]		Appliance with pressure jet burner	Appliance with vaporising burner
A	Below an opening[2][3]	600	[5]
B	Horizontally to an opening[2][3]	600	[5]
C	Below a plastic/painted gutter, drainage pipe or eaves if combustible material protected[4]	75	[5]
D	Below a balcony or plastic/painted gutter, drainage pipe or eaves without protection to combustible material	600	[5]
E	From vertical sanitary pipework	300	[5]
F	From an external or internal corner or from a surface or boundary alongside the terminal	300	[5]
G	Above ground or balcony level	300	[5]
H	From a surface or boundary facing the terminal	600	[5]
J	From a terminal facing the terminal	1200	[5]
K	Vertically from a terminal on the same wall	1500	[5]
L	Horizontally from a terminal on the same wall	750	[5]
M	Above the highest point of an intersection with the roof	600[7]	1000[6]
N	From a vertical structure to the side of the terminal	750[7]	2300
O	Above a vertical structure which is less than 750mm (pressure jet burner) or 2300mm (vaporising burner) horizontally from the side of the terminal	600[7]	1000[6]
P	From a ridge terminal to a vertical structure on the roof	1500	[5]

[1] Terminals should only be positioned on walls where appliances have been approved for such configurations when tested in accordance with BS EN 303-1:1999 or OFTEC Standards OFS A100 or OFS A101.

[2] An openable element, such as an openable window, or a permanent opening such as a permanently open air vent.

[3] Notwithstanding the dimensions above, a terminal should be at least 300mm from combustible material, e.g. a window frame.

[4] A way of providing protection of combustible material would be to fit a heat shield at least 750mm wide.

[5] Should not be used.

[6] Where a terminal is used with a vaporising burner, the terminal should be at least 2300mm horizontally from the roof.

[7] Outlets for vertical balanced flues in locations M, N and O should be in accordance with manufacturer's instructions.

J.5.4 Flue gas temperature

The temperature of flue gases depends on the appliance type and its age: older appliances are likely to produce gases at temperatures greater than 250°C, while more modern, CE-marked boilers will not usually exceed 250°C. Condensing appliances will usually have flue gases well below 100°C. Where data on flue gas temperature is not available the temperature should be assumed to be greater than 250°C.

For temperatures above 250°C the guidance in **J.2** and **J.3** for connecting fluepipes, masonry or flueblock chimneys or factory-made metal chimneys should be followed.

Where temperatures are lower than 250°C:

- for new appliances, use independently certified factory-made components corresponding to the designation in Table J.15, for appliance type, installed in accordance with the manufacturer's instructions; or

- follow the guidance for chimneys given below.

Table J.15 Minimum performance designations for chimney and fluepipe components for use with new oil-fired appliances with flue gas temperature less than 250°C

Appliance type	Fuel type	Minimum designation[1]
Condensing boiler, including combination boiler, range cooker, range cooker/boiler – with pressure-jet burners.	Class C2 oil (kerosene) Liquid biofuel to EN 14213:2003	T120 N2 W1 O
	Class D oil (heating oil)	T160 N2 W2 O
Non-condensing boiler, including combination boiler, range cooker, range cooker/boiler – with pressure-jet burners.	Class C2 oil (kerosene) Liquid biofuel to EN 14213:2003	T250 N2 D1 O
	Class D oil (heating oil)	T250 N2 D2 O
Cooker and room heater – with vaporising burner.	Class C2 oil (kerosene)	T160 N2 D1 O
	Class D oil (heating oil)	T250 N2 D2 O

[1] Default designations. Follow appliance manufacturer's instructions if a higher designation is specified.

Connecting fluepipes should be:

- any of the options in **J.2.2.2**;
- sheet metal fluepipes to BS EN 1856-2:2004;
- fibre cement pipes as BS EN 857:2003+A1:2008;
- or any other material or component which has been certified as suitable.

Masonry chimneys should be as **J.2.2.3**. Flueblock chimneys should be to **J.2.2.4** or factory-made systems to:

- BS EN 1858:2008 for concrete flueblocks;
- BS EN 1806:2006 for clay/ceramic flueblocks, with designation appropriate to the appliance.

Flueblock chimneys should be installed as per the manufacturer's instructions, with sealed joints and with bends and offsets formed with factory-made matching components.

Factory-made metal chimneys should be as **J.2.2.6**.

The building fabric should be protected from heat from flues. The measures in Table J.16 apply if the flue gas temperature is not above 250°C.

A fluepipe or chimney which penetrates a fire compartment wall or floor should not breach the fire separation requirements of Part B (**B.5.2**). It should be guarded if it would be at risk of damage or could present a hazard to occupants.

Further guidance

BS EN 1856-1:2003. Chimneys. Requirements for metal chimneys. System chimney products. [Withdrawn, replaced by 2009 edition.]

BS EN 1856-2:2004. Chimneys. Requirements for metal chimneys. Metal liners and connecting fluepipes. [Withdrawn, replaced by 2009 edition.]

BS EN 1857:2003+A1:2008. Chimneys. Components. Concrete flue liners. [Withdrawn, replaced by 2010 edition.]

BS EN 1806:2006. Chimneys. Clay/ceramic flue blocks for single wall chimneys. Requirements and test methods.

BS EN 1858:2008. Chimneys. Components. Concrete flue blocks. [Now +A1:2011.]

Table J.16 Protecting building from hot flues for flue gas temperatures no more than 250°C

Flues within	Protecting measures
Connecting fluepipes	Flues at least 25mm from any combustible surface. When passing through a combustible wall, floor or roof (other than a compartment wall, floor or roof) this separation can be achieved by enclosing the fluepipe or chimney with a 25mm air space to the relevant flue wall).
Factory-made chimney appropriately designated to BS EN 1856-1:2003	
Factory-made chimney appropriately designated to BS EN 1856-1:2003 and BS EN 1856-2:2004	Install in accordance with **Table J.2** with separation distances according to flue designation.
Masonry chimney	Provide at least 25mm of masonry between flues and any combustible material.
Flue block chimney	Provide flueblock walls at least 25mm thick.
Flue assemblies for room-sealed appliances	Flues passing through combustible walls should be surrounded by at least 50mm of insulating material. Provide minimum 50mm clearance from the edge of the flue outlet to any combustible wall cladding.

J.5.5 Re-lining flues in chimneys

Re-lining of flues should follow the guidance in **J.2.3.2**. Where flue gases are likely to be over 250°C liners should be:

- liners as **J.2.2.3**;
- liners as **J.3.7**;
- flexible stainless steel liners to BS EN 1858:2008;
- other independently certified systems.

For flue gas temperatures under 250°C, liners should be:

- any of the liners listed above;
- for a new appliance of known type, a lining system independently certified to have performance to required designation in Table J.15.

Flues expected to serve appliances burning Class D oil should be made of materials which are resistant to acids of sulphur (minimum designation D2 for non-condensing appliances, or W2 for condensing appliances, to BS EN 1443:2003).

Flexible metal liners should be installed as specified at **J.4.8**.

Further guidance
BS EN 1443:2003. Chimneys. General requirements.

BS EN 1858:2008. [See **J.5.4**.]

J.5.6 Hearths

If the operation of the appliance is unlikely to raise the temperature of the floor beneath to above 100°C (when tested to, for example, OFS A100 and OFS A101) then no special measures are required beyond a rigid, imperforate, non-absorbent sheet of non-combustible material, such as a steel tray – which may be provided as an integral part of the appliance.

Above 100°C a more substantial hearth is required, such as for solid fuel appliances (**J.3.10**) shown in Figures J.24 and J.25, but with the distance to any combustible material as Figure J.35.

Further guidance
OFS A100. *Heat boilers with atomising burners. Outputs up to 70kW. Maximum operating pressures of 3 Bar.* OFTEC. 2004.

OFS A101. *Oil fired cookers with atomising or vaporising burners with or without boilers. Heat outputs up to 45kW.* OFTEC. 2004.

Figure J.35 Location of an oil-fired appliance in relation to its hearth

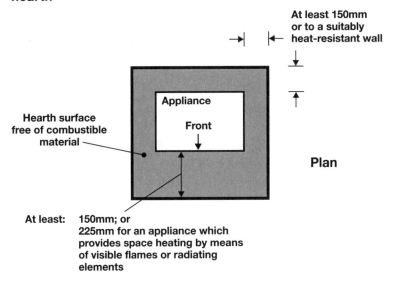

At least 150mm
or to a suitably
heat-resistant wall

Appliance

Front

Hearth surface
free of combustible
material

Plan

At least: 150mm; or
225mm for an appliance which
provides space heating by means
of visible flames or radiating
elements

J.5.7 Shielding of appliances

Combustible materials adjacent to an oil-fired appliance may need to be protected from heat. Appliances independently certified as having a surface temperature during operation of not more than 100°C should not normally require shielding. Otherwise there should be:

- a shield of non-combustible material, for example, insulating board with fire-resistant surface; or

- an air space of at least 75mm (Figure J.32).

J.6 Liquid fuel storage and supply

Oil and LPG storage installations and connecting pipework should be located and constructed so as to be reasonably protected from fires in buildings or beyond boundaries. Oil storage tanks and connecting pipework to combustion appliances in private dwellings should also be:

- reasonably resistant to physical damage and corrosion, and designed and installed to minimise risk of oil escape during filling or maintenance; and

- incorporate secondary containment if there is a significant risk of pollution; and

- be labelled with information on how to respond to a leak.

J.6.1 Oil storage – protection against fire

The guidance here applies to above-ground or semi-buried storage tanks of 3500 litre capacity or less, used exclusively for heating oils (Classes C2 and D to BS 2869:2006, liquid biofuels to BS EN 14213:2003 and mixtures of those oils and liquid biofuels). Additional guidance is given in BS 5410-1:1997.

For tanks over 3500 litres the advice of the fire authority should be sought.

Table J.17 Fire protection for oil storage tanks

Location of tank	Protection usually satisfactory
Within a building	Locate tanks in a place of special fire hazard which should be directly ventilated to outside. Particular care should be taken in complying with Part B.
Less than 1800mm from any part of a building	(a) Make building walls imperforate[1] within 1800mm of tanks with at least 30 minutes' fire resistance (**B.2.1**) to internal fire and construct eaves within 1800mm of tanks and extending 300mm beyond each side of tanks with at least 30 minutes' fire resistance to external fire and with non-combustible cladding; or (b) Provide a fire wall[2] between the tank and any part of the building within 1800mm of the tank and construct eaves as (a). Fire wall should extend at least 300mm higher and wider than affected parts of the tank.
Less than 760mm from a boundary	Provide a fire wall between the tank and the boundary or boundary wall, having at least 30 minutes' fire resistance to fire on either side. Fire wall should extend at least 300mm higher and wider than the top and sides of the tank.
At least 1800mm from the building and at least 760mm from a boundary	No further provisions necessary.

[1] Ignoring small openings such as air bricks.

[2] Fire wall: Imperforate non-combustible walls or screens, such as masonry walls or fire-rated composite panel screens.

Appropriate fire resistance may be provided by means of fire walls constructed to Table J.17. Fire walls should be stable and not present a danger to people around them. To prevent the installation becoming overgrown, there should be a hard surface beneath the tank – of concrete or 42mm thick paving slabs – extending to at least 300mm beyond the perimeter of the tank (or the external skin if it is integrally bunded).

Pipework should be fire-resistant and have a proprietary fire valve system to BS 5410-1:1997, sections 8.2 and 8.3.

J.6.2 Risk of oil pollution

For tanks to which Requirement J7 applies (above ground, domestic, smaller than 3500 litres capacity), secondary containment should be provided where there is a significant risk of oil pollution, if the installation:

- has a capacity more than 2500 litres; or
- is within 10m of inland fresh waters or coastal waters; or
- is located where spillage could run into an open drain or loose-fitting manhole cover; or
- is within 50m of sources of potable water, such as wells, boreholes and springs; or
- is located where oil spilled could reach the waters listed above by running across hard ground; or
- is located where tank vent pipe outlets cannot be seen from the intended filling point; or
- is within Zone 1 (inner protection zone) of an Environment Agency groundwater Source Protection Zone (SPZ).

Further guidance

BS 2869:2006. Fuel oils for agricultural, domestic and industrial engines and boilers. Specification. [Withdrawn, replaced by BS 2869:2010+A1:2011.]

BS EN 14213:2003. Heating fuels. Fatty acid methyl esters (FAME). Requirements and test methods. [Withdrawn, replaced by BS EN 14214:2012. Liquid petroleum products. Fatty acid methyl esters (FAME) for use in diesel engines and heating applications. Requirements and test methods.]

BS 5410-1:1997. Code of practice for oil firing. Installations up to 45kW output capacity for space heating and hot water supply purposes.

Your garden walls: Better to be safe than sorry. ODPM. 2004. [Guidance on wall thicknesses, based on BRE Good Building Guides 13 and 14.]

Note that 'inland fresh waters' includes streams, rivers, reservoirs, and lakes, as well as ditches and ground drainage pipes that feed into them.

Secondary containment could be provided by the use of an integrally bunded prefabricated tank, or constructing masonry or a concrete bund. Where the bund walls are part of the walls of a chamber or building enclosing the tank, any door through such walls should be above bund level. Specialist advice should be sought where the bund plays a structural role in the building.

Bunds should have a capacity of at least 110 percent of the largest tank they contain. Integrally bunded oil tanks will meet that provision if they comply with:

* OFS T100 Oil Firing Equipment Standard – Polyethylene Oil Storage Tanks for Distillate Fuels (2008); or
* OFS T100 Oil Firing Equipment Standard – Steel Oil Storage Tanks and Tank Bunds for use with Distillate Fuels, Lubrication Oils and Waste Oils (2008).

The oil installation should be prominently labelled with advice on what to do if an oil spill occurs and the telephone number of the Environment Agency's Emergency Hotline.

J.6.3 LPG storage installations

LPG storage installations are controlled by legislation enforced by the Health and Safety Executive (HSE). The amount of building work necessary for compliance depends upon the capacity, whether the storage tanks are above or below ground, and the nature of the premises served. A storage installation built in accordance with the industry Code of Practice will comply with legislation. For an installation up to 1.1 tonne capacity with a tank in the open, the guidance below and in Part B will usually be sufficient.

The storage system should comply with UKLPG Code of Practice 1 Bulk LPG Storage at Fixed Installations Part 1 (2009) and BS 5482-1:2005. The tank should be outdoors and not within an open pit. It should be separated from buildings, the boundary and any fixed sources of ignition, in accordance with the distances given in Table J.18 and Figure J.36. Drains, gullies and cellar hatches within the separation distances should be protected from gas entry.

Further guidance

www.environment-agency.gov.uk/research/library/maps [The Environment Agency's Groundwater Sources map, which shows the location of SPZs.]

Pollution Prevention Guide 2 (PPGs) *Above Ground Oil Storage Tanks*. Environment Agency. 2004. [Replaced by 2011 edition. Contains guidance on constructing masonry and concrete bunds.]

Masonry Bunds for Oil Storage Tanks. CIRIA/ Environment Agency Joint guidelines.
Concrete Bunds for Oil Storage Tanks. CIRIA/ Environment Agency Joint guidelines.

Table J.18 Fire protection for LPG storage tanks		
	Minimum separation distances from buildings, boundaries or fixed sources of ignition (m)	
(A) Capacity of tank not exceeding (tonnes):	**(B) To a tank with no fire wall or to a tank around a fire wall**	**(C) To a tank shielded by a fire wall**
0.25	2.5	0.3
1.1	3	1.5

Figure J.36 Separation or shielding of LPG tanks of up to 1.1 tonne capacity

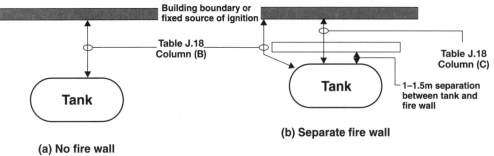

Building boundary or fixed source of ignition

Table J.18 Column (B)

Table J.18 Column (C)

1–1.5m separation between tank and fire wall

Tank

(a) No fire wall

Tank

(b) Separate fire wall

Boundary or building incorporating fire wall

Table J.18 Column (C)

Table J.18 Column (B)

Tank

(c) Boundary incorporating fire wall
or
Building incorporating fire wall
(see also Diagram (d) below)

Example

a 1.1 tonne tank could be located:

3m from a boundary
(Diagram (a))
or
2m from a boundary with an intervening fire wall. The fire wall would stand between 1m and 1.5m from the tank and be wide enough to ensure that the shortest path from tank to boundary remains 3m (Diagram (b))

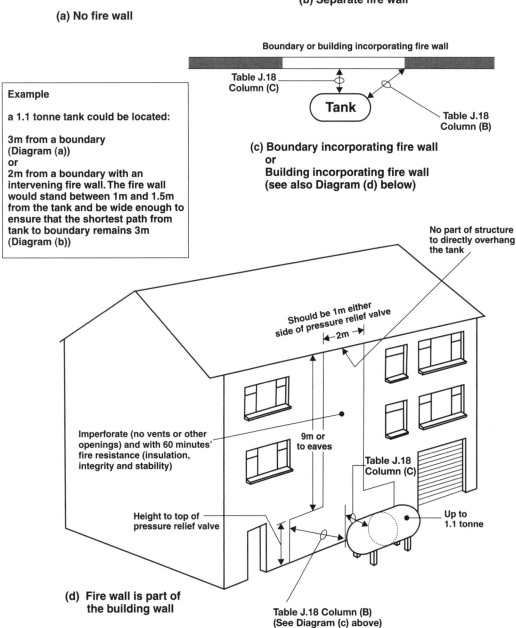

No part of structure to directly overhang the tank

Should be 1m either side of pressure relief valve

|←2m→|

Imperforate (no vents or other openings) and with 60 minutes' fire resistance (insulation, integrity and stability)

9m or to eaves

Table J.18 Column (C)

Height to top of pressure relief valve

Up to 1.1 tonne

Table J.18 Column (B) (See Diagram (c) above)

(d) Fire wall is part of the building wall

Fire walls may be free-standing or part of the building or a boundary wall, but should not be built to more than one side of the tank. Fire walls should be of solid masonry, concrete or similar construction and be imperforate, with fire resistance (REI) (see **B.2.1**) of 30 minutes if free-standing, or 60 minutes if part of the building.

The fire wall should be at least as high as the pressure relief valve and should extend horizontally so that the separation distance in Table J.18 column B is maintained when measured either:

- around the ends of the fire wall (Figure J.36(b)); or
- to the ends of the fire wall as Figure J.36(c) where it forms the boundary or part of the building.

Storage for LPG cylinders should ensure cylinders are:

- upright and secured by chains or straps against a wall outside the building in a well-ventilated position;
- readily accessible;
- protected from damage and not obstructing exit routes.

There should be a firm level base such as 50mm of concrete, or paving slabs bedded on mortar, arranged so the cylinder valves will be:

- at least 1m horizontally and 300mm vertically from openings and heat sources such as flue terminals and tumble-dryer vents; and
- at least 2m horizontally from drains without traps, unsealed gullies or cellar hatches, unless there is an intervening wall at least 250mm high.

Further guidance
BS 5482-1:2005 Code of practice for domestic butane- and propane-gas-burning installations. Installations at permanent dwellings, residential park homes and commercial premises, with installation pipework sizes not exceeding DN 25 for steel and DN 28 for corrugated stainless steel or copper.

Protection from falling, collision and impact

K.1 Scope

Part K is intended to ensure safe circulation for people in and about buildings. It addresses stairs and ramps, guarding, the risk of harm from impact with glazing, doors and windows, and includes provisions for the safe operation and cleaning of windows and other glazing.

Part K: Protection from falling, collision and impact

Requirements	Limits on application
Stairs, ladders and ramps	
K1 Stairs, ladders and ramps shall be so designed, constructed and installed as to be safe for people moving between different levels in or about the building.	Requirement K1 applies only to stairs, ladders and ramps which form part of the building.
Protection from falling	
K2 (a) Any stairs, ramps, floors and balconies and any roof to which people have access; and (b) any light well, basement area or similar sunken area connected to a building, shall be provided with barriers where it is necessary to protect people in or about the building from falling.	Requirement K2(a) applies only to stairs and ramps which form part of the building.
Vehicle barriers and loading bays	
K3 (1) Vehicle ramps and any levels in a building to which vehicles have access shall be provided with barriers where it is necessary to protect people in or about the building. (2) Vehicle loading bays shall be constructed in such a way, or be provided with such features, as may be necessary to protect people in them from collision with vehicles.	
Protection against impact with glazing	
K4 Glazing, with which people are likely to come into contact whilst moving in or about the building shall: (a) if broken on impact, break in a way which is unlikely to cause injury; or (b) resist impact without breaking; or (c) be shielded or protected from impact.	
Protection from collision with open windows etc.	
K5.1 Provision shall be made to prevent people moving in or about the building from colliding with open windows, skylights or ventilators.	Requirement K5.1 does not apply to dwellings.
Manifestation of glazing	
K5.2 Transparent glazing, with which people are likely to come into contact while moving in or about the building, shall incorporate features which make it apparent.	Requirement K5.2 does not apply to dwellings.

Safe opening and closing of windows etc.	
K5.3 Windows, skylights and ventilators which can be opened by people in or about the building shall be so constructed or equipped that they may be opened, closed or adjusted safely.	Requirement K5.3 does not apply to dwellings.
Safe access for cleaning windows etc.	
K5.4 Provision shall be made for any windows, skylights, or any transparent or translucent walls, ceilings or roofs to be safely accessible for cleaning.	Requirement K5.4 does not apply to: (a) dwellings; or (b) any transparent or translucent elements whose surfaces are not intended to be cleaned.
Protection against impact from and trapping by doors	

K6 (1) Provision shall be made to prevent any door or gate:
   (a) which slides or opens upwards, from falling onto any person; and
   (b) which is powered, from trapping any person.
(2) Provision shall be made for powered doors and gates to be opened in the event of a power failure.
(3) Provision shall be made to ensure a clear view of the space on either side of a swing door or gate.
	Requirement K6 does not apply to:
	(a) dwellings, or
	(b) any door or gate which is part of a lift.

The standard of provision appropriate for a building depends on the circumstances; for example:

- Public buildings used by large numbers of people – most of whom will not be familiar with them – will require higher standards of provision than dwellings.

- Provision for maintenance access may be to a lower standard, as greater care can be expected from those carrying out the work.

Approved Document K therefore contains different standards of provision for dwellings, common access areas in buildings containing flats (referred to in this chapter as *common access areas*) and buildings other than dwellings.

K.1.1 Application

The installation of new glazing where previously there was no glazing – whether in a new building, extension or change of use – is subject to Requirements K4 and K5.2, as is the replacement of a whole unit (frame and glazing). However the replacement of glazing, as a repair, is not building work and therefore beyond the scope of Building Regulations.

Access and circulation routes which form part of a means of escape should comply with Requirement B1, Means of warning and escape (see **B.3**), whilst external access routes to a building should comply with Requirement M1 (see **M.3**).

K.1.2 Other regulations

Section 23(3) of the Health and Safety at Work, etc. Act 1974 prevents an inspector from requiring improvement measures more onerous than those necessary to meet Building Regulations, unless the specific requirements of health and safety regulations are more onerous. As a result, complying with the Requirements listed in Table K.1 will prevent the serving of related improvement notices.

2013 changes

Until 2013 the requirements of Part K and the associated guidance conflicted at points with those of Parts M (Access) and N (Glazing). The 2013 revisions have consolidated the requirements and guidance of Parts K and N into an expanded Part K (Part N no longer exists) and conflicts with Part M have been resolved.

Approved Document K has been entirely revised and edited to Plain English standards and set out in a new single column format. There have been no technical changes in requirements or guidance, except for the elimination of minor errors and inconsistencies. However, the 'Alternative approach' of compliance based on standards (for example at paragraph 1.7 of AD K 1998) is no longer in the Approved Document.

Table K.1 Interaction between Part K and health and safety regulations		
Part	Health and safety regulations	Provisions
K1	Regulation 17 – Workplace (Health, Safety and Welfare) Regulations 1992	Permanent stairs, ladders and ramps in workplaces, including for maintenance access
K2	Regulation 6 – Work at Height Regulations 2005	Avoidance of risk of falling
K3	Regulation 17 – Workplace (Health, Safety and Welfare) Regulations 1992	Design of vehicle barriers and loading bays
K4	Regulation 14(1)(a) – Workplace (Health, Safety and Welfare) Regulations 1992	Prevention of personal injury
K5.1	Regulation 15(2) – Workplace (Health, Safety and Welfare) Regulations 1992	Projecting windows, skylights and ventilators
K5.2	Regulation 14(1)(b) – Workplace (Health, Safety and Welfare) Regulations 1992	Marking windows and transparent/translucent doors, gates and walls
K5.3	Regulation 15(1) – Workplace (Health, Safety and Welfare) Regulations 1992	Opening, closing and adjusting windows, skylights and ventilators
K5.4	Regulation 16 – Workplace (Health, Safety and Welfare) Regulations 1992	Cleaning of windows and skylights, etc.
K6	Regulation 18 – Workplace (Health, Safety and Welfare) Regulations 1992	Doors and gates

K.2 Stairs, ladders and ramps (Requirement K1)

Stairs, ladders and ramps should enable people to move safely between different levels in and around the building. External stairs and ramps at a building's entrance should meet Requirement K1, but those which do not form part of a building – for example, those on an access route – need not (although they must still comply with M1).

2013 changes
There is now no minimum change of level at which Requirement K1 applies. Previously the minimum change of level was 600mm in dwellings and 380mm in other buildings.

K.2.1 Stairs

There are three categories of stair:

- private stair – a stair intended to be used for only one dwelling;
- general access stair – intended for all users of a building as a normal day-to-day route between levels; and
- utility stair – used typically for escape or access for maintenance, but not as the usual day-to-day route between levels.

K.2.1.1 Rise, going and pitch

The rise and going of all stairs in a flight should comply with the minimum and maximum figures given for that category in Table K.2, so that the sum of twice the rise plus the going (2R + G) falls in the range of 550–700mm. Rise and going are measured as Figure K.1 (but see **K.2.2.1** for tapered tread stairs).

The dimensions in Table K.2 also apply to work on existing buildings. Where dimensional constraints prevent their application, an alternative proposal should be agreed with the building control body and form part of the access strategy (**M.1.5**).

Table K.2 Rise and going					
Stair type	Rise (mm)		Going (mm)		Notes
	Minimum	Maximum	Minimum	Maximum	
Private stair	150	220	220	300	Maximum pitch 42° External tapered steps which are part of a dwelling should have a minimum going of 280mm
General access stair	150	170	250	400	For school buildings, the preferred rise and going are 150 and 280mm respectively
Utility stair	150	190	250	400	

Figure K.1 Measuring rise and going

DWELLINGS

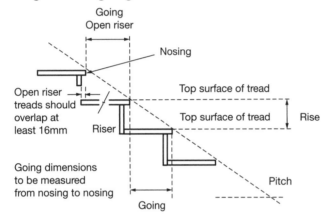

Note: Two examples of tread profiles have been shown together for illustrative purposes only

BUILDINGS OTHER THAN DWELLINGS

(For tread profiles see Figure K.2)

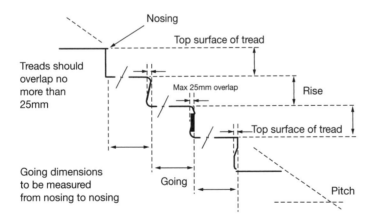

Note: Four examples of tread profiles have been shown together for illustrative purposes only

K.2.1.2 Construction

For all stairs, treads should be level, and rise and going consistent for a flight.

In dwellings, risers may be open, provided:

• treads overlap by at least 16mm; and

• a 100mm diameter sphere cannot pass between treads.

In buildings other than dwellings:

• risers must not be open (to prevent feet or walking aids becoming trapped beneath the stair and causing a fall, and to avoid users feeling insecure when looking through open risers);

• nosings must not protrude over the tread below by more than 25mm, but preferably should not protrude at all (Figure K.2);

• nosings must have permanent contrasting material at least 55mm wide on both tread and riser;

• where the soffit of a stair is less than 2m above floor level the area beneath it must be protected either by guarding and low level cane detection, or by a barrier giving equivalent protection.

For common access areas:

• risers should not be open;

• nosings should have a profile as Figure K.2 and have permanent contrasting material 50–65mm wide on the tread and 30–55mm on the riser.

2013 changes
Most of the guidance here is new to AD K, but has been moved out of AD M. The requirement for risers not to allow a 100mm sphere through now applies only to dwellings, because in all other buildings risers must be solid. The vague test of likely use by a five year old child has been removed from this section.

Figure K.2 Examples of suitable tread nosing profiles

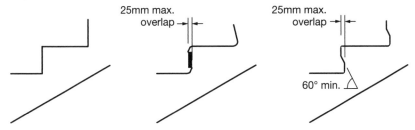

K.2.1.3 Dimensions

The minimum headroom for access between levels is 2m, measured floor to ceiling for landings and pitch line to ceiling for stairs. In buildings other than dwellings and for common access areas, escape routes should have minimum clear headroom of 2m, except in doorways. In loft conversions in dwellings, where space constraints make 2m headroom impracticable, it is permissible to have a minimum height of 1.9m at the centre line, which may reduce to 1.8m at one side.

In buildings other than dwellings:

• stairs that form part of a means of escape should be sized as **B.3.5.2**;

• otherwise, flights should be at least 1.2m wide between walls, strings or upstands and 1m wide between handrails; and

• flights more than 2m wide should be divided into flights at least 1m wide.

Figure K.3 Change of direction in flights

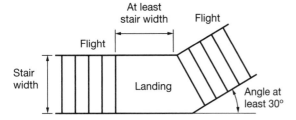

Any stepped change of level within the entrance storey of a dwelling should have a minimum clear width of 900mm.

Where a stair has more than 36 risers in consecutive flights then there should be at least one landing with a 30° change of direction (Figure K.3).

For buildings other than dwellings and common access areas the maximum number of risers on flights between landings is:

- utility stairs – 16 risers;
- general access stairs – 12 risers, but exceptionally no more than 16 in small premises with restricted plan area.

There should not be single steps.

K.2.1.4 Landings

There should be a landing at the top and bottom of every flight: the floor of the building can count towards the area of landing. Landings should be level, except where formed by the ground at the top or bottom of a flight, when a maximum gradient of 1:60 along the direction of travel is permitted provided the ground is paved or made firm.

The length and width of a landing should be at least equal to the narrowest width of the flight: in buildings other than dwellings landings should be at least 1.2m long. Landings which form part of escape routes should comply with **B.3.5.2**.

In all buildings, landings must be clear of permanent obstructions. Doors to cupboards and ducts may open over a landing at the top of a flight provided there is a clear space at least 400mm deep between the door edge and the top step, and the doors are kept shut or locked shut in normal use.

In buildings other than dwellings, no other doors are permitted to swing across landings. In dwellings, a door may open across a landing at the bottom of a flight, but only if there is a clear space of at least 400mm deep between the swing of the door and the first step.

K.2.1.5 Handrails

Handrails should be provided in accordance with Table K.3. In addition, for buildings other than dwellings:

- Where there is full-height structural guarding and a second, lower, handrail is provided, its top surface should be 60mm above the pitch line.

2013 changes
AD K 1998 made no recommendations for minimum stair width, but referred to AD B and AD M. AD K now incorporates guidance originally in AD M.

2013 changes
Door swings across landings at the bottom of stairs are no longer permitted in buildings other than dwellings.

Table K.3 Design of handrails			
Provision	Buildings other than dwellings	Common access areas	Dwellings
Location of handrails	Continuous handrails to each side of flights of stairs, ramps and landings	Continuous handrails to each side of flights of stairs and landings	Both sides of stairs 1000mm or wider Each side of flight and intermediate landings on a stepped change of level in an entrance storey with three or more risers
Height to top of handrail	900–1100mm from landing 900–1000mm from pitch line of stairs	1000mm from landing 900mm from pitch line of stairs	900–1100mm from pitch line or landing
Relation to guarding	Handrail may form part of guarding if heights match		
Other requirements	Extending at least 300mm beyond top and bottom of ramped access or top and bottom nosing of steps	Extending at least 300mm beyond top and bottom nosing of steps	

- A handrail should either be circular (32–50mm diameter), or oval (50mm wide and 39mm deep, with rounded edges of 15mm minimum radius), with ends which will not catch on clothing. The surface should contrast visually with the background, but not be highly reflective; it should be slip-resistant, but not cold to the touch.
- There should be 50–75mm clearance between the rail and an adjacent wall surface, and 50mm to any cranked support. The inner face of the rail should be set no more than 50mm from the edge of ramps or steps, and the rail should not project into an access route.

2013 changes
Most of the guidance on handrails has been translated from AD M.

K.2.1.6 Guarding

Guarding should be provided to stairs and landings:

- in dwellings: where there is a drop greater than 600mm;
- in buildings other than dwellings and common access areas: where there are two or more risers.

The height of guarding should conform to Table K.5. In buildings likely to be used by children under five, guarding should be designed so a 100mm sphere cannot be passed through any opening, to prevent children being trapped; it should not be readily climbable.

K.2.2 Special stairs

K.2.2.1 Tapered treads

On stairs less than 1000m wide, the going should be measured along the centre of the curved stair line and should comply with Table K.2: the narrow end of each stair should have 50mm minimum tread. On wider stairs the going should be measured 270mm in from each side of the stairs; on the wider side the going should not exceed the maximum value in Table K.1, while on the narrow side it should not be less than the minimum value. Landing length should be measured along the centre line.

Consecutive tapered tread should have the same going. On a stair with tapered and straight treads the going of the tapered treads should not be less than that of the straight treads.

Table K.4 Stepped gangways

Feature	Requirement
Pitch	Maximum pitch for gangways to seating areas for spectators is 35°
Steps	The rise of each step in a gangway to be 100–190mm Multiple steps on a single row of seats to have the same rise In stepped tiers, maintain same level between the seatway and the nearest step
Length of flight	A tier uninterrupted by cross-gangways with pitch greater than 25° to have no more than 40 steps
Gangways	Align end of all rows of seats to provide a constant gangway width Minimum gangway width: • for not more than 50 persons: 900mm • for more than 50 people: 1100mm
Handrails	For stepped gangways provide as **K.2.1.5**
Transverse gangways	Provide transverse gangways to give side access to storey exits within the seating layout Transverse and radial gangways should not cross: offset connections between them to enable a smooth flow of people to the exits
Landing	Where an exit is approached from a stepped gangway provide a landing the width of the exit and minimum 1100mm deep, immediately in front of the exit doors

K.2.2.2 Stepped gangways in assembly buildings

Gangways to spectator areas in assembly buildings (e.g. stadia, theatres or cinemas) may need to be at different pitches to maintain sightlines: steps and gangways should comply with Table K.4.

K.2.2.3 Spiral stairs

Spiral and helical stairs should be designed to BS 5395-2.

K.2.2.4 Alternating tread stairs

Alternating tread stairs have paddle-shaped treads with the wide portion on alternate sides on consecutive treads. They may only be used in loft conversions where:

- there is not enough space for other straight flights; and
- they give access to no more than one habitable room with bathroom and/or WC (which must not be the only WC in the dwelling).

Alternative tread stairs should have:

- uniform alternate treads, with parallel nosings and slip-resistant surfaces;
- treads which comply with Table K.1 at the wider part, with a maximum rise of 220mm and minimum going of 220mm: going is measured between alternate treads;
- construction must be as **K.2.1.2**;
- minimum clear headroom of 2m;
- handrails to both sides.

2013 changes
The relaxation on the going for conversions with limited space has been removed.

Further guidance
BS 5395-2:1984. Stairs, ladders and walkways. Code of practice for the design of helical stairs. + AMD 6076, Corrigenda July 2008, C2, C3.

K.2.2.5 Fixed ladders

These may only be used for access to a loft conversion of one habitable room, when there is not enough space to accommodate a standard stair (but see **B.3.6.3**). There must be a fixed handrail to each side. Retractable ladders may not be used as a means of escape.

K.2.2.6 Industrial buildings

Stairs, ladders and walkways should be designed to meet BS 5395-3 or BS 4211.

K.2.2.7 Access for maintenance

Where frequent maintenance access is expected (more than once a month), stairs should comply with the guidance for private stairs in dwellings, or BS 5395-3. Less frequent access may be achieved by temporary means of access, such as portable ladders, which should comply with the provisions of the Construction (Design and Management) Regulations 2007.

K.2.3 Ramps

For buildings other than dwellings, where the change of level is less than 300mm a ramp should be provided instead of a single step. For changes of level of 300mm or more, a ramp should be supplemented by two or more clearly signposted steps.

K.2.3.1 Layout and construction

Ramps should be readily apparent or clearly signposted. The going and gradient of a ramp should be as Figure K.4: a floor level with a gradient of 1:20 or steeper should be designed as a ramp.

Further guidance

BS 5395-3:1985. Stairs, ladders and walkways. Code of practice for the design of industrial type stairs, permanent ladders and walkways. + AMD 14247 [Current, but partly replaced by BS EN ISO 14122 and proposed for withdrawal.]
BS 4211:2005. Specification for permanently fixed ladders. +AMD A1:2008, Corrigenda C1, C2.

Further information

BS 5395-3:1985. See **K.2.2.6**.

2013 changes

The guidance on ramps from AD M 2004 has largely replaced that in AD K 1998.

Figure K.4 Relationship of ramp gradient to going of a flight

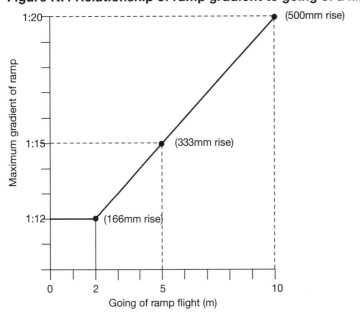

NOTE: For goings between 2m and 10m, it is acceptable to interpolate between the maximum gradients i.e. 1:14 for 4m going or 1:19 for 9m going

In buildings other than dwellings:

- On the open side of any ramp or landing there should be a visually contrasting kerb at least 100mm high, in addition to any guarding.
- The ramp surface should be slip-resistant, especially when wet. It should contrast visually with the surface of the landings but have similar frictional characteristics.
- Where the soffit of a ramp is less than 2m above floor level, the area beneath it must be protected either by guarding and low level cane detection, or by a barrier giving equivalent protection.

K.2.3.2 Dimensions

Ramps should have clear headroom of at least 2m and be clear of permanent obstructions.

In buildings other than dwellings, ramps that provide access for people should be at least 1.5m wide, measured between walls, upstands or kerbs. Ramps forming a means of escape should be sized as **B.3.5.2**.

K.2.3.3 Landings

In dwellings and common access areas, landings for ramps should follow the applicable guidance for landings for stairs in **K.2.1.4**.

In other buildings, landings at the foot and head of a ramp should be 1.2m long and intermediate landings should be 1.5m long. Landings should be level, or have a maximum gradient of 1:60, and be clear of door swings or obstructions. Intermediate passing places should be provided if a wheelchair user cannot see from one end of the ramp to the other, or if the ramp has three or more flights. Passing places should be at least 1.8m wide and 1.8m long.

K.2.3.4 Handrails and guarding

In dwellings and common access areas, ramps 600mm or less in height do not require handrails. Higher ramps require a handrail to at least one side if they are less than 1m wide, or to both sides, if wider. The top of the handrail should be 900–1000mm above the ramp surface, and may form the top of guarding if heights match. Handrails should give firm support and allow firm grip. In other buildings there should be a handrail to each side of the ramp, which should follow **K.2.1.5**.

Ramps and their landings should be guarded in the same way as stairs (see **K.2.1.6**).

K.3 Protection from falling (Requirement K2)

Guarding should be provided:

- in dwellings, where falls of more than 600mm are possible;
- in buildings other than dwellings where falls of more than two risers or 380mm are possible.

2013 changes

The main change in this section is the introduction of Eurocode 1 and the associated Published Document for calculating loading.

It may be required at:

- the edges of any part of a floor (including below an opening window), gallery, balcony or roof;
- the edges of light wells, basements or other sunken areas;
- vehicle parks.

Guarding is not required on ramps used only for vehicle access or where it would obstruct normal use, for example at loading bays.

Guarding, which may be formed by walls, parapets and balustrades, should meet the minimum height requirements in Table K.5 and should be strong enough to resist the loads given in BS EN 1991-1-1 (with UK National Annex) and PD 6688-1-1. Glazing used in guarding should comply with Requirement K.4 (see section **K.5**).

Table K.5 Design of guarding		
Building category	**Location**	**Minimum height**
Single family dwellings	Stairs, landings, ramps, edges of internal floors	900mm for all elements
	External balconies, including Juliette balconies and roof edges	1100mm
Factories and warehouses (light traffic)	Stairs, ramps	900mm
	Landings and edges of floors	1100mm
Residential, institutional, educational, office and public buildings	All locations	900mm for flights, otherwise 1100mm
Assembly	Within 530mm in front of fixed seating	800mm
	All other locations	900mm for flights, otherwise 1100mm
Retail	All locations	900mm for flights, otherwise 1100mm
Glazing in all buildings	At opening windows*	800mm
	At glazing to changes of levels to provide containment	Below 800mm

*Except roof windows in loft extensions (see **B.3.6.1**)

In buildings likely to be used by children under five, guarding should be designed so a 100mm sphere cannot be passed through any opening: to prevent climbing, it should not include horizontal rails.

For areas where only maintenance access is required, but more frequently than once a month, the provision of guarding should meet the standard for dwellings. For less frequent access, temporary guarding or warning notices may be sufficient. Provisions should comply with the Construction (Design and Management) Regulations 2007 and the Work at Height Regulations 2005. Provide signs as specified in the Health and Safety (Safety Signs and Signals) Regulations 1996.

Further guidance
BS EN 1991-1-1:2002. Eurocode 1. Actions on structures. General actions. Densities, self-weight, imposed loads for buildings.
UK National Annex to Eurocode 1. 2002. Actions on structures. General actions. Densities, self-weight, imposed loads for buildings.
PD 6688-1-1:2011. Recommendations for the design of structures to BS EN 1991-1-1.
BS 6180:2011. Barriers in and about buildings. Code of practice.

K.4 Vehicle barriers and loading bays (Requirement K3)

Pedestrians must be protected from collisions with vehicles by impact-resistant barriers. Where vehicles have access to a floor, roof or ramp which forms part of a building there must be barriers at the perimeters of vehicle routes which are level with, or above, the floor, the ground or another vehicle route.

The barriers must be at least 375mm high at the edge of a floor or roof, and at least 610mm high at the edges of ramps. Walls, parapets and balustrades can serve as barriers. The barriers should be strong enough to resist loads given in BS EN 1991-1-1 (and UK National Annex) and PD 6688-1-1.

To prevent people being struck or crushed by vehicles, a loading bay should have at least one exit point from its lower level, preferably set near the centre of its rear wall. Loading bays which can accept three or more vehicles should have at least one stepped exit point to each side or have a stepped exit point and a safety refuge (see Figure K.5).

Guarding should be provided as section **K.3**, or alternative safeguards should be agreed with the building control body.

2013 changes
The main change in this section is the introduction of Eurocode 1 and the associated Published Document for calculating loading.

Further guidance
BS EN 1991-1-1. [See **K.3**.]
PD 6688-1-1. [See **K.3**]

Figure K.5 Layout of loading bays

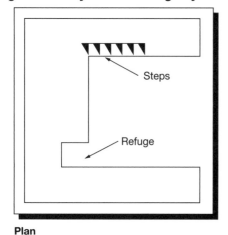

Plan

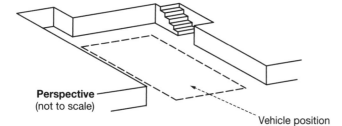

Perspective (not to scale)

K.5 Protection against impact with glazing (Requirement K4)

K.5.1 Glazing in critical locations

In order to prevent injury to people moving about a building, glazing in locations where the risk of collision is high (*critical locations*) should:

- if broken by impact, break safely; or
- resist breakage, being robust or in small panes; or
- be permanently protected from impact.

The risk of injury is greatest at doors and door side panels, from low level to shoulder height, but particularly high near door handles and push plates. The risk at walls and partitions is predominantly at a lower level, with children being particularly vulnerable.

Critical locations for glazing are defined as (Figure K.6):

- for internal and external walls and partitions – from finished floor level to 800mm above that level;
- for doors and side panels – a zone 1500mm from finished floor level and extending 300mm either side of the door.

Figure K.6 Critical locations for glazing in internal and external walls

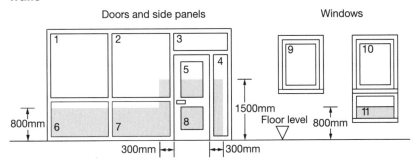

Shaded areas show critical locations to which requirement K4 applies (i.e. glazing in areas numbered 2, 4, 5, 6, 7, 8, 11)

K.5.2 Safe breakage

Glazing breaks safely if the result of an impact is limited to:

- a small clear opening only, with small detached particles; or
- disintegration, with small detached particles; or
- breakage into separate pieces that are not sharp or pointed.

Safe breakage is tested and classified to BS EN 12600 section 4 and BS 6206 clause 5.3:

- BS EN 12600 Class 3, or BS 6206 Class C glazing material is suitable for critical locations.
- BS EN 12600 Class 2, or BS6206 Class B glazing material is suitable for use in doors or door side panels with pane width greater than 900mm.

Further guidance

BS EN 12600:2002. Glass in building. Pendulum test. Impact test method and classification for flat glass. + Corrigendum April 2010.
BS 6206:1981. Specification for impact performance requirements for flat safety glass and safety plastics for use in buildings. + AMDs 4580, 5189, 7589, 8156, 8693.

K.5.3 Robustness

Some materials are inherently strong (e.g. polycarbonate sheet or glass blocks); others, such as annealed glass, are stronger when thicker. Annealed glass may therefore be used in large areas in the frontages of shops, showrooms, offices, factories and public buildings provided it is sufficiently thick. See Figure K.7 for dimensional limits for common thicknesses fully supported on all edges.

Figure K.7 Dimension limits for annealed glass of various thicknesses

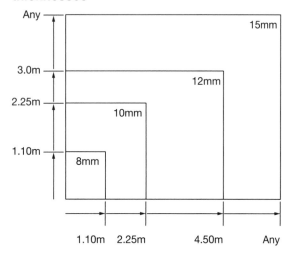

K.5.4 Glazing in small panes

A small pane may be an isolated pane or one of a number of panes within glazing bars, or traditional leaded- or copper-lights. The area of a small pane should not exceed 0.5m², and the smaller dimension should not exceed 250mm.

Annealed glass in small panes should be not less than 6mm nominal thickness, or 4mm for leaded- or copper-lights.

K.5.5 Permanent screen protection

A permanent screen that protects glazing in a critical location should:

- prevent a sphere of 75mm diameter coming into contact with the glazing; and
- be robust; and
- be difficult to climb, if it protects glazing that forms part of protection from falling (Figure K.8).

Glazing with such protection need not, of itself, comply with Requirement K4.

Figure K.8 Permanent screen protection

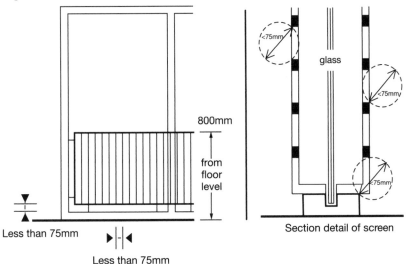

Less than 75mm

Less than 75mm

800mm

from floor level

glass

<75mm

<75mm

<75mm

Section detail of screen

K.6 Protection from collision with open windows etc. (Requirement K5.1)

Where parts of a window, skylight or vent project more than 100mm inside or outside a building and are less than 2m above the floor or ground surface, projecting parts should be:

- guarded by a rail or barrier 1100mm high which will prevent people walking into the projecting part, with cane detection on access routes; or
- marked by a tactile surface which guides people away, such as cobbles and slight change of level.

The requirement does not apply to dwellings. Where only infrequent, maintenance access is expected, it would be sufficient to mark clearly the projecting part.

K.7 Manifestation of glazing (Requirement K5.2)

Large areas of transparent glazing which present a risk of collision to people moving in or around a building must have features to make them apparent, such as manifestation. The risk of collision is most severe where people might reasonably expect direct access between locations on the same level.

To prevent collisions, glazing should be indicated by permanent manifestation or by features such as mullions, transoms, door framing or large handles. Manifestation normally would not be required for:

- door-height transparent glazing less than 400mm wide;
- door-height transparent glazing with a rail 850–1000mm and 1400–1600mm above the floor;

- a single pane glazed door with a substantial frame;
- glazed doors with no frame or a narrow frame, but with a large handle or push plate to each door.

Where manifestation is necessary, it should:

- be provided at two levels (Figure K.9);
- contrast visually (see **M.1.6.3**) with the background, when viewed from either side in all lighting conditions;
- take the form of a logo or sign at least 150mm high (repeated on glazed screens) or a decorative feature (such as bands or broken lines) at least 50mm high.

Figure K.9 Height of manifestation for glass doors and glazed screens

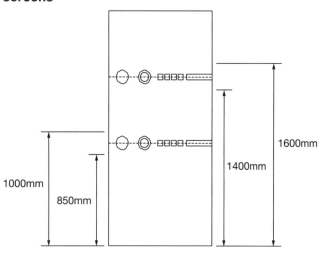

Manifestation can take various forms, e.g.
broken or solid lines, patterns or company logos

Glazed doors which are beside or part of a glazed screen should be clearly marked with a high-contrast strip at the top or both sides. Glass doors which may be held open should be guarded to prevent collisions with the leading edge.

2013 changes
The guidance from AD M has replaced the guidance originally contained in AD N.

K.8 Safe opening and closing of windows, skylights and ventilators (Requirement K5.3)

It must be possible to operate safely windows, skylights and ventilators. Controls such as handles and catches should be sited within safe reach of a permanent stable surface, as Figure K.10. Where that is not possible, safe remote operation should be provided.

Any window above ground floor level should have a limiter or guarding if there is a risk of anyone falling through.

Figure K.10 Height of controls

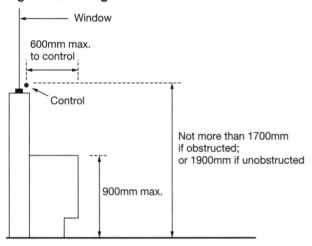

Window

600mm max.
to control

Control

Not more than 1700mm
if obstructed;
or 1900mm if unobstructed

900mm max.

K.9 Safe access for cleaning windows etc. (Requirement K5.4)

Any windows, skylights and transparent or translucent walls, ceilings or roofs which are intended to be cleaned should be safely accessible for cleaning on both sides (the requirement does not apply to dwellings). Where a glazed surface cannot be cleaned safely by someone standing on the floor, ground or other permanent stable surface, other provision is required:

- Windows which allow the outside surface to be cleaned safely from inside the building (Figure K.11): reversible windows should have a mechanism which holds them in the reverse position.
- Access ladders set at 75° from the horizontal:
  - ladders up to 6m long require a suitable firm level base;
  - ladders 6–9m long require a permanent stable surface away from traffic and tying or fixing points.
- Walkways at least 400mm wide with either 1100mm high guarding or anchorages for sliding safety harnesses.

2013 changes
The performance guidance to what was Requirement N4 referred to danger of a fall of more than 2m. There is no limiting distance associated with Requirement K.5(4).

Figure K.11 Safe reaches for cleaning

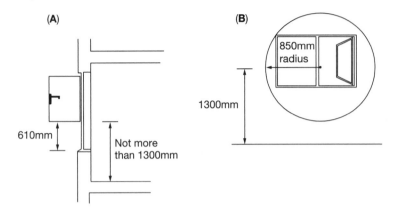

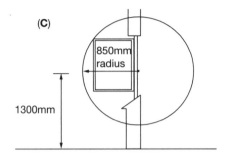

Typical safe reaches for cleaning windows:

(**A**) downwards reach through an opening light;
(**B**) side reach through an opening light;
(**C**) reach for cleaning an open casement with reflex hinges.

- Access equipment such as suspended cradles or travelling ladders, with attachments for safety harnesses.
- Anchorage points for safety harnesses or abseiling hooks.
- Where other provision is not possible, provide space for scaffolding towers.

Further guidance
BS 8213-1:2004. Windows, doors and rooflights. Design for safety in use and during cleaning of windows, including door-height windows and roof windows. Code of practice.

K.10 Protection against impact from and trapping by doors (Requirement K6)

The following requirements are intended to provide safe movement around and through doors and gates:

- Door leaves and side panels more than 450mm wide should have vision panels with minimum zones of visibility as Figure K.12.
- Any sliding door or gate must have stops to prevent it falling off the end of the track, and retaining rails to prevent it falling, should the suspension system fail or its rollers leave the track.
- Any upward-opening door or gate must be fitted with a device to prevent it falling in a way that may cause injury.
- Powered doors and gates should be fitted with safety devices – such as pressure-sensitive door edges – which will prevent people from being trapped. The doors and gates should also have a readily identifiable and accessible stop switch, and provision for manual and/or automatic opening should the power fail.

Doors which, in normal use, swing out onto access routes by more than 100mm should be protected as Figure K.13.

The requirements in this section do not apply to dwellings; nor to a door or gate which is part of a lift.

2013 changes
The guidance on protecting doors on access routes has been transferred to this section from AD M.

Figure K.12 Visibility requirements of doors

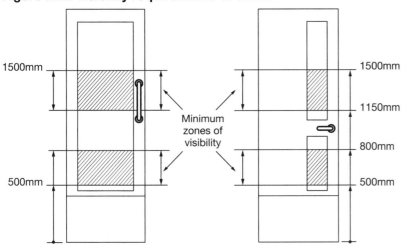

1500mm

500mm

Minimum zones of visibility

1500mm

1150mm

800mm

500mm

Figure K.13 Avoiding doors on access routes

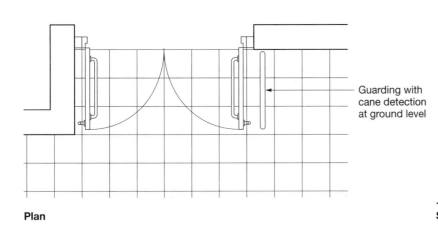

Guarding with cane detection at ground level

Plan

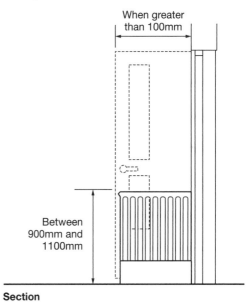

When greater than 100mm

Between 900mm and 1100mm

Section

Conservation of fuel and power

L.1 General considerations

L.1.1 Scope

Part L is intended to ensure that buildings have reasonable provision for the conservation of fuel and power. In addition to requirements of Part L of Schedule 1, the following Regulations also apply:

- Regulation 23 – requirements relating to thermal elements;
- Regulations 24–32 – carbon dioxide emissions calculations, consequential improvements and Energy Performance Certificates;
- Regulation 40 – information about use of fuel and power;
- Regulation 43 – air pressure testing.

Part L: Conservation of fuel and power	
Requirement	**Limits on application**
L1 Reasonable provision shall be made for the conservation of fuel and power in buildings by: (a) limiting heat gains and losses – (i) through thermal elements and other parts of the building fabric; and (ii) from pipes, ducts and vessels used for space heating, space cooling and hot water services; (b) providing fixed building services which – (i) are energy efficient; (ii) have effective controls; and (iii) are commissioned by testing and adjusting as necessary to ensure they use no more fuel and power than is reasonable in the circumstances.	

The requirements apply to building work to, or in connection with, a building which uses energy to condition the indoor climate, which includes:

- new buildings;
- extensions;
- material changes of use;
- material alterations to existing buildings;
- change of energy status;
- provision or extension of controlled services or fittings;
- replacement or renovation of thermal elements.

Under Regulation 21 a number of building types are exempt from the energy efficiency requirements; they include places of worship, unheated agricultural buildings and industrial sites. (For a full list see **I.3.2**).

2013 changes

The 2013 revisions to Part L address the requirements of the recast Energy Performance of Buildings Directive (2010/31/EU) and take a further step towards the zero carbon standards required in 2016 (dwellings) and 2019 (other buildings). The main changes are:

- A reduction in permitted carbon dioxide emissions of 6% for dwellings and an aggregate 9% for buildings other than dwellings (non-dwellings);
- The introduction of fabric energy efficiency standards for new dwellings (**L.2.2**);
- A requirement to assess the feasibility of high-efficiency alternative systems for new buildings (**L.3.1.7**).
- Minor revisions to the SBEM and SAP calculation methodologies;
- Tightening of some of the limiting values for the efficiency of building fabric and services.

In addition, the language of Approved Documents L1A and L2A has been revised to Plain English standards. The documents have been re-structured and now have a single column layout.

There have been only minor changes to the requirements for work on existing buildings covered in Approved Documents L1B and L2B.

The requirements distinguish between dwellings and other buildings, and between new buildings and work to existing buildings. Guidance is given in four Approved Documents:

- L1A New dwellings;
- L1B Existing dwellings;
- L2A New buildings other than dwellings;
- L2B Existing buildings other than dwellings.

In addition, minimum standards for building services are set out in:

- *Domestic Building Services Compliance Guide*;
- *Domestic Ventilation Compliance Guide*;
- *Non-Domestic Building Services Compliance Guide*.

Further guidance
www.planningportal.co.uk
[For downloadable versions of the Approved Documents and compliance guides.]

L.1.2 Definitions

Change of energy status A change which makes a building subject to the requirements of Part L where previously it was not.

Display lighting Lighting to highlight displays of exhibits or merchandise, or used in spaces for public leisure and entertainment.

Display window An area of glazing (including glazed doors) intended for the display of products or services, which: is at access level immediately adjacent to a pedestrian thoroughfare; or has no permanent workspace within one glazing height of perimeter (discounting glazing more than 3m above access level). Planners may require a greater height of glazing to match an existing façade.

Fit-out work Work to complete partitioning and building services within the external fabric of the building. Fit-out can take place as the shell is constructed, or subsequently.

Fixed building services Any part of, or controls to, fixed systems for: internal or external lighting (excluding emergency escape lighting or specialist process lighting); heating, hot water, air-conditioning or mechanical ventilation; any combination of such systems.

High-usage entrance door The door to an entrance primarily for use of people, which is expected to experience large volumes of traffic.

Principal works Work necessary to achieve the client's purpose in extending a building and/or increasing the installed capacity of any fixed building services.

Renovation Provision of a new layer in a thermal element or the replacement of an existing layer, but excluding decorative finishes and a new layer provided solely to repair a flat roof.

Simple payback The time taken to recover initial investment through energy savings. Calculated by dividing the marginal additional cost of implementing an energy efficiency measure by the value of the energy saving. Costs and energy prices should be those current at time of application to the BCB.

Specialist process lighting Lighting, such as theatre spotlights and medical lighting, intended to illuminate specialist tasks.

Thermal element A wall, roof or floor which separates a conditioned space from: the external environment; unconditioned spaces including extensions in Class VII; a part of a building conditioned to a different temperature.

Total useful floor area The areas of all enclosed spaces, measured to the internal face of external walls, with sloping surfaces such as staircases and raked auditoria measured as plan area, and excluding unenclosed areas such as open floors and balconies. (Equivalent to the RICS Gross Floor Area.)

L.1.3 Special cases

L.1.3.1 Shell and core developments

First fit-out of shell and core developments should be treated as new build (**L.3.3.2**). Subsequent fit-out work should comply with the standards for existing buildings.

L.1.3.2 Modular and portable buildings

A building composed of sub-assemblies from a centrally held stock, or from the disassembly or relocation of a building at other premises is treated as a new building (**L.3.3.2**). Erecting a separate unit on a site with an existing building is an extension only if the new unit is permanently linked to it.

L.1.3.3 Buildings with low energy demand

Buildings with low energy demand are those where fixed building services condition only a localised area rather than the entire enclosed volume; or heat spaces to temperatures less than those required for human comfort.

For guidance on new buildings see **L.3.3.1**, and for existing buildings see **L.4.1.2**.

L.1.3.4 Common areas in buildings with multiple dwellings

Common areas which are:

* heated – should be treated as a building other than a dwelling (**L.3.3**);

* unheated – should have fabric which meets the limiting fabric standards in **L.3.2.2** and Table L.2.

L.1.3.5 Conservatories

Under Regulation 9 conservatories and porches are exempt from the energy efficiency requirements of the Regulations, provided:

* they are at ground level; and

* have a floor level of less than 30m^2; and

* the glazing complies with the Requirements K4, K5.1, K5.2, K5.3 and K5.4 (see **K.5** to **K.9** – for dwellings only K4 applies); and

* the existing walls, doors and windows which separate the building from the conservatory are retained, or if removed, are replaced by walls, doors and windows which meet energy efficiency requirements; and

* the heating system of the building is not extended into the conservatory or porch.

A non-exempt conservatory or porch constructed at the same time as a dwelling, which has adequate thermal separation from the dwelling and is not served by its heating system should comply with guidance in Approved Document L1B (see **L.4.1.4**). Where the thermal separation is inadequate, or the heating system serves the conservatory or porch, the conservatory or porch must comply with Approved Document L1A (See **L.3.2**) and be included in the TER/DER and TFEE/DFEE calculations.

Conservatories and porches constructed as extensions to existing buildings should comply with Approved Documents L1B or L2B (see **L.4.1.4**). If any of the thermal separation to an existing exempt extension is removed, or the heating system is extended into it, the extension loses its exemption and must be treated as a conventional extension (**L.4.2**).

L.1.3.6 Swimming pools

The U-values of the walls and floor of the pool basin should be no worse than 0.25W/m²K (calculated to BS EN ISO 13370) and the building should be assessed with the pool replaced with an area of floor having the same U-value as the pool surround.

L.1.4 Energy Performance Certificates

Under Regulation 29 an Energy Performance Certificate (EPC) must be provided when a building is:

- erected; or
- modified to have greater or fewer number of parts designed or altered for separate use than previous, and the modifications include the provision or extension of fixed services for heating, hot water, air-conditioning or mechanical ventilation.

EPCs are not required for:

- places of worship;
- temporary buildings;
- buildings of less than 50m² total useful floor area; and
- unconditioned buildings, or those with low energy demand.

Every dwelling (including one in a mixed-use building) requires its own EPC; other buildings can have common certification for areas served by a common heating system.

The EPC shows:

- the building's energy efficiency;
- benchmark ratings for the building type;
- recommendations for cost-effective improvement measures.

The EPC must be produced by an energy assessor accredited for that type of building. The EPC must be given to the owner of the building within five days of completion of the work, and notice of that should be given to the BCB.

2013 changes
The glazing of exempt conservatories and porches must now comply with the relevant requirements of Part K, rather than Part N. Removing thermal separation from an existing conservatory or porch, or extending the heating system into it, no longer constitutes a change of energy status, but the requirements of Part L will still apply to the conservatory or porch. There is no guidance on non-exempt conservatories or porches constructed at the same time as new buildings other than dwellings.

Further guidance
BS EN ISO 13370:2007. Thermal performance of buildings. Heat transfer via the ground. Calculation methods.

Further guidance
Improving the energy efficiency of our buildings – A guide to Energy Performance Certificates for the construction, sale and let of non-dwellings. CLG. 2008. [Useful summary of the requirements for non-domestic EPCs.]

L.1.5 Commissioning fixed building services

Fixed building services should be commissioned by testing and adjustment to ensure that they use no more fuel and power than is reasonable. A commissioning plan should be prepared, identifying systems which require testing, and tests to be carried out; a copy should be provided with the design stage submission to the BCB. The templates in the BSRIA Model Commissioning Plan offer a way of documenting the commissioning process. The plan should also identify:

- systems which cannot be commissioned (e.g. those with on/off controls); and

- systems for which commissioning will not affect energy use.

Commissioning should follow the approved procedure. For dwellings:

- heating and hot water – *Domestic Building Services Compliance Guide*;

- ventilation – *Domestic Ventilation Compliance Guide*.

For other buildings:

- *CIBSE Commissioning Code M: commissioning management*; and

- the procedures for leakage testing of ductwork in **L.3.3.5**.

Commissioning should be carried out by a suitably qualified person. For non-domestic heating, ventilation and air-conditioning (HVAC) and lighting systems, it would be helpful for the BCB if the declarations supplied with the commissioning notice were signed by a member of the:

- Commissioning Specialists Association;

- Commissioning Group of the Building & Engineering Services Association (B&ES – formerly HVCA);

- Lighting Industry Commissioning Scheme.

Following commissioning, the BCB should be given a notice confirming:

- the commissioning plan has been followed;

- every system has been inspected and commissioned in an appropriate sequence and to a reasonable standard; and

- test results confirm that performance is reasonably in accordance with the building design.

The notification should be given within five days of completion of commissioning, or thirty days where work has been carried out by a member of a competent person scheme.

A sustained period of fine tuning of services following occupation, such as the Soft Landings process, is recommended as a means of enhancing energy efficiency in practice.

L.1.6 Nearly zero-energy buildings

Under Regulation 25B, where a building is erected it must be a nearly zero-energy building, which is defined as: a building with very high energy performance, where the nearly zero or low amount of energy required is covered to a very significant extent by energy from renewable sources, including energy produced on-site or nearby. The regulation is not due to come into force until 2019.

Further guidance
BG 8/2009 *Model Commissioning Plan*. BSRIA.

Domestic Building Services Compliance Guide. CLG. 2013.

Domestic Ventilation Compliance Guide. CLG. 2013.

CIBSE Commissioning Code M: *Commissioning management*. CIBSE. 2003.

http://www.bsria.co.uk/services/design/soft-landings/ [Guidance on the Soft Landings initiative.]

2013 changes
Regulation 25B transposes article 9 of the recast Energy Performance of Buildings Directive into English regulations. It has no practical effect at present.

L.1.7 Ecodesign Directive

The Ecodesign Directive (2009/125/EC) is a framework for establishing regulations for energy-related products on EU markets. Products covered by an ecodesign regulation must meet the stated test standards and be CE-marked. Some construction products are subject to ecodesign regulations, including space heaters and combination heaters, water heaters and hot water storage tanks, and water pumps, although the standards may not yet be in force (the hot water storage tank standards do not come into force until 2017).

It is intended that the minimum energy efficiency standards in the government's compliance guides will match those of the relevant ecodesign regulations as they come into force.

Further guidance
http://ec.europa.eu/energy/efficiency/ecodesign/eco_design_en.htm
[An overview of the Ecodesign Directive.]
http://ec.europa.eu/energy/efficiency/ecodesign/doc/overview_legislation_eco-design.pdf.
[A summary of ecodesign legislation.]

L.2 Methods of calculation and test

L.2.1 Carbon emission rates

The overall energy efficiency of a building is expressed by its carbon dioxide emission rate – that is, the predicted mass of CO_2 resulting from the operation of fixed building services for heating, cooling, domestic hot water, ventilation and lighting. It is expressed as kilograms per square metre of total floor area ($kgCO_2/m^2$) per year.

Carbon dioxide emission rates must be calculated using an approved methodology. For dwellings that is an approved software implementation of SAP 2012. For other buildings, an appropriate tool that is either:

- iSBEM – an implementation of SBEM (Simplified Building Energy Model); or

- other approved software tools, such as those which use Dynamic Simulation Modelling (DSM).

L.2.2 Fabric energy efficiency

The Fabric Energy Efficiency rate (FEE) measures the thermal performance of the fabric of a dwelling. It represents the amount of energy required to heat and cool the building, expressed in kilowatt hours per square metre of floor area per year ($kWh/m^2/year$) and is calculated using SAP 2012. The FEE takes account of heat losses and gains through the fabric: it takes no account of fixed building services.

L.2.3 U-values

U-values express the rate of heat loss by conduction through building elements or components, and should be calculated in accordance with BR 443. U-values for windows, roof windows, rooflights and doors are based on the whole unit, including any glazing and the frame. The U-value for a window may be calculated for:

- the actual unit; or

- the smaller of the two standard windows in BS EN 14351-1; or

- the standard windows in BR 443.

The U-value for a door may be calculated for:

- the standard size as defined in BS EN 14351-1; or

- the specific size and configuration of the actual door.

The limiting U-values for roof windows and roof-lights presume that the units have been assessed in a vertical plane: where units have been assessed in a different plane, the limits should be adjusted for the slope, using the procedure in BR 443.

L.2.4 Window and doorset energy rating (WER and DSER)

The window energy rating (WER) is an energy efficiency rating, running from A–G, which is calculated from the window's solar gain, U-value and air infiltration performance. The Doorset Energy Rating (DSER) is a similar measure for doors. The rating schemes are run by the British Fenestration Rating Council (BFRC).

L.2.5 Linear thermal transmittance (psi-values)

The linear thermal transmittance, or psi-value, expresses the rate of conduction heat loss through a junction between two elements (e.g. wall to floor), or at the edges of elements (e.g. around door and window openings).

Psi-values should be calculated in accordance with BR 497 by someone with appropriate expertise and experience (for example, a person who has been trained in using the software and has applied that model to the sample calculations in BR 497 to achieve results within the stated tolerances).

L.2.6 Air permeability

Air permeability is a measure of air leakage through the building fabric expressed as the volume of air passing through a square metre of the building envelope per hour, at a standard pressure differential between inside and outside of 50Pa ($m^3/(h.m^2)$ @ 50Pa).

Part L considers three different air permeability measures:

- limiting air permeability – the highest permissible value;

- design air permeability – the target value at design stage;

- assessed air permeability – the final value at completion.

When required, pressure testing should follow the procedure described in the appropriate Air Tightness Testing and Measurement Association (ATTMA) standard, and results should be recorded as set out in section 4 of that standard. The envelope area is the total area of external elements bordering the internal volume, including the areas of junctions with internal elements. Test results must be notified to the BCB within seven days.

Pressure testing should be carried out by a person registered by the British Institute of Non-destructive Testing or ATTMA for the appropriate class of building. Test equipment should have been calibrated at a UKAS accredited facility within the last twelve months.

Further guidance
BR 443 *Conventions for U-value calculations*. BRE. 2006.

BS EN 14351-1:2006+A1:2010. Windows and doors. Product standard, performance characteristics. Windows and external pedestrian doorsets without resistance to fire and/or smoke leakage characteristics.

2013 changes
The Doorset Energy Rating is now used in Approved Documents L1B and L2B. Some publications refer to it as the Door Energy Rating (DER). Approved Document L1B no longer contains the calculation method and rating levels for the WER.

Further guidance
BFRC Ratings calculations, and *BFRC Guidance Note*. British Fenestration Rating Council. [Available from www.bfrc.org]

Guide to the Calculation of Energy Ratings for Windows, Roof Windows and Doors. Glass and Glazing Federation. 2013.

Further guidance
BR 497 *Conventions for calculating linear thermal transmittance and temperature factors*. BRE. 2007. [Amended 2010.]

Further guidance
Measuring air permeability in the envelopes of dwellings, Technical Standard L1. ATTMA. 2010.

Measuring air permeability of building envelopes, Technical Standard L2. ATTMA. 2010.

L.2.7 Ductwork leakage

Ductwork leakage testing should be conducted to DW/143 by a suitably qualified person, such as a member of:

- the B&ES (formerly HVAC) specialist ductwork group; or
- the Association of Ductwork Contractors and Allied Services.

L.2.8 Efficiency data for building services

Efficiency values for building services should be derived from the test standards listed in the Building Services Compliance Guides and certified by notified bodies. In the absence of certified data, the BCB should satisfy itself that the claimed performance is justified.

The minimum efficiency of a system that is not listed in the relevant compliance guide should be no less than a comparable one which is listed.

L.3 New buildings – L1A and L2A

All new buildings must comply with five criteria, although the requirements for demonstrating compliance differ between dwellings and other buildings.

L.3.1 Common considerations

L.3.1.1 Criterion 1 – Meeting the TER

The target emission rate (TER) is the annual rate of CO_2 emissions from a notional building of the same size and shape as the actual building, but using a set of reference values for the performance of the fabric and fixed building services. The predicted annual CO_2 emission rate for the building must not be worse than its TER. The TER may be met using a combination of fabric, fixed building services and low- or zero-carbon (LZC) technologies. To facilitate future integration of LZC technologies, designers should consider:

- adopting heating and/or cooling systems with low distribution temperatures;
- organising the controls for multiple systems which feed the same end so the least carbon-intensive option is given priority;
- making buildings 'LZC ready', to aid subsequent installation of LZC technologies.

Notification

At least one day before work starts the BCB must be given a notice which specifies the target and predicted CO_2 emission rates for the building, together with a list of specifications to which the building is to be constructed. Features critical to achieving compliance should be highlighted to help the BCB prioritise risk-based inspection.

The emissions calculation for the completed building should be given to the BCB within five days of the completion of the work, together with a list of changes to the initial specifications. The BCB can accept as evidence of compliance a certificate to that effect produced by an energy assessor accredited for that category of building.

Further guidance
DW/143 *A practical guide to ductwork leakage testing.* B&ES. 2013.

DW/144. *Specification for Sheet Metal Ductwork*. B&ES. 2013.

L.3.1.2 Criterion 2 – Limiting trade-off

To prevent inappropriate trade-offs, the building fabric and fixed building services must provide reasonable overall standards of energy efficiency.

L.3.1.3 Criterion 3 – Limiting heat gain

Solar gain in the summer must be limited, to prevent overheating and reduce the need for, or installed capacity of, air-conditioning systems. Solar gain can be limited by window size and orientation (while still providing adequate daylighting as BS 8206), shading and other passive solar control measures, ventilation and fabric with high thermal capacity.

L.3.1.4 Criterion 4 – As-built performance

The actual performance of a building must be consistent with its predicted performance; in a final 'as-built' calculation the emission rate must meet the TER.

Insulation should be reasonably continuous over the whole building envelope, with no avoidable thermal bridging within elements, at junctions between elements, or between elements and components; and air infiltration should be limited. To reduce convection heat losses, air barriers and insulation layers should be contiguous, or the space between them filled with solid material.

L.3.1.5 Criterion 5 – Information

Under Regulation 40, within five days of the completion of the work, the person carrying out the work must provide the building owner with information about the building, its fixed services and their maintenance requirements: that information should be sufficient to enable the building to be operated efficiently. The information should include the recommendations report that accompanies the EPC, together with the data used in the CO_2 emissions calculations, which preferably should also be retained in electronic format.

L.3.1.6 Criterion 6 – Model designs

A building constructed to the specifications used for the notional building will meet the TER and pass criterion 1. The specifications can be found in the NCM documentation. However, the notional building specifications may not be the most economic specification.

Some builders may prefer to adopt model design packages of fabric U-values, boiler efficiencies, and window opening allowances which, within certain constraints, would achieve compliance. However, even with model designs, it would still be necessary to demonstrate compliance with the five criteria.

2013 changes
The approved documents to Part L now refer more broadly to heat gain rather than just solar gain, to include the effects of unwanted gains from fixed building services which are described in **L.3.2.3**.

Further guidance
BS 8206-2:2008. Lighting for buildings. Code of practice for daylighting.

Further guidance
NCM Modelling Guide. BRE. 2013.
[Available at www.2013ncm.bre.co.uk. Contains the notional building specifications for buildings other than dwellings.]

The Government's Standard Assessment Procedure. SAP 2012. DECC. 2013.
[Available at: www.bre.co.uk/sap2012. Contains the notional dwelling specification.]

www.modeldesigns.info

L.3.1.7 High efficiency alternative systems

Before work begins on any new building, the technical, environmental and economic feasibility of using high-efficiency alternative systems must be analysed, in accordance with Regulation 25A. High-efficiency alternative systems include:

- decentralised energy supply based on renewable energy sources;
- cogeneration (CHP);
- district or block heating or cooling, particularly those based on renewable energy sources;
- heat pumps.

The analysis can be performed for individual buildings, groups of similar buildings or all the buildings connected to a district energy system, and should state whether such systems have or have not been included in the building design.

Notice that the analysis has been undertaken must be given to the building control body at least a full day before work begins. The analysis must be documented and the documentation made available for inspection by the building control body.

L.3.2 New dwellings – L1A

L.3.2.1 Criterion 1 – Whole dwelling performance

New dwellings must meet performance standards for fabric energy efficiency and carbon dioxide emissions at the design stage and on completion. Both standards are based on the performance of a notional dwelling which has the same size and shape as the actual building, but fabric and services specification taken from SAP 2012 Appendix R (summarised in AD L1A Table 4).

The fabric and services standards used for the notional dwelling are concurrent standards, which may be used in the design process as a guide to the performance necessary to meet the fabric energy efficiency and carbon dioxide standards.

Fabric energy efficiency – TFEE/DFEE

The fabric energy efficiency rate of the actual dwelling – the DFEE – must not be greater than its target fabric energy efficiency rate – the TFEE. The TFEE is the fabric energy efficiency of the notional dwelling, increased by 15%. Both DFEE and TFEE are calculated using SAP 2012.

Carbon dioxides emissions – TER/DER

The carbon dioxide emission rate for the dwelling – the DER – must not exceed the target carbon dioxide emission rate – the TER. Both the DER and TER are calculated using SAP 2012. The TER is based on the carbon dioxide emissions of the notional dwelling, adjusted by a fuel factor to compensate for the use of heating fuels which have higher carbon dioxide emission rates than mains gas.

2013 changes
The new requirement to assess the feasibility of high efficiency systems, is a transposition of Article 4 of the recast Energy Performance of Buildings Directive.

2013 changes
The fabric energy efficiency requirement has been introduced in Part L 2013 to address building fabric performance. As the TFEE and DFEE are unaffected by the building services specification for the the dwelling, it is no longer possible to mask poorly-performing fabric by renewables or high-efficiency services. In many cases, achieving the TFEE will require significantly more than the 6% improvement over 2010 standards required for the TER.

Table L.1 Secondary heating

Condition	Secondary heating appliance
Secondary heating appliance installed	The installed appliance, using the appropriate fuel.
Chimney or flue, but no appliance fitted: gas point adjacent to hearth	A decorative fuel-effect gas fire, open to chimney/flue, with 20% efficiency.
Chimney or flue, but no appliance fitted: no gas point	An open fire in grate burning multi-fuel, with 37% efficiency – smokeless solid mineral fuel in smoke control areas.
All other conditions	The secondary heating has the same efficiency and fuel as the main heating (effectively no secondary heating).

The DER is based on:

- the dimensions and fabric of the actual building;
- the fixed building services as proposed, but with some of the heating demand provided by a secondary heating system (Table L.1) according to the secondary heating fraction in SAP 2012;
- the design air permeability.

Where a community energy system is connected to a number of dwellings, the percentage of heat supplied from each heat source should be the same for each newly-connected dwelling. When calculating the percentage of heat supplied, the effect of all dwellings to be newly connected in the first twelve months can be considered.

Notification

Prior to construction, the builder must provide the BCB with the fabric energy efficiency (TFEE/DFEE) and carbon dioxide emissions (TER/DER) calculations for the proposed dwelling, together with the input data. After construction, a final set of TFEE/DFEE and TER/DER calculations must be carried out, taking account of any changes made during construction. The dwelling must still meet the TFEE and TER standards.

The post-construction calculations should be carried out using the the assessed air permeability, which is:

- for a dwelling which has been pressure tested – the measured air permeability;
- for a dwelling which has not been pressure tested – the average test result from dwellings of the same type on the development, increased by a margin of $2m^3/(h.m^2)$ @ 50Pa (tested dwellings will therefore need to achieve air permeabilities better than $8.00m^3/(h.m^2)$);
- for a dwelling on a small development, taking the option not to test – $15m^3/(h.m^2)$.

Buildings containing multiple dwellings

Mid-floor flats and mid-terrace houses are disadvantaged by the comparative compliance methods of the TFEE and TER. To compensate, blocks of flats or terraces of houses may be considered as one unit, allowing the better performance of some dwellings (ground and top floor flats, or end-terrace houses) to counter-balance the poorer performance of others.

2013 changes
The 2010 TER was based on emissions a notional dwelling with Part L 2002 fabric and services standards, modified by improvement factors, emissions factor adjustments and a fuel factor. The 2103 TER is based on emissions from a notional dwelling with concurrent fabric and services standards, modified by a fuel factor. The notional dwelling specification has been set to produce an aggregate 6% reduction in emissions across all dwellings.

The dwellings in a building containing multiple dwellings will comply when either:

- every individual dwelling has a DFEE no greater than its TFEE and a DER no greater than its TER; or
- the average DFEE for the dwellings is no greater than their average TFEE and the average DER for the dwellings is no greater than their average TER.

The average TFEE/DFEE and TER/DER figures are floor-area-weighted averages of the individual TFEE/DFEE and TER/DER values, so:

$$TFEE_{av} = \frac{(TFEE_1 \times A_1) + \ldots + (TFEE_n \times A_n)}{A_1 + \ldots + A_n}$$

and:

$$TER_{av} = \frac{(TER_1 \times A_1) + \ldots + (TER_n \times A_n)}{A_1 + \ldots + A_n}$$

Even if the average method is used, TFEE/DFEE and TER/DER data must still be submitted for each dwelling.

L.3.2.2 Criterion 2 – Limiting trade-off

The building fabric should meet the standards in Table L.2 and each fixed building service, including lighting, should meet the appropriate efficiency value in the *Domestic Building Services Compliance Guide*.

Table L.2 Limiting fabric parameters – dwellings

Parameter	Limiting value
Roof U-value	0.20W/m²K
Wall U-value	0.30W/m²K
Floor U-value	0.25W/m²K
Party wall U-value	0.20W/m²K
Swimming pool basin U-value	0.25W/m²K
Windows, roof windows, glazed rooflights[1], curtain walling and pedestrian doors (U-value)	2.00W/m²K
Air permeability	10m³/(h.m²) at 50Pa

[1] Based on the developed area of rooflight, not the areas of the roof aperture. See NARM Technical Document NTD 2. 2010.

L.3.2.3 Criterion 3 – Limiting heat gain

The solar gain calculation in SAP 2012 Appendix P should indicate that there is not a high risk of high internal temperatures in summer. The assessment should be carried out using reasonable assumptions about air change rates, opening windows and the like, but ignoring any cooling system.

Heat losses from pipework should also be limited by insulating primary circulation pipes for domestic hot water along their whole length. In apartment blocks insulating primary space heating circulation pipes in communal areas can also reduce unwanted heat gains and overheating.

2013 changes
Minimum performance standards in the 2013 edition of the Domestic Building Services Compliance Guide are largely unchanged. However, the guide now defines five types of oil central heating boiler, with a slight relaxation of standards for some types of boiler. Heat pump efficiency is now set as COP levels (Coefficient of Performance levels) rather than SPF (Seasonal Performance Factor), making it difficult to compare new and existing standards.

Further guidance
Domestic Building Services Compliance Guide. DCLG. 2013.
[Available from www.planningportal.gov.uk]

2013 changes
The contribution of space heating and hot water services pipework to overheating has been recognised.

L.3.2.4 Criterion 4 – Performance as-built

Party walls

Heat loss from party cavity walls can be substantial. The rate of heat loss can be reduced by restricting air movement through the cavity, either by fully filling the cavity, or by effective sealing around the perimeter. The extent of the reduction depends on the design and on the quality of construction.

Edge sealing (either on its own, or in conjunction with a fully filled cavity) must restrict air flow; a cavity barrier provided for Part B may not be effective. The sealing system must be aligned with the thermal envelope. For example, the sealing system in a room-in-roof should follow the line of the insulation in sloping and horizontal ceiling constructions, even though the cavity barrier will need to follow the slope to the ridge. For flats, the sealing system should follow party floors and other party structures, as well as the main thermal envelope. Designers should note that these measures may conflict with Part E (**E.2**).

In the absence of independent evidence, U-values in Table L.3 should be adopted in the DER calculation, although in order to claim a reduced U-value, it must be demonstrated that the design is likely to be robust on site. Thermal bridging must be assessed for all party wall junctions.

Further guidance
http://www.buildingcontrolalliance.org

Table L.3 U-values for party walls

Party wall construction	U-value
Solid	$0.0W/m^2K$
Unfilled cavity, no effective edge sealing	$0.5W/m^2K$
Unfilled cavity, effective edge sealing around all exposed edges and aligned with insulation in abutting elements	$0.2W/m^2K$
Fully-filled cavity, effective edge sealing around all exposed edges and aligned with insulation in abutting elements	$0.0W/m^2K$

Thermal bridges

Reasonable provision for minimising thermal bridging at junctions between elements and around openings would be to:

- use approved design details from the DCLG Approved Construction Details or others formally recognised by DCLG. The psi-values may be used in DFEE and DER calculations.
- use details which have been calculated by a person with suitable expertise to BR 497. Temperature factors for the details should be no worse than those given in IP 1/06 and the psi-values may be used in DFEE and DER calculations. (Suitable expertise would be evidenced by having been trained in the software use and having modelled the test examples in BR 497 within the stated tolerances.)
- use psi-values in the 'default' column of Table K1 of SAP 2012 directly in DFEE and DER calculations.
- using a y-value of $0.15W/m^2K$ in the DFEE and DER calculations, instead of psi-values.

Psi-values from the first three methods may be combined on the same DFEE and DER calculations. Where approved design details or calculated psi-values are used the builder must be able to demonstrate to the BCB that an appropriate system of site inspection is in place to ensure a consistent standard of construction.

Air permeability and pressure testing

Pressure tests should be carried out on a sample of dwellings on each site (each block of flats should be treated as a separate development). For each type of dwelling testing should be carried out on the least of: three units; or 50% of units. (Criteria for establishing dwelling types are given in AD L1A Appendix A.)

The dwellings to be tested should be selected by the BCB in consultation with the pressure tester so that about half of the scheduled tests are carried out during construction of the first 25% of each dwelling type.

A dwelling will comply if:

- the assessed air permeability (**L.2.6**) is not worse than 10m³/(h.m²) @ 50Pa; and
- the DFEE and DER calculated using the assessed air permeability are not worse than the TFEE and TER.

If a dwelling fails, remedial measures and further testing should be carried out until it complies, and an additional dwelling of that type should be tested. Other dwellings of the same type should be examined and, where appropriate, similar remedial measures applied.

Small developments

Air pressure testing is not required for developments of one or two dwellings, providing:

- a dwelling of the same type constructed by the same builder can be shown to have achieved the design air permeability during the preceding 12 months; or
- the DFEE and DER are calculated using a design air permeability of 15m³/(h.m²) @ 50Pa (that will require compensating measures elsewhere in the dwelling).

Commissioning heating, hot water and ventilation systems

Fixed building services must be commissioned in accordance with the approved procedure and notice of commissioning given as **L.1.5**. The BCB may withhold the completion certificate until the commissioning notice has been received.

L.3.2.5 Criterion 5 – Efficient operation

The operating and maintenance instructions should be specific to the dwelling. The documentation should:

- explain the essential design principles and key features of the dwelling;
- have floor plans showing the location of the main heating and ventilation components.
- explain how to operate, control and maintain the space heating, hot water and ventilation systems and any other low or zero carbon technologies.

Further guidance
IP 1/06. *Assessing the effects of thermal bridging at junctions and around openings in the external elements of buildings*. BRE. 2006.

BR 497. *Conventions for calculating linear thermal transmittance and temperature factors*. BRE. 2007 [Amended 2010.]

2013 changes
The performance penalty for using calculated psi-values (an increase of the greater of 25% or 0.02W/mK) has been removed.

- signpost other important documentation such as appliance manuals, the data from the compliance calculations and the on-construction EPC recommendation report.

The documentation should be durable and be in an easily understood format.

L.3.3 New buildings other than dwellings – L2A

L.3.3.1 Buildings with low energy demand

No target emission rate or building emission rate (BER) calculation is required, but the building envelope should be insulated to a reasonable degree. Where some heat is provided, no part of the opaque fabric should have a U-value worse than $0.7W/m^2K$. Fixed building services should comply with the *Non-Domestic Building Services Compliance Guide*.

Any part of the building which is partitioned off and heated normally (e.g. an office area in a warehouse) should be treated as a separate 'building' and normal compliance procedures observed.

Where a building is designed as a low-energy-demand building but the first occupier wants to install a fixed building service such as heating, this should be treated as a first fit-out.

L.3.3.2 Criterion 1 – TER/BER

The BER and TER are calculated using the same software tool (**L.2.1**). The TER is based on a notional building with:

- the size, shape and zoning arrangements of the actual building;
- other properties, including glazing class, as specified in the *NCM modelling guide*.

The BER is based on:

- the dimensions and fabric of the actual building;
- fixed building services as proposed;
- the design air permeability.

The BER must be no worse than the TER at the design stage and on construction.

Prior to construction, the builder must provide the BCB with the BER and TER calculations, together with the construction specification and input data. After construction, the final BER/TER calculations must be carried out, taking account of:

- any changes to performance specifications made during construction;
- the measured air permeability;
- 'as commissioned' ductwork leakage and fan performance.

Further guidance
National Calculation Methodology (NCM) modelling guide (for buildings other than dwellings in England and Wales). BRE. 2013.
A summary of the fabric and services standards for the notional building can be found in Table 5 of Approved Document L2A.

2013 changes
The properties for the notional building have been modified to give an aggregate 9% reduction in carbon dioxide emissions against 2010 standards. The reductions vary across building types, with small warehouses requiring a 3% reduction, while shallow plan offices require a 13% reduction.

CO$_2$ emission factors

BER calculations should be based on the CO$_2$ emission factors published in Table 12 of the SAP 2012 document. If a system can be fired by more than one fuel, the fuel with the highest emission factor should be used, except for:

- a biomass heating appliance supplemented by an alternative appliance – use an average CO$_2$ emission factor for the fuels, weighted for anticipated use;
- an appliance capable of burning biomass or fossil fuel – use the emission factor for dual-fuel appliances, or anthracite for smoke control areas.

Emission factors for energy from community heating or cooling systems should be calculated for the annual average performance of the scheme, taking account of combined heat and power (CHP), waste heat recovery and heat dumping. To account for increased operation of any marginal plant the effect of all buildings newly connected to the system can be included in any calculation of heat supplied.

Electricity from CHP or from trigeneration should be credited at an emission rate equal to the grid average, with CO$_2$ emissions for thermal energy allocated proportionally by output.

Where emission rates are calculated, the BER submission should be accompanied by a report – signed by a suitably qualified person – detailing how they have been derived.

Further guidance
The Government's Standard Assessment Procedure for energy rating of dwellings, SAP 2012.
www.bre.co.uk/sap2012

Management features

Management features which offer improved energy efficiency will reduce the BER. The reduction is equal to the CO$_2$ emission rate for the system affected, multiplied by the adjustment factor given in Table L.4. For example, a building with emissions from electrical consumption of 70kg CO$_2$/m^2 per year with a power correction factor of at least 0.95 would have its BER reduced by 70 × 0.025 = 1.75kg CO$_2$/m^2 per year.

Table L.4 Enhanced management and control features	
Feature	**Adjustment factor**
Automatic monitoring and targeting with alarms for out of range values[1]	0.050
Power factor correction to achieve a whole building power factor >0.90[2]	0.010
Power factor correction to achieve a whole building power factor >0.95[2]	0.025

[1] An installation that measures and communicates meaningful energy management information to the operator.

[2] Power factor correction must apply to the whole building: the two power factor adjustments are not cumulative.

Modular and portable buildings

The delivery of an existing module to a new site is considered to be a new building. However, it is not always appropriate to expect a relocated unit to meet new building standards.

Modular or portable buildings with a planned life of more than two years at a given location should meet all five compliance criteria, but if more than 70% of the external envelope consists of sub-assemblies manufactured prior to 6 April 2014 then the TER should be multiplied by the appropriate factor from Table L.5.

For a modular building with an intended time of use in a given location of less than two years a TER/BER calculation should be carried out when the module is first constructed, and may be based on a generic configuration. That calculation can be used to demonstrate compliance whenever the module is moved. The supplier should confirm, in writing, that the modules as provided meet the elemental energy standards of the generic module, and that the activities assumed in the generic calculation are representative of the planned use of the actual module.

Where the intended time in use is less than two years electrical resistance heating is the only practicable heating technology. In such cases the BER calculation for the generic configuration should be based on a gas boiler with 77% efficiency, giving energy efficiency measures 15% better than conventional fossil fuel heating. If it is necessary to carry out a TER/BER calculation the TER should be adjusted by the appropriate figure from Table L.5.

In both cases, any refurbishment (such as replacement windows or new lighting) should follow **L.4**.

2013 changes
The TER multiplying factors in Table L.5 have been revised to allow for the 9% aggregate improvement in carbon dioxide emissions required for buildings other than dwellings.

Table L.5 TER multiplying factors for modular and portable buildings

Date of manufacture of 70% of modules making up the external envelope	TER multiplying factor
After 6 April 2014	1.00
1 October 2010 – 5 April 2014	1.10
6 April 2006 – 30 September 2010	1.47
1 April 2002 – 5 April 2006	1.93
Pre 1 April 2002	1.93 [2.59][1]

[1] Use the figure in brackets for buildings with a planned use on site of less than two years.

Shell and core developments

The developer of a building offered to market for sale or let as a shell for subsequent fit-out, must demonstrate by a TER/DER submission how the building shell, as offered, could meet the TER. The submission to the BCB should identify those services which have not been provided and should give the assumed efficiencies used in the calculation together with the efficiencies for comparable systems in the notional building. A predicted EPC rating should be made available to prospective occupiers.

When fixed services for heating, hot water, air-conditioning or mechanical ventilation are provided or extended on first fit-out of all or part of the building, a revised TER/BER submission for that part of the building should be made to the BCB. The submission should be based on the shell, as constructed, and the services, as installed. Where no work is done to those services it will be sufficient to show that any lighting systems are at least as efficient as those in the initial submission. The fitted-out part of the building will require a new EPC.

Industrial sites, workshops and non-residential agricultural buildings

Special considerations may apply to industrial sites, workshops and non-residential buildings which are not low energy demand buildings, where:

- the CO_2 target is established through another regulatory framework, such as the carbon reduction commitment; or
- the generic National Calculation Methodology cannot account adequately for industrial processes or agricultural use.

In such cases reasonable provision would be to provide fixed building services to the standards for existing buildings set out in **L.4.5**.

L.3.3.3 Criterion 2 – Limiting trade-off

Building fabric should meet the standards in Table L.6. Fixed building services should meet the appropriate efficiency value in the *Non-Domestic Building Services Compliance Guide*.

Heating, ventilation and air-conditioning systems should be designed so that:

- areas of the building with significantly different usage patterns or solar exposure have separate control zones;
- each control zone is capable of independent control of timing and temperature and, if appropriate, ventilation and air recirculation rate;
- services respond to the spaces they serve (heating and cooling should be controlled so as not to operate simultaneously);
- central plant should only operate as and when the zone systems require it, with the default condition being 'off'.

Energy meters should:

- enable at least 90% of the estimated annual energy consumption of each fuel to be assigned to end use categories (heating, lighting etc.);
- enable the output of any renewable energy system to be separately monitored;
- include automatic meter reading and data collection facilities in buildings with over 1000m² total useful floor area;
- facilitate benchmarking of energy performance.

Designers should consider the provision of centralised switching which would enable facilities managers to turn off appliances when they are not needed.

2013 changes
While the minimum efficiency standards in the Non-Domestic Building Services Compliance Guide are largely unchanged, standards have been tightened for gas heating boilers under 2 MW output and most comfort cooling systems. The minimum efficiency for general lighting has been increased from 55 to 60 luminaire lumens/circuit-watt. Lighting efficiency may now be assessed using the LENI methodology (Lighting Energy Numerical Indicator) as defined in BS EN 15193:2007.

Further guidance
Non-Domestic Building Services Compliance Guide 2013 edition. DCLG.
TM 39 Building energy metering. CIBSE. 2009.
TM 46 Energy benchmarks. CIBSE. 2008.
NTD 2 Assessment of thermal performance of out-of-plane rooflights. NARM. 2010.

Table L.6 Limiting fabric parameters – buildings other than dwellings

Parameter	Limiting value
Roof	0.25W/m²K
Wall	0.35W/m²K
Floor	0.25W/m²K
Swimming pool basin	0.25W/m²K
Windows, roof windows, rooflights[1], curtain walling and pedestrian doors[2][3]	2.2W/m²K
Vehicle access and similar large doors	1.5W/m²K
High usage entrance doors	3.5W/m²K
Roof ventilators (including smoke vents)	3.5W/m²K
Air permeability	10.0m³/(h.m²) @ 50Pa

[1] Based on the developed area of rooflight, not the areas of the roof aperture. See NARM Technical Document NTD 2. 2010.

[2] Excluding display windows and similar glazing.

[3] In buildings with high internal heat gains a higher average weighted U-value for glazing may reduce CO_2 emissions. However, the value should not be relaxed beyond 2.7W/m²K.

L.3.3.4 Criterion 3 – Limiting heat gain

For each occupied space in the building, the aggregated solar gains for April to September inclusive should be no greater than would occur through the appropriate reference glazing systems in Table L.7. For a naturally ventilated building, meeting this criterion is not evidence that its internal environment will be satisfactory.

An occupied space is one intended to be occupied by the same person for a substantial part of the day. The requirement excludes areas such as circulation spaces and toilets, and spaces not intended for occupation such as display windows.

Further guidance
BS EN 410:2011. Glass in building. Determination of luminous and solar characteristics of glazing.
TM 37 Design for improved solar shading control. CIBSE. 2006.
BB101 Ventilation of school buildings. DfE. 2006.

Table L.7 Reference glazing systems for solar gain

Requirements	Space which the NCM database defines as predominantly:		
	Side lit	Top lit – average zone height ≤6m	Top lit – average zone height >6m
Reference case	East facing façade	Horizontal roof of same total area	Horizontal roof of same total area
Glazing area	1m × length	10% of roof [1]	20% of roof [1]
Framing factor	10%	25%	15%
Solar energy transmittance (g-value)[2]	0.68	0.68	0.46

[1] Viewed from inside to outside.

[2] To BS EN 410.

L.3.3.5 Criterion 4 – Performance as-built

Building fabric

There are two methods of addressing thermal bridging at joints between elements and at the edges of elements:

- use construction joint details for which linear thermal transmittances have been calculated by a suitably qualified person to the guidance in BR 497, following a process flow sequence in their construction. The details should achieve a temperature factor no worse than the standard required by BRE IP 1/06.

- unaccredited details with no specific quantification of thermal bridge values – the BER calculation should use the generic psi-values in IP 1/06 increased by the greater of 0.04W/mK or 50%.

Air permeability and pressure testing

All new buildings, including extensions which are being treated as new buildings for Part L compliance purposes, must be pressure tested. The only exceptions are:

- Buildings of less than 500m² total useful floor area – the developer may avoid pressure testing by using air permeability of 15m³/(h.m²) @ 50Pa in the BER calculation.

- Factory-made modular buildings of:
  - less than 500m² floor area; with
  - planned life of more than 2 years at more than one location; and
  - no site assembly work, except for linkages between standard modules made using standard link details.

  The builder should give the BCB a notice which confirms that the building as installed conforms to a standard configuration of module/link details for which the installer has a minimum of five in situ pressure measurements, with an average test result at least 1m³/(h.m²) better than the design air permeability used in the BER calculation.

- Large extensions which cannot be sealed from the existing building – subject to the agreement of the BCB, the extension should be treated as a large complex building.

- Large complex buildings, where testing is impracticable – developers must produce, in advance of construction work, a detailed justification of why pressure testing is impracticable, which should be endorsed by a suitably qualified person. One method of demonstrating compliance would be to appoint a suitably qualified person, such as an ATTMA member, to undertake detailed design development, component testing and site supervision to give confidence that a continuous air barrier will be achieved. The claimed air permeability must not be less than 5m³/(h.m²).

- Compartmentalised buildings divided into self-contained units with no internal connections – pressure testing should be carried out on a representative area. In the event of failure, in addition to the measures below, a further test should be carried out on another representative area to confirm the expected standard is achieved in all parts of the building.

A building will comply if:

- the assessed air permeability (**L.2.6**) is not worse than the limiting value of 10m³/(h.m²); and

- the BER calculated using assessed air permeability is not worse than the TER.

2013 changes
The reference to accredited construction details has been removed, as has the 25% performance penalty for using calculated linear thermal transmittance values.

Further guidance
IP 1/06 *Assessing the effects of thermal bridging at junctions and around openings in the external elements of buildings*. BRE. 2006.
BR 497 *Conventions for calculating linear thermal transmittance and temperature factors*. BRE. 2007 [amended 2010].

If the building fails, then remedial measures and re-testing should be carried out until it passes. Provided the measured air permeability is less than $10m^3/(h.m^2)$, other improvements may be made to bring the building DER below the TER.

Commissioning

Fixed building services must be commissioned and a notice of commissioning be provided to the BCB within the required timescale (see **L.1.5**).

Air leakage testing of ductwork

Where required by DW/143, ductwork of systems served by fans with a design flow rate greater than $1m^3/s$ should be tested (see **L.2.6**). Ductwork should reach the standard for the appropriate pressure class in Table L.8.

Remedial work should be carried out on ductwork which fails to meet the leakage standard, following by re-testing, and testing of further sections of ductwork.

DW/143 does not require testing of low-pressure ductwork (class A), however, if 10% of such ductwork is tested at random and meets the standard there will be an improvement in the BER.

Further guidance
Measuring air permeability of building envelopes, Technical Standard L2. ATTMA. 2010.
[Available from www.attma.org]

2013 changes
Testing is now required only when specified by DW/143. The benefit of testing low-pressure ductwork has been clarified.

Further guidance
DW/143 A practical guide to ductwork leakage testing. B&ES. 2013.

Table L.8 Ductwork pressure classes

Duct pressure class	Design static pressure (Pa)		Maximum air velocity (m/s)	Air leakage limits (l/(s.m²) of duct surface area[1])
	Maximum positive	Maximum negative		
Low pressure (Class A)	500	500	10	$0.027 \times \Delta p^{0.65}$
Medium pressure (class B)	1000	750	20	$0.009 \times \Delta p^{0.65}$
High pressure (class C)	2000	750	40	$0.003 \times \Delta p^{0.65}$
High pressure (Class D)	2000	750	40	$0.001 \times \Delta p^{0.65}$

[1] where Δp is the differential pressure in pascals

L.3.3.6 Criterion 5 – Efficient operation

Operating and maintenance information should be provided in a building log book which follows TM 31. The log book could draw on documents, such as the Operation and Maintenance manuals and the Health and Safety file required by the CDM Regulations.

Further guidance
TM 31 Building Log Book Toolkit. CIBSE 2006.

L.4 Existing buildings – L1B and L2B

L.4.1 Special cases

L.4.1.1 Large extensions

A large extension is treated as a new building if its total useful floor area is:

- greater than $100m^2$; and
- greater than 25% of the total useful floor area of the existing building.

The extension of a building with total floor area of at least $1000m^2$ will also trigger a requirement for consequential improvements (**L.4.7**).

2013 changes
The requirements for work to existing buildings are largely unchanged, with only minor changes to standards for controlled fittings (**L.4.4**) and the treatment of thermal elements (**L.4.6**).

L.4.1.2 Buildings with low energy demand

Where a building with low energy demand is extended or parts of the fabric are renovated, the new or renovated fabric need be insulated only to the degree that is reasonable in a particular case; where some general heating is provided (for example, for frost protection or on an infrequent basis) then no part of the opaque fabric should have a U-value worse than $0.7W/m^2K$. Fixed building services should meet the energy efficiency standards of the *Non-Domestic Building Services Compliance Guide*.

Any area which is partitioned off and heated normally (such as an office area in a warehouse) should be treated as a separate 'building' and normal standards followed for the enclosure.

A change of use or energy status which results in the space being generally conditioned is likely to result in the need for consequential improvements (**L.4.7**). If the first occupier wants to install a service such as heating that is treated as first fit-out (**L.3.3.2** Shell and core developments).

L.4.1.3 Historic and traditional buildings

The energy efficiency of historic and traditional buildings should be improved as far as is reasonably possible, but without prejudicing the character of the building or increasing the risk of long-term deterioration. In arriving at a balance between conservation and energy efficiency it would be appropriate to take account of advice from English Heritage and/or the local authority conservation officer.

L.4.1.4 Conservatories and porches

A conservatory or porch subject to Part L should have:

* effective thermal separation, with walls, doors and windows between the conservatory/porch and the existing building being insulated and draughtproofed to at least the same extent as in the existing dwelling;

* glazed elements to Table L.10 and thermal elements to Table L.11 (see **L.4.6.3**). The limitations on areas of windows, roof windows and doors do not apply;

* any heating system at least as efficient as minimum standards in the appropriate *Building Services Compliance Guide*, with automatic on/off controls which need not default to same schedule as the main building.

L.4.1.5 Swimming pools

The design of swimming pools should take account of the loading on insulation boards and should address thermal bridging at junctions between the basin wall, floor and foundations.

L.4.2 Extensions

There are three methods of demonstrating an extension meets Part L, with more complex methods giving greater design flexibility.

L.4.2.1 Reference method

The extension should meet the following standards:

* newly constructed thermal elements to **L.4.6.1**;

Further guidance
Energy Efficiency and Historic Buildings. English Heritage. 2011.
http://www.english-heritage.org.uk/publications/energy-efficiency-historic-buildings-ptl/

Other guidance documents are available at:
http://www.english-heritage.org.uk/professional/advice/advice-by-topic/climate-change/energy-efficiency/

2013 changes
Additional guidance has been supplied for the design of swimming pools.

- doors, windows, rooflights and smoke vents to **L.4.4**;
- fabric elements which become thermal elements to **L.4.6.3**;
- areas of openings in the extension:
  - in dwellings, windows, doors and rooflights not to exceed 25% of floor area of the extension, plus the area of any openings which no longer exist or are no longer exposed.
  - in other buildings, the areas of windows and rooflights should generally not exceed Table L.9, but may have the same proportion of glazing as that part of the building to which the extension is attached;
- fixed building services provided or extended should meet **L.4.5**.

Table L.9 Opening areas in extensions

Building type	Windows and personnel doors as % of exposed wall	Rooflights as % of area of roof
Residential buildings where people temporarily or permanently reside	30	20
Places of assembly, offices and shops	40	20
Industrial and storage buildings	15	20
Vehicle access doors, display windows and similar glazing	As required	Not applicable
Smoke vents	Not applicable	As required

L.4.2.2 Area-weighted U-value method

The area-weighted U-value of all elements in the extension should be no greater than for an extension of the same dimensions that conforms to the fabric standards for the reference method. The area-weighted U-value equals:

$$((U_1 \times A_1) + (U_2 \times A_2) + \ldots + (U_n \times A_n))/(A_1 + A_2 + \ldots + A_n)$$

Fixed building services should comply with **L.4.5**.

L.4.2.3 Whole building calculation

The CO_2 emission rate from the building with the proposed extension (calculated with an approved calculation tool) is no greater than that of the building plus a notional extension built to the reference method.

For dwellings:

- openings should conform with **L.4.4**, with the door area set equal to that of the proposed extension and other openings classified as windows;
- values in SAP 2012 Appendix S can be used to estimate performance of existing fabric; and
- any upgrades proposed to the existing fabric should meet **L.4.6.3**.

For other buildings:

- the notional building should include all upgrades required for consequential improvements;
- upgrades (other than consequential improvements) should be no worse than **L.4.6.3**.

L.4.3 Material change of use and change of energy status

Where a building undergoes a material change of use, or there is a change to a building's energy status:

- controlled fittings, controlled services and thermal elements should comply with the guidance in **L.4.5–L.4.7**;

- where the area of openings in a newly created building exceeds 25% of the total floor area, either that area should be reduced to 25%, or compensatory measures introduced;

- existing windows, doors, rooflights, and roof windows which separate a conditioned space from an unconditioned space or outside, and which have U-values worse than 3.3W/m²K should be replaced with units which comply with **L.4.4**, although display windows or high usage entrance doors may have higher U-values.

Alternatively, an approved calculation tool may be used to demonstrate that emissions from the building as it will become are no worse than if it had been improved following the guidance above.

In buildings other than dwellings the work may also result in a need to make consequential improvements.

L.4.4 Controlled fittings

Controlled fittings – windows, roof windows, roof lights and doors – consist of the whole unit, including the frame (consequently, replacing glazing within an existing frame or a door leaf within an existing frame, is not covered by Part L). The units should comply with Table L.10, should be draught-proofed and, where appropriate, have insulated cavity closers.

Where replacement windows or fully glazed external pedestrian doors cannot meet Table L.10 because of the need to maintain the appearance or character of the building they should have a centre pane U-value no higher than 1.2W/m²K (making no allowance for edge spacers or frame). Alternatively, single glazing should be supplemented with low-e secondary glazing: weather stripping should be on the secondary glazing to minimise condensation risk between primary and secondary glazing.

Where thicker glass is required to meet enhanced performance requirements, for example to address wind loading or acoustic attenuation, it is sufficient to demonstrate the window with the equivalent standard glazing thickness would comply.

In dwellings, the creation or enlargement of a window, roof window, rooflight or door should not increase their total area above 25% of the floor area of the dwelling, without compensating measures to reduce heat loss.

In other buildings:

- the creation or enlargement of a window, door or rooflight should not increase their total areas above the relevant values in Table L.9, without compensating measures;

- in a building with high internal gains, the average U-value figure can be relaxed to 2.7W/m²K in order to reduce overall emissions.

2013 changes
There have been minor changes to the standards for controlled fittings (Table L.10): there have now include DSER standards for doors; the proportion of glazing which defines glazed doors has been increased from 50% to 60%; for buildings other than dwellings that percentage of glazing is assessed on the external face.

Table L.10 Standards for controlled fittings

Building type	Fitting	Standard[1]
Dwelling	Window, roof window or roof-light[2][3]	WER = Band C or better; or U-value ≤ 1.6W/m²K
	Doors with >60% of internal face glazed	DSER = Band E or or better; or U-value ≤ 1.8W/m²K
	Other doors	DSER = Band E or better; or U-value ≤ 1.8W/m²K
Other buildings	Windows in buildings that are essentially domestic in character (e.g. student accommodation and care homes)	WER = Band C or better, or U-value ≤ 1.6W/m²K
	All other windows, roof windows and rooflights (excluding display windows)[2][3]	U-value ≤1.8W/m²K for the whole unit
	Curtain walling	U-value ≤1.8 W/m²K[4]
	Pedestrian door with >60% external face glazed	DSER = Band E or better; or U-value ≤ 1.8W/m²K
	All other pedestrian doors	DSER = Band E or better; or U-value ≤ 1.8W/m²K
	High usage entrance doors for people	U-value ≤ 3.5W/m²K
	Vehicle access and similar large doors	U-value ≤ 1.5W/m²K
	Roof ventilators (including smoke extract ventilation)	U-value ≤ 3.5W/m²K

[1] U-values for roof windows and rooflights measured in vertical position. The limiting U-value should be adjusted using the procedure in BR 443 (Conventions for U-value calculations, BRE 2006) if the unit's U-value has been measured in another plane.

[2] As U-values are determined for standard configurations the effects of Georgian bars and/or leaded lights can be ignored.

[3] Based on the developed area of rooflight, not the areas of the roof aperture. See NARM Technical Document NTD 2. 2010.

[4] Alternatively, the limiting U-value may be calculated from: $U = 0.8 + \{(1.2 + (FOL \times 0.5)) \times GF\}$, where FOL is the fraction of opening lights and GF is the glazed fraction.

L.4.5 Controlled services

Fixed building services should comply with the appropriate Compliance Guide. Where an existing appliance is replaced, the new appliance should be at least as efficient as the one being replaced. If there is a change of fuel then the relative emissions of new and existing fuel must be considered. Similarly, replacement energy generators should not have electrical output significantly less than the original installation.

Once installed, fixed building services must be commissioned (**L.1.5**).

L.4.5.1 Non-dwellings

New HVAC systems should comply with the design principles for fixed building services in new buildings (**L.3.3.3**). Energy meters for monitoring newly installed plant should meet the same criteria as those in new buildings, although the assignment to end use of 90% of energy consumption for the building is an aim, rather than a requirement.

New or refurbished ductwork should be tested for leakage where fans have design flow rates greater than 1m³/s, or DW/143 recommends testing for that class of duct (**L.2.6**).

Information on new services should be supplied in a new log book, or incorporated into the existing one.

L.4.6 Thermal elements

L.4.6.1 New thermal elements

New and replacement thermal elements should comply with Table L.11. There should be no reasonably avoidable thermal bridges within elements and at junctions, and unwanted air leakage should be limited. For buildings other than dwellings, there should be no gaps between air barriers and insulation (see L.3.3.5). Reasonable provision would be to adopt accredited construction details, or to demonstrate that the specified details provide adequate protection against surface condensation (see IP 1/06 and BR 497).

Where the replacement of the thermal element constitutes a major renovation or involves more than 50% of the element's surface area, the whole element must be replaced to the standards in Table L.11, so far as that is technically, functionally and economically feasible.

L.4.6.2 Renovation of thermal elements

Renovation may include adding a new layer to a thermal element (for example, cladding or drylining) or removing and replacing an existing layer by stripping down and rebuilding a thermal element, or replacing the waterproof membrane on a flat roof. Where renovation constitutes a major renovation, or affects 50% of the surface area of an element or 25% of the total building envelope (measured from the work side) thermal performance of the whole element should be improved.

Thermal elements should be improved to the values in Table L.11 column (b), provided that is technically and functionally feasible and achieves simple 15 year payback. Otherwise, it should be improved as much as possible within those constraints.

L.4.6.3 Retained thermal elements

Thermal performance of an existing element should be upgraded where:

- the building is subject to a material change of use;
- an existing element becomes part of the thermal envelope where previously it was not.

A thermal element with a U-value worse than column (a) of Table L.11 should be upgraded to column (b), provided it achieves a 15 year payback and is technically and functionally feasible. Otherwise it should be improved as far as possible within those constraints, but generally to no worse than $0.7 W/m^2 K$.

2013 changes

The requirements for replacement and renovation of thermal elements in regulation 23 have been clarified. If the work to replace or renovate a thermal element constitutes a 'major renovation' (a term not defined in the Regulations) or affects more than 50% of the surface of the element, then the whole element must be replaced or renovated.

Further guidance

IP 1/06. BRE. 2006. [See **L.3.3.5**.]

BR 497 *Conventions for calculating linear thermal transmittance and temperature factors*. BRE. 2007: [amended 2010].

Table L.11 Standards for new and retained thermal elements

Element[1]	New thermal elements	Upgrading retained thermal elements	
	Limiting U-value (W/m²K)	(a) Threshold U-value (W/m²K)	(b) Improved U-value[2] (W/m²K)
Wall – cavity insulation	0.28	0.70	0.55[3]
Wall – external or internal insulation	0.28	0.70	0.30
Floor[4]	0.22	0.70	0.25
Pitched roof – insulation at ceiling level	0.16	0.35	0.16
Pitched roof – insulation at rafter line	0.18	0.35	0.18
Flat roof or roof with integral insulation	0.18	0.35	0.18
Swimming pool basin	0.25	N/A	N/A

[1] Roof includes roof parts of dormer windows and walls includes dormer cheeks. Curtain walling is a controlled fitting.

[2] Lesser provisions may be appropriate where meeting the standards would:

- cause a reduction of more than 5% in total floor area;
- create significant problems with floor levels;
- create limitations on headroom;
- exceed the loadbearing capacity of the frame.

[3] Only where suitable for installation of cavity insulation, in all other cases as wall external or internal insulation.

[4] The U-value of the floor of an extension can be calculated using the exposed perimeter and floor area of whole enlarged dwelling.

L.4.7 Consequential improvements

Additional work to improve the energy efficiency (consequential improvements) will be required where building work to an existing building with a total useful floor area over 1000m² involves:

- an extension;
- initial provision of any fixed building services (other than a renewable energy generator);
- increase to the installed capacity of any fixed building services (other than renewable energy generator).

The additional work should ensure the building complies with Part L, to the extent that the improvements are technically, functionally and economically feasible (see Approved Document L2B Table 6). Improvements will be economically feasible if the simple payback time does not exceed 15 years (unless there are unusual circumstances, such as a building with a remaining service life of less than 15 years).

Improvement works other than those 'trigger' items listed above can count towards consequential improvements, provided they are not being carried out to compensate for a poorer standard of extension (**L.4.2**).

L.4.7.1 Extending a building

When a building is extended, consequential improvements should be made up to a value of at least 10% of the principal works.

L.4.7.2 Installing building services

When a fixed building service is first installed or its installed capacity is increased:

- the fabric of those parts of the building it serves should be improved to Table L.11 where economically feasible (but not limited by the 10% threshold); and

- additional improvements made as Table L.12 (the costs of the fabric improvements are ignored when evaluating the 10% threshold).

The installed capacity of a fixed building service is the design output of the distribution system output devices serving the space, divided by the total useful floor area of the space.

Further guidance
TM 39 Building energy metering. CIBSE. 2009.

Table L.12 Consequential improvements to fabric when increasing the installed capacity of services		
Fixed building service	**Thermal elements**	**Openings and lighting**
Heating system	Thermal elements worse than **Table L.11** column (a) should be upgraded as **L.4.7.2**.	Existing windows, roof windows, rooflights and doors (but not display windows or high usage entrance doors) should be upgraded as **L.4.4**.
Cooling system	Thermal elements worse than **Table L.11** column (a) should be upgraded as **L.4.7.2**.	If design solar load exceeds 25W/m^2, and the area of windows and roof windows (excluding display windows) exceeds 40% of the façade area, or the area of rooflights 20% of the roof area, then upgrade solar control provisions to satisfy one of the following: • Solar gain per unit floor area averaged over the period 0630-1630 GMT does not exceed 25W/m^2 when the building is subject to solar irradiancies for July (CIBSE Design Guide A). • Design solar load is reduced by at least 20%. • The effective g-value is no worse than 0.3. • The zone or zones satisfy Criterion 3 for new buildings other than dwellings. General lighting systems with average lamp efficiency less than 45 lamp-lumens/circuit watt should be upgraded to meet the Non-Domestic Building Services Compliance Guide.

L.4.8 Provision of information

On completion of the work the building owner should be provided with sufficient information about the building, its services and their operating and maintenance requirements to enable the building to be operated using a reasonable amount of fuel and power. The requirement only applies to work which has been carried out. The information should be similar to that described in **L.3.1.5**, **L.3.2.5** (dwellings) and **L.3.3.6** (other buildings).

1. Access to and use of buildings

M.1 General considerations

M.1.1 Scope

Part M is intended to ensure that buildings and their facilities are accessible by all people, regardless of age, disability or gender. Part M is not intended to address all the requirements for fully independent living for all people with disabilities.

2013 changes
The main changes to Part M are:
- Much of the guidance for stairs, ramps, handrails, guarding, vision panels and manifestation of glazing has been removed from Approved Document M, which now makes reference to the relevant sections of Approved Document K. However, guidance on access to buildings is still contained in Approved Document M.
- Guidance on meeting the Equality Act 2010, replaces guidance on the Disability Discrimination Act (**M.1.3**).
- There is no longer a requirement to submit a written Access Statement on every project: instead, there is a more general obligation to demonstrate to the Building Control Body (BCB) how the chosen approach will satisfy the requirements of Part M (**M.1.5**).
- Some references have been updated.

Part M: Access to and use of building

Requirement	Limits on application
Access and use	
M1 Reasonable provision shall be made for people to – (a) gain access to; and (b) use the building and its facilities.	The requirements of this Part do not apply to – (a) an extension of or material alteration of a dwelling; or (b) any part of a building which is used solely to enable the building or any service or fitting in the building to be inspected, repaired or maintained.
Access to extensions to buildings other than dwellings	
M2 Suitable independent access shall be provided to the extension where reasonably practicable.	Requirement M2 does not apply where suitable access to the extension is provided through the building that is extended.
Sanitary conveniences in extensions to buildings other than dwellings	
M3 If sanitary conveniences are provided in any building that is to be extended, reasonable provision shall be made within the extension for sanitary conveniences.	Requirement M3 does not apply where there is reasonable provision for sanitary conveniences elsewhere in the building, such that people occupied in, or otherwise having occasion to enter the extension, can gain access to and use those sanitary conveniences.
Sanitary conveniences in dwellings	
M4 (1) Reasonable provision shall be made in the entrance storey for sanitary conveniences, or where the entrance storey contains no habitable rooms, reasonable provision for sanitary conveniences shall be made in either the entrance storey or principal storey. (2) In this paragraph 'entrance storey' means the storey which contains the principal entrance and 'principal storey' means the storey nearest to the entrance storey which contains a habitable room, or if there are two such storeys equally near, either such storey.	

M.1.2 Application

M.1.2.1 New non-domestic buildings

All the relevant requirements of Part M apply to the whole building and its access routes, with the exception of areas only intended for access for building and services maintenance.

M.1.2.2 Extension of an existing non-domestic building

An extension to a non-domestic building is treated as a new building. The requirement for suitable independent access need not require separate provision, if it can be demonstrated that the extension will have suitable access through the existing building, which may be modified to provide access. The building access strategy (**M.1.5**) may be used to demonstrate either that independent access is not required, or is neither practicable nor cost-effective.

M.1.2.3 Material alteration of non-domestic buildings

Alteration work to existing buildings must comply with Requirement M1, and the building overall must be no less compliant than it was prior to the work being undertaken. However, where an alteration does not affect access there is no need to upgrade access to meet Requirement M1.

M.1.2.4 Material change of use

Where the whole building is subject to material change of use the whole building must be upgraded to comply with Requirement M1.

Where only part of the building is subject to change of use that part must be upgraded to comply with M1. Sanitary conveniences in, or connected with, that part must comply with M1, as should those in other parts of the building to which users have access. There should be suitable access to that part of the building, either by a route to and through other parts of the building, or independent access.

If the change of use results in a building which includes both non-domestic and domestic parts then the non-domestic and common parts should comply with non-domestic guidance.

M.1.2.5 New dwellings

All the relevant requirements of Part M apply.

M.1.2.6 Extensions and alterations to dwellings

Part M does not apply to the extension or alteration of an existing dwelling. Work carried out need not comply with Part M, neither is there any requirement to bring the dwelling to the standards of Part M.

Nonetheless, should an alteration or extension result in the dwelling either being non-compliant where it previously was compliant, or being less compliant than before, then the work constitutes a material alteration and measures must be taken to prevent the degradation (**I.2.2**). For example, removing the only WC from the entrance storey of a dwelling would constitute a material alteration, because the building would no longer meet Requirement M4.

M.1.2.7 Historic buildings

Accessibility should be improved as much as is practically possible, without prejudicing the character of the historic building or increasing the risk of long-term deterioration of fabric or fittings.

M.1.3 The Equality Act 2010

The Equality Act 2010 imposes duties on employers and those who provide services to the public to make reasonable adjustments to those physical features of a building which place a disabled person at a substantial disadvantage compared with people who are not disabled. Following the guidance in Approved Document M may not be sufficient to comply with duties imposed by the Act, as they may require provisions beyond the scope of the Approved Document.

Under the Equality Act 2010 (Disability) Regulations 2010, it is not reasonable for a physical feature to be removed or altered if the feature was provided to assist people to access the building or use its facilities, and it satisfied the provisions of the then current edition of Approved Document M (the 'relevant design standard'). However, the exemption does not apply if more than ten years have elapsed since the construction or installation of the feature.

2013 changes
In 2010 the Disability Discrimination Act (DDA) was replaced by the Equality Act, with the intention of strengthening and harmonising existing anti-discrimination provisions. Under the DDA a service provider had to take steps if a physical feature made it unreasonably difficult for disabled people to use their services: the Equality Act requires measures where a disabled person might be at a substantial disadvantage to a non-disabled person.

Further guidance
The Equality Act 2010.
www.legislation.gov.uk/ukpga/2010/15

The Equality Act 2010 (Disability) Regulations 2010.
www.legislation.gov.uk/uksi/2010/2128

M.1.4 BS 8300

The guidance given in Approved Document M is based largely on the same research as BS 8300:2001, although in a few cases, the recommendations of the Approved Document differ from the guidance in the standard.

The 2009 edition of BS 8300 (amended 2010) contains some recommendations based on new and re-evaluated research; adopting those recommendations would be an acceptable alternative to following the guidance in Approved Document M. However, such a decision should be agreed with the BCB early in the design process. Guidance for dwellings is now given in DD 266 and not BS 8300:2009.

Further guidance
BS 8300:2001. Design of buildings and their approaches to meet the needs of disabled people. Code of practice. [Withdrawn and replaced by BS 8300:2009+A1:2010.]

BS DD 266:2007. Design of accessible housing. Lifetime home. Code of practice.

M.1.5 Access strategy

The guidance in Approved Document M is only one way in which the requirements of Part M may be met. Where alternative solutions are proposed, it must be demonstrated that they will satisfy those requirements, which may be achieved by reference to British Standards or research evidence. The access strategy to achieve the required standard of provision should be agreed with the BCB before work begins.

A written access strategy is not required, although may be useful in some circumstances, particularly where proposals diverge from Approved Document M. In smaller works, agreement may be achieved by a conversation to review proposals, which is then recorded by correspondence. Larger, more complex works – particularly where an existing site imposes constraints – may require a written document supported by annotated drawings.

2013 changes
There is no longer a requirement to submit a written access statement to the BCB. The essential requirement is to agree the appropriate standard of provision with the BCB.

M.1.6 Provision groups

Approved Document M provides for the access requirements of people with a range of impairments.

M.1.6.1 Wheelchair users

Wheelchair users require level or ramped access to buildings and enough space within circulation areas to permit unobstructed movement around the building, either on their own or with a helper. Lifting devices are required to enable vertical circulation.

Wheelchair users have limited reach, so handles, controls and switches should be set at a convenient height. Facilities such as reception desks, ticket desks and bar counters should also be usable by someone in a wheelchair.

WCs and other sanitary facilities should be accessible and should facilitate transfer from and to a wheelchair.

M.1.6.2 Ambulant disabled

Ambulant disabled people, who may use sticks, crutches, walking frames or have callipers, are likely to be limited in the distances they can travel. They will often find stairs safer to negotiate than ramps. They may move more slowly than other people, so they will take longer to get through doors. They may also require more space in sanitary accommodation.

M.1.6.3 Impaired vision

People with visual impairment may be blind, or may have poor or partial vision. The partially sighted will benefit from well-designed natural and artificial lighting which provides even illumination without glare: for example, low-level uplighters can disorientate some visually impaired people and should be avoided.

The use of visually contrasting surface finishes will assist people with visual impairment to get a sense of the spaces within the building, to distinguish doors and items such as control panels against the background, and to identify access routes and information. For the purposes of Part M, surfaces contrast visually if there is a difference of more than 30 points in surface light reflectance between them. Where illuminance on surfaces is greater than 200 lux the difference should be at least 20 points, and if door opening furniture projects beyond the door or otherwise enhances differentiation a difference of 15 point will be adequate.

There should be visual warning of hazards, particularly those likely to cause collisions and falls. Door edges should be visually distinct, glass screens and doors should have manifestation, and steps should have high contrast edging.

Guarding, with cane detection, will prevent collision with obstacles protruding onto access and circulation routes. Some hazards, including steps or kerbs, require tactile warnings – such as corduroy surfaces – which should extend sufficiently to give users time to respond to the warning.

2013 changes
There are now different limits for acceptable levels of light reflectance values for two particular conditions.

The provisions for manifestation and guarding are now predominantly addressed in Part K, rather than Part M.

Signage and lettering on controls should be visually contrasting and symbols on controls, such as those for lifts, should be raised to facilitate tactile reading.

M.1.6.4 Impaired hearing

For people with impaired hearing the main provisions address the use of a building's facilities and active participation in activities taking place within it.

Hearing impaired people who rely on lip-reading or signing for communication require good visibility. Therefore, good levels of lighting are essential. However, the design should avoid features such as glazed screens in front of desks, or light sources and glazing behind desks, which can produce glare and so impair lip-reading and signing. Large repeating patterns should also be avoided at reception desks and speakers' rostrums.

For those with some degree of hearing, communication can be hindered by background noise, so the design of facilities such as reception areas and ticket offices should minimise intrusive noise. Good acoustic conditions throughout the building will also promote intelligibility of speech.

Hearing enhancement systems would be beneficial at reception desks and in meeting rooms and auditoria.

Warning alarms must include visual indicators.

M.1.6.5 Impaired strength/manual dexterity

Some building users may not have sufficient strength to open self-closing doors or have sufficient manual dexterity to use standard controls and switches, such as those for operating lights. To assist them, doors should only require a limited amount of force to open them, and controls should not require high levels of strength or dexterity.

M.1.6.6 Other requirements

Many of the provisions for wheelchair users and the ambulant disabled will benefit other building users – particularly those with small children in prams, buggies and double buggies – as they move round the building and also when they use sanitary facilities (double buggies require wider openings than wheelchairs). People with large amounts of luggage will also benefit from the space provisions for ambulant disabled people.

Further guidance
BS 8300:2009+A1:2010 Appendix B. [For guidance on the use of light reflectance values (LRVs) to assess visual contrast.]

Colour, contrast and perception for internal built environment. K. Bright, G. Cook and J. Harris. University of Reading, 1997. [Guidance on the use of colour to assist the visually impaired.]

M.2 Common provisions

Much of the guidance in Approved Document M is common to several requirements.

M.2.1 Surfaces

Access routes should be level and even. Their slope should not exceed 1:60, and any cross-fall should not exceed 1:40. Routes surfaced with formless materials should have variation of no more than 3mm across a distance of 1m. Paved units with flush joints should have no more than 5mm height difference between units: joints should be recessed by no more than 5mm, but may be up to 10mm wide; unfilled joints may be no more than 5mm wide.

M.2.2 Ramps

Ramps are suitable for wheelchair users, people pushing prams and those with wheeled luggage. However, they may be unsuitable for some ambulant disabled people because they may increase the risk of slipping, so stairs should generally be provided as well. Ramps should be readily apparent or well signed.

Ramps within buildings should comply with Approved Document K Section 2 (see **K.2.3**). Ramps on access routes to buildings other than dwellings should follow the same requirements together with the additional items listed in **M.3.3**.

2013 changes
For internal ramps, Approved Document M now refers directly to the revised guidance in Approved Document K section 2 (**K.2.3**). However, the guidance for external ramps on access routes is still contained in Approved Document M, despite the requirements being almost identical.

M.2.3 Stairs

Stairs within buildings should comply with Approved Document K Section 1. Stairs on access routes to buildings other than dwellings should follow the same requirements, together with the additional items listed in **M.3.4**.

2013 changes
For internal stairs, Approved Document M now refers directly to the revised guidance in Approved Document K section 1 (**K.2.1**). However, the guidance for external stairs on access routes is still contained in Approved Document M, despite the requirements being almost identical.

M.2.4 Handrails

Handrails assist people who have difficulty negotiating changes of level. They should therefore be easily gripped, comfortable to hold and, where possible, provide good forearm support. Handrails should comply with Approved Document K sections 1–3 (**K.2.1.5** and **K.2.3.4**). In addition, handrails on access routes to buildings should protrude no more than 100mm into the surface width of a ramp or stepped access where that would interfere with a means of escape (**B.3.5.2**).

2013 changes
Although guidance for handrails on internal access routes is now given in Approved Document K, the guidance for handrails on external access routes to buildings has remained in Approved Document M. The guidance is identical, except for the 100mm protrusion limit for external access routes.

M.2.5 Doors and screens

To provide sufficient space for wheelchair users, the minimum clear width of a single leaf door, or one leaf of a double leaf door, should be as shown in Table M.1, when measured according to Figure M.1.

Table M.1 Minimum effective clear width of doors		
Direction and width of approach	New buildings (mm)	Existing buildings (mm)
Straight-on (no turn or oblique approach)	800	750
At right angles to an access route ≥1500mm	800	750
At right angles to an access route ≥1200mm	825	775
External doors to buildings used by the general public	1000	775

Note: Clear width as **Figure M.1**.

Figure M.1 Clear width requirements for doors

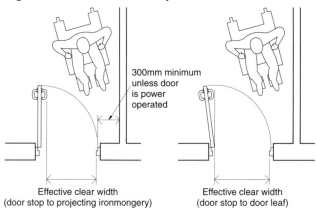

300mm minimum unless door is power operated

Effective clear width (door stop to projecting ironmongery)

Effective clear width (door stop to door leaf)

To prevent collisions as people approach doors from both sides, door leaves and side panels should have vision panels as Approved Document K section 10 (**K.10**). Glass doors and screens should have manifestation as Approved Document K section 7 (**K.7**).

Doors which require a force to open of more than 30N at 0° (closed) to 30° open, and 22.5N for 30–60° open will be an obstacle to people with impaired strength and to wheelchair users. Such doors (e.g. those with self-closers fitted) will require a powered opening and closing system.

To aid orientation, where sets of double doors on a corridor have unevenly sized leaves, the wider ones should be on the same side of the corridor for its whole length.

M.2.5.1 Manually operated doors

Manually operated doors need enough space for wheelchair users to reach the handle and open the door without colliding with the door or the wall. At the pull side of the door, there should be 300mm unobstructed space between the return wall and the leading edge of the door.

The opening furniture on doors with latches should be operable with one hand using a closed fist, for example a lever handle. The door furniture should contrast visibly with the door, and should not be cold to the touch.

Where a manually operated entrance door has a self-closing device the force required to open the door is likely to exceed 30N at 0° (closed) to 30° open, and 22.5N for 30–60° open; consequently, a manually operated door is unlikely to be suitable for such a location.

2013 changes
The guidance on the acceptable force for opening doors has been modified from the single maximum limit of 20N, to a two-stage limit, making it identical with that in BS 8300:2009+A1:2010. Section 6.5.2 of that standard notes that wheelchair users experienced difficulty in opening doors against the initial force of the closer and further difficulty when the door was opened beyond approximately 30°.

2013 changes
The guidance on the acceptable force for opening doors has been modified, making it identical with that in BS 8300:2009+A1:2010.

M.2.5.2 Powered entrance doors

Powered doors may have sliding, swinging or folding action and should be controlled manually (for example, by push pad), or automatically, by motion or proximity sensors. Any controls should be set 750–1000mm above floor level and, if on the opening side of the door, be set back 1400mm, to prevent the user having to move to avoid the door as it opens. The controls should be operable with a closed fist, and should contrast visually with the background.

The door must open early enough, and stay open long enough, to permit safe entry and exit, and should incorporate a safety feature to prevent the door closing on someone passing through. In the event of power failure the door should revert to manual, or failsafe open.

When open, the doors should not project onto any adjacent access route. Doors which swing open towards people approaching should have visible and audible warnings of opening and closing.

M.2.6 Obstructions and low soffits

Access routes should, as far as possible, be clear of obstructions. Where obstructions such as doors or windows project more than 100mm onto an access routes they should be guarded as Approved Document K sections 6 and 10 (**K.6** and **K.10**). Obstructions such as full-height columns, ducts, radiators and fire hoses which project more than 100mm into corridors or lobbies should be protected with visually contrasting guarding.

2013 changes
Approved Document M now refers to Approved Document K for guidance regarding hazards on access routes and areas with low soffits below stairs and ramps.

M.3 Access to buildings other than dwellings (Requirement M2)

There should be suitable means of access to the building from entrance points at the site boundary, or from on-site car parking; buildings on the same site should also be accessible.

Changes of level should be avoided as far as practicable, in order to give level access from the boundary or disabled parking to: the principal entrance; any entrance used exclusively by staff; or an alternative accessible entrance. The design should minimise level differences between the entrance storey and the site entrance point. Similarly, access between entrances or alternative accessible entrances should, as far as possible, be level.

Where there are gradients, these should be as gentle as possible, and should either have one long, gentle gradient, or several short lengths at a steeper gradient with level landings as rest points. Any part of an approach with a gradient steeper than 1:20 should be designed as ramped access.

Surfaces should allow easy travel and present no risk of tripping or falling.

M.3.1 Car parking

Car parking provision should enable a disabled person or a person with a pushchair or luggage to leave the vehicle, access the rear of the vehicle if necessary, then travel by an easy access route to the principal entrance, staff entrance or alternative accessible entrance.

There should be at least one disabled person's parking bay as close as is feasible to the principal entrance. The bay should measure 2400mm × 4800mm, with a 1200mm safety zone to the end closest to the vehicular access route and a 1200mm access zone to the side. The bay should have a firm, even, durable surface; sand and gravel are unlikely to be suitable.

If a ticket machine is necessary, its plinth should not prevent wheelchair users reaching it, and the controls should be 750–1200mm from the ground.

A clearly signposted setting down point should be provided on firm, level ground, as close to the principal or alternative accessible entrance as possible, and it should be clearly signposted.

M.3.2 Level access

Access routes should provide sufficient space for travelling, and passing. Routes should be at least 1.5m wide, with passing places at least 1.8m wide and 2m long, within sight of each other, but no more than 50m apart. Any route with a width of 1.8m or more does not require passing places.

The route should have a gradient no greater than 1:60, or no greater than 1:20 for a distance not exceeding 10m, provided there is a level landing for each 500mm rise. Cross-falls for drainage should not exceed 1:40.

The surface should be firm, durable and even. All materials should have similar frictional properties. The route should be free of obstructions up to 2.1m above its surface.

M.3.3 Ramped access

Ramped access should be provided where the approach is 1:20 or steeper. Ramps should comply with the guidance in Approved Document K Section 2 (**K.2.3**). In addition, no flight should have a going greater than 10m, or a rise of more than 500mm, and ramps may have a cross fall of up to 1:40. Where the total rise is greater than 2m an alternative means of access for wheelchair users should be provided (e.g. a lift).

2013 changes

Although the guidance for ramps within buildings has been transferred to Approved Document K, the provisions for ramps on access routes have remained in Approved Document M. However, the only significant variations between the two sets of guidance are those listed in this section.

M.3.4 Stepped access

Stepped access routes should follow the general guidance for stairs (**M.2.3** and **K.2**), but with the following modifications:

- Landings at the top and bottom of flights must be level.
- No door swings across landings are permitted.
- There should be corduroy hazard warning surfaces on the top and bottom landings of a series of flights (Figure M.2). Where access to the landing is from the side, the corduroy surface should extend 400mm beyond the line of the steps.

- The going of each step should be 280–425mm.
- A rise outside the standard range of 150–170mm may be permissible adjacent to an existing building. The case for such a variation should be made in the access strategy.
- A flight with a going of less than 350mm may have no more than 12 risers, while a flight with a going of 350mm or more may have no more than 18 risers.
- The maximum width between handrails is 1.8m.

Further guidance:
Guidance on the use of tactile paving surfaces. DfT. 2005. [Updated 2007.]
https://www.gov.uk/government/publications/guidance-on-the-use-of-tactile-paving-surfaces

2013 changes
Despite the consolidation of the guidance for internal stairs to Approved Document K, the guidance for stairs on access routes to buildings remains in Approved Document M. However, apart from the points listed in this section the guidance is identical.

Figure M.2 Stepped access – key dimensions

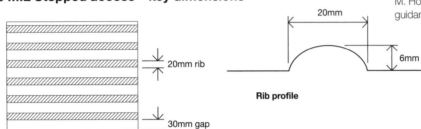

20mm rib

30mm gap

20mm

6mm

Rib profile

'Corduroy' hazard warning surface (with 8mm ribs)

Note: Full details of tactile paving are in *'Guidance on the use of tactile paving surfaces.'*

'Corduroy' hazard warning surface at top of stairs to extend at least 400mm at each side of stairs and to stop 400mm from nosing

Closed end to handrail at top and bottom

Handrail to be continuous across intermediate landings

400mm min.

Stair width

400mm min.

Handrail to be terminated in a way that reduces the risk of clothing being caught

800mm when the approach is straight on and 400mm when a conscious turn is needed to reach the step

400mm

1200mm min.

400mm

800mm

1200mm min. bottom landing

M.3.5 Hazards on the access route

Access routes should be clearly marked, well lit and separated from vehicular access routes. Any crossings should be marked by a buff-coloured blister surface. Projections onto the access route should be guarded (see **M.2.6**).

M.4 Access into buildings other than dwellings

The principal entrance(s) and main staff entrances of the building, together with their lobbies, should be accessible to all. Where that is not possible – either with existing buildings or buildings on steeply sloping or restricted sites – an alternative accessible entrance should be provided.

M.4.1 Accessible entrances

An accessible entrance should be clearly signposted from the edge of the site or from the principal entrance, using the international symbol for access (Figure M.3). The entrance should be easily identifiable from the rest of the building and its environment by means of lighting and/or visual contrast. Structural elements, such as canopy supports, can be used to identify the entrance but they must not present a hazard to those with impaired vision.

Figure M.3 International symbol for access

There should be a level landing in front of the entrance door measuring at least 1500mm × 1500mm, which is clear of door swings, having a surface which does not impede wheelchairs, and weather protection where the entrance doors are non-powered and manually operated. Door entry systems should be accessible to those with impaired hearing or speech.

The threshold should preferably be level, particularly if it is going to be frequently used, or alternatively it should be no more than 15mm total height, with a minimum number of upstands and slopes. Any upstand greater than 5mm should be chamfered or rounded.

Internal floor surfaces should not impede wheelchairs, and changes of flooring material should not form a trip hazard. At matwells, the surface of the mat should be level with the floor surface.

Where access is provided by means of an alternative accessible entrance there should be an accessible internal access route to all areas served by the principal entrance.

M.4.2 Doors to accessible entrances

The door to an accessible entrance may be manual, but should preferably be powered, with manual or automatic control, and should be capable of being held closed when not in use. Automatic sliding doors avoid many of the collision risks associated with automatic swing doors. Revolving doors are not considered accessible and should be supplemented with a well-signed, accessible door adjacent to it.

When open, doors should be wide enough to give unrestricted access for a variety of users, including wheelchair users and parents with prams or buggies (see Table M.2 and Figure M.2). It may be difficult to obtain the required width with existing buildings. The case for a narrower door may be made in the access strategy.

Doors should have vision panels to avoid collisions, unless there are requirements for privacy or security. Arguments for that should be made in the access strategy. Glass entrance doors which swing outwards should have guarding to prevent collisions, in particular with the leading edge.

M.4.3 Entrance lobbies

A lobby should be large enough for a wheelchair user with a companion, or a person pushing a pram to be able to get into the lobby and have the door close behind them before opening the second door. Consequently, the size of the door swing will have a significant effect on the lobby's size (see Table M.2 and Figure M.4).

Table M.2 Sizing of lobbies		
Lobby type	Dimension	Minimum requirement
Single swing doors	Length	As **Figure M.4**
	Width	The greatest of: • 1200mm • DL1 + 300mm • DL2 + 300mm
Double swing doors	Length	Dimensions DP1 + DP2 + 1570mm
	Width	1800mm

Note: Dimensions DL and DP measured as shown on **Figure M.4**.

The flooring should not impede wheelchairs and should help remove rainwater from shoes and wheelchairs. Any change of material should not create a trip hazard. At matwells, the surface of the mat should be level with the floor surface.

The lobby should have minimal obstructions, and full height elements such as ducts and columns which project more than 100mm should have visually contrasting guarding. Glazing should not create distracting reflections.

Figure M.4 Key dimensions for lobbies

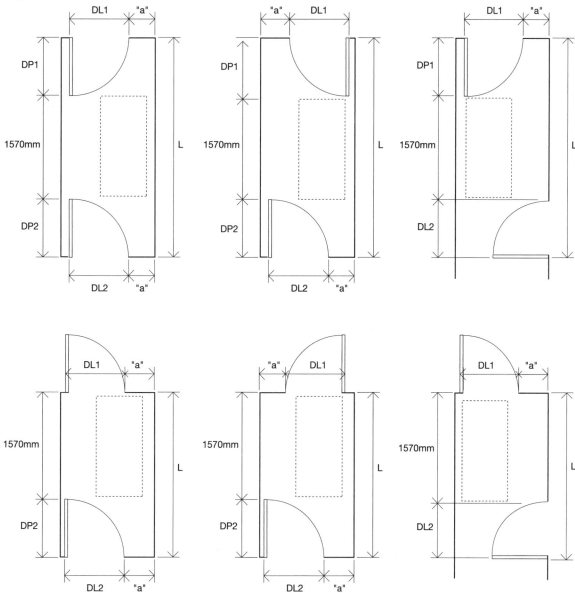

DL1 and DL2 = door leaf dimensions of the doors to the lobby
DP1 and DP2 = door projection into the lobby (normally door leaf size)
L = minimum length of lobby, or length up to door leaf for side entry lobby
"a" = at least 300mm wheelchair access space (can be increased to reduce L)
1570mm = length of occupied wheelchair with a companion pushing (or a large scooter)

NB: For every 100mm increase above 300mm in the dimension "a" (which gives a greater overlap of the wheelchair footprint over the door swing), there can be a corresponding reduction of 100mm in the dimension L, up to a maximum of 600mm reduction.

M.5 Circulation around buildings (Requirement M1)

All users should be able to travel conveniently within the building in order to use its facilities.

M.5.1 Entrance hall and reception area

As the first point of contact with the building, the entrance hall and reception area should be accessible and convenient to use. Signage should make it easy to find information about the building; and the floor should be slip-resistant.

The reception point should be easily identifiable from the entrance doors or lobby and have an unobstructed approach. Where high levels of external noise are expected the reception point should be sited away from the principal entrance, but within view of it. The reception point should have a hearing enhancement system.

Any reception or sales counter should be accessible, with a manoeuvring space in front of it of 1400mm × 2200mm (1200mm × 1800mm if there is a 500mm deep knee recess in the counter). A section of counter at least 1500mm wide should be at a height suitable for wheelchair users; this should be no more than 760mm high, with a knee recess extending at least 700mm above floor level.

Further guidance
BS 8300:2009+A1:2010 [Section 9.2 has guidance on signage.]

M.5.2 Internal doors

Doors form potential barriers to access, and should be avoided whenever appropriate. Similarly, the use of self-closers should be avoided where they require an opening force on the leading edge in excess of 30N at 0° (closed) to 30° open, and 22.5N for 30–60° open.

Fire doors, particularly those to circulation routes, should be held open with electromagnetic devices which self-close when activated by local or central smoke and/or fire detection systems. Swing-free devices should be used for doors to individual rooms. Low-energy powered doors with slow action may be specified in areas of infrequent use, or light traffic; and these should be able to operate in manual, powered or power-assisted mode.

A manual door requires 300mm unobstructed space between its leading edge and the return wall on the pull side of the door, unless it gives access to a standard hotel bedroom.

The guidance on doors in **M.2.5** applies with regards to sizing, visual differentiation, manifestation, vision panels and door opening furniture.

M.5.3 Corridors and passageways

Corridors should be wide enough for free circulation and to enable people on crutches or with buggies or cases to pass each other. Wheelchair users should have access into adjacent rooms and spaces, and should be able to pass other people and turn through 180°.

Generally, corridors and passageways should have an unobstructed width of 1200mm, although narrow corridors may be permissible for short distances, for example to pass through archways in existing buildings. Where the corridor is less than 1800mm wide there should be 1800mm × 1800mm (minimum) passing places at reasonable intervals to allow wheelchair users to pass. Those passing places could be at corridor junctions. In schools, corridors with lockers should be at least 2700mm wide.

Floors should generally have a gradient no greater than 1:60. Where the gradient is between 1:60 and 1:20 there should be no more than a 500mm rise without a level (less than 1:60) rest area 1500mm long. Any sections steeper than 1:20 should be designed as a ramp (**M.2.2**).

Doors which open onto major traffic routes and escape routes should be recessed so that they do not project into the corridor space when fully open. Small store rooms and locked duct cupboards are exempt from that requirement. Doors from unisex, wheelchair-accessible toilets can project onto other corridors, provided the corridor is at least 1800mm wide at that point. Projecting columns and ducts should have visually contrasting guarding.

M.5.4 Internal lobbies

Internal lobbies should follow the same guidance as entrance lobbies (**M.5.1**), but there are no requirements for matwells, nor for flooring to remove rainwater from shoes and wheelchairs.

M.5.5 Vertical circulation

The most suitable means of vertical circulation is the passenger lift, which should be provided wherever possible. In a limited number of circumstances other means may be suitable. The case for providing a lifting device other than a passenger lift should be made in the access strategy.

New developments should have passenger lift access to all storeys, although on constrained sites (such as an infill site) a lifting platform (platform lift) may be acceptable. Existing buildings should either have passenger lift access to all storeys, or have a lifting platform. Exceptionally, a wheelchair stairlift may be acceptable, for example to access a staff room, but the case should be set out in the access strategy.

Lifting devices for mobility impaired people must be clearly signed from the building's entrance; and each floor landing should have visually contrasting floor indicators which can be clearly seen from the lifting device.

Irrespective of the type of lifting device that is provided, there should also be internal stairs, suitable for ambulant disabled people and those with impaired sight. Where unavoidable, the route to a lifting device may include a ramp.

M.5.5.1 Lifting devices

Common provisions

All users, including those in wheelchairs, should be able to reach and use controls to summon and direct the lifting device. The buttons and face plate should contrast visually with each other and with the background, and the buttons should have raised symbols for tactile reading.

The car or platform should be clearly illuminated, without confusing shadows, glare or reflections. The lift landing and the car doors should be visually distinguishable from adjoining walls; areas of glass should be readily identifiable as such.

The floor should not be a dark colour and, to prevent tripping, should have similar frictional properties to that of the landing.

Acoustic and visually reflective surfaces should be avoided to prevent discomfort for those with visual or hearing impairment.

Passenger lifts

Lifts should be sized to match both the expected density of use and the needs of disabled people. The minimum size allows for a wheelchair user and one accompanying person (see Figure M.5). However, a larger lift (w × d: 2000 × 1400mm) takes more people and allows a wheelchair user or someone with a walking frame to turn within the lift ready to exit. Where a lift is too small for turning, there should be a mirror for a wheelchair user to see the space behind the wheelchair. Alternatively, the provision of doors on opposite sides of a lift would allow a wheelchair user to exit the lift without having to turn.

Figure M.5 Key dimensions for passenger lifts

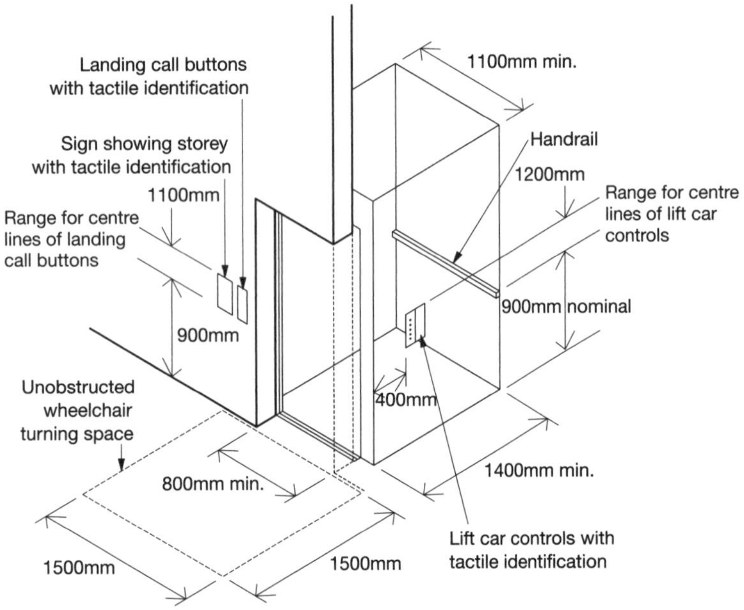

Any lift intended to be used to evacuate disabled people in an emergency should conform to BS 5588-8. The lift should meet the requirements listed in Table M.3.

Lifting platforms

Lifting platforms are suitable only to transfer wheelchair users, people with impaired mobility and their companions between levels or storeys. As they are slow travelling they may not be suitable for lone users who are easily fatigued. Careful consideration should be given to their intended use and the product's designed duty cycle, particularly in an unsupervised environment.

The provision of opposing doors on the platform would avoid wheelchair users having to reverse, although a second door set at 90° to the first may be more convenient. The lifting platform should meet the requirements listed in Table M.4.

Wheelchair platform stair lifts

Wheelchair platform stair lifts can be used independently by wheelchair users when seated. They travel slowly, so are not suitable for people who are easily fatigued. They are likely to be suitable only as a last resort, in locations where users can be instructed, and management supervision ensured. Their use must be justified in the Access Statement.

In a building with a single stairway, the clear width of the flight and landings required for means of escape must be maintained when the platform is parked (**B.3.5.2**). As it travels the platform should not interfere with the safe use of the stair by others. The platform stair lift should meet the requirements listed in Table M.5.

Further guidance
BS 5588-8:1999. Fire precautions in the design, construction and use of buildings. Code of practice for means of escape for disabled people. [Withdrawn, replaced by BS 9999:2008. Code of practice for fire safety in the design, management and use of buildings. Clause 46 covers the Evacuation of disabled people.]

Table M.3 Specification for passenger lifts

Feature	Provision
Layout	Clear landing: 1500 × 500mm, or 900mm wide straight access route. Car size (minimum, w × d): 1100mm × 1400mm. Clear opening width (minimum): 800mm. Handrail: at least one, 900mm above floor. Not obstructing mirrors or controls.
Controls	Landing: 900–1100mm from floor, and 500mm from return wall. Car: 900–1200mm from floor (preferably 1100mm), and 400mm from front wall.
Signalling system	Landing: Visual and audible indication of lift's arrival and its location. Car: Visual and audible indication of arrival and floor reached. Emergency communication system required.
Operation	Timing devices and re-opening activators give enough time for people and assistance dogs to enter and leave lift.

Table M.4 Specification for lifting platforms

Feature	Provision
Layout	Clear landing: 1500 × 1500mm, or 900mm wide straight access route. Handrail: at least one, 900mm above floor. Not obstructing mirrors or controls.
Dimensions (minimum w × d)	Not enclosed, intended for unaccompanied use: 800mm × 1250mm, with 800mm door. Enclosed, intended for unaccompanied use: 900mm × 1400mm with 800mm door. Enclosed with doors at 90° or accompanied use: 1100mm × 1400mm with 900mm door.
Rise	No enclosure or floor penetration: 2m. With enclosure: No limit.
Rated speed (maximum)	0.15m/s
Controls	Landing: 900–1100mm from floor. 500mm from return wall. Platform: Continuous pressure controls. 800–1100mm from floor. 400mm from return wall. Clear instructions for use.
Signalling system	Audible and visual indicator of arrival and floor reached. Emergency communication system required.

Table M.5 Specification for platform stair lifts	
Feature	**Provision**
Layout	Clear landing: 1500mm × 1500mm, or 900mm wide straight access route. Handrail: at least one, 900mm above floor. Not obstructing mirrors or controls.
Dimensions (minimum w × d)	800mm × 1250mm
Rated speed (maximum)	0.15m/s
Controls	Landing: 900–1100mm from floor. 500mm from return wall. Platform: Continuous pressure controls, e.g. joystick, which prevent unauthorised use.
Signalling system	Emergency communication system required.

M.5.5.2 Internal stairs

Internal stairs should comply with the standard requirements for stairs at **M.2.3**, with handrails as **M.2.4** (see **K.2.1** for the guidance).

M.5.5.3 Internal ramps

Internal ramps should comply with the standard requirements for ramps at **M.2.2**, with handrails as **M.2.4** (see **K.2.3** for the guidance).

M.6 Facilities within buildings (Requirement M1)

M.6.1 Audience and spectator facilities

A building must enable all people to take part in proceedings at lecture or conference facilities, and at entertainment, leisure, social and sports venues, as spectators, participants and members of staff.

Wheelchair users and those with mobility or sensory impairment may need to sit at a particular side, or at the front for lip-reading or signing. There should be spaces into which wheelchair users can manoeuvre easily, which provide a clear view, and which give them the choice of sitting next to a conventionally seated person or companion wheelchair user.

General provisions:

- Routes to wheelchair spaces and ancillary accommodation should be accessible by wheelchair users.
- Stepped access routes to seating should have fixed handrails (**M.2.4**).
- The minimum provision of wheelchair spaces should be as set out in Table M.6.
- Wheelchair spaces should be level, and offer a 900mm × 1400mm clear space, with a 900mm clear access route. Figure M.6 shows one method of provision suitable for terraced seating.
- Where more than two spaces are provided they should give a range of views at each side as well as at the front and back of seating.

- Some wheelchair spaces should be provided in pairs, with standard seating to at least one side (this may be achieved by using removable seating).

- Standard seats at row ends next to wheelchair spaces should have detachable or lift-up arms.

- Some seats are located so an assistance dog can accompany its owner and rest in front of or under the seat.

- Seating should contrast visually with its surroundings.

Table M.6 Provision of wheelchair spaces in audience seating		
Seating capacity	**Minimum provision of wheelchair spaces**	
	Permanent	**Removable**
Up to 600	1% of total seating capacity, rounded up	Remainder to make a total of 6
601–10,000	1% of total seating capacity, rounded up	Additional provision, if desired
10,001+	Consult Sports Grounds and Stadia Guide no. 1. *Accessible stadia*, Football Stadia Improvement Fund, 2003	

Figure M.6 Example of wheelchair provision in a cinema or theatre

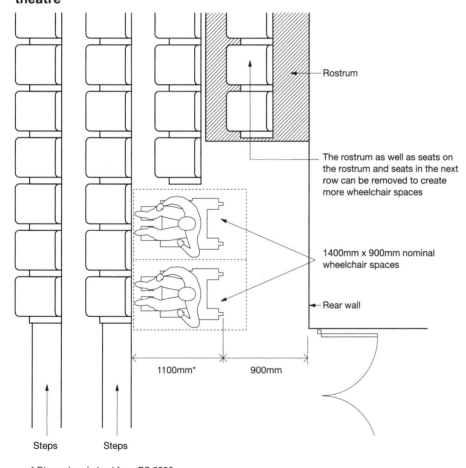

Rostrum

The rostrum as well as seats on the rostrum and seats in the next row can be removed to create more wheelchair spaces

1400mm x 900mm nominal wheelchair spaces

Rear wall

1100mm*   900mm

Steps   Steps

* Dimension derived from BS 8300

Lecture and conference facilities:
People with hearing impairments should be able to participate fully in conferences, committee meetings and study groups and all people should be able to use presentation facilities.

The podium or stage should be accessible by wheelchair, either by means of a ramp or a lifting platform.

The design and location of lecture equipment should ensure that the background and/or lighting conditions do not prevent a person with hearing impairment from receiving information from a sign language interpreter or lip speaker. A hearing enhancement system should be provided (**M.6.5**).

Entertainment, leisure and social:
Seating is generally more tightly packed in such venues and the design and location of wheelchair spaces requires considerable care.

M.6.2 Refreshment facilities

Refreshment facilities such as restaurants and bars, including staff areas, should be designed to be accessible by all (either independently or with companions), with all users being able to access self-service and waiter service areas. Changes in floor level within the facility are permitted, provided those different levels are accessible.

Public areas, including WCs and external terraces, should all be accessible. The threshold between interior and external seating areas should be wheelchair-accessible.

The working surface of each bar or serving counter must have a section which is permanently accessible to wheelchair users and no more than 850mm high. In shared refreshment facilities (e.g. for tea-making) the worktop should be 850mm high with a 700mm high clear space beneath and any taps should be operable with a closed fist.

M.6.3 Sleeping accommodation

Sleeping accommodation provided for a significant number of people, such as in hotels, motels or student accommodation, should be convenient for all. A proportion of rooms should be designed for people using wheelchairs, while the remaining rooms should have features to facilitate their use by people with other disabilities.

In student accommodation the provision of a wheelchair-accessible WC for disabled visitors would be beneficial.

M.6.3.1 All bedrooms

All bedrooms should have the following provisions:
- Doors should have clear widths to Table M.1, to enable wheelchair users to visit companions in other bedrooms.
- Swing doors for storage should open through 180°.

Further guidance
Technical standards for places of entertainment. District Surveyors Association/ Association of British Theatre Technicians. 2002. [Revised edition, 2009.]

Access for disabled people. Sport England. 2002. [Replaced by: *Accessible sports facilities*. 2010.]

Guide to safety at sports grounds. TSO. 1997. (Fifth edition. DCMS. 2008.)

Sports Grounds and Stadia Guide no. 1. *Accessible stadia*.
Football Stadia Improvement Fund. 2003. [Guidance on providing accessible spectator facilities.]

- Handles on hinged and sliding doors should contrast with the door surface and be easy to grip and operate.
- Controls for openable windows should be 800–1100mm from the floor and should not require the use of both hands.
- There should be a visual fire alarm signal in addition to those required in Part B.
- Room numbers should be embossed.
- Electronic card-locks and lever taps would be advantageous for those with poor manual dexterity.

M.6.3.2 Wheelchair-accessible bedrooms

There should be one wheelchair-accessible bedroom for each 20 bedrooms or part thereof. The bedrooms should offer a choice of location, be on accessible routes, and be of a standard which matches the other rooms. It is useful for some wheelchair-accessible bedrooms to have a connecting door to an adjoining room for a companion.

The bedrooms should be sufficiently spacious for a wheelchair user to transfer to one side of the bed with or without assistance, and to have enough room for the occupant to manoeuvre and use all facilities in the room (a suitable layout is shown in Figure M.7). Sanitary accommodation should be accessible, with en-suite provision preferred and an equal number of en-suite shower-rooms as en-suite bathrooms.

Figure M.7 Example layout of a wheelchair-accessible bedroom

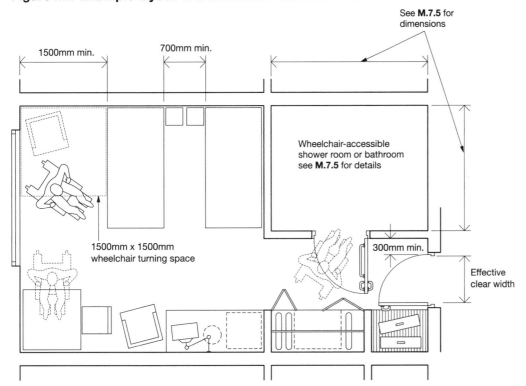

Wheelchair-accessible bedrooms should have the following provisions:

- The access door should meet the requirements for internal doors and be sized to Table M.1. A 300mm clear space is required between the leading edge and side wall, unless the door is powered.

- Any wide-angle viewers on doors should be set 1050–1500mm above the floor to enable their use by people who are standing or seated.

- The door to the en-suite shower-room or bathroom should be sized to Table M.1.

- The sanitary facilities should meet the requirements in **M.7.5**. It may be beneficial to have a finger rinse basin next to the WC as well as a washbasin or sink in a vanity unit.

- Switches and controls should comply with **M.6.4**.

- Curtains and blinds should have automatic or remote control devices, such as rods or pull cords.

- Built-in wardrobes and shelving should be accessible.

- There should be an emergency assistance alarm, with reset button, which can be operated from the bed and the adjacent floor area. The call signal should be audible and visible both to those immediately outside the bedroom, and to a central control point.

- Any balcony to the room should be accessed by a door sized to Table M.1, with a level threshold and with no horizontal transoms 900–1200mm above the floor. There should be no permanent obstructions in a zone 1500mm back from the door.

M.6.4 Switches, outlets and controls

All users should be able to locate a control, tell which setting it is on and use it, without inadvertently changing its setting. The usability of switches and controls is affected by their ease of operation, visibility, height and freedom from obstruction.

Controls and switches will comply with Part M if they are located as shown in Table M.7 (with the exception of those set into floors of open-plan offices), and they meet the following conditions:

- Controls should visually contrast with their surroundings.

- Lights should preferably be operated by push-button pads.

- Individual switches on multiple panels should either be well separated, or be large touch plates, in order to prevent inadvertent selection of an adjacent control by a person with visual impairment or limited dexterity.

- Red and green are the most commonly confused colours for partially sighted or colour blind people; they should not be used together as on/off indicators.

- Text or pictograms can be used to clarify multiple controls and switches.

- Controls should not require simultaneous use of both hands, unless necessary for safety reasons.

- Switched socket outlets should indicate when they are 'on'. Mains and circuit isolator switches should clearly indicate whether they are 'on' or 'off'.

- Consistent positioning in relation to doors and corners will assist people to use controls and switches.

Table M.7 Locations for switches, outlets and controls	
Item	**Location**
Light switches for the public (alternatively pull cords)	900–1100mm from floor – aligned with door handles 50mm bangle at 900–1100mm from floor
Wall-mounted socket outlets, telephone points, TV sockets	400–1000mm from floor – preferably towards lower end of the range Sockets at least 350mm from corners
Switches for permanently wired appliances	400–1200mm from floor – unless particular appliance requires higher switch
Switches and controls requiring precise hand movement	750–1200mm from floor
Simple push button controls requiring little dexterity	≤1200mm from floor
Red alarm pull cords	Close to wall – two red 50mm diameter bangles at 100mm and 800–1000mm above floor
Controls needing close vision	1200–1400mm – thermostats towards top of range

M.6.5 Aids to communication

An integrated system for wayfinding, public address and hearing enhancement offers the greatest benefit for building users. Hearing enhancement and telephone systems should be chosen carefully to ensure intelligibility. Any public address system should be clearly audible and supplemented by visual information systems.

M.6.5.1 Hearing impairment

In order to take part in discussions and enjoy public performances people with impaired hearing need to receive a signal which is amplified both in volume and in signal-to-noise ratio. That may be achieved using induction loop, infrared or radio-based hearing enhancement systems.

Hearing enhancement systems should be installed at service or reception counters in noisy areas or behind glass screens, and also in rooms and spaces designed for:

- meetings;
- lectures;
- classes;
- performances;
- spectator sport;
- film screening.

Large spaces should have permanent systems, but portable induction loops are suitable for small meeting rooms. Where there are systems in adjacent rooms, these should be designed to avoid interference. Artificial lighting should not interfere with other electronic and radio-frequency installations.

M.6.5.2 Signage

The presence of an induction loop or infrared system should be indicated by the standard symbol. Telephones for hearing aid users should be indicated by the standard ear and T-symbol and the telephones should incorporate an inductive coupler and volume control. Text telephones for people who have a hearing impairment should be clearly indicated by the standard symbol.

Further guidance
BS 8300:2009+A1:2010. [Section 9 contains comprehensive guidance on communication aids.]

M.7 Sanitary accommodation

There should be suitable sanitary accommodation for everyone using the building, including wheelchair users, ambulant disabled, people of either sex with babies and small children, and people with luggage. The design of sanitary accommodation should address the needs of people with:

- visual or hearing impairment;
- learning difficulties;
- lack of tactile sensitivity, who may inadvertently touch hot surfaces;
- limited strength and/or dexterity who may have difficulty operating taps and opening doors.

Table M.8 sets out the general provisions for sanitary accommodation.

Table M.8 General requirements for sanitary accommodation	
Feature	**Requirements**
Taps	Bath or washbasin tap either controlled automatically or can be operated with closed fist (e.g. lever action). In schools and public facilities thermostatic mixing valves must prevent discharge water temperatures exceeding 43°C.[1]
Doors	Compartment doors and doors to wheelchair-accessible toilets have light action privacy bolts. The force required to open self-closing doors should be no more than 30N at 0° (closed) to 30° open, and 22.5N for 30–60° open. Handles operable with a closed fist and visually contrast with the background. Doors should have an emergency release mechanism enabling them to be opened outwards from the outside. Doors should not block emergency exits.
Fire alarms	Visual and audible signal.
Emergency assistance alarm	Visual and audible indicators to confirm a call has been received. Reset control within reach from a wheelchair, WC or shower/changing seat. Signals visually and audibly distinguishable from the fire alarm.
Lighting controls	As **M.6.4**.
Heat emitters	Screened, or with external surface temperature less than 43°C.
Visual contrast	Wall and floor finishes visually contrasting. Sanitary fittings and grab bars contrast visually with wall and floor finishes.
Layout	Consistent layout in multi-storey buildings helps people with learning difficulties to locate facilities.

[1] Guidance note G18.5 of the Guidance Document to Schedule 2: Requirement for Water Fittings, of the Water Supply (Fittings) Regulations 1999.

M.7.1 Toilet accommodation

Toilet accommodation must be suitable for all who use the building. Although provision for disabled people may take the form of a specially designed cubicle in a separate-sex washroom, a self-contained unisex toilet is to be preferred, because it allows a partner or carer of the other sex to assist. A wheelchair-accessible unisex toilet should therefore always be provided, in addition to any wheelchair-accessible toilet in a separate-sex washroom (wheelchair-accessible unisex toilets should not be used for baby changing).

2013 changes
Approved Document M now makes specific reference to Changing Places Toilets.

An enlarged cubicle in a separate-sex washroom can be useful for ambulant disabled people, and parents with children. In large buildings separate facilities for baby changing and an enlarged unisex toilet with adult changing table are desirable (facilities with adult changing tables are commonly known as Changing Places Toilets).

Basic provision:

- Where there is only one toilet in a building it should be wheelchair-accessible and unisex, and should be wide enough to accommodate a standing-height washbasin.

- At every location where sanitary accommodation is provided – whether for visitors, customers, or staff – there should be at least one wheelchair-accessible unisex toilet.

- In separate-sex toilet accommodation there should be at least one WC cubicle suitable for use by ambulant disabled people.

- Where there are four or more WC cubicles in separate-sex toilet accommodation at least one should be enlarged for use by people needing extra space.

Further guidance

www.changing-places.org [website of the Changing Places Campaign.]
BS 8300:2009+A1:2010 [Section 12.7 and Annex G contain guidance on Changing Places Toilets.]

M.7.2 Wheelchair-accessible unisex toilets

Wheelchair-accessible unisex toilets should be separate from other sanitary accommodation, in order to improve identification and availability. They should be reached from the rest of the building within a reasonable time and should be laid out so that wheelchair users can manoeuvre into the toilet and then transfer to the WC, either with or without assistance.

Table M.9 sets out the requirements, together with Figures M.8–M.10.

Table M.9 Requirements for wheelchair-accessible unisex WCs	
Feature	**Requirements**
Location	One located as close as possible to the entrance and/or waiting area of the building. Location not to compromise the privacy of users. In a multi-storey building located in a similar position on each floor, allowing for right- and left-hand transfer on alternate floors. In other buildings, a choice of layouts suitable for left-hand and right-hand transfer is provided.
Travel	• No more than 40m on the same floor, unless the circulation route is unobstructed; or • No more than 40m combined horizontal distance on two floors where accessible by lift (vertical travel limited to one storey where a lifting platform is installed).
Dimensions	Minimum dimensions and arrangement comply with **Figure M.8** and heights and arrangement of fittings comply with **Figures M.9** and **M.10**. When it is the only toilet facility in the building it should be 2m wide with a standing height washbasin, in addition to the finger rinse basin associated with the WC. Heat emitters not to restrict manoeuvring or transfer space.
Rails	An additional drop-down horizontal support rail is provided on the wall side 320mm from centre line of WC if the horizontal support rail is set at the minimum distance from the wall.
Emergency assistance alarm	Provided as **Table M.8** with an easily identifiable pull cord reachable from the WC and the floor close to the WC. Call signal outside the toilet compartment easily seen and heard by those able to give assistance.
WC	Pan conforms to key dimensions of BS EN 997:2012 to accommodate variable height toilet seat riser. Cisterns have their flushing mechanism on the open, or transfer side, of the space.

Figure M.8 Layout of wheelchair-accessible toilet

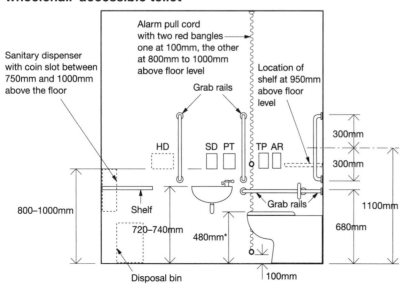

Alternative door position

Sanitary dispenser

1500mm x 1500mm wheelchair turning space

Disposal bin

Shelf

Mirror

Wall A

Finger rinse basin

2200mm min.

Clothes hooks

Vertical grab rails

Alarm pull cord

140–160mm

Drop-down rail

Wall-mounted grab rail

750mm

60–85mm

600mm

Sanitary disposal unit

250mm

Alternative position for alarm pull cord

150mm   320mm   500mm

Zone for shelf for standing users

Vertical grab rail

970mm

1000mm min.

1500mm min.

(excluding any projecting heat emitters)

Note
Layout for right-hand transfer to WC

Figure M.9 Height and arrangement of fittings in a unisex wheelchair-accessible toilet

Alarm pull cord with two red bangles one at 100mm, the other at 800mm to 1000mm above floor level

Sanitary dispenser with coin slot between 750mm and 1000mm above the floor

Grab rails

Location of shelf at 950mm above floor level

HD   SD PT   TP AR

300mm

300mm

800–1000mm

Shelf

720–740mm   480mm*

Grab rails

1100mm

680mm

Disposal bin

100mm

*Height subject to manufacturing tolerance of WC pan

HD: Possible position for automatic hand dryer (see also Figure M.10)
SD: Soap dispenser
PT: Paper towel dispenser
AR: Alarm reset button
TP: Toilet paper dispenser

Height of drop-down rails to be the same as the other horizontal grab rails

Figure M.10 Heights of fittings in toilet accommodation

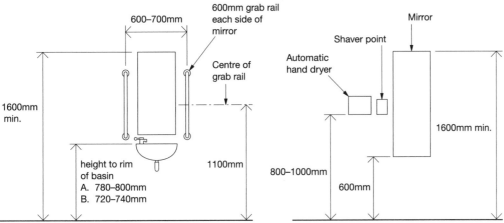

Height of independent washbasin
and location of associated fittings, for
wheelchair users and standing people

A. For people standing
B. For use from WC

Mirror located away from washbasin
suitable for seated and standing people
(mirror and associated fittings used
within a WC compartment or serving a
range of compartments)

M.7.3 Toilets in separate-sex washrooms

Separate-sex washrooms should have provision for ambulant disabled people,
by means of a larger WC compartment which gives enough room for those with
crutches or impaired leg movement, and is fitted with support rails. In larger
washrooms, there should be an enlarged cubicle for those requiring extra space,
such as parents with children and babies.

A fold-down table for baby changing would also be beneficial, as would low-level
urinals for children in male washrooms. Where separate-sex washrooms are
accessible to wheelchair users it should be possible for them to use a urinal, where
appropriate, and a washbasin.

Table M.10 and Figure M.11 set out the main requirements.

Figure M.11 WC cubicle for ambulant disabled people

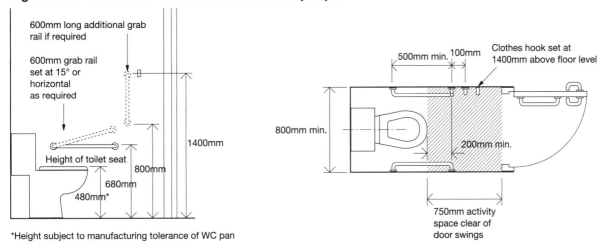

*Height subject to manufacturing tolerance of WC pan

Table M.10 Requirements for separate-sex toilet washrooms

Facility	Requirement
Standard WC compartments	450mm diameter manoeuvring space between WC pan, door swing and compartment wall (based on inward opening door).
Compartments for ambulant disabled people	Dimensions and arrangement of fittings as **Figure M.11**. Doors preferably outward opening with horizontal closing bar on side face. WC pan to BS EN 997:2012 to accept variable height toilet seat riser.
Enlarged compartment	1200mm wide. Horizontal grab bar next to WC. Vertical grab bar on rear wall. Space for shelf and fold-down changing table.
Wheelchair-accessible compartment (where provided)	Same layout as unisex wheelchair-accessible toilet (**Table M.9**).
Wheelchair-accessible washroom	At least one washbasin with rim 720–740mm above floor. For men, one urinal with rim 380 above floor, and 600mm vertical grab bars to either side of the urinal, centre lines 1100mm above floor.

M.7.4 Wheelchair-accessible changing and shower facilities

Where changing and shower facilities are associated, some disabled people will be content to use open facilities with sub-divisions, while others will prefer self-contained cubicles or compartments. As it may be difficult to provide the appropriate arrangements of rails, seat and controls in an open facility, individual cubicles are preferred.

Changing and shower facilities should meet the requirements in Table M.11 and Figures M.12 to M.14. Changing facilities not associated with showering should match the requirements for sports changing. Large developments such as retail parks and large sports centres should have one wheelchair-accessible unisex toilet capable of including an adult changing table.

Table M.11 Requirements for wheelchair-accessible changing and shower facilities

Facility and feature	Requirement
Changing and shower facilities	
General provision	Sports facilities with communal separate-sex facilities should also have individual facilities. Where multiple compartments are provided they offer a choice of left- and right-hand transfer. Communal changing and shower facilities have sub-divisions with same configuration as individual compartments, but without doors.
Layout	Wall-mounted, drop-down support rails and wall-mounted, slip-resistant, tip-up seats. Emergency assistance cord, easily identifiable and reachable from wall-mounted seat or floor. Alarm system itself as **Table M.8**. Limb storage facilities included for benefit of amputees.
Changing facilities	
Layout	Arrangement and dimensions as **Figure M.12**. Where associated with a shower, the floor of the changing area is level and slip-resistant wet or dry.[1] 1500mm manoeuvring space in front of lockers.
Shower facilities	
General provision	Showers for staff in commercial developments include at least one wheelchair-accessible shower compartment.
Layout	Arrangement and dimensions as **Figure M.13**. The shower curtain should be operable from the shower seat. A shelf for toiletries should be provided, accessible from the shower seat or the wheelchair. The floor of the shower and shower area should be slip-resistant[1] and self-draining. Markings on shower control should be clear and logical. The temperature of water discharged by the shower outlet must be controlled by thermostatic mixing valves so as not to exceed 43°C.[2]
Wheelchair-accessible shower facilities in communal areas	Shower controls 750–1000mm above ground.
Shower facilities with WC	Arrangement and dimensions as **Figure M.14**. Left- and right-hand layouts available where more than one such facility provided.

[1] Annex C of BS 8300:2001 includes guidance on slip resistance. The 2009 (amended 2010) edition contains guidance in Annex E, and suggests reference be made to clause 7 of BS 5395-1:2010. Stairs. Code of practice for the design of stairs with straight flights and winders.

[2] Guidance note G18.5 of the Guidance Document to Schedule 2: Requirement for Water Fittings, of the Water Supply (Fittings) Regulations 1999.

Figure M.12 Self-contained changing room for individual use

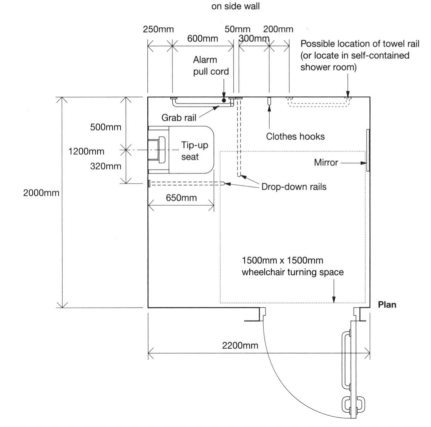

Alarm pull cord

2100mm minimum unobstructed height

Vertical grab rail length 500mm min.

Clothes hooks at 1400mm and 1050mm above floor level

Horizontal grab rail

Back rest

Alarm reset

Drop-down rail

680mm

480mm

Tip-up seat

800mm

Possible location of towel rail

Drop-down rail on side wall

Elevation

250mm

600mm

50mm

300mm

200mm

Alarm pull cord

Possible location of towel rail (or locate in self-contained shower room)

Grab rail

500mm

1200mm

320mm

Tip-up seat

Clothes hooks

Mirror

2000mm

Drop-down rails

650mm

1500mm x 1500mm wheelchair turning space

Plan

2200mm

Figure M.13 Self-contained shower room for individual use

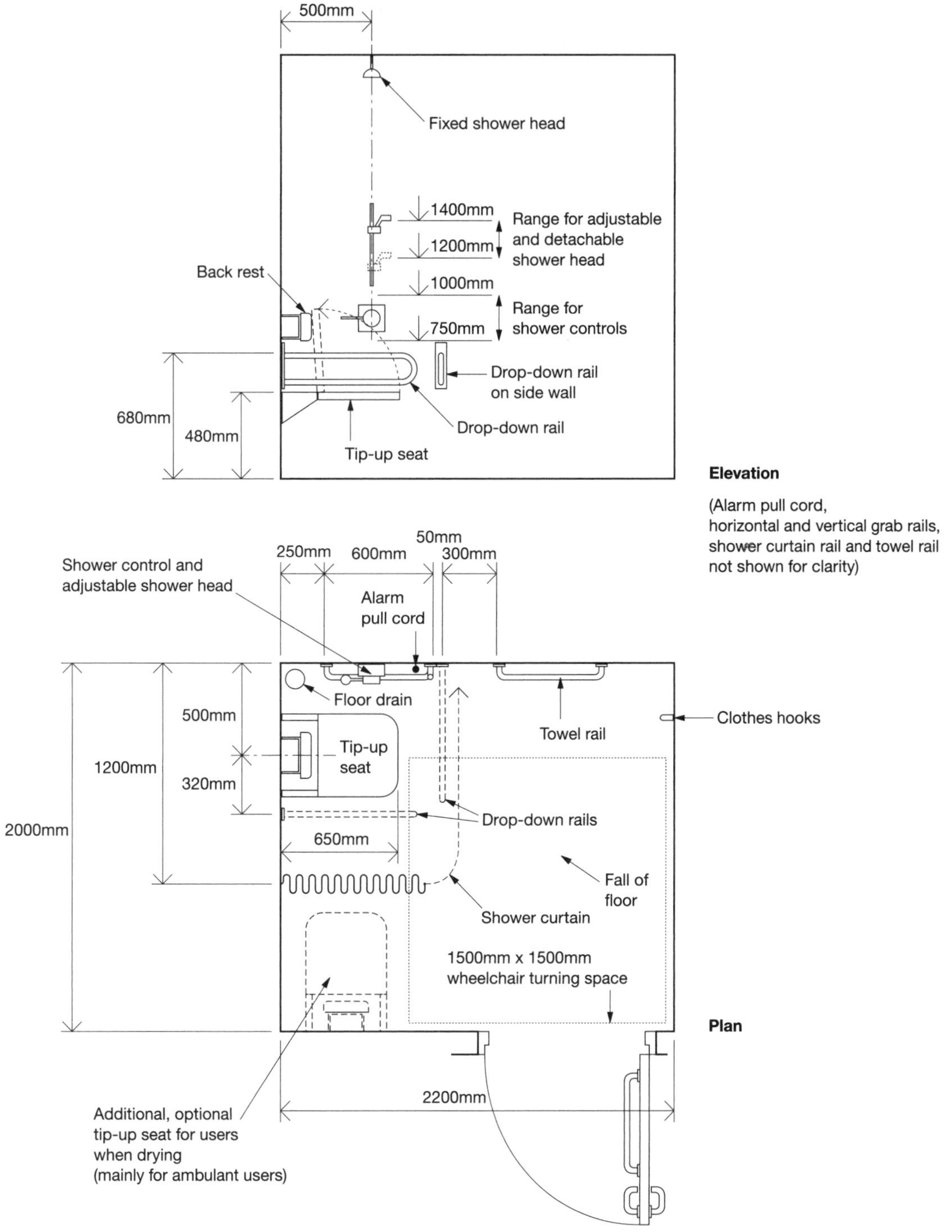

Fixed shower head

1400mm
1200mm — Range for adjustable and detachable shower head

Back rest

1000mm

750mm — Range for shower controls

Drop-down rail on side wall

Drop-down rail

680mm

480mm

Tip-up seat

Elevation

(Alarm pull cord, horizontal and vertical grab rails, shower curtain rail and towel rail not shown for clarity)

Shower control and adjustable shower head

250mm   600mm   50mm
300mm

Alarm pull cord

Floor drain

500mm

Tip-up seat

1200mm

320mm

2000mm

Towel rail

Clothes hooks

Drop-down rails

650mm

Fall of floor

Shower curtain

1500mm x 1500mm wheelchair turning space

Plan

Additional, optional tip-up seat for users when drying (mainly for ambulant users)

2200mm

Figure M.14 Shower room with corner WC for individual use

The arrangement of shower controls
and ancillary fittings is as Figure M.13

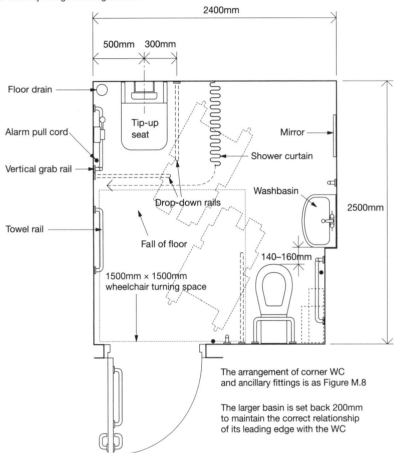

2400mm

500mm   300mm

Floor drain

Tip-up
seat

Alarm pull cord

Vertical grab rail

Drop-down rails

Towel rail

Fall of floor

1500mm × 1500mm
wheelchair turning space

Mirror

Shower curtain

Washbasin

2500mm

140–160mm

The arrangement of corner WC
and ancillary fittings is as Figure M.8

The larger basin is set back 200mm
to maintain the correct relationship
of its leading edge with the WC

Note:
Layout shown for right-hand transfer to shower seat and WC

M.7.5 Wheelchair-accessible bathrooms

Wheelchair-accessible bathrooms should enable wheelchair users or ambulant
disabled people to wash and bathe either independently or with assistance.
The organisation of the space and facilities is critical. Table M.12 sets out the
requirements for wheelchair-accessible bathrooms in buildings such as hotels,
motels and student accommodation; for en-suite wheelchair-accessible bathrooms
see **M.6.3**. Figure M.15 shows one way in which those requirements might be met.

Table M.12 Requirements for bathrooms	
	Requirement
Layout	Dimensions and arrangement as **Figure M.15**. A choice of left- and right-hand layouts available where more than one such facility provided. Doors preferably outward opening with horizontal closing bar to inner face.
Bath	Has transfer seat, 400mm deep, equal to width of bath.
Floor	Slip-resistant when wet or dry (see note [1] to **Table M.11**).
Emergency alarm	Emergency assistance pull cord easily identifiable. Cord accessible from bath or floor. Alarm system itself as **Table M.8**.

Figure M.15 Bathroom incorporating corner WC

(a)

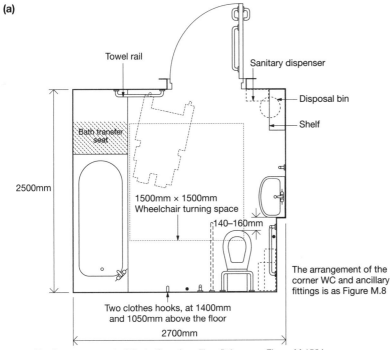

Towel rail

Sanitary dispenser

Disposal bin

Shelf

Bath transfer seat

2500mm

1500mm × 1500mm
Wheelchair turning space

140–160mm

The arrangement of the corner WC and ancillary fittings is as Figure M.8

Two clothes hooks, at 1400mm
and 1050mm above the floor

2700mm

For the arrangement of the bath and ancillary fittings see Figure M.15(b)

Note: Layout shown for right-hand transfer to bath and WC

(b)

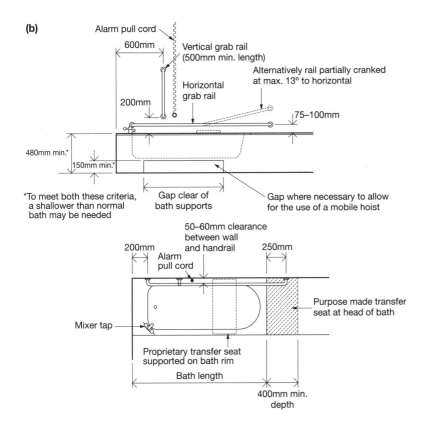

Alarm pull cord

600mm

Vertical grab rail
(500mm min. length)

Alternatively rail partially cranked
at max. 13° to horizontal

Horizontal
grab rail

200mm

75–100mm

480mm min.*

150mm min.*

*To meet both these criteria,
a shallower than normal
bath may be needed

Gap clear of
bath supports

Gap where necessary to allow
for the use of a mobile hoist

50–60mm clearance
between wall
and handrail

200mm

250mm

Alarm
pull cord

Purpose made transfer
seat at head of bath

Mixer tap

Proprietary transfer seat
supported on bath rim

Bath length

400mm min.
depth

M.8 Dwellings

M.8.1 Access to, and into the dwelling

A disabled person should be able to approach and gain access to a dwelling from the point of alighting from a vehicle, which may be within or outside the plot. On reasonably level plots wheelchair users should be able to reach the principal entrance, and gain entrance to a dwellinghouse and entrance level flats. On more steeply sloping sites it may be acceptable to provide a stepped approach suitable for ambulant disabled people, or to provide access to an alternative entrance. A driveway may be used to provide an access point on the plot, to give visitors a level or ramped approach.

- **A level approach** should have a gradient less than 1:20 and be at least 900mm wide, with a firm even surface and cross-falls of no more than 1:40. All or part of the approach may be formed by a driveway.

- **A ramped approach** is permitted if the route has a plot gradient exceeding 1:20 but not exceeding 1:15. Flights may be up to 10m long on ramp gradients not steeper than 1:15 and up to 5m long on ramp gradients not steeper than 1:12. Flights should be 900mm wide, with top, bottom and any intermediate landings at least 1200mm long, clear of any door or gate swing. Surfaces should be firm and even.

- **A stepped approach** is acceptable on plots with a gradient steeper than 1:15. Flights should have a rise between landings no greater than 1800mm and an unobstructed width of 900mm, with top, bottom and any intermediate landings at least 900mm long. Steps should have a uniform rise of 75–150mm and a going of at least 280mm (measure tapered treads 270mm from the 'inside' of the tread). Treads may overlap by 15–25mm. Flights of three or more risers require a handrail with a grippable profile, 850–1000mm above the line of pitch and extending 300mm beyond the top and bottom nosings.

Where a driveway forms part of a level or ramped approach, car parking should not reduce the access width below 900mm.

A dwelling with level or ramped approach should have an accessible threshold, as should flats on the entrance level. Dwellings with stepped approaches should generally have an accessible threshold: in exceptional circumstances a step with a maximum 150mm rise is permitted. Accessible thresholds must comply with Part C (**C.5.3.6**).

Entrance doors should have a minimum clear opening width of 775mm, measured from the face of the doorstop on the latch side, to the face of the door when open 90°.

M.8.2 Circulation around the dwelling

On the entrance or principal storey, corridors and doorways which give access to habitable rooms and a room containing a WC should be wide enough for wheelchair access. Corridors must be at least 900mm wide; obstructions such as radiators may reduce the width of a corridor for part of its length, but never below 750mm, and not so as to obstruct a door.

Table M.13 Minimum corridor widths for the entrance or principal storeys of dwellings

Doorway – clear opening width (mm)	Approach	Corridor/passageway width (mm)
750 or wider	Head on	900
750	Lateral	1200
775	Lateral	1050
800	Lateral	900

The width of a corridor will be constrained by the width of any door opening, because access through narrower doors requires wider corridors. Table M.13 gives minimum corridor widths for a number of doorway widths.

Where a change of level within the entrance storey is unavoidable, stairs are permissible, and should meet Requirement K1 (**K.2**).

Where access to the storey is by an alternative entrance, rather than the principal entrance, wheelchair users should be able to access the rest of the storey.

M.8.3 Accessible switches and outlets

Wall-mounted switches, sockets and outlets should be located at heights suitable for people with limited reach, 450–1200mm above finished floor level.

M.8.4 Passenger lifts and common stairs

In a building containing flats, disabled people should be able to visit occupants on any storey. A passenger lift is the most suitable means of access between storeys, but there is no requirement to provide one.

Where there is no lift a general access stair should be provided, suitable for ambulant disabled people and people with impaired vision. Where there is a lift, a utility stair should be provided, suitable for people with impaired vision. Stairs should comply with section 1 of Approved Document K (**K.2**).

Where a lift is provided it should be suitable for an unaccompanied wheelchair user, and have provision for those with impaired vision or hearing. Table M.14 gives one specification which would meet that requirement.

2013 changes
The requirements for stairs are now given in Approved Document K rather than Approved Document M.

2013 changes
The guidance now refers to general access and utility stairs where previously it referred only to stairs.

Table M.14 Passenger lifts for blocks of flats

Feature	Provision
Capacity (minimum)	400kg
Layout	Clear landing (minimum): 1500 × 1500mm Clear opening width (minimum): 800mm Car size (minimum w × d): 900 × 1250mm
Location of controls	900–1200mm from landing and car floor 400mm from front wall
Tactile indicators	To identify storey: On landing and adjacent to call button. To confirm floor selected: On or adjacent to lift buttons within car.
Signalling system	Visual indication that lift is answering landing call. Visible and audible indication of floor reached in buildings of more than three storeys.
Operation	A dwell time of 5 seconds from door being fully open. A door re-activating device is allowed to override that, to a minimum of 3 seconds.

M.8.5 WC provision

The entrance storey of a dwelling must have a WC. Where there are no habitable rooms in the entrance storey then the WC may be provided in the principal storey. The WC may be provided in a bathroom.

The door to the WC compartment should open outwards and be wide enough for wheelchair users to access the WC. The dimensions shown in Table M.13 would be sufficient. While it may not always be practical for the wheelchair to be accommodated fully within the WC compartment, there should be enough clear space for a wheelchair user to reach the WC, without the washbasin impeding access (see Figure M.16).

Figure M.16 Access to WC

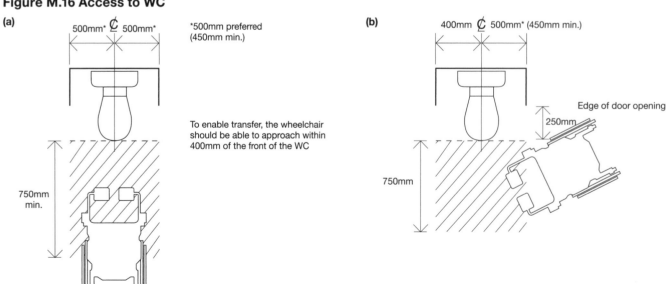

(a) 500mm* ₵ 500mm* *500mm preferred (450mm min.)

To enable transfer, the wheelchair should be able to approach within 400mm of the front of the WC

750mm min.

(b) 400mm ₵ 500mm* (450mm min.)

Edge of door opening

250mm

750mm

P. Electrical safety

P.1 General considerations

P.1.1 Scope

Part P is intended to protect people operating, maintaining or altering electrical installations in dwellings from fire or injury.

Part P: Electrical safety	
Requirement	**Limits on application**
Design and installation	
P1 Reasonable provision shall be made in the design and installation of electrical installations in order to protect persons operating, maintaining or altering the installations from fire or injury.	The requirements of this Part apply only to electrical installations that are intended to operate at low or extra-low voltage and are: (a) in or attached to a dwelling; (b) in the common parts of a building serving one or more dwellings, but excluding power supplies to lifts; (c) in a building that receives its electricity from a source located within or shared with a dwelling; or (d) in a garden or on land associated with a building where the electricity is from a source located within or shared with a dwelling.

Part P applies to electrical installations in:

- dwellinghouses or flats, including:
  - parts that are outside the dwelling, such as fixed lighting, photovoltaic panels, garden lighting and pond pumps;
  - parts in outbuildings including sheds, detached garages and domestic greenhouses, even if those buildings are otherwise exempt from the regulations under Schedule 2;
- lift installations in single dwellings;
- common access areas of blocks of flats;
- shared amenities of blocks of flats, such as laundries and kitchens;
- business premises connected to the same meter as an installation in a dwelling (such as a shop beneath a flat): but not an agricultural building.

Part P does not apply to electrical installations:

- in business premises in the same building as a dwelling, but with separate metering;
- that supply power to lifts in blocks of flats.

Figure P.1 illustrates the scope of Part P.

2013 changes

There have been two major changes to Part P, both intended to reduce the cost of regulation:

- The range of notifiable electrical installation work has been reduced.
- An installer who is not a registered competent person may use a registered third party to certify notifiable work, instead of using a Building Control Body (BCB).

The Approved Document to Part P has been re-structured and revised; Appendices A–E, which contained additional guidance, have been removed.

Figure P.1 Scope of Part P

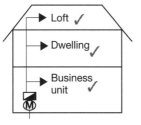

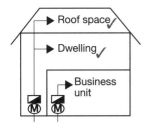

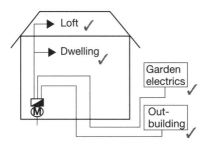

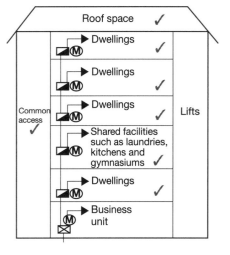

⊠ Intake switchgear

◪ Source of electricity supply

Ⓜ Electricity supply meter

Reproduced with the permission of the Electrical Contractors' Association

Electrical installations will also be affected by other parts of the Building Regulations, including:

- Part A: depths of chases and sizes of notches in joists (**A.2.2.3**);
- Part B: fire safety of electrical installations (**B.3.3.5**), provision of alarm systems (**B.3.2**) and fire resistance of service penetrations (**B.5.4**);
- Part C: resistance of service penetrations to rainwater and contaminants, including radon (**C.3.5**) and moisture transfer into roof voids (cold roofs) through gaps around services penetrations (**C.5.5**);
- Part E: soundproofing of service penetrations (**E.2.3.2** and **E.2.3.3**);
- Part F: dwelling ventilation rates (**F.3.1**);
- Part L: provision of energy efficient lighting (**L.3.3.2**);
- Part M: height of socket outlets and switches (**M.6.4**).

P.1.2 Definitions

- **Electrical installation** Fixed electrical cables or fixed electrical equipment on the consumer's side of the electricity meter.
- **Extra-low voltage** Voltage not exceeding 50V AC, or 120V DC, whether between conductors or to earth.
- **Low voltage** Voltage greater than extra-low voltage, but not exceeding 1000V AC or 1500V DC between conductors, or 600V AC or 900V DC between conductors and earth.

P.2 Design and installation

P.2.1 General

All electrical installations should be designed and installed in accordance with BS 7671. Information should be provided to enable the installation to be operated, maintained or altered safely: the information should consist of items required by BS 7671 and other information including:

- electrical installation certificates;
- permanent labels, including those on items such as consumer units and residual current devices (RCDs);
- operating instructions and log books;
- for large or complex installations, detailed plans.

P.2.2 New dwellings

The location of wall-mounted socket outlets and switches should comply with Part M (**M.6.4**), and be 450–1200mm above finished floor level. Consumer units should be accessible and located with switches 1350–1450mm above floor level.

P.2.3 New dwellings formed by change of use

Under Regulation 6, a dwelling created by a material change of use must comply with the requirements of Part P. The existing electrical installation may need to be upgraded to meet current standards. There is no need to replace adequate existing cables, even if they use old colour codes.

P.2.4 Work to existing electrical installations

New work should follow BS 7671. There is no need to upgrade existing installations, unless:

- the new work adversely affects the safety of the existing installation;
- the condition of the existing installation prevents the new work being operated safely.

The existing installation should be checked to ensure that:

- the rating and condition of the existing equipment, both consumer and electricity distributor, is suitable for carrying additional loads from the new work;
- protective measures are adequate;
- earthing and equipotential bonding arrangements are satisfactory.

P.3 Inspection, testing and certification

All electrical work should be inspected and tested to the procedures in BS 7671 to ensure the design and installation is adequate and the installation will be safe to use, maintain and alter. Local authorities have the power to take enforcement action where non-notifiable work is found to be non-compliant.

Further guidance
BS 7671:2008+A1:2011. Requirements for Electrical Installations. [IET Wiring Regulations 17th Edition]

2013 changes
The guidance on the siting of consumer units is new and addresses the absence of guidance in Approved Document M.

Inspection and test forms should generally be given to the person ordering the work. Building Regulations certificates should be given to the occupier; or for rented properties to the person ordering the work with copies to the occupier.

P.3.1 Notification

Electrical installation work is notifiable under Regulation 12(6A) if it consists of:

- installation of a new circuit;
- replacement of a consumer unit;
- any addition to, or alteration of, existing circuits in a special location.

A special location is defined as:

- the space surrounding a bath tap or shower head as defined in Figure P.2;
- a room containing a swimming pool or sauna heater.

All other electrical installation work is non-notifiable, that is:

- additions and alterations to existing installations outside special locations;
- replacements, repairs and maintenance anywhere.

Figure P.2 Extent of special locations in bath or shower rooms

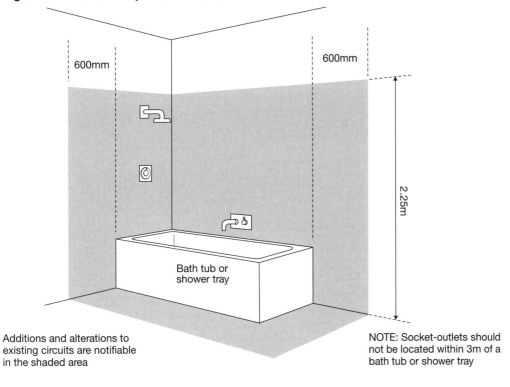

600mm   600mm

2.25m

Bath tub or shower tray

Additions and alterations to existing circuits are notifiable in the shaded area

NOTE: Socket-outlets should not be located within 3m of a bath tub or shower tray

Installing fixed electrical equipment is within the scope of Part P, even if the final connection is by a 13A plug; however, the work is only notifiable if it comes under Regulation 12(6A). For example, the installation of a built-in cooker comes under Part P, but would only be notifiable if a new cooker circuit were needed. The same principle applies to prefabricated modular wiring systems connected by plug and socket.

P.3.2 Certification of notifiable work

There are three methods for demonstrating that notifiable work complies with the requirements of the Building Regulations:

- self-certification by a registered competent person (**P.3.2.1**);
- third-party certification by a registered third-party certifier (**P.3.2.2**);
- certification by a Building Control Body (BCB) (**P.3.2.3**).

P.3.2.1 Self-certification by a registered competent person

Electrical installers who are registered competent persons should complete a BS 7671 certificate for each job. The installer or their registration body must, within 30 days of the work being completed:

- give a copy of the Building Regulations compliance certificate to the occupier; and
- give the certificate, or a copy of the information on the certificate, to the BCB.

P.3.2.2 Certification by a registered third party

An installer who is not a registered competent person may, before work begins, appoint a registered third-party certifier to inspect and test the work. The installer must notify the certifier within five days of completion of the work. The certifier should then inspect and test the work and, if it is satisfactory, complete an electrical inspection condition report and give it to the person ordering the work.

Within 30 days of a satisfactory condition report being issued, the registration body of the third party certifier must:

- give a copy of the Building Regulations compliance certificate to the occupier; and
- give the certificate, or a copy of the information on the certificate, to the BCB.

P.3.2.3 Certification by a building control body

An installer who is not a registered competent person and has not appointed a third-party certifier must notify a BCB before work begins. The BCB will determine the extent of inspection and testing required and may either carry that out itself, or appoint a specialist to prepare an electrical condition report.

An installer who is competent to carry out inspection and testing should give the appropriate BS 7671 certificate to the BCB which will take it into account when determining the extent of any further inspection. That may result in lower building control charges.

Once the BCB has determined that, so far as can be ascertained, the work meets all Building Regulations requirements it will issue a completion certificate (local authority) or final certificate (approved inspector).

Appendices

List of Figures

List of Figures

List of Tables

List of Tables

Sources of information

Acts of Parliament	www.opsi.gov.uk/acts
Air Tightness Testing and Measurement Association (ATTMA)	www.bindt.org
British Board of Agrément (BBA)	www.bbacerts.co.uk
British Wood Preserving and Damp-Proofing Association	www.wood-protection.org
BSRIA	www.bsria.co.uk
Building & Engineering Services Association	www.b-es.org
Building Regulations and related documents	www.planningportal.gov.uk
CIBSE	www.cibse.org
CIRIA	www.ciria.org
Construction Industry Council	www.cic.org.uk
Construction Information Service	http://uk.ihs.com/
Department for Communities and Local Government (CLG)	www.communities.gov.uk
Department for Education (DfE)	www.education.gov.uk
Electrical Contractors' Association (ECA)	www.eca.co.uk
Environment Agency	www.environment-agency.gov.uk
Glass and Glazing Federation	www.ggf.org.uk
Health and Safety Executive (HSE)	www.hse.gov.uk/
Institution of Electrical Engineers (IEE)	www.theiet.org
OFTEC	www.oftec.org
The Institution of Structural Engineers	www.istructe.org
The Stationery Office (TSO)	www.tso.co.uk
TRADA	www.trada.co.uk
Water Regulations Advisory Scheme (WRAS)	www.wras.co.uk

Index

Note: page numbers in *italics* refer to figures; page numbers in **bold** refer to tables.

Index

Index